Global Commodity Chains and Labor Relations

# Studies in Global Social History



VOLUME 42

The titles published in this series are listed at *brill.com/sgsh*

# Global Commodity Chains and Labor Relations

*Edited by*

Andrea Komlosy and Goran Musić

BRILL

LEIDEN | BOSTON

This volume is published in collaboration with the International Conference of Labour and Social History (ITH) and arose out of the 52nd International Conference of Labour and Social History (ITH) which took place in Steyr, Austria on 15–17 September 2016.

ITH International Conference of Labour and Social History
Internationale Tagung der HistorikerInnen der Arbeiter- und anderer sozialer Bewegungen
Conférence internationale d'histoire ouvrière et sociale

The language of this book was edited by Harriet Trautsch.

Cover illustration: "Loading of a Ship in the Creek of Dubai", February 2010. © Andrea Komlosy.

Library of Congress Cataloging-in-Publication Data
Names: Komlosy, Andrea, editor. | Musić, Goran, 1981- editor.
Title: Global commodity chains and labor relations / edited by Andrea Komlosy and Goran Musić.
Description: Leiden ; Boston Brill, [2021] | Series: Studies in global social history, 1874-6705 ; volume 42 | Includes bibliographical references and index. | Summary: "This edited volume provides a collection of historical and contemporary commodity chain studies by placing labor at the centre of analysis. A global historical perspective demonstrates that splitting production processes to different, hierarchically connected locations are by no means new phenomena. The book is thus an important and valuable contribution to commodity chain research, but also to the fields of social-economic and global labor history"– Provided by publisher.
Identifiers: LCCN 2020048766 (print) | LCCN 2020048767 (ebook) | ISBN 9789004448032 (hardback ; alk. paper) | ISBN 9789004448049 (ebook)
Subjects: LCSH: Labor. | Production control. | Business logistics. | International business enterprises.
Classification: LCC HD4901 .G545 2021 (print) | LCC HD4901 (ebook) | DDC 331–dc23
LC record available at https://lccn.loc.gov/2020048766
LC ebook record available at https://lccn.loc.gov/2020048767

Typeface for the Latin, Greek, and Cyrillic scripts: "Brill". See and download: brill.com/brill-typeface.

ISSN 1874-6705
ISBN 978-90-04-44803-2 (hardback)
ISBN 978-90-04-44804-9 (e-book)



This book is printed on acid-free paper and produced in a sustainable manner.

# Contents

## PART 6
## *Conclusion*

# Maps, Figures and Tables

## Maps



## Figures

## Tables

# Notes on Contributors

*Christin Bernhold*
is a Postdoctoral Researcher at the Institute of Geography, University of Hamburg, Germany. Her research interests include agro-industries and the economic geographies of class relations and uneven development. While in recent years her (doctoral) research has focused on agribusiness, corporate strategies and class dynamics in Argentinian grain and oilseed commodity chains, she has recently also started to look into the meat industry in Europe.

*Karin Fischer*
is a Senior Lecturer and Head of the Global Sociology and Development Research Unit at the Institute of Sociology at Johannes Kepler University Linz, Austria. Her research focuses on neoliberal transformation, global commodity chains and uneven development in historical and transnational perspective. Her recent publications include: *Handbuch Entwicklungsforschung*, Springer 2016 (co-edited with Gerhard Hauck and Manuela Boatcă); *Clases dominantes y desarrollo desigual: Chile entre 1830 y 2010*, Ediciones Universidad Alberto Hurtado 2017; Globale Ungleichheit. *Über Zusammenhänge von Kolonialismus, Arbeitsverhältnissen und Naturverbrauch*, Mandelbaum 2019 (co-edited with Margarete Grandner); *Capitalism in Transformation: Movements and Countermovements in the 21st Century*, Edward Elgar 2019 (co-edited with Roland Atzmüller, Brigitte Aulenbacher, Ulrich Brand, Fabienne Décieux and Birgit Sauer).

*Tamás Gerőcs*
is a political economist who is currently pursuing his PhD at the State University of New York Binghamton. His research field of interest is semi-peripheral dependent development in Eastern Europe and labor relations in the automotive industry in Hungary. Gerőcs is a research fellow at the Institute of World Economics, Centre of Economic and Regional Studies. He graduated from the Corvinus University of Budapest (CUB) in 2008 with an MA degree in International Relations. Gerőcs is also a member of the Budapest-based Working Group for Public Sociology "Helyzet". His most recent publications are: "*Relocation, standardization and vertical specialization: core-periphery relations in the European automotive value chain*" (Co-authored along with András Pinkasz), "*Central and Eastern Europe's Dependent Development in German automotive value chains*" (Co-authored along with András Pinkasz), "*The Formation of a New Patrie in the Multipolar World-System*" (In: Gerőcs, T. – Szanyi, M. (eds): Market Liberalism

and Economic Patriotism in the Capitalist World-System), "*Conflicting Interests in the Comecon Integration: State Socialist Debates on East-West-South Relations*" (Co-authored along with András Pinkasz), "*Debt-Ridden Development on Europe's Eastern Periphery*" (Co-authored along with András Pinkasz).

*Jan Grumiller*
is a Researcher at the Austrian Foundation for Development Research (ÖFSE) in Vienna. His work focuses on Global Production Networks, Industrial Policy and Trade Policy. Recent publications include: "*Delivering on promises? The expected impacts and implementation challenges of the Economic Partnership Agreements between the European Union and Africa*", in the Journal of Common Market Studies (2020); "*Commodity dependence, global commodity chains, price volatility and financialisation*", in ÖFSE Working Paper 62 (2019); and "*Towards an Institutional Setup for Industrial Policy in Late Industrialization in the 21st Century*", in ÖFSE Working Paper 61 (2019).

*Santosh Hasnu*
teaches undergraduate History at Hansraj College, University of Delhi. His research focuses on the history of transport systems (roadways, railways & airways) and its closed linkages with labor, war and political legitimacy. He has recently, published on labor mobilization for road construction in colonial India: "*Disciplining the Hill Tribes into Coolie Labour for Road Construction*", in Gwyn Campbell and Alessandro Stanziani (eds.). *The Palgrave Handbook of Bondage and Human Rights in Africa and Asia* (New York 2020); "*Inception of Aviation Routes between India and China*" (Economic & Political Weekly, August 2017).

*Klemens Kaps*
is a Senior Lecturer at the Department for Social and Economic History, Johannes Kepler University, Linz. His research focuses on social and economic inequalities and trade in Central Europe and Spain between the seventeenth and nineteenth centuries in a trans-regional and global framework. He has published on trade history, merchant communities and mercantile networks, uneven development, nationalist and anti-Semitic stereotypes. His most recent publications include: "*Cores and Peripheries Reconsidered: Economic Development, Trade and Cultural Images in the Eighteenth-Century Habsburg Monarchy*", Hungarian Historical Review 7/2 (2018) and "*A Gateway to the Spanish Atlantic? The Habsburg Port City of Trieste as Intermediary in Commodity Flows between the Habsburg Monarchy and Spain in the Eighteenth Century*", in Weber,

Klaus and Wimmler, Jutta (eds), Globalized Peripheries. *Central and Eastern Europe in a Rethinking of the Atlantic World, 1680–1860* (Rochester 2020).

*Andrea Komlosy*
is a Professor at the Department for Economic and Social History, University of Vienna, Austria, where she is one of the Global History and Global Studies program coordinators. She has published on work and labor, migration, borders and uneven development on a regional, a European and a global scale, recently: "*Work and Labour Relations*", in Jürgen Kocka and Marcel van der Linden (eds.). *Capitalism: The Re-Emergence of a Historical Concept* (London 2016); *Work: The Last 1000 Years* (London and New York 2018); *Grenzen. Räumliche und soziale Trennlinien im Zeitenlauf* (Wien 2018).

*Miroslav Lacko*
Having graduated in Archive and Auxiliary Historical Sciences from the Comenius University, Bratislava (Slovakia) in 2011, he became a Doctoral Fellow at the Institute of History at the Slovak Academy of Sciences, Bratislava and completed his PhD in History at Comenius University in 2015. His research focus areas are the economic and social history of the Early Modern Age, Central European mining history from the Late Middle Ages to 1945, the economic history of the Habsburg Monarchy, and environmental history. Since 2016, he has been a research associate at the Center for Economic and Social History of the Faculty of Arts at the University of Ostrava (Czech Republic) and has been an editor of *Montánna história* "The Mining History: A Yearbook for History of Mining and Metallurgy" since acting as one of its founders in 2008. Since 2018, he has been a postdoctoral fellow at the Friedrich Christian Lesser College of East-Central Europe at Friedrich Schiller University, Jena (Germany).

*Ernst Langthaler*
is a Professor of Social and Economic History at the Johannes Kepler University, Linz and head of the Institute of Rural History in St. Pölten. He works on global commodity chains and frontiers with a focus on agriculture and food. His recent publications include: "*The Soy Paradox: The Western Nutrition Transition Revisited, 1950–2010*," Global Environment 11 (2018); "*Food Regimes and their Trade Links: A Socio-ecological Perspective*," Ecological Economics 160 (2019) (with Fridolin Krausmann); "*Broadening and Deepening. Soy Expansions in a World-Historical Perspective*," HALAC – Historia Ambiental Latinoamericana y Caribeña 10 (2020).

*Tibor T. Meszmann*
is a Research Fellow at the Central European Labour Studies Institute, Bratislava, a research affiliate at the CEU Center for Policy Studies, and member of the Public Sociology Working Group "Helyzet", Budapest. His research and publications center on industrial relations and the sociology of work, with a focus on developments in Hungary. His recent publications include: "*Precarization via Digitalization? Work Arrangements in the On-Demand Platform Economy in Hungary and Slovakia*" Frontiers in Sociology 5:3. February 2020 (with Marta Kahancova and Maria Sedlakova) "*Snakes or Ladders? Job Quality Assessment among Temp Workers from Ukraine in Hungarian Electronics*" Central and Eastern European Migration Review 5(2): 135–153, 2019 (with Olena Fedyuk).

*Goran Music*
is an Associated Researcher at the Research Centre for the History of Transformations (RECET) at the University of Vienna. His fields of interest include global labor history, the comparative history of workers under state socialism, and the everyday history of socialist Yugoslavia. His most recent publication is: "*Making and Breaking the Yugoslav Working Class: A Story of Two Self-Managed Factories*" (CEU Press).

*Jörg Nowak*
is a visiting Professor at the University of Brasilia. He has published on labor conflict in the Global South, logistics and infrastructure, and Althusserian Marxism. His recent publications are: "*Mass Strikes and Social Movements in Brazil and India*" (2019), and "*Logistik, Machtressourcen und die politische Ökonomie des Rohstoffexports. Der Streik der brasilianischen Trucker im Jahr 2018*" (2020).

*Franziska Ollendorf*
is a Research Associate at the Leibniz Institute of Agricultural Development in Transition Economies (IAMO), Halle. Her current research interests include corporate social responsibility and power dynamics in global value chains, the political economy of cocoa, as well as rural change and livelihood systems.

*András Pinkasz*
is a Head of Section at the Business Statistics Directory and the secretary of the Union at the Hungarian Central Statistical Office. He is a member of the Public Sociology Working Group "Helyzet". His research interests focus on the political economy of Eastern Europe, especially the changing types of integration

relating to the international division of labor. His most recent publications are: "*Relocation, standardization and vertical specialization: core-periphery relations in the European automotive value chain*" (Society and Economy, 41(2), 2019) and "*Conflicting Interests in the Comecon Integration: State Socialist Debates on the East-West-South Relations*" (East Central Europe, 45(2–3), 2018). Both of them co-authored by Tamás Gerőcs.

*Stefan Schmalz*
is currently a visiting Professor of Sociology at the Institute for Latin American Studies, Freie Universität Berlin. He has published on uneven development, work and labor and political economy in Europe, China and Latin America. Among his recent publications are: Schmalz, Stefan/ Sommer, Brandon (eds.) (2019): *Confronting Crisis and Precariousness: Organized Labour and Social Unrest in the European Union* (Lanham: Rowman & Littlefield); Ramírez, Martín/ Schmalz, Stefan (eds.) (2018) *¿Fin de la bonanza? Entradas, salidas y encrucijadas del extractivismo* (Buenos Aires: Editorial Biblos).

*Johanna Sittel*
works as a Researcher at the Department of Sociology of Work, Industry and Economy at the Friedrich Schiller University, Jena. She is currently writing her PhD dissertation on informal work in the Argentine automotive industry and has published on informal and precarious work in Latin America, uneven development, public sociology and current transformation processes in the automotive industry. Her most recent publications are: Neuhauser, Johanna/ Sittel, Johanna/ Weinmann, Nico (eds.) (2019): *Arbeit und Geschlecht im Wandel. Impulse aus Lateinamerika* (Frankfurt/New York: Campus).

*Uwe Spiekermann*
is an associate lecturer at Georg-August-University Göttingen, Germany. His research interests include the history of consumption, retailing, nutrition, and knowledge. Among his thirteen books are: *Künstliche Kost. Deutsche Ernährung von 1840 bis heute* (2018) and *Immigrant Entrepreneurship: The German-American Experience* (Co-editor, 2016). For additional information visit Uwe-Spiekermann.com.

CHAPTER 1

# Chains of Labor

## *Connecting Global Labor History and the Commodity Chain Paradigm*

*Andrea Komlosy and Goran Musić*

The Global Commodity Chain approach has developed within social sciences parallel to the globalization of industrial production flows in the 1970s and 1980s. The build-up of production chains beyond national borders has picked up pace especially in the last three decades. The stock of foreign direct investment increased from around 10 percent of global GDP in 1990 to 35 percent in 2015.[1] Over one-half of all exports (by value) cross a border twice before reaching the end-customer. This rising complexity inspired the economist Jagdish Bhagwati to visualize the transforming trade flows and their supporting network of international trade agreements metaphorically as a "spaghetti bowl".[2] It is important to recognize that the multiplication of locations and forms of labor organization across the globe did not affect all companies and industrial branches in a direct way. Still, almost all economic actors were put under competitive pressure by the productivity and cost standards dictated by outsourcing and just-in-time production. Governments and businesses that favored local, regional and national markets and their protection found themselves lagging behind a global trend. The economic and political forces, which required free movement of capital and commodity flows in the world economy for their operations, put pressure on governments and international organizations to liberalize. As a result, we witnessed a shift from the national welfare state towards a regulatory framework of global governance.

At present, the negative consequences of workflows going global are finding growing echoes in Western media and public debates. The growing attention given to the impacts of deregulation, flexibilization and labor fragmentation is due to the fact that they do not only affect developing countries in the Global South but have been increasingly stamping their mark on the old industrialized North. The decline of traditional industrial regions, loss of stable incomes and social benefits for the working class, social polarization and lacking futures

1 "The Retreat of the Global Company," *The Economist*, 28 January 2017, pp. 14–17, referring to Arvind Subramanian and Martin Kessler.

2 Term coined by Jagdish Bhagwati in 1995.

 | DOI:10.1163/9789004448049_002

for lower and middle classes stir popular dissatisfaction. While transnational companies, global buyers, international retailers and their cosmopolitan stakeholders still promote the free movement of capital and commodities, the less mobile "losers of globalization" argue against the proclaimed benefits of constant liberalization.

During the relocation of production to low wage regions, many economies formerly referred to as the "developing countries" came to be seen as the "Newly Industrializing Countries" (NIC). The former "Second World" of socialist Eastern Europe witnessed a reverse change in outside and self-perception based on the structural alterations in their economies. The attempts of these countries to nurture self-reliant development and industrial catching-up by state planning and control were halted as they became transformed into suppliers of Western companies, similar to "developing countries". Some big size emerging NICs, which had a long domestic industrial tradition before coming under Western dominance in the eighteenth and nineteenth centuries, above all China and India, were able to profit from the globalization of production. These countries have moved up from low end to high end in a number of chains, depriving the old cores of the world-economy from their monopoly in research, development and chain logistics. In some instances, they were even able to take command over chain logistics, enter sectors with higher adding value and become agents of outsourcing themselves by relocating production to cheaper locations in "developing countries" or internal peripheries.

As a consequence of the new geopolitical production landscape, political positions vis-à-vis liberalism and protectionism have been reversed. The politicians from the old, or maybe more precisely, "Former Industrial Countries" (FIC) are increasingly divided about the benefit of globalization. The dilemma for the political elites in these countries is whether they should push for further globalization or give priority ("We first") to domestic industries and markets, in order to defend their privileged position in the world-economy against competitors. Conversely, the Newly Industrialized Countries promote the liberal economic world order. These emerging cores embrace the free movement of capital and commodities, while at the same time avoiding the adoption of liberal political rights, usually associated with economic liberalism and the traditional core nations.

Based on a more authoritarian political regime, China can set new standards for global competitiveness, putting pressure on the "Former Industrial Countries" to adapt. However, the overstretched nature of Global Commodity Chain logistics, combined with the new breakthroughs in individualized (opposed to standardized) technologies of mass production, could reverse the global organization of commodity chains. According to recent statistics about direct foreign investment and shares of cross-border supply chains controlled by multinational firms, we face a stagnation of investment and a decline of returns. Conversely, in the FICs, the manufacture based on national production and consumption is increasing compared to globalized arrangements.[3] It is too early to draw definite conclusions, but these findings might be an indicator of the upcoming change and reorientation in the global economy. A critical juncture in the development of Global Commodity Chains is a good moment to reflect and take a closer look at how the concept evolved over time and the limitations it met on the way.

The investigations in this volume stem from a conference on Global Commodity Chains and Labor Relations, organized by the International Conference on Labor and Social History (ITH) in the mining and industrial town of Steyr (Austria) in 2017. The conference topic was motivated by a recognition that tracing single products through manufacturing stages, taking place at different locations under a plethora of institutional, social and legal environments, has proven to be a particularly fruitful way to research the seemingly opaque networks of global capitalism. Yet, the organizers also pointed out that the commodity chain research tends to have a narrow focus on firms and governability, offering very little insight regarding the workers, their conditions and the actual production process. The volume aims to help correct this oversight by gathering papers engaging with commodity chains from the perspective of labor relations and work experience in various locations through history, as well as the possibility of workers' agency within these complex spatial arrangements. The idea is to test the advantages and limits of a Global Commodity Chains approach in the study of labor. Conversely, the volume poses the question how a greater emphasis on labor and labor relations could contribute to the commodity chain literature.

## 1 Global Commodity Chains: The Concept and Its Adaptations

Sourcing from and outsourcing to peripheries and combining locations with different price and legal structures is not a novel strategy. The phenomenon has a long history (manifold systems of putting out on a local, a regional and a global level) and can be traced through time in a cyclical pattern. As in the

3 "The Retreat of the Global Company," *The Economist*, 28 January 2017, pp. 14–17. In the spring of 2020, when the last changes were made to this contribution, global commodity chains were more severely disturbed by the protectionist measures that most governments ordered to hinder the spread of the SARS-CoV-2 virus.

case of business[4] or accumulation cycles,[5] the cycle metaphor does not claim a comeback of older modes of production in the same or in a similar way. Rather we can observe shifts between decentralization and centralization of production, between periods of geographically expanding arrangements of location that form a chain and periods when flows of production concentrate next to each other in a single workshop or factory. Moreover, the shifts between outsourcing and in house-tendencies do not usually concern the whole economy but rather occur in specific sectors.

Historization can help us avoid attributing teleological continuity and inevitability to globalizing tendencies.[6] While medieval merchant or urban trade networks reached beyond state borders, the formation of the modern state put pressure on the manufacturing companies to perform within the borders of the developing territories of the political or national economies. Trans-national production networks only appeared on the agenda again as the leading principle of organizing flows of production, when the confines of the states did not offer favorable conditions for value creation at the end of the post-Second World War reconstruction period, and big companies went for multi-national workflows, pushing states to pave the way towards the globalization of commodity chains.[7]

Organizing the flow of production between various forms of division of labor – on the inter-firm level, as well as between firms, on the local level, as well as in trans-local organizational arrangements – has been a key issue from the beginning of economic thought. Methodological approaches in the investigation of chains differ between focusing on the reproduction of inequalities in historical capitalism,[8] contemporary global commodity chains, and production networks[9] or the possibilities of upgrading on a firm or state level.[10] A major shift can be identified at the moment when the Old International Division of Labor between manufacturing in the Global North and raw material production in the Global South gave way to a New International Division of Labor, in which peripheral locations in the South were transformed into manufacturing sites supplying the western-based multinational companies with

4 Schumpeter, *Business Cycles.*

5 Arrighi, *The Long 20th Century*, pp. 28–36.

6 Feldbauer et al., *Rhythmen der Globalisierung*; Komlosy, "Spatial Division of Labour."

7 Sassen, *Territoriality – Authority – Rights.*

8 Wallerstein, "Introduction."

9 Gereffi and Korzeniewicz, *Commodity chains and global capitalism*; Bair, "The Political Economy of Commodity Chains" and Bair, "Global Capitalism and Commodity Chains."

10 Gereffi et al., "The Governance of Global Value Chains."

cheap industrial labor.[11] This shift is embedded in changing organizational frameworks shaped by transnational commodity chains. The global commodity chains today are made up of headquarters, technology-intensive sites, usually combined with research and development functions, at their "high" ends (realizing high added value) and standardized, labor-intensive functions at their "low" ends.[12]

A basic distinction in the study of global chains can be observed between commodity chains set up by the "producer", who is outsourcing certain operations from the central company (producer-driven commodity chains), or from the side of the retailing company (or global "buyer") that is contracting and sourcing from various producers in order to achieve the final product (buyer-driven commodity chains).[13] If operations at different locations are combined to realize the final product, the management of flows is of vital importance: single parts and components have to be sent and to arrive "just in time" to be ready for further processing or assembling at the next production site. Inspired by the more sophisticated ways of distributing works in a global just-in-time framework, coordination of inputs and outputs within commodity chains has acquired a distinctive status both in management and in economic research, giving way to logistics studies.[14] More recently, the concept of commodity frontiers contributed to the assessment of global capitalism as a system of expansion that constantly extends its reach into new territories, thus commodifying nature, raw material, and labor. In a situation where geographical expansion is not possible anymore, the capitalist logic brings new needs to the process of commodification.[15] In this process, new locations are incorporated into global commodity chains, while previous commodity chains are constantly being restructured.

Although global commodity chains rely on labor, this aspect does not play a key role in most of the research. If it is included, labor and labor movements are often reduced to cost factors, accounting for (re)locating single steps of the work-process to specific locations from the perspective of the

11 The term "New International Division of Labor" was coined by Fröbel et al., *Umbruch in der Weltwirtschaft*.

12 Stöllinger, "Change in functional specialisation in CESEE."

13 The distinction between producer-driven and buyer-driven commodity chains was coined by Gary Gereffi and Miguel Korzeniewicz and taken over in business and business studies, see: Gereffi and Korzeniewicz, *Commodity chains and global capitalism*.

14 Bonacich and Wilson, *Getting the Goods*; Cowen, *The Deadly Life of Logistics*; Altenried et al., *Logistische Grenzlandschaften*.

15 Altvater, *Die Grenzen der Globalisierung*; Moore, *Capitalism in the Web of Life*; Moore and Patel, *A History of the World in Seven Cheap Things*; see also Langthaler in this volume.

profitability for chain organizers, while a social and economic analysis of labor conditions has been widely neglected for a long time, not least due to the success of Global Production Network and Global Value Chain models. This was not always the case. Within the world-systemic modeling, from which the commodity chain paradigm originated, labor relations were considered a key factor in splitting up locally integrated production and relocating work-flows to locations with different cost profiles.[16] The world-system origins of the concept were refined in the 1980s to comply with the global industrial relocations that took place in the wake of the global crisis in the 1970s.[17] While world-systems analyses focused the imbalances in the division of labor and the appropriation of value by combining different labor regimes, they often did not undertake in-depth research into the conditions of specific chain arrangements in single sectors and companies. By investigating business and logistic organization of specific chains, more focused commodity chain analyses were able to offer empirical data. Research interest moved to examine the possibilities to develop commodity chains and improve output, productivity, and growth in different forms or organization and management (governance). Imbalances were seen as barriers to be overcome instead of representing the fundamental functioning principle of chain management.

Global value distribution along the flow of production and the chains of location became a useful tool to analyze business organization, both on the producer-firm level, between firms and subcontractors, as well between "buyers" and their respective suppliers.[18] Equally, it was taken up by development planning in order to discover strategies to upgrade single locations, regions, or states within a commodity chain or by including local production in a chain.[19] Development studies broadly agreed that entering a global commodity chain risked transforming regional production into suppliers of cheap raw material or into "extended workbenches". At the same time, they emphasized the positive aspects, e.g. upgrading from a low end supplying position ("Original Equipment Manufacture" OEM) to a more value creating position ("Original

16 Hopkins and Wallerstein, "Patterns of Development of the Modern World-System"; Hopkins and Wallerstein, "Commodity Chains in the World Economy."

17 Fröbel et al., *Die neue internationale Arbeitsteilung*; Fröbel et al., *Umbruch in der Weltwirtschaft*; Gereffi and Kornzeniewicz, *Commodity chains and global capitalism.*

18 Fischer et al., "Einleitung."

19 Bair, "Global Capitalism and Commodity Chains"; Bair, "The Political Economy of Commodity Chains."

Design Manufacture" ODM or "Original Brand Manufacture" OBM).[20] As the concept gained currency and entered international business, finance and development organizations, it risked being transformed from a critical to a mainstream tool. Development was shaped in terms of upgrading, while the reproduction of imbalances and polarizations between high- and low-end positions along the chain disappeared from sight. Moreover, commodity chains were seen as inevitable arrangements of global production. Due to the permanent re-arrangement, entering the chain at the low end was seen as the only way for developing countries to move up the chain.

According to the product-cycle model,[21] advanced industrial producers moved into new, more value adding products, offering developing countries access to manufacturing in less profitable sectors. Once a part of a commodity chain, technological upgrading seemed feasible and trickle-down effects were expected within the national economies. However, upgrading was perceived only from the perspective of those who were successful, not taking into consideration the fact that only some could improve their chain position, while others were at the same time pushed into a supplier position that fixed them on a low level. Even in cases where success in upgrading was guaranteed, the development from a technological middle position to a high one failed because of the structural barriers preventing industrial suppliers in emerging countries from moving into chain controlling positions – a limit coined as a middle-income or – more precisely – middle level development trap.[22] Single exceptions, usually due to historical conditions (e.g. the East Asian "tigers" and other follow-up "tigers" in South East Asia or Brazil), the size of a company or state, geographic location, and a supportive regulatory framework, do not allow generalizing successful examples. In general, the modernization paradigm of "everybody can move up" lost sight of those who failed to do so or were caught in a mid-way trap.

The approaches mentioned above assumed an automatic and positive correlation between the successful upgrading of single companies, regions or states, and the improvement of labor relations and standard of living. What they ignored is the fact that low wages, low taxes, and other incentives to foreign investors to save costs, were part of the development strategy, often preventing technological upgrading from translating into higher wages and better

20 Distinguishing the different positions and concentrating on upgrading for single companies, chains or states, channeled discussions among experts into the given labels preventing research from embedding commodity chains into the global division of labor.

21 Vernon, *International Investment*.

22 Krasilshchikov, *The Malaise from Success*.

living conditions. Hereby the Global Commodity Chain analyses lost critical impact vis-à-vis the structural inequalities of global capitalism within and between states. Indeed, states can change position or even restructure the global division of labor in the course of their industrial upgrading. In the same vein, individual firms can upgrade their position in a chain or network and increase their share of value creation. However, capital accumulation, that is a precondition for capitalism to work as a global system, cannot exist without regional imbalances, neither on the macro-economic nor on the micro-economic level.

## 2 Global Labor History: Bringing Labor Back

Scholars have reacted in different ways to the co-optation of Global Commodity Chain and Global Production Network concepts into mainstream economics: Some, who nurtured a critical position towards the liberal international order, neglected the Global Commodity Chain concept[23] or rejected it altogether; others revisited its critical potential and developed new approaches. Faced with the realization that economic upgrading does not necessarily translate into an advancement of workers' wellbeing, there is an increased emphasis on the importance of "social upgrading" within recent Global Value Chain literature. Authors are becoming more attentive to the governance roles of states, trade unions, and social movements, but also businesses, mainly through the corporate social responsibility paradigm.[24] The 2013 collapse of the Rana Plaza garment production building in Bangladesh, which killed 1,134 people,[25] prompted the ILO to spotlight the research of working conditions inside the global value chains, giving birth to a number of articles in scientific journals, reports and policy papers focused especially on the lower tiers of labor intensive sectors with poor records regarding respect for labor rights, such as the garments and agriculture industry.[26]

With most of the social upgrading literature tending to observe workers' exploitation within production chains as a contingent phenomenon to be overcome within the existing international division of labor, and adopting

23 Harvey, *Seventeen Contradictions*.

24 Barrientos, et al., "Economic and social upgrading in global production networks."

25 For the interdisciplinary overview of Rana Plaza tragedy and its impact on the South Asian garment industry see: Saxena, *Labor, Global Supply Chains, and the Garment Industry in South Asia*.

26 For an overview of this research see: Delautre, "Decent work in global supply chains: An internal research review."

top-down approach that neglects workers' agency, a more critical strand of research has evolved, highlighting structural inequalities and workers' collective action.[27] The neglect of a labor perspective within Global Production and Value Chain studies has also propelled new interest in studying the agency of labor and labor movements in shaping commodity chains from a more historical perspective.[28] These authors usually built up their research on the broader literature that Global Labor History had produced since the 1980s. Global Labor History, substantially shaped by the initiatives of the International Institute for Social History, Amsterdam, under its scientific directors Jan Lucassen and Marcel van der Linden, aimed at overcoming the narrow notion of work that had become dominant at the turn of the nineteenth to the twentieth century.[29] With this concept, work was reduced to regular gainful employment, while all labor relations that did not comply with this definition, were not classed as work. As the codification of work to gainful employment was based upon developments in Western industrialized states, it included social securities that were built in the formalization and regulation of labor. Therefore, the brunt of the research on work, workers, and labor movements during the twentieth century concentrated mainly on the conditions of commodified labor, ideally entitled to social security, seen as the future of work.

These labor relations were analyzed with regard to exploitation, surplus value realization, labor struggles and labor organization aiming at reform or revolution. Accordingly, unpaid, house and subsistence, irregular, informal, casual work, as was performed by the vast majority of the world population, were seen as relics of pre-capitalist modes of production that would give way to commodification in the course of a further deepening and expansion of capitalism. In the same way, serfdom, slavery and forced labor were not included in capitalist labor relations. Global Labor History opened the horizon for the synchronicity of labor relations – commodified and reciprocal, free and unfree, formal and informal – to the functioning of global capitalism. From this perspective, it is only consequent to look at their combination in local, regional and global commodity chains.

27 Selwyn, *Workers, State and Development in Brazil*; Selwyn "Social Upgrading"; Bair and Bernstein, "Labor and the Wal-Mart Effect"; Cumbers, et al. "Labour agency and union positionalities"; Mezzadri, *The Sweatshop Regime*.

28 Silver, Forces of Labour; Selwyn, "Beyond firm-centrism"; Newsome et al., *Putting Labour in its Place*; Cowen, *The Deadly Life of Logistics*.

29 *Hofmeester and Van der Linden, Handbook*; Lucassen and Van der Linden, *Working on Labor*; Roth, *On the Road to Global Labour History*.

World-system analyses concentrate on the functional side of coexistence and combination of different labor relations in different parts of the world, giving way to the categories of core, periphery, and semi-periphery to represent the axial division of labor in global capitalism beyond single locations and states. Labor relations are seen as one important expression of centrality or peripherality, with free, proletarized labor developing (in combination with other labor relations) in the core regions, while peripheries, both global or within states, show a larger amount of unfree, informal or subsistence labor.[30] Once these regions are incorporated into the unequal division of labor of global capitalism, they are drawn into a process of unequal and combined development.[31] World-systems analyses thus offers a framework for embedding commodity chain and labor analyses into global capitalism and the changing manifestations of its axial division of labor. It requires cooperation with other approaches from business history, industrial relation studies, and from global labor history in particular. Global Labor History takes greater interest in the empirical side of what concrete labor looked like and how it was organized at each location, at the same time keeping in mind the composition of different labor relations on a local, national or global scale.[32]

The Global Commodity Chain concept focuses on chains, or networks, of locations with different institutional, legal and social conditions that are combined in order to achieve a single product. The network involves companies, governments, households, and labor. In contrast to ahistorical, purely organizational models that do not include power relations, more historically-oriented approaches ask for the hierarchy among the combined locations (low end, intermediary, high end with their different positions in a functional division of labor with regard to wage, costs, qualification and value added) and their different part in value creation. This hierarchy is also related to political power and state support, which is causing social inequalities and imbalances in state revenue and workers' income along the chain. From this perspective, successful catching up involves more than becoming an industrial location, increasing manufacture output and export, or using new technologies. It relies on the capacity to create governance, organization, and innovation, in a combination of state and enterprise efforts.[33] This is why the catching up of

30 Wallerstein, *Historical Capitalism*.

31 Much criticism of the world-system approach has been expressed for focusing exchange over production, economic determinism, neglect of agency, etc. For a review and discussion of critiques as well as for recent developments within world-system paradigms, see: Kaps and Komlosy "Centers and Peripheries Revisited."

32 Komlosy, *The Last 1.000 Years*; Roth, *On the Road to Global Labour History*.

33 Grumiller and Raza, "Towards an Institutional Setup for Industrial Policy."

one participant may overcome chain or network hierarchies, while imbalances re-appear in new sectorial and regional arrangements.

The Global Labor History concept draws from relating different social environments with their specific forms of labor. For instance, unfree labor (serfdom, slavery, servitude) is seen as a constitutive component of capitalism, adapting to changing conditions, e.g. the factory system (and its demand for cotton in the first half of the nineteenth century, giving way to a Second Slavery), or forced labor camps, whenever unwanted or politically prosecuted layers of the population are pushed into forced labor institutions (under mercantilism, forced industrialization programs of various political projects, dealing with political adversaries or prisoners of war).[34] Both slave and convict labor have been integrated into commodity chains in different periods of history until today, together with free labor contributing to the same product, e.g. in the sugar or cotton industries.

If the variety of work relations is to be fully assessed, a household perspective is necessary, as also suggested by world-systems and feminist concepts.[35] Households are places, where paid and unpaid, various forms of gainful work – wage-work, self-employed activities or precarious jobs – meet subsistence agriculture, unpaid house, reproduction and care work, performed by household members. Households pool resources and incomes and they do so in a single place, or in the form of trans-national households, if income pooling is not possible at home – thus linking global labor studies to global migration studies.[36]

Another branch of global labor studies that intersects with commodity chain approaches are informality and informalization studies.[37] From a company-perspective, informalization aims to reduce costs and (expensive) regulations by outsourcing activities to workers who do not have access to regulated, secure jobs. From a worker's and household perspective, informal activities compensate for the lack of regular, i.e. formal employment or business opportunities. For them, informalization circumvents formal labor contracts and relations, leading to more precarious, unstable and unsecured forms of

34 See ITH Conference volume on coerced labor: Van der Linden and Rodriguez, *On Coerced Labor*.

35 Compare Global household studies: Smith and Wallerstein, *Creating and Transforming Households*; Dunaway, "The Semi-Proletarian Household"; Mies et al., *Women – the last colony*; Mies at al., *The Subsistence Perspective*; Komlosy, "Re-assessing Labour"; Komlosy, *Work. The Last 1.000 Years*.

36 Compare Global migration studies: Lucassen and Lucassen, *Globalizing Migration History*.

37 Compare informalization studies: Portes et al., *The Informal Economy*; Komlosy et al., *Ungeregelt und unterbezahlt*; Cerda-Becker et al., "Grauzonen der Arbeit" and Sittel and Schmalz in this volume.

employment, including the tendency of transforming dependent employment into dependent self-employment.

Last but not least, sociologists have begun to enter the booming field of logistics, extending logistic studies from the organization of production-flows to labor issues. The logistics perspective can help our understanding of, not only how trans-national production-flows are organized, but also how labor is composed at different locations and which kind of labor-power is mobilized to fit into specific work-profiles.[38]

## 3 Connecting Approaches

As we have pointed out, commodity chain studies primarily focus on production networks and how location and specialization contribute to accumulation of value, whereas labor studies focus on labor relations in commodified contexts. The latter tend to emphasize wage-workers' exploitation as well as the influence of wage-workers' organizations, often attributing success to workers' struggles, while neglecting how improvement at one location fits into the overall necessity of maintaining income and labor regime differentials between the "high" and the "low ends" of a commodity chain, that is connecting core, semi-peripheral and peripheral parts of the world-system. This is why Commodity Chain – Production Network Analyses have to be inter-related with the diversity and hierarchical connection of labor relations at different locations – the more so, if these sites and jobs are connected by a transregional commodity chain. The combination of the two approaches can help assess the importance of differentials in labor relations for the functioning of global chains or networks.

This volume proposes a theoretical and methodological framework for connecting existing studies and further inter-disciplinary research that bring together Global Labor and Commodity Chain/Production Network and Value Chain studies. The main question is: How does the combination of different labor relations along a chain allow profit realization, i.e. make capital accumulation feasible? This requires looking at single locations and how labor is organized locally. At the same time, the overall arrangement of the work-flow along a chain (network) is important, because it impacts on each participating location – on owners, workers, and governments – from an entrepreneurial, developmental, as well as from a labor perspective.

38 Bonacich and Wilson, *Getting the Goods*; Mezzadra and Brett, *Border as Method*; Cowen *The Deadly Life of Logistics*.

Different from most commodity chain literature until now, this volume follows a historical approach, offering historical case studies, longitudinal analysis and contemporary investigations, focusing on specific regions, sectors, branches or networks that rely on transregional commodity chains. The chain character differs from case to case and requires defining the specific set of conditions that produce and re-arrange different types and combinations of labor relations to be combined along the chain. From a methodological point of view, we have to keep in mind the work steps and production flows on all locations along a chain/network, including raw material production, research & development, administration, logistics, manufacturing, transport, marketing, merchandizing and distribution. In the long run – although not part of this book –, consuming also gives way to a flow of waste deposits, reuse or recycling that can be organized in a separate circle or end up in the same commodity chain. Labor relations at all locations along a chain/network include both commodified (paid) labor (different modes of contracts, qualifications, control, wage levels and levels of social protection) and reciprocal (unpaid) work (within parental, household and solidarity groups, providing reproduction, care, subsistence agriculture etc.) and their inter-relationship.

Just as any production relies on human beings, human reproduction cannot be separated from the product-cycle. Both cycles are linked by a continuum of paid and unpaid, formal and informal labor with their different levels of wage, income and social provisions of state and companies, which vary according to business cycles, conjunctures and a region's position within the functional transregional division of labor. This means that, according to space and time, workers and their families either rely more on monetary income, on unpaid subsistence activities, or on state support.

Labor protests and movements are important factors in shaping the solidarity networks among workers. They strive for the improvement of working conditions of individual companies, whole branches, as well as for national labor regulations. Outsourcing steps of production to other legal spaces (states or special processing zones exempt from national legislation) is therefore a widespread means of circumventing local and national agreements. Globalizing trade-unions is a means of exercising pressure on transnational companies and organizers of commodity chains; as a matter of fact, transnational unions lag behind business strategies pitting different groups of workers against each other. From a worker's perspective, it is therefore highly beneficial, if political and economic space are identical.[39]

39 Becker and Komlosy, "Grenzen und Räume," p. 48.

The legal, institutional, and the technological framework of commodity chain, production network and labor organization has to be included on a national, an international, and a transnational scale. These levels may compete with each other, coexist, or get actively combined by division of labor and commodity chain work-flows. They also compete with each other, coexist or become intentionally coalesced by the regulatory political frameworks that enable, encourage, support, restrict, or set up conditions for transregional commodity production flows. We meet variations and shifts of more or less regulation (laws, prohibitions, incentives), supporting, hindering, or structuring flows of capital, goods, and labor, such as taxation, duties, trade agreements, regulations for outsourcing and contract manufacturing, labor regulation, environment and health regulations, or social security obligations. Regulatory measures vary according to the specific conditions, constitutions, and competences attributed to the different regulating polities from the local community to the transnational organization level. Depending on the interests, keeping regulation to a lower level or transferring it from community and district to national levels, or from national to international levels, is used as a means of protection or competition. Unlike as presented in liberal main stream economics, protection and competition are strongly interrelated: Protection is used as a means of improving competitiveness at a specific moment of international business relations, while shifts between advanced producers and industrial late-comers often provoke a change of economic policy from protections to free trade on the side of the initial leaders and from free-trade to protectionism on the side of the emerging, lately industrializing countries.[40]

Chain controlling representatives exercise pressure on national legislation, policies and international regulations in order to allow the flow of capital, commodities (eventually also labor) as well as the transfer of profits without legal restrictions and at low costs (taxes, tolls and other trade barriers). They exercise pressure on trade unions, labor and social movements, as well as on participating companies by opening and closing affiliates, engaging or disengaging contractors, transferring activities to other locations, by subcontracting, outsourcing etc.

At the same time, local arrangements, traditions, the struggles and demands of social movements affect how commodity chains are organized, which location is included in or excluded from the chain. Although global business actors, national governments and international institutions tend to present constraints that do not allow alternative paths to be pursued, production

40 Bairoch, *Economics and World History*; Chang, *Kicking Away the Ladder*.

arrangements are not exempt from restructuring and renewal on different ethical and political grounds. The historical approach proves that constant re-arrangement has been the rule, not the exception.

Establishing transregional commodity-chains is a way to make use of, and moreover, to contribute to the rise of, legal, social, technical, cultural, and wage differentials. Although transregional commodity-chains do represent an indispensable condition of capital accumulation, they do not characterize capitalist production at all places at all times. Whether or not they are established depends on technologies (production, transport, communication, logistics), on the coincidence of capital interests (profits) with state interests (taxes, jobs, export promotion, technological upgrading, regulatory framework), as well as the coincidence of capital interests with workers' interests (social advent, participation, consumption). They are dependent on economic conjunctures and on international political relations that are favorable to transregional cooperation across state-borders.

## 4 Chain Actors

Controlling a chain/network means permanent restructuring according to changing economic and technological requirements and to changing legal and political environments at the participating places, respectively nodes. Chains/networks reflect hierarchies, dependencies and conflicts, not only between employers and workers, but more so between different kinds of employers and different kinds of workers. Moreover, agency goes beyond the capital – labor antagonism and includes regions or populations that are not part of transregional commodity chains. Why is it that specific regions become part of the chain, while others remain outside? This question requires combining a transregional approach of global producers' or global buyers' demand with the specific conditions offered at single locations, made up from labor, social, tax, financial, legal, and environmental requirements.

First of all, selecting specific locations for a commodity chain depends on the chain controlling company, which considers legal conditions, qualifications and costs at different locations as well as transport possibilities. Their decision depends on local conditions, i.e. whether or not infrastructure, incentives, subsidies or privileges like the unlimited (in- and out-)flow of capital are offered to them by local governments. This opens a sphere for local political actors to exercise influence on investment. Still, the local conditions are weighed against each other by investors, allowing them to choose between different offers or combine different locations for different tasks, hence reducing the impact of local agents. Historical relations and established co-operations play a prominent role in selecting partners, but long-term alliances can also be given up if circumstances change.

Eastern Europe serves as a good example for shifting participation in transregional commodity chains. Eastern European regions have been delivering raw materials or semi-processed products to Western firms, both within the Habsburg (or the German) Empire, or in an international framework in the seventeenth, eighteenth and nineteenth centuries. When, mostly in 1918, nation-building broke up established imperial and interimperial cooperations, trading and investment partners were replaced, e.g. French capital replaced Austrian and German ownership in the 1920s, until NS-Germany used the Western withdrawal from global trade in the 1930s to expand its influence and incorporated Eastern Europe, supplying the German Reich with raw materials and (forced) labor. When socialist Eastern Europe delinked from the capitalist West in 1945, the Great German chains broke down, giving way to catching up industrialization in the framework of COMECON, until the breakdown of state socialism reintegrated Eastern Europe into Western corporate governance again in 1989/90.[41]

Second, local or national governments may also opt to prevent firms from including their territory in a commodity chain (fearing economic downgrading, de-qualification, pressure on wages, loss of added value, etc.), under the condition that international agreements (world or regional trade agreements) do not hinder them. Investigating the composition of commodity chains therefore requires looking at how state and investors' interests intersect or are pressed to converge. On the one hand, governments face pressure from investors and the transnational institutions (customs and free trade unions, international organizations and agreements, investment protection agreements and global investment tribunals) that replace politics with codified juridical constraints to open markets. On the other hand, international organizations and their – more or less binding – legal frameworks and road maps could strengthen a single government against entrepreneurial claims. Governments also face pressure from social movements that is sometimes welcomed, and, if not, there are refined political strategies either to suppress protest movements or to transform opposition into procedures of controlled participation (governance).

Third, local/national companies may be interested in joining a production network for export promotion and technological upgrading. Or they might

41 Hofbauer and Komlosy, "Capital Accumulation."

oppose such a development, in fear of being outcompeted, lose markets, go bankrupt or face a take-over, therefore trying to persuade governments to grant them privileges, subsidies and market protection. Governments then have to decide between favoring or discriminating against local/national or transnational firms, and accordingly support international agreements that allow or forbid national priorities. It goes without saying that political parties that represent local entrepreneurs will be more protective, while parties that represent transnational capital and the transnational managerial class will fight state interference and promote international agreements that prevent it. Socialist or social-democratic parties are squeezed between a managerial approach that promises modernization and upward mobility for the middle-classes and a labor-oriented approach that is devoted to social commitments, that do not fit into (neo)liberal conditions favored by the organizers/commanders of global commodity chains.

Fourth, local workers do not own enough (if any) capital in order to make decisions on investment. It may be useful to differentiate workers' agency according to the sources and conditions of their power into structural, associational, and marketplace power.[42] In the framework of global commodity chains, workers' agency is equally dependent on their chain position, i.e. whether or not they work in a company on the low end, the high end or in a medium position, corresponding with added value realization, technological equipment, labor conditions and wages. This means that their relationship with capital is overarched by how their local employer fits into the hierarchy of the chain, on the one hand giving way to a joint capital-labor interest vis-à-vis other chain positions, and, on the other hand, subordinating workers' interests in decent pay and living wages to cost reduction strategies that are imposed on their employer to maintain their position as a supplying firm. In fact, workers' agency is restricted – either work for a specific company or find a new employer; this decision includes migrating or commuting to a work place, if job offers and migration and labor market regulations allow them to do so. Usually the workforce of a company consists of long-term residential workers, complemented by temporary workers who do not enjoy the same wages and benefits, often lacking residence permission or security. Once employed, workers can put organized pressure on the company to offer better working conditions, pay, and social coverage, especially if their skills empower them. They form trade unions that usually support the skilled workforce and protect them against competition from temporary workers, often migrants, who are ready to accept

42 According to: Selwyn, "Beyond firm-centrism."

worse conditions. Management can either put pressure on trade unions or it can co-opt them to maintain order and hierarchy among workers – a position that eventually leads to the collaboration of management and trade unions to prevent workers from making more radical claims.[43] The maneuvering space of trade unions depends on the freedom of association, guaranteed by state constitution, is usually broader in times of economic upswings than during recessions, and is more developed in core regions of the world-system, where workers are not only seen as cost factors but also as consumers, than in outward processing peripheries. Transition form developing to emerging country, as we can most successfully observe in contemporary China, does not imply greater liberties for trade unions. Nevertheless, increasing social polarization and inequality is driving workers to protest, pushing the government to open new fields of negotiation, arbitration and shop-floor participation for workers.[44]

Fifth, labor migration flows should also be taken into consideration. As long as there are job alternatives, workers can choose another employer and find maneuvering space for collective bargaining and trade union activities. When job alternatives do not exist, workers will rather have to accept the given conditions, unless they want to migrate to another place. Usually workers' households are rooted in their living community: they try their best to get a job at home or within a commutable distance, even if wages and careers might be less attractive. The more workers are uprooted and do not have a home-community to which they are attached, the more they will be prepared to follow jobs and careers.

The practices of deregulation and precarization, by replacing permanent with temporary contracts, exchange of direct contracts with a company by labor leasing, and swapping in-house production for outsourcing to subcontractors, do not guarantee workers a secure future. One solution may consist of joining the migrant workforce and moving to a place where more decent work is available than at home – a strategy that may prove successful for the worker and his/her family at home that rely on remittances. At first, local governments might also appreciate these remittances as a major part of their national products. In the long run, out migration causes brain drain, which undermines the possibilities for more and more regions to upgrade their economies and overcome crises, resulting in peripheralization. These regions risk losing their ability to host even the lower positions of a commodity chain; instead they indirectly contribute to lowering costs by sending cheap migrant workers, who

43 Meszmann et al. in this volume.

44 Zhang, *Inside China's Automobile Factories*.

were raised, trained, and eventually taken back, when their labor is not needed any more. Family households and neighborhoods at home are an important safety net in caring for them.

Decision making over the location of production sites and the arrangement of commodity chains therefore involves local and national governments, supra-state and international organizations, local/national and transnational capital, as well as workers and their organizations, albeit with different levels of bargaining power. They compete and collaborate against the background of shifting conjunctures and technological change. Therefore commodity chains can never be stable. They require permanent adjustment to conjunctures and cycles, government, workers' and social movements' claims and resistance. For this reason, a thorough research of the phenomena of commodity chains cannot follow a fixed script but requires empirical analyses and case studies across time and space.

## 5 Chapter Overview

This volume encompasses a wide range of commodity types and forms of labor in various world regions during vastly different time periods. It combines historical with contemporary social science perspectives, organized in five distinct thematic sections. Unlike most studies of commodity chains and production networks, which focus on the recent tendency of outsourcing industrial operations to cheaper locations and informal sectors in global peripheries, this book has a very broad understanding of commodity chains. It takes up the initial world-systemic understanding of capitalism as an uneven mode of production combining different work and labor relations within and across regions, inviting the authors to define and develop the specific mechanisms, which connect local production to arrangements and institutions that signify transregional commodity chains. Some authors argue in the framework of world-system analyses, others do not.

The commodity chains studied in this volume do not always have a global reach. They are often set up in local and regional contexts, for example, the Austrian and Slovakian mining districts, Galician agriculture and food industries, Assam tea and Brazil soy plantations or Argentinian car manufacturing. In some cases, they remain within the local and regional framework, which does not prevent them from being a global phenomenon, occurring locally. In other cases, local commodity chains are inscribed in transregional flows and networks, either continental or transcontinental. So commodity chains reflect and therefore are a good analytical tool for studying the interaction of various spatial levels of the capitalist system. This is only possible if the specific work operations and labor relations at each step of the workflow are taken into consideration. Such an approach underlines the fact that the unequal web of commodity chains requires transcending business perspectives and opening up to work.

The volume shows a clear commitment to introduce a commodity chain and labor perspective for early modern periods. The chapters on Austria, Slovakia and Galicia deal with the sixteenth to eighteenth centuries; other chapters, like the ones on soybeans, textiles or sugar show commodity chains and labor relations in a longitudinal perspective. Their findings do not support a linear and inevitable tendency towards growing distance, pace and intensity of commodity chains, or chain building at all; they rather show cyclical shifts between periods of organizing production by combining different producers and locations on the one hand and periods of centralizing production in a single company and location on the other.

The set of contributions allows commodity chains to be grasped in a broad range of sectors, from agriculture (wheat, soy, sugar, tea, cocoa, cotton, hides), mining (iron, copper) and the following manufacturing into the industrial products (textiles, leather products, metals and cars). They include regions, political regimes and labor relations that are often neglected in global economic history, such as: Central, Eastern and South Eastern Europe, along with Asian, African, North and South American regions. Conversely, Western Europe, which often dominates the narrative, remains in the background and is only included, if Western European investors, merchants or multinational companies enter the scene. The case studies hardly touch regions where the metropolitan version of capitalism, characterized by wage labor entitling to social security, is dominant. They rather explore internal peripheries of empires, feudal economies, colonial or post-colonial regions. The chapters also include subsistence agriculture, family economies, peasantry, serfdom, slavery, socialist wage-work, informal sectors and housework in a range of work and labor relations to be taken into consideration. The volume is far from giving a complete overview, but it is outstanding in the range of cases included in the investigation of commodity chains and labor relations.

The first section consists of two broad historical and theoretically informed overviews of global commodity chains rooted in textile production and soya cultivation, as well as a contribution on the contemporary upgrading strategies in Argentine agriculture. Andrea Komlosy presents the formation and constant restructuring of textile chains from the eighteenth century all the way up until the present with a special focus on the interaction between European and Asian producers. Komlosy's chapter shows how the organization of global textile production has evolved in cyclical oscillations between the centralization of production stages inside the single factory, and decentralization through outsourcing towards less regulated sectors and the households. Komlosy notices how the former trend usually gives rise to "formal labor relations that provide social security for their permanent workforce", while the latter favors "informal labor without social provisions, mobilizing unpaid household and family support in order to survive."

Ernst Langthaler compares three main global soya production formations in the course of the twentieth century, located in Northeast China, the American Midwest, and Brazil's savanna and rainforest regions. China, in the interwar period, and the present-day Brazil are chosen as the embodiments of two radically different models of soya production based respectively on labor-intensive farming by individual peasants in China and industrial plantation farming dependent on cheap wage labor in Brazil. The evolution of US soya production since the 1950s illustrates that small-scale peasant farming can successfully evolve into a more capital-intensive model, while the ongoing struggle of landless peasants' movements in Brazil is exerting pressure for a transition in the opposite direction. Both chapters thus show that contrasting dynamics are always present on the ground and that local socio-economic constellations brought about by the global commodity chains are not irreversible.

Christin Bernhold presents a contemporary case of the Argentine agricultural business model, which avoids employing a permanent workforce with fixed salaries, rather opting to camouflage capital relations by forwarding the small farmers commercial capital as their "partners" and offering income sharing deals. This scheme promises decentralized opportunities for individual upgrading to individual farmers, thus creating a network of dependencies and masking exploitative labor relations. Bernhold effectively shows how these exploitative labor relations in peripheral societies are not only the remnants of an underdeveloped past, but often serve as the very bases of the modern upgrading strategies.

The contributors in the second section convincingly apply the commodity chain model to agriculture and copper mining in early modern Europe. Klemens Kaps follows the succession of various agricultural commodity chains between the late eighteenth and early twentieth century in order to explain the reasons for the peripheral position of Galicia in the context of the Habsburg Monarchy, to which the province was annexed in the eighteenth century. Kaps demonstrates the changing combination of labor relations in producing export crops, grain, and alcohol, relying of unfree (apparently feudal) labor, wage-labor, independent entrepreneurship, peasant and landlord agriculture. By grasping the regional formation and re-configuration of commodity chains it is possible to assess the transregional position of Galicia, qualifying the region as "peripheral" instead of "backward", as the modernist mainstream claims. Miroslav Lacko shows how copper producers in the Habsburg monarchy between the seventeenth and nineteenth century utilized state support for workforce recruitment and transport logistics to export their product as far as Asia and Africa. Together, these two chapters challenge the standard view of preindustrial producers as isolated units untouched by global exchange and free from competitive pressures.

The third section inspects the lasting effects of global commodity chains on colonial and post-colonial societies. Uwe Spiekermann charts the transfer of private investment into the sugar industry back and forth between Hawaii and California. Santosh Hasnu's chapter presents the case of colonial Assam, where the British rulers were forced to construct a railway and mobilize coolie labor from other regions for tea plantations after failing to discipline the local hill tribes into permanent wage labor. These two contributions, focusing on coolie labor, show how global commodity chains have radically altered both the physical landscape and demographic features of the peripheral territories. The third contribution in this section presents the evolution of leather industry in Ethiopia during the previous three decades in the context of different industrial policy regimes and the leather global commodity chain. The industrial policy regime implemented since the 1990s is characterized by a relative marginalization of labor in the context of an export-oriented industrialization strategy, limiting the workers' ability to transform their structural power to associational power. A key finding of this chapter is that the structural power of labor in the contemporary leather industry differs depending on the market integration and strategies of different groups of manufacturing firms, which explains the large diversity of labor relations in the industry.

The fourth section covers post-(socialist) East and South Eastern Europe, a region which has so far been underrepresented in both global labor history and commodity chain studies. This region differs from other global peripheries because of the state socialist experience, such as progress in industrial transformation and social welfare for workers, even if the transformation back to capitalism after 1989/90 shows some similarities with the Global South. Goran Musić explores the expansion of outward processing trade in Yugoslavia's textile industry during the 1980s. The chapter shows how global textile chains influenced labor in Eastern Europe years before the transformation into market economies, leaving direct consequences for the work relations between different sections of workers and the relationship between the working class and the ruling communist party. Tamás Gerőcs, Tibor T. Meszmann and András Pinkasz take the industrial relations approach to study the present day Hungarian automotive industry. They pose the question why labor is unable to strongly represent its interest in Central and Eastern Europe's manufacturing sector. Their findings focus on changes in value-added production and labor relations caused by the hybrid rent seeking strategies of multinationals. These strategies reinforce fragmentation of labor, which in turn fortifies weak interest representation of labor.

The fifth section covers the question of workers' agency, the impact of informalization on workers' social positions as well as political attempts to steer or resist the pressures of commodity chain marketization. Jörg Nowak looks at the trade union cooperation and solidarity beyond the nation-state as one of the possible ways to overcome the challenges that atomized, the place-bound working classes face when attempting to organize against transnational and globalized capital. Franziska Ollendorf inspects the role of corporate social responsibility campaigns within the global cocoa production chain in Ghana. She observes that corporations are increasingly implementing corporate social responsibility programs, not only because of consumer pressure for ethical production, but also because of the need to improve the sustainability of their commodity supplies. Johanna Sittel and Stefan Schmalz show how the present-day automotive industry chains in Argentina are creating a tiny layer of relatively well-off workers in final production plants, while at the same time reproducing informal work among their component suppliers positioned lower along the chain.

Post scriptum: The chapters of this book were finished before the outbreak of the so-called COVID-19 crisis in the spring of 2020. This event revealed to the public the extent to which contemporary life is dependent on global trade and just-in-time deliveries in global commodity chains, but also the fragility of these networks and their susceptibility to crisis. The sudden interruption and reduction of communication and trade by most state authorities, up to the suspension of mobility and freedom of movement, demonstrated that commodity chains can be shortened, and indeed cut completely, in the face of a global pandemic, economic downturn and state protectionism. Keeping in mind that every crisis is also an opportunity for change, and the longstanding grievances against the unequal relations of power within the dominant production and distribution channels in today's world, we hope that the critical historical overview and the focus on labor presented in this volume can serve as a modest contribution to the conceptualization of more socially sustainable local, regional, and global arrangements of production and distribution.

## Bibliography

Adelman, Jeremy. "Is global history still possible or has it had its moment," Aeon Essays, March 2, 2017, online available at: <https://aeon.co/essays/is-global-history-still-possible-or-has-it-had-its-moment>; last accessed November 11, 2018.

Altenried, Moritz, Manuela Bojadzijev, Leif Höfler, Sandro Mezzadra and Mira Wallis (eds). *Logistische Grenzlandschaften. Das Regime mobiler Arbeit nach dem Sommer der Migration* (Münster: Unrast, 2017).

Altvater, Elmar and Birgit Mahnkopf. *Die Grenzen der Globalisierung. Ökonomie, Ökologie und Politik in der Weltgesellschaft* (Münster: Westfälisches Dampfboot, 1996).

Bair, Jennifer. "Global Capitalism and Commodity Chains: Looking Back, Going Forward," *Continuity and Change* 9, 2 (2005), pp. 153–180.

Bair, Jennifer (ed.). "The Political Economy of Commodity Chains," *Journal of World-Systems Research*, Special Issue, 20, 1 (2014), pp. 1–10.

Becker, Joachim and Andrea Komlosy. "Grenzen und Räume – Formen und Wandel. Von der Stadtmauer bis zum 'Eisernen Vorhang'," in Joachim Becker and Andrea Komlosy (eds), Grenzen weltweit. Zonen, Linien, Mauern im historischen Vergleich (Wien: Promedia, 2004), pp. 21–54.

Bonacich, Edna and Jake B. Wilson. *Getting the Goods. Ports, Labor, and the Logistics Revolution* (Ithaca, NY: Cornell University Press, 2008).

Cerda-Becker, Claudia, Johanna Sittel and Stefan Schmalz (eds). "Grauzonen der Arbeit," *Journal für Entwicklungspolitik*, Special Isssue, XXXI, 4 (2015).

Cowen, Deborah. *The Deadly Life of Logistics: Mapping Violence in Global Trade* (Minneapolis, MI: University of Minnesota Press, 2014).

Dunaway, Wilma A. "The Semi-Proletarian Household over the Longue Durée of the World System," in Richard E. Lee (ed.). The Longue Durée and World-System Analysis (Albany, NY: SUNY Press, 2012), pp. 97–136.

Fischer, Karin, Christian Reiner and Cornelia Staritz. "Einleitung," in Karin Fischer *et al.* (eds), *Globale Güterketten. Weltweite Arbeitsteilung und ungleiche Entwicklung* (Wien: Promedia, 2010), pp. 7–23.

Frank, Andre Gunder. *ReOrienting the 19th Century: Global Economy in the Continuing Asian Age*; edited and introduced by Robert A. Denemark; afterword by Barry K. Gills (Boulder, CO: Paradigm Publishers, 2015).

Fröbel, Volker, Jürgen Heinrichs and Otto Kreye. *Die neue internationale Arbeitsteilung* (Reinbek bei Hamburg: Rowohlt, 1977).

Fröbel, Volker, Jürgen Heinrichs and Otto Kreye. Umbruch in der Weltwirtschaft. *Die globale Strategie: Verbilligung der Arbeitskraft/Flexibilisierung der Arbeit/Neue Technologien* (Reinbek bei Hamburg: Rowohlt, 1986).

Gereffi, Gary and Miguel Korzeniewicz (eds). *Commodity Chains and Global Capitalism* (Westport, CT: Praeger, 1994).

Gereffi, Gary, John Humphrey and Timothy Sturgeon. "The Governance of Global Value Chains," *Review of International Political Economy* 12, 1 (2005), pp. 78–104.

Harvey, David. *Seventeen Contradictions and the End of Capitalism* (Oxford and New York: Oxford University Press, 2014).

Hopkins, Terence K. and Immanuel Wallerstein. "Patterns of Development of the Modern World-System," *Review*, 1, 2 (1977), pp. 111–145.

Hopkins, Terence K. and Immanuel Wallerstein. "Commodity Chains in the World Economy prior to 1800," *Review* 10, 1 (1986), pp. 157–170.

Komlosy, Andrea. "Work and Labour Relations," in Jürgen Kocka and Marcel van der Linden (eds), *Capitalism: The Re-Emergence of a Historical Concept* (London: Bloomsbury, 2016) pp. 33–69.

Komlosy, Andrea. "Re-assessing Labour and Value Transfer under Capitalism," in Karl-Heinz Roth (ed.). *On the Road to Global Labour History: A Festschrift for Marcel van der Linden* (Leiden and Boston: Brill, 2017), pp. 241–262.

Komlosy, Andrea. *Work. The Last 1.000 Years* (London and New York: Verso, 2018).

Komlosy, Andrea, Christof Parnreiter, Irene Stacher and Susan Zimmermann (eds). *Ungeregelt und unterbezahlt. Der informelle Sektor in der Weltwirtschaft* (Frankfurt and Wien: Brandes & Apsel, 1997).

Van der Linden, Marcel and Leo Lucassen (eds), *Working on Labor. Essays in Honor of Jan Lucassen* (Leiden and Boston: Brill, 2012).

Van der Linden, Marcel and Magalay Rodriguez Garcia (eds), *On Coerced Labor. Work and Compulsion After Chattel Slavery* (Leiden and Boston: Brill, 2016).

Lucassen, Jan and Leo Lucassen (eds), *Globalizing Migration History. The Eurasian Experience (16th to 21st Centuries)* (Leiden and Boston: Brill, 2014).

Mezzadra, Sandro and Brett Neilson. *Border as Method, Or, the Multiplication of Labor* (Durham, NC: Duke University Press, 2013).

Mies, Maria, Veronika Bennholdt-Thomsen and Claudia von Werlhof. *Women – The Last Colony* (London: Zed Books, 1988).

Mies, Maria and Veronika Bennholdt-Thomsen. *The Subsistence Perspective* (London: Zed Books, 1999).

Moore, Jason W. *Capitalism in the Web of Life. Ecology and the Accumulation of Capital* (London and New York: Verso, 2015).

Moore, Jason and Raj Patel. *A History of the World in Seven Cheap Things. A Guide to Capitalism, Nature, and the Future of the Planet* (London and New York: Verso, 2018).

Newsome, Kirsty, Philip Taylor, Jennifer Bair and Rainnie, Al (eds). *Putting Labour in its Place. Labour Process Analysis and Global Value Chains* (London: Palgrave Macmillan, 2015).

Portes, Alejandro, Manuel Castells and Lauren Benton (eds). *The Informal Economy. Studies in Advanced and Less Developed Countries* (Baltimore: Johns Hopkins University Press, 1989).

Roth, Karl-Heinz and Marcel Van der Linden (eds). *Beyond Marx: Theorising the Global Labour Relations of the Twenty-First Century* (Leiden and Boston: Brill, 2014).

Selwyn, Ben. "Beyond firm-centrism: Re-integrating labour and capitalism into global commodity chain analysis," *Journal of Economic Geography* (2011), pp. 1–22.

Silver, Beverley. *Forces of Labour. Workers' Movements and Globalization since 1870* (Cambridge: Cambrigde University Press, 2003).

Smith, Joan and Immanuel Wallerstein (eds). *Creating and Transforming Households: The Constraints of the World Economy* (Cambridge, UK: Cambridge University Press, 1992).

Wallerstein, Immanuel. "Introduction," *Review,* 23, 1 (2000), pp. 1–13.

# PART 1

## *Theorizing Commodity Chains, Labor Relations and Upgrading*

CHAPTER 2

# Cycles of Global Expansion and Contraction

## *Global Commodity Chains and Labor Relations in Textiles and Garments from the 17th to the 21st Century*

*Andrea Komlosy*

In this chapter, global commodity chains are not reduced to a recent phenomenon, but traced back into the history of capitalism. Moreover, they are not assessed as a linear development with a tendency of increasing density, geographical reach and complexity, but rather as a cyclical phenomenon with alternating periods of rise, decline, as well as non-synchronicity between the sectors and regions involved. A particular focus is on the work and labor relations in the single steps of production that are combined in a chain arrangement. Tackling work and labor relations requires looking at the specific operations carried out at work. They vary from product to product, and, depend on the raw material inputs, technology, division of labor, and work flow organization in each economic sector. The findings in one sector of production can therefore not be generalized for all industrial products. This chapter takes textiles – i.e. the production of yarn and cloth – as well as garments – i.e. the manufacturing of cloth into clothes – to analyze the cyclical development of global commodity chains and the labor relations involved across time and space.

Textiles serve as a good topic for the application of chain analysis as they were among the first products in human history to be exchanged over long distances. They were also the first craft to make use of outsourcing work steps to (more or less) distant locations, assembling workers in different places into a single chain, controlled by a merchant. Conversely, garments were produced in family households or in local craft workshops until the nineteenth century, when mass production of clothes gained momentum in Western countries and local commodity chains were set up in urban fashion industries. Textiles promoted mechanization and centralization in the early factory system in Western Europe and became the leading sector of the Industrial Revolution.

Although textile production was replaced as the leading sector of the factory system in the nineteenth century, textiles still remain a major industrial product that faces permanent restructuring, opening up to permanent product, process and logistical innovation. As soon as other sectors took over the lead in global productivity growth from the 1840s onwards (steel, railways etc.),

 | DOI:10.1163/9789004448049_003

the development of textiles had to cope with competition from more profitable investments, driving textile locations into rural and peripheral regions. In this way, textile transformed from a leading sector of the Industrial Revolution to a sector that promoted the catching-up measurements of developing countries to set up domestic factory industries. In the twentieth century, garment manufacturing became an important driver of global outsourcing and restructuring of global commodity chains because of its high labor-intensity and limits of automation.

This chapter will approach the chronological outline of the formation and restructuring of textile commodity chains along the following pattern. The description of each historical period starts with a short overview of global commodity production (technology, organization). The spotlight is then placed on the labor relations involved in different parts of the production flow, including material (food, housing) and social reproduction (giving birth, care, psychological support, styling, self-representation) of the workers and their family or household members.[1] This chapter also looks into the forms of value transfer that are characteristic for each period. After the chronological overview of all the major periods of global textile production and exchange, the final section sketches some of the most recent developments, such as online trade and online shopping and projects some of the possible development in the future. This section explains the latest tendencies to expand the textile commodity chain through new forms of paid and unpaid work performed by transport workers and consumers.

Textiles for global markets: Scheme of periodization:[2]

- Until 1700 (Asia: until the nineteenth century): Global interaction based on trade
- Eighteenth century onwards: Commodity production based on the trans-regional combinations of labor relations, since 1800 including the factory system
- Nineteenth century: Western industrializing states: Development of national factory industries (according to the British model): Centralizing, mechanizing and concentrating production in a single factory location (except: raw material, hand-weaving, home-works)

1 A major part of the chain, raw material production (wool, flax, silkworms, cotton, hemp, jute, synthetics) will only be addressed at the margins. This is also true for the related operations, like administration, training, research & development, design and logistics.

2 The periodization is following Komlosy 2010. The characteristics of each period build up on Komlosy, "Spatial Division" and Komlosy, *Work*.

- Nineteenth century: Asian perception re-oriented: Commodity chains combining industrial (factory) and industrious (handicraft, home industry) work
- Twentieth century: Vertically integrated textile production on the factory level, serving as the model for national catching up industrialization in peripheries and former colonies
- 1970s: New International Division of Labor: Re-location of industrial mass production from Global North to Global South
- To date: Upgrading of (selected) semi-peripheries in Global Commodity Chains and return of precarity and informality to the old Western cores

## 1 Before 1700: Artisan Production, Linked by Trade

Before 1700, textile export production took place in artisans' workshops. Each producer specialized in a specific product that the artisan and his team (consisting of partners, apprentices, journeymen production workers, servants and family members maintaining the household) controlled from beginning to end. When artisanal workshops were rather big and belonged to aristocratic courts, family integration of the workers was less close. Commodity chains proper did not exist. Conversely, independent producers were linked by merchants, i.e. in the framework of trade relations. However, there was a division of labor between highly specialized producers, e.g. weavers of different fabrics, fullers, dyers and other final refinements that can also be interpreted as a commodity chain.

There was no overarching producer or merchant-buyer, skimming off profits. The handicraft and artisan producers were thus in full control of the workflow, as far as cloth manufacturing is concerned. However, fiber cultivation and spinning were not integrated into the artisan system. They were part of agricultural fieldwork, livestock breeding or homework before the raw or semi-finished produce (raw fiber, yarn) was sold to artisans at local markets, or – in the case of remote materials – by merchants. In this respect, primary material producers were linked to the artisan in a commodity chain. Apart from certain processes that were carried out with water driven machines (e.g. fulling mills, silk winding mills, etc.), technologies were based on hand-driven devices (the spinning wheel, hand loom etc.), which were constructed by weavers with the help of specialists in metal and wood work. There existed a broad range of local varieties of devices that were constantly improved and adapted, giving way to technology and knowledge transfer on the one hand, while being kept top-secret on the other hand.

Labor relations involved:

- Artisan workshop: Characterized by co-living and working of artisan employers and employees (master; journeymen's and apprentices' employment based on formal contracts and regulations under guild or court control), housewife and house-servants providing lodging and food within the household economy. The guild system provided institutionalized social relief in case of disease, accident or death to members and their families.
- Raw material production and spinning was part of the rural household economy that consisted of agricultural and industrial activities, carried out on manorial estates or peasant households. Landowners or their representatives were assigning peasants, servants, laborers, family members with raw fiber production or spinning in the framework of their overall corvée or household duties; food, lodging and social care was provided in the framework of the household.

Variations of this system of textile export production, involving rural household economies for primary materials, everyday provisioning and manufacturing, existed all over the world. They did not rely on commodity chains, but were based on the autonomy and responsibility of separate independent producers. Employees, family and servants were members of the household economy that combined subsistence and market production, reciprocal work and paid labor. Surplus appropriation was realized by drawing rents. Transfer of value to the master was not only exercised through employment, but was based on personal relations that allowed the master and head of the household to assign specific activities to employees and family members. All members were linked in a mutual, personal dependency, based on reciprocity, patterns of distribution of provision following unequal and hierarchical conceptions of kin, gender and age status. As value transfers were not based on exploiting surplus labor, but on rent collection, employees did not serve as the link that allowed appropriation of their families' household and subsistence work. Paid, as well as unpaid work, was an integral part of the production process and both were objects of surplus appropriation.

The single artisanal workshops in different regional centers of export production were independent and connected via trade relations, not commodity chains. Profits depended on opportunities to exploit market positions, allowing single producers, and merchants, more gains than others did. In other words, the involved actors did not fit into a pattern of structural inequality of exchange.

## 2 1700–1820 Manufacture and Putting Out Systems: Central Headquarters Relocating Work to Rural Households

The beginning of the eighteenth century roughly marks the transition from inter-regional trade to inter-regional division of labor, based on commodity chains. Instead of independent artisan producers in control of the complete process, production became divided into single operations that were coordinated by a general entrepreneur. As a rule, the general coordinator was a merchant or a merchant company, acting as a "buyer", organizing the flow of production in more or less far-reaching networks. Prominent and well researched examples are trans-regional textile networks in the Lake Zurich and Lake Constance region, Austrian and Bohemian regions, Indian and Chinese regions, as well as trans-continental networks, often set up by Western trade companies that were able to integrate local and regional putting out systems into global trade (e.g. East Indian Company Thread and Money System in South Asia).

The textile merchant-manufacturers of this period usually had a central headquarter, where they kept employees for administration, trade, preparation, distribution, collection and finishing operations, while labor-intensive spinning and weaving was subcontracted or outsourced to local producers, who obliged family and household members to carry out the work. Contracts between a general "buyer" and local producer included purchase, putting out or wage systems, leaving different degrees of autonomy to their suppliers. Within the rural household economy, textile production for trans-local "buyers" ranged from being the primary source of income (especially for rural poor) to an additional occupation for young or old family members, especially outside of the agricultural peak seasons, besides other sources of income.

Labor relations involved:

- Trans-regional putting out systems: On top there was a putting out merchant or central manufactory (often controlled by a merchant or trade company) that formally employed in-house employees (administration, logistics, preparation and finalizing, marketing). Spinning, weaving and knitting was put out to peasants' and rural poor households, who combined income from putting out-labor for the merchant/manufacturing company with other wage-incomes and with unpaid household and subsistence work, allowing them to keep spinning and weaving wages, or piece-rates, low. Putting out manufactories enabled a steady increase in market and export production, requiring a permanent increase of rural labor. This led to the lifting of the existing feudal restrictions to marriage and new settlement and guilds' limitations for new workshops. The family household provided social care to all its members according to their status.

- Supply of raw materials: Similar to the artisan system, local fibers and yarn were sourced in agricultural households. As artisan production coexisted with the putting out system, both artisans and merchant-manufactories competed for the local supply of raw material. Rise of production led to an increasing demand for more raw materials on local and distant markets. Along with changing consumer habits, cotton that had been used in cotton-growing regions ever since its cultivation, entered European textile manufacture. In the eighteenth century, cotton cloth was imported alongside raw cotton that was manufactured in European textile regions. The demand for cotton grew as more finished textile imports were substituted by domestic production, only to explode at the turn from the eighteenth to the nineteenth century, when factory spinning led to an even bigger demand. Former textile regions in West and South Asia came under pressure from import restrictions and colonial interference to replace a mixed domestic economy, that grew and manufactured cotton cloth, with export of raw cotton or – until the mechanization of spinning – cotton yarn as well.[3] Moreover, new land was turned into cotton plantations in the Caribbean, Brazil, and in the US South, where indigenous people were driven westwards and their land transformed into plantations on which white farmers employed slave labor.
- Trade and re-export: Trans-regional putting out systems required transport and trading networks that connected the different locations of primary production, manufacture and consumption. While South Asia was the major region of cotton manufacturing in the eighteenth century, logistics, transport and re-export was in the hands of European trade companies, foremost the East-Indian Company (EIC). This company started as a global merchant in the seventeenth century; slowly it took over the headquarter functions of a global commodity chain that placed orders, financed producers and managed trade flows, until Asian producers came into a dependent position. EIC agents replaced local organizers of putting out networks, thus transforming formerly independent participants in trans-continental trade into "low end" suppliers within a global commodity chain.

The shift from artisanal production to a putting out system marks the beginning of trans-regional commodity chains in manufacturing. Putting out

3 Beckert, *Empire.*

merchants and manufacturers, whose company headquarters were located in urban centers, took over and increased textile production for export markets. They were able to put local artisans under pressure, by competing for local fiber and by saving wage costs by outsourcing spinning and weaving to rural poor households, whose living relied on the household economy. Once they worked for putting out merchants, their unpaid labor entered the commodity chain. Putting out textile work in the family household allowed appropriating unpaid subsistence work, transferring values to those who were in command of the chain.

Putting out merchants and manufacture companies combined formal employment of workers in their headquarters with putting out work in rural households. Putting out can be regarded as informal work, because it was a way to overcome existing community, municipal and guild regulations on employment and working conditions. At the same time, rural textile manufacture offered the rural poor the opportunity to earn a living beyond a subordinate existence as servant or family co-resident. Their desire to marry and establish independent households was exploited by the putting out agents, who put pressure on wages and piece-rates, which further undermined the regulations provided by the artisan system. Moreover, manufacturing companies set up trans-continental networks to source raw materials, beginning with their demand the transformation of local mixed economies in cotton growing regions into suppliers of raw materials. Reluctance of Indian cotton weaving peasants to introduce or increase raw cotton production, motivated the search for new cotton frontiers in other world regions that relied on labor coercion.[4]

It is difficult to answer the question who was in control and benefited most once the local commodity chains became part of global trade networks. It depends on the perspective and the period under consideration. In the first phase of trans-continental commodity chains between Indian regions and the EIC, Indian putting out merchants and their supplying weavers, dyers, painters, and printers shared the profits with the English merchant-company that profited from trade, transport and re-export. From 1700 onwards, the EIC increased its influence on how the flow of production and labor was organized and financed in Indian workshops. The EIC moved from a cooperative into a dominant position, restructuring the commodity chain according to its interests.[5]

4 Beckert, *Empire*, ch. 5.

5 Rothermund, *Europa*.

## 3 1800–1914: New Combinations of Factory Labor with Craft, Home and Subsistence Work in the "Industrial" (West) and the "Industrious" System (East)

The standard (Western) narrative of textile innovation and modernization is concentrated on the rise of the factory system in nineteenth century Western Europe and the US-North, addressed as the "industrial revolution" that became the benchmark for development. Asian scholars have offered a different interpretation by insisting on the ongoing developments of technology and work organization in the framework of artisan and putting out manufacture that had fostered a steep rise in productivity and production throughout the eighteenth century in Asian – as well as in Western – textile regions. It relied on labor-intensity instead of capital and technology-intensity.[6] This "industrialization before industrialization" period was also coined as "proto-industrialization".[7] Following the eighteenth century-contemporary term "industriousness" to describe the efforts to increase output based on diligence, Jan de Vries introduced the – less teleological – term "industrious" revolution for this period of innovation, juxtaposed with the "industrial" revolution that was characterized by centralization and mechanization of production in factories.[8]

Asian industrious advantage motivated European textile entrepreneurs to introduce labor-saving machines, convincing their governments to secure internal and export markets for cloth made in Europe against Asian competition. For quite a while, Asian industrious textile production continued to be competitive, especially within domestic markets, while Western industrial textiles replaced Asian cloth within global export markets.[9] The result was a steady decline of West, South and East Asian shares in global textile production: first in South Asia, where the East Indian Company moved from textile putting out manufacture to a triangular opium and tea trade between India, China and Britain.[10] China remained a dominant textile producer, replacing Indian textiles in British re-export trade in the first half of the nineteenth century. Andre Gunder Frank claims that the British and West European advance in (textile) manufacture only became dominant after 1860, when the unequal treaties imposed after the Opium Wars opened the Chinese internal market for Western imports.[11]

---

6 Chaudhuri, *Asia*; Sugihara, "The East Asian Path."
7 Kriedte, Medick and Schlumbohm, *Industrialisierung*.
8 De Vries, *Industrious Revolution*.
9 Roy, *Rethinking Economic Change*.
10 Rothermund, *Europa*.
11 Frank, *ReOrienting*.

Labor relations involved in the "industrial" system, North, West and Central Europe and North America:

- Factory labor in the West[12]: The industrial system was characterized by the mechanization and centralization of major steps of textile production on factory premises. Factories started in the spinning sector from the 1780s onwards, entering weaving and knitting 30 to 50 years later, England being ahead of continental Europe and the US North. While putting out was based on relocating the labor-intensive steps of the workflow into the workers' homes, workers now left their homes to work in the factory. As a consequence, market relations that were embedded into the household economy and its status related distribution of income and social care, were replaced by individual labor contracts. Except for leading positions, labor contracts offered low pay and virtually no social provisions, leading to rapid exhaustion and frequent rotation of the factory workers. High mortality was a typical feature of the early industrial age due to miserable conditions, no limits to working hours and age, no social care, and lack of access to reciprocal work and subsistence. From the mid-century onwards, legal regulation (i.e. formalization) of hiring, working conditions and social security provisions by company-owners, workers' associations and state became necessary in order to stabilize the industrial workforce. Moreover, new skilled textile professions arose in engineering and the design, art, management and merchandizing sector, offering carrier opportunities for a skilled, specialized workforce.
- Home-weavers and other home-workers (including the garment industry) supplied factories with manual operations carried out in the family household. In this way, factories became putting out agents in those sections of the work-flow that were impossible or difficult to be carried out by power-driven machines. While spinning moved from home-wheel-spinning into mechanized factory production in the first half of the nineteenth century, weaving was still predominantly carried out by hand-weavers in their homes. As a consequence, the textile geography changed, concentrating spinning mills in regions with a water or steam power supply next to places of mass consumption, while home-weaving faced a boom in more remote rural regions, with weaving compensating for the loss of spinning as the central source of income for the rural poor. Mechanical weaving mills only became commonplace from the 1830s onwards, with Great Britain and the

12 Factories were only introduced in a few regions of South America and Asia, while the majority of textile production was carried out in these parts of the world in the "industrious" mode, see: van Voss et.al., *The Ashgate Companion.*

US North leading the transformation, while European textile regions lagged behind. When both spinning, weaving (as well as knitting) was carried out in factories, home-work faced re-structuring: On the one side it moved into new sectors, e.g. garment and home textile production that required a lot of specialized manual operations (finishing applications, sewing), along with the introduction of putting out systems into urban fashion industries. On the other side, home-weaving survived because of the flexibility of the rural workforce to be mobilized in periods of high demand, while being dismissed when demand was low. Home-workers – neither employed nor self-employed – were not included in public or company social security systems, relying on household and family for social support. Family households served as reproductive and income pooling units, often on a trans-regional basis, including migrant workers who sent home remittances and were taken care of when they lost their jobs or fell ill. In villages and small towns, subsistence agriculture and agricultural wage-work helped with survival, while big cities offered begging, precarious makeshift jobs or poor relief to people in need.

– Expansion of raw material frontiers: The increase in Western factories' demand for raw fibers depended upon the further expansion of the cotton frontier of Egypt, the US-South, the Caribbean, Brazil and the wool frontier of Australia and New Zealand. This expansion was based largely on complementary labor relations with the manufacturing sector, such as: slavery; indentured labor; agricultural wage-labor; and independent farming.

Labor relations involved in the "industrious" system:

– In the "rest" of the world: While Western regions (Western and Central Europe, US North) faced a transition to the factory system, the vast majority of textile producers in the Global South – and in peripheral regions of Europe as well – maintained subsistence, artisan, small workshop or putting out production, marking the industrious system. Due to the high numbers and density of population, wages were low, while high agricultural productivity and subsistence background kept workers' living costs low, allowing them to reach a standard of living that was supposedly higher than that of Western factory workers.[13] Hence, there was no need to mechanize and centralize production. Instead of home spinning, local weavers introduced European factory yarn into their workflow, opening a commodity chain that allowed

13 For comparisons of living standards between European and Asian textile regions, compare Pomeranz, *The Great Divergence*; Parthasarathi, "Agriculture"; Roy, *Rethinking Economic Change*.

them to combine the high productivity of factory spinning with the high productivity of handloom weaving.

The tendency of proletarianization, entitling workers to social security services instead of household care, was restricted to a relatively small percentage of the textile workforce that was concentrated in Western factories. For them, the Marxian model of exploitation through employment (surplus value) gained momentum. The majority of textile producers all over the world continued to work in putting out and artisan systems, relying on household cooperation for production and reproduction. In the West, handicraft and home-workers became incorporated into a commodity chain that was dominated by the factory, supplying industrial production with cheap and flexible industrious components and services. This demonstrates how commodity chains adapted to technological change, on the one side integrating former putting out spinners into formal factory work, while on the other side opening other parts of the workflow to informal suppliers. In a similar way, the expansion of factory textile output led to an enormous increase in demand for raw materials, incorporating new regions into the supply chain, as shown by the expansion of the cotton frontier.

Cotton plantations and European rural textile regions moved into the position of low-end positions in a production network that was controlled by the most advanced factories at the high ends. From an Asian perspective, the question of chain governance is highly contested. While the standard narrative continues to underline Western industrial companies' out-competing of Asian industrious producers on domestic and export markets (de-industrialization), a revisionist narrative has been gaining ground, downsizing the significance and the onset of the "Great Divergence"[14] at a later moment in the nineteenth century, especially with regard to China.[15] One main argument is based on the assumption that the industrious mode of production was able to restructure previous global commodity chains, by including industrial modes in the flow of production. These voices do not deny Western industrial competitive pressure; instead of simply acknowledging the Western leading position, they rather stress the flexible way Asian industrious producers make use of Western spinning technology without themselves taking over the industrial mode. From this perspective, it is far from evident to identify control, amount, direction and beneficiaries of value transfers. Conversely, to the European homeweavers, who were driven into extreme poverty by the restructuring of the

14 The term was coined by Pomeranz, *The Great Divergence.*

15 Frank, *ReOrienting*; Sugihara, "The East Asian Path."

production networks, Asian weavers were able to maintain control over their changing position in the chain – at least for a while.

From a theoretical perspective, there are two options when modeling the Asian-European relationship in the framework of the Global Commodity Chain concept:

- We consider factory production as the "high end" that withdrew from global commodity chains in manufacturing by substituting Asian cloth and print imports with domestic factory production (which became a synonym for "industry"). It limited putting out to technological niches, flexible nearby home-workers to meet peak demand or supply new fashion industries. The Western factory-driven system out-competed Asian producers, who faced a decline in industrial output and opened their markets for Western imports.
- Or, we consider industrious weaving to continue representing the "high end", making use of cheap European factory yarn, allowing Asian manufacturers to concentrate on their on-going competitive advantage in hand weaving and printing. In this scenario, the low wages of the Western factory workers indirectly benefited the Asian producers, making use of Western workers' impoverishment for their industrious advance. Moreover, Asian producers indirectly profited from the exploitative labor conditions in global raw cotton production elsewhere that was processed in Western spinning factories.

In practice, the two options overlapped and led to an entanglement of unilateral advantages for both West and East, as long as the industrial and industrious modes coexisted. As soon as Western export advances finally not only conquered Asian export, but also equally Asian domestic markets, Asian industrial output faced a sharp decline. Asian economies were transformed into raw material exporters in exchange for manufacture import. From the 1870s to the 1970s, the first option seemed to prevail. The Asian surrender gave way to ideas and efforts of catching up with the Western factory system from the late nineteenth century onwards.

## 4 1918–1973: Catching Up the Factory System after Decolonization: Industrial Factory Labor Gaining Grounds

The very short twentieth century sees a constant decline in Western textile production that is replaced by new leading industries. At the same time, new states in Eastern Europe and the Global South have taken over textile production, partly starting from an agricultural background, with others from reviving existing textile capacities. They hoped that the textile factory industry would have spin-off effects on other industrial branches, on infrastructure and service industries, finally leading to a diversified self-reliant economic structure. (Colonial) dependency on raw material exports was to be overcome by import substitution aiming to build up domestic industries. Hence, the Western factory model was established as a global model. It was based on the centralization, mechanization and proletarization of the workforce.

Labor relations involved:

- Western textile industries: While textile and garment industries faced a relative decline and wages were among the lowest, factory as well a homework that was outsourced to rural household was still a dominant source of employment in old textile regions.
- Post-colonial textile industries: Textile industry moving from core to semi-peripheral locations, gave rise to labor organizations and labor movements. Although formal employment contracts increased, they usually did not include social benefits for workers, who had to rely on family support. Factory work was often limited to young men and women, who were replaced by new generations after some years. Workers' struggles clashed with employers, who rejected mechanisms of dispute settlement or trade union participation. Improvements of labor and social regulations were often limited to state enterprise.
- State-socialism: Employment was compulsory and included access to social benefits from companies and state care institutions. Social services were based on professional work; subsistence, family and other networks compensated for shortages of consumer goods.

In the course of Newly Industrializing Countries' catching up, we face a multiplication of labor relations: In the West, textile workers ranged among the low pay branches. Moreover, textile factories were concentrated in rural regions, where income pooling and subsistence farming complemented wages. Big companies coexisted with smaller ones that produced for local markets and survived on product niches, as well as on the readiness of both employers and employees to accept low wages and low profit. Small weaving workshops as well as small suppliers of looms and various devices that were widely spread up to the first decades after the Second World War, did not find a successor. Workers benefited from the rise of the welfare state after the First and Second World War, enlarging social security to a broad range of services from health care, maternity leave, unemployment and old age pension, complementing unpaid household care. This does not account for "Third World" countries, while East European COMECON states had a highly developed welfare system, based on state, company and family support.

Except for raw materials, in-house production was prevailing over putting out or outsourcing. The division of labor took place within the central premises' departments, containing the complete flow of production from preparation, spinning, weaving or knitting until refinement, control and distribution. Garments were often part of a separate production flow. In the West, more and more local producers were taken over by multinational companies that operated within highly protected national markets, restricting competition from developing countries where textiles and garments were among the leading sectors of import-substituting industrialization. These efforts were state-driven and supported by subsidies and protective tariffs, aiming at as much self-reliance as possible.

The global textile landscape faced a new geography: It comprised old textile regions in South and East Asia and Turkey as well as new locations in South America, Northern and Subsaharan Africa, where textile factories for local markets were established. However, the globalization of textile production did not go hand in hand with the globalization of commodity chains. In the Western, the socialist Eastern European and the developing world, industries primarily produced within the framework of local, regional and national markets. Due to the lack of capital and knowledge, postcolonial industrial development relied on technologies, machinery and credits, establishing new dependencies from the former colonial powers. COMECON countries faced technology embargos from the West after the Second World War, unintentionally encouraging them to engage in independent technological research and development and cooperation with developing countries.

## 5 1970s Onwards: Re-globalization of Commodity Chains

The world economic crisis of 1973/74 gave way to a new cycle of globalization. A general reaction to the crisis consisted in relocating industrial mass production into developing countries, while former industrial countries were supposed to switch from industrial to knowledge based post-industrial activities to recover in a new cycle. Textile and garments companies were among the first to go South, reviving commodity chains in manufacturing. Centralizing the command at the high end, while selecting the best available location according to the interest of the headquarters to keep costs low, undermined the self-reliant maneuvering space of import-substituting industries in developing countries. The introduction of commodity chains was accompanied by the establishment of new forms of global trade regulations and trade agreements that were beneficial for developing countries. The Lomé Agreement between the European Communities and the ACP (Africa, Caribbean, Pacific) states of 1975 had guaranteed ACP exports duty free access to EC-markets, while accepting import barriers for European manufactures in order to protect national industries.[16] In 2000 Lomé was replaced by the Cotonou Agreement, which introduced a new trade regime. Preferential treatment was declared incompatible with free trade, imposing market opening for European exports in exchange for developing countries' access to Europe. While making a formal pretense at trade equality, it de facto ended import-substitution.

The first wave of globalization was characterized by producer-driven commodity chains, set up by multinational companies, maintaining headquarters, logistics and technology-intensive high-value operations in the cores, while outsourcing labor-intensive operations to low wage – low tax countries. From the 1990s, the command of commodity chains moved from manufacturing companies to retailers, brand owners and owners of supermarket chains: the so-called global "buyers".[17] "Buyer"-driven chains were characterized by an even bigger flexibility of the chain organizers to make use of different legal frameworks and labor regimes at different locations, putting producers in strong competition with each other. Producers reacted by passing the pressure to subcontractors and workers. Some Eastern European COMECON countries, especially Poland, Hungary and Romania, as well as socialist Yugoslavia,[18] became locations for Western outsourcing from the 1970s onwards, until the whole region was transformed into a supplier of cheap manufacture for companies who kept logistics, research and development at their Western headquarters after the change of system in 1989/90.[19]

The relocation of production to the Global South and Eastern Europe was accompanied by international trade regulations (1974 Multifiber Agreement, 1995–2004 Agreement on Textile and Clothing), privileging companies in the old industrial cores by a progressive regime of duties escalating with the number of operations added during manufacturing.[20] This protectionist environment allowed old cores to slowly restructure their economies, while developing and emerging countries remained in a subordinate position. As long as access to Western markets was the object of quotas, guaranteed by the textile agreements, strong emerging producers increased their export shares by "quota-hopping", i.e. China relocating production to developing countries that were

16 Taylor and Smith, *UNCTAD*.
17 Gereffi and Korzeniewicz, *Commodity Chains*.
18 See Goran Musić in this volume.
19 Hofbauer, *EU-Osterweiterung*.
20 Ferenschild and Wick, *Globales Spiel*, pp. 28–48.

not able to make full use of their export quotas.[21] When the restrictive duty and quota regime of the Agreement on Textile and Clothing was abolished in 2004, full liberalization set in, polarizing between a few emerging countries, who could increase output and make use of global relocations themselves, while most developing countries fell back in their industrializing efforts.

It was primarily China that was able to make use of the new deregulation and upgrade its position in global textile manufacturing. In the process of their own catching up, Chinese companies integrated South-East Asian as well as African textile producers as suppliers of raw-material (cotton) and cheap labor in Chinese-controlled commodity chains. Take the example of the Shanghai based knit and sportswear company Jiale, who opened affiliates for low-end productions not only in the Chinese interior (2007), but also in Indonesia (2011) throughout the course of their upgrading from contract manufacturing to a higher value creating position.[22] In the case of Subsaharan Africa, Chinese companies moved up into a controlling position by importing African raw cotton, manufacturing cloth in China, while relocating the labor-intensive Cut-Make-Trim operations back to Africa. Apparel manufactured in the least-developed Subsaharan countries, like Lesotho, enjoy duty free entry into the United States under the African Growth and Opportunity Act (AGOA), set up in 2005. While China, with its triangular commodity chain, is a beneficiary of this program, African countries like Lesotho, one of the leading participants, face the downgrading of domestic industries to suppliers of low value components.[23]

Labor relations involved:

- Newly industrializing countries (NICs): The advancement of social care was lagging behind the relocation of textile production to NICs. Factory work often did not include social securities; workers had to rely on household support and families on migrants' remittances. Labor struggles and trade unions had little impact, nor were certification systems that were imposed by Western "buyers" on their NIC suppliers able to overcome the wage and social gap between core and semi-periphery. However, in the case of China, the introduction of labor and social security regulations from the early 2000s onwards represented the move from a low to a medium income country, providing more and more workers with higher wages, social benefits and purchasing power.[24] In the meanwhile, China's industrial core areas are

21 Komlosy, "China's Move," p. 366.

22 Ibid., p. 370.

23 Komlosy, "China's Move," p. 366; Traub-Mertz and Jauch, "African Textile."

24 Scherrer, *China's Labour Question*.

suffering from the lack of workforce. While Chinese core workers face better conditions and upward mobility, improvements do not include workers in supplying and subcontracting firms, especially in developing countries.

- Former (old) industrial countries (FICs West and East): The old (former) industrial world is facing competition from low wage manufacturing from NIC. Global "buyers" use their central coordinating position to select locations and suppliers according to their legal and social conditions and involve them in a competitive race against each other. They are putting pressure on regulations in FICs, contributing to the decline of labor and relatively high social security standards acquired during the industrial age between 1880 and 1980, especially after the Second World War. Deregulation, informalization and precarization, gaining momentum from the 1990s onwards, completely changed the working and living conditions. These tendencies contributed to a strong polarization between representatives of the old working-class (in decline), the new upward middle strata and the growing new poor, who cannot live from their wage and therefore have to combine multiple jobs and incomes, low price – low quality consumption, public transfers and new ways of subsistence (based on recycling, gardening, waste economy, etc.).

The commodity chains were thus re-activated on local and global levels. With the rise of informal, precarious labor relations in sweatshops and subcontracted suppliers instead of stable employment entitling workers to social benefits, household and family safety networks gain importance. So far, capitalist crises have cyclically led to the reactivation of non-capitalist, non-commodified and informal resources, making up for the loss of formal occupation and income revenues. However, we must not forget that non-capitalist or non-commodified resources can never be a safety net for all. Some lack access and in times of war they are destroyed. Conversely, post-war reconstruction fosters growth again and allows rebuilding capacities. There are serious doubts that capitalism's capacity of regeneration and flexible adaptation to new cycles of growth will go on, both from the demographic and the ecological side, as well as from the fact that massive urbanization has been depriving more and more people of basis means of reproduction and subsistence, necessary for resilience in times of crisis.[25] If these means are lacking, massive impoverishment is destroying the availability of the workforce, risking the feasibility of capitalist accumulation.

25 Immanuel Wallerstein, among others, has therefore predicted a culmination of crises leading to the end of capitalist civilisation, see: Wallerstein, "Structural Crisis". Even if the symptoms may seem plausible and the collapse of the capitalist world-system may happen, it is equally likely that Wallerstein will share the fate of his predecessors in announcing an end to capitalism, while the system merely adapts to a new regime of accumulation.

## 6 Latest Developments, Contradictions and Perspectives

Until recently, a commodity chain or global production network perspective would find its end, when the final product, a coat or pair of trousers, reached the retail shop. Shopping, dressing and choosing a product were the subjects of consumption or fashion studies. Home-repair is no longer common practice, as the quick change of fashion, the cheap price of ready-to-wear and the loss of home tailoring skills turned garments into short-lived consumer goods that were frequently replaced with new ones. This sits in contrast with the growing number of tailor shops specializing in size and style adaption or repair of factory-ware not only in developing countries, but in the Western world as well. We consider adaption and repair to be a continuation of the commodity chain. In the Western world, these tasks are usually performed in small workshops, run by self-employed migrants, making use of family networks and chain-migration from their home regions.

Another prolongation of the commodity chain takes place in the second hand trade. It is often annexed to small repair workshops and exists all over the world. In the framework of charity, social work, disaster and development assistance, second hand trade developed into a business niche opening new markets for used Western garments in developing countries. In contrast to the charity image mobilized for the donators of used textiles in the Global North, these clothes, once transferred to developing countries, interfere with the local textile markets. They create a dependency on Western garments. Studies on African recipient countries stress the creativity of used garment dressmakers and shopkeepers, who adapt European textiles to African tastes,[26] neglecting that these „donations" are Janus-faced. They outcompete and undermine local crafts and factories' capacities to supply the population with self-made garments. Rwanda's President, Paul Kagame, for instance, spoke out against the misuse of his fellow citizens for a final valorization of Western textiles and increased the tariffs on imported used clothes in April 2018.[27]

Another recent example of a prolongation of the commodity chain is online-trade. Since the late 1990s, e-commerce sales have been increasing their shares from year to year. Online trade-platforms are replacing retail stores. They started to set up corporate clouds for advertising and taking orders, while

26 Brooks, "Stretching Global Production Networks"; Ezeoha, Okoyeuzu, Onah and Uche, "Second-hand."

27 David Pilling, "America must allow Rwanda to make its own choices," Financial Times, June 20, 2018, online available at: < https://www.ft.com/content/44b5cb2e-73a9-11e8-b6ad-3823e4384287>; last accessed 10 July, 2020.

outsourcing storage, packing, payment and transport to others. In the meanwhile, e-commerce companies enlarged their activities, building warehouses, logistical networks and transport systems and hiring large numbers of workers.[28] E-commerce gave way to a competitive race between store and online trade, urging smaller retailers to move into e-commerce to avoid losing customers to the big companies. Monopolization tendencies in online trade exceed retail store trade. In 2017, the biggest e-commerce company, Amazon, was employing more than 230,000 workers and many more during high seasons. Other platforms, like Zalando, specialize in apparel.

Labor conditions in big warehouses for online-retailers, packing and delivery departments like Amazon have become a prominent topic of a labor studies and labor struggles, with regard to precarious employment, as well as the effects of digitalization on the work process.[29] They form the node of the network that links textile productions, among others, with the consumer. Ordering online implies that the item has to be delivered to the customer's home. In this way, postal, delivery and transport services explode and entail a myriad of movements of planes, trains, vehicles and people, increasing traffic in an unprecedented way. The growth of package waste is a related problem. New systems of delivery, storage and transport are being developed, giving way to a sharp competition between different services for concepts, market shares and profits. These movements increase the more the customer has the right to return. A Zalando spokeswoman explained in 2018 that 50 percent of orders go back to the warehouse.[30] Bold visions have conceived of delivering by drones as a solution to traffic jams. Others dream of developing 3-D-printing as a way to sell software instead of products and outsource production to the consumer.

Already today, online-trade is also a way of outsourcing consulting and fitting services from shop assistants to the consumer. The consumer takes on the work, previously carried out by professional salespeople, when he or she is studying the website, selecting, paying, unpacking and repacking the ordered pieces. The consumer tries them on, eventually including the assistance of family or friends. By replacing employees, consumers are prolonging the commodity chain to their private desktop and living room. Maybe the consumer is not aware of the work that he or she is doing and would object to calling it

---

28 Srnicek, *Platform Capitalism*, p. 60.

29 The German trade union Verdi has a long history of struggle with the US e-commerce company Amazon over wages, collective labor agreements and the right to collective actions in Amazon firms.

30 Rainer Hennig, "Wie kommt das T-Shirt zu seinem Träger," *Die Presse, Fokus: Logistik*, September 19, 2018, p. F8.

work. E-consumers are nevertheless saving costs for the company by replacing former sales personnel and increasing turnover and profit. In order not to confound consumer operations with home-work in the productive or service sector, we rather call it "shadow work" – following Ivan Illich's definition of unproductive work necessary to survive in a commodified society.[31] Any activity that is outsourced from professionals to one's personal digital device represents such a "shadow".

However, e-commerce companies do not only trade merchandise. They trade data. By accessing a website, searching for specific products and placing orders, every consumer delivers data that are used for the product portfolio, advertisements and specific product placements during searches. Online shops are in a position to generate such information about their consumers and can sell it to other firms. Additionally, they buy data from advertising platforms like Facebook or Google, whose free communication service is paid for by customers' data profiles. These data are used for the communication platforms' own gains in selling advertisement space and product placements, and they are sold to other e-companies, enabling them to find the best access to their customers. Online trade is inseparably linked to the e-communication networks. Amazon expanded its field of operation by developing its own cloud computing service, Amazon Web Services (AWS), that is also rented out to smaller firms. In this way, they get access to an ever increasing amount of data. Currently, AWS is the most rapidly growing part of Amazon, generating more profit than from its core retail business.[32] Data can thus be seen as a new resource incorporated into the commodity chains. In other words, data represent a commodity frontier. Access to that frontier relies on the control of platforms that connect producers, networks, retailers, users and consumers. As data require data collection, data storage, data analysis and data application, data themselves represent a value chain.[33]

As we have seen, e-commerce meets customer demands. In exchange, companies do not only receive voluntarily given shadow work, but also a resource that helps them to direct advertisements according to specific consumer profiles. This knowledge of consumer profiles and preferences does not only serve e-retailers, but also supports producers designing their products according to customer profiles. For a long time, the search for customers only started, when

31 Illich, *Shadow Work*, also see Lambert, *Shadow Work*; Komlosy, *Work*, p. 70, 210.

32 Srnicek, *Platform Capitalism*, p. 61, 64.

33 Edd Dumbill, "Understanding the Data Value Chain," *IBM Data & Analytics Hub*, October 11, 2014, online available at: <https://www.ibmbigdatahub.com/blog/understanding-data-value-chain>, last accessed January 29, 2019.

a product was finished. In the near future, with the help of specific information about consumers' tastes, data collection will precede product development and product planning. In an accelerating product cycle, the interaction between consumer profile and product profile intermingles into a permanent flow of adaptions, customizing every item according to individual taste. Individual customization corresponds to new technologies allowing the production of small product series or the changing of the product in the course of the workflow according to changing consumer demands. Just-in-time supply chains adapt to these changes, corresponding and interacting with new work and information flows in distribution and data collection. Hence, expanding data frontiers gives companies direct access to information regarding the wishes and desires of the consumer, which are shaped by permanent monitoring and surveillance: in this way, commodity chains take control of the consumers themselves, making them virtual-employees, so to speak. The concept of "shadow work" can be applied to data delivery itself.

At this point, the flows of production in just-in-time arrangements are likely to enter a new regime, labeled "platform capitalism".[34] The manufacturing is most affected by industrial platforms, also known as the "Internet of things", the "industrial Internet" or "Industry 4.0." It means embedding sensors and computer chips into the production process at each step of the workflow and the implementation of trackers into the logistic process through connections over the Internet. The overall aim of reducing labor, energy, maintenance and other costs by optimizing the production process does not differ from previous just-in-time arrangements. What is novel is the idea of interlinking each component in the workflow, establishing communication between machines and components without the guidance of working people. By interlinking production with consumer data, product design is supposed to incorporate consumer feedback, drawn from their surveillance in e-commerce.[35] Nobody can predict to what extent these developments will become practice. Some enthusiastic observers expect the rise of direct computer-based interaction to be the beginning of a post-capitalist or a post-work era. Conversely, Srnicek reminds us of the monopolizing tendencies, systematically inherent to platform capitalism and cyber-competition. He refers to a World Economic Forum Report, stating that with the industrial Internet "the big winners will be platform owners."[36]

When extending commodity chains into ever far-reaching domains of demand, with repercussive effects on production and distribution, the "spaghetti

34 Srnicek, *Platform Capitalism*, p. 49.
35 Ibid., p. 66.
36 World Economic Forum, *Industrial Internet of Things*.

bowl" of global inter-connectedness is likely becoming more and more dense and intense. Conversely, monopolization is leading to increasing polarization into winners and losers of those developments, and provoking countertendencies. This is why we face contradicting movements of more and more entangling of commodity-chains on the one hand, while, on the other hand, groups of producing and retailing companies, states and regions, and consumers oppose and resist the pressure to participate in a competition that they cannot win. We witness re-locations of final operations from distant locations to workshops and factories that are close to the consumer. We witness new demands for products of local origin, appreciating production flows under one roof or in one – qualified responsible – hand. Finally, we witness regional and national governments' political and legal interventions aiming at re-centering commodity flows within their confines.

When commodity chains expand beyond production and distribution, starting points and moments where one can shape, reform or oppose chain and labor organization multiply. Activities to bring about change can equally depart from factory-owners, "global producers" as well as the "global buyers", from workers at all levels, steps and flows of production, transport and logistics and from the consumers, both in their capacity to buy the final product and in their capacity to deliver "shadow work" and data resources. Each actor has his or her specific role in more or less strategic places of the flow or network, from where they can best challenge the power and the capability of value realization by those who are in control of the chain, as well as other parties involved. This is why commodity chain organization and logistics is a contested field.[37]

There is a wide range of options for how commodity chains are being contested from each of the different positions within the chains. Generally speaking, and without considering the chances of success, there are two possible directions. From the side of workers' organizations, one option is to adapt their struggles to the changing flows, coordinate actions across boundaries and make use of strategic vulnerable points in the flow of production, in transport and logistics, to enforce their claims for higher wages and better working conditions.[38] Another option is to oppose existing chains and their expansion by giving priority to arrangements of supply and demand at the local, regional or national level, subjecting transnational commodity chain arrangements to regional and national regulations and giving priority to smaller vis-à-vis bigger spatial flows and networks. Realizing a re-regionalization of global commodity

37 Bonacich and Wilson, *Getting the Goods*; Cowen, *Deadly Life*.
38 See Jörg Nowak in this volume.

chains equally requires international coordination and cooperation – otherwise delinking would suffer from boycott and isolation. Using delinking from "platform capitalism" as a starting point for global restructuring could maybe reconcile and combine global and local action in the end.

## 7 Conclusion

From a long-durée perspective, we can observe a long continuity of commodity chains in manufacturing from at least the eighteenth century onwards. If we include the acquisition of raw materials, commodity chains already existed even before this time. Although the degree and intensity of global interactions has been constantly growing, commodity chains do not show a linear increase. Commodity chains were also subject to changes in government structure: they started with artisans' search for semi-finished products – mainly yarn – in the time before 1700, then transformed from artisan-driven chains to merchant-driven chains, while the artisan system was suppressed and finally replaced by putting out manufacture. Outsourcing to rural households overcame local (urban, artisan) restrictions of growth, multiplying output and geographical reach of production and trade during the eighteenth century. The nineteenth century faced a restructuring of global commodity chains combining the West European industrial system (supplying factory yarn) with industrious handicraft and home industries (especially weaving) in Asian textile regions. The fully integrated textile production that mechanized and centralized the complete flow of production was a Western way to compete with Asian labor-intense productivity – raw materials sourced in the Global South notwithstanding: cotton in the US and in Egypt, wool in Ireland and Australia.

During the nineteenth century, factory centralization was still an exception, until power-driven machines outcompeted the labor-intense industrious mode and the factory succeeded to become the model for catching-up industrialization in peripheries and former colonies from the late nineteenth century onwards. During interwar and post Second World War reconstruction and decolonisation periods, the nation-state was the reference for successful economic development in the Western and catching-up in the socialist and the developing world. The 1970s saw a re-globalization of commodity chains, overcoming a profit squeeze in the cores by outsourcing labor-intense operations to the peripheries. Along with the liberalization of international trade, commodity chains became the leading form of organizing trans-local flows of production, first under the control of Western multinational companies and their international financial organizations, later transforming into a renewed form of merchant capitalism under global "buyers" command that was reviving the putting out system on a global scale. Big emerging nations have been combining state and business power to challenge the power balance of global commodity chains in their favor, initiating protectionist reactions from the part of the former industrially developed Western cores to maintain economic control and hegemonic positions.

Global textile production is thus characterized by cyclical shifts of in-house centralization and putting out decentralization, the first favoring formal labor relations that provide social security for their permanent workforce, the second favoring informal labor without social provisions, mobilizing unpaid household and family support in order to survive. Moreover, formal and informal labor relations show uneven distribution along commodity chains, the "low ends" facing the lowest pay and job security, activating a "below zero" subsistence level in order to make up for the misery of the working poor. Core locations are not excluded from informal and precarious labor relations: on the one hand, there is a gap between the permanent skilled and temporary unskilled workforce, the latter relying on household networks' unpaid support. On the other hand, global crises contribute to the decline of formal regulations and give way to an increase in informal labor and subsistence regimes.

## Bibliography

Beckert, Sven. *The Empire of Cotton. A Global History* (New York: Alfred A. Knopf, 2015).

Bonacich, Edna and Jake B. Wilson. *Getting the Goods. Ports, Labor, and the Logistics Revolution* (Ithaca, NY: Cornell University Press, 2008).

Brooks, Andrew. "Stretching global production networks: The international second-hand clothing trade", *Geoforum*, 44 (2013), pp.10–22.

Chaudhuri, Kirti Narayan. *Asia before Europe. Economy and Civilisation of the Indian Ocean from the Rise of Islam to 1750* (Cambrigde, UK: Cambridge University Press, 1990).

Cowen, Deborah. *The Deadly Life of Logistics: Mapping Violence in Global Trade* (Minneapolis, MI: University of Minnesota Press, 2014).

De Vries, Jan. *The Industrious Revolution. Consumer Behaviour and the Household Economy* (Cambridge, MA: Cambridge University Press, 2008).

Ezeoha, Abel, Chinwe Okoyeuzu, Emmanuel Onah and Uche, Chibuike. "Second-hand Vehicle Markets in West Africa: A Source of Regional Disintegration, Trade Informality and Welfare Losses", *Business History* (May 2018), pp. 1–18.

Ferenschild, Sabine and Ingeborg Wick. *Globales Spiel um Kopf und Kragen. Das Ende des Welttextilabkommens verschärft soziale Spaltungen* (Siegburg-Neuwied: Südwind Texte, 2004).

Frank, Andre Gunder. *ReOrienting the 19th Century: Global Economy in the Continuing Asian Age*; edited and introduced by Robert A. Denemark; afterword by Barry K. Gills (Boulder, CO: Paradigm Publishers, 2015).

Gereffi, Gary and Miguel Korzeniewicz (eds). *Commodity Chains and Global Capitalism* (Westport, CT: Praeger, 1994).

Hofbauer, Hannes. *EU-Osterweiterung. Historische Basis – ökonomische Triebkräfte – soziale Folgen* (Wien: Promedia, 2007).

Illich, Ivan. *Shadow Work* (London: Marion Boyars Publishers, 1981).

Komlosy, Andrea. "Re-assessing Labour and Value Transfer under Capitalism", in Karl-Heinz Roth (ed.). *On the Road to Global Labour History: A Festschrift for Marcel van der Linden* (London and Boston: Brill, 2017), pp. 241–262.

Komlosy, Andrea. "Spatial Division of Labour, Global Inter-Relations and Imbalances in Regional Development," in Lex Heerma van Voss, Els Hiemstra and Elise van Nederveen Meerkerk (eds.). *The Ashgate Companion to the History of Textile Workers, 1650–2000* (Aldershot, GB: Ashgate, 2010), pp. 621–646.

Komlosy, Andrea. "China's Mowe Towards a Global Economic Core in the 21st Century? Prospects, Constraints, Consequences," in Centers and Peripheries revisited, *Review Fernand Braudel Center*, Special Issue, XXXVI, 3–4 (2013, published in 2017), ed. by Klemens Kaps and Andrea Komlosy, pp. 351–386.

Komlosy, Andrea. *Work. The Last 1.000 Years* (London and New York: Verso, 2018).

Kriedte, Peter, Hans Medick and Jürgen Schlumbohm. *Industrialisierung vor der Industrialisierung. Gewerbliche Warenproduktion auf dem Land in der Formationsperiode des Kapitalismus* (Göttingen: Vandenhoeck & Ruprecht, 1977).

Lambert, Craig. *Shadow Work. The Unpaid Unseen Jobs that Fill Out Our Day* (Berkeley: Conterpoint, 2015).

Parthasarathi, Prassanan. "Agriculture, Labour, and the Standard of Living in Eighteenth-Century India," in Robert C. Allen, Tommy Bengtsson and Martin Dribe (eds), *Living Standards in the Past: New Perspectives on Well-Being in Asia and Europe* (Oxford: Oxford University Press, 2005).

Pomeranz, Kenneth. *The Great Divergence. China, Europe and the Making of the Modern World Economy* (Princeton and Oxford: Princeton University Press, 2001).

Rothermund, Dietmar. *Europa und Asien im Zeitalter des Merkantilismus* (Darmstadt: Wissenschaftliche Buchgesellschaft, 1978).

Roy, Tirthankar. *Rethinking Economic Change in India. Labour and Livelihood* (London and New York: Routledge, 2005).

Roy, Tirthankar. *Artisans and Industrialization: Indian Weaving in the 20th Century* (New Delhi: Oxford University Press, 1993).

Scherrer, Christoph (ed.). *China's Labor Question* (München: Rainer Hampp Verlag, 2011).

Srnicek, Nick. *Platform Capitalism* (Cambridge, UK: Polity Press, 2017).

Sugihara, Kaoru. "The East Asian Path of Economic Development: A Long-Term Perspective," in Giovanni Arrighi et. al. (eds), *The Resurgence of East Asia: 500, 150 and 50 Year Perspectives* (London and New York: Routlegde, 2003), pp. 78–123.

Taylor, Ian and Karen Smith. *United Nations Conference on Trade and Development (UNCTAD)* (London and New York: Routledge, 2007).

Traub-Mertz, Rudolf and Herbert Jauch. "The African textile and clothing industry: From import-substitution to export orientation," in Herbert Jauch and Rudolf Traub-Mertz (eds), *The Future of the Textile Industry in Sub-Saharan Africa* (Cape Town: Friedrich Ebert Foundation, 2006), pp. 9–35. online available at: <http://library.fes.de/pdf-files/iez/03796/02article.pdf>; last accessed June 10, 2020.

Van Voss, Lex Heerma, Els Hiemstra and Elise van Nederveen Meerkerk (eds.). *The Ashgate Companion to the History of Textile Workers, 1650–2000* (Aldershot, GB: Ashgate, 2010).

Wallerstein, Immanuel. "Structural Crisis, or Why Capitalists Can no Longer Find Capitalism Rewarding", in Immanuel Wallerstein, Randall Collins, Michael Mann, and Calhous Derluguan. *Does Capitalism have a Future?* (Oxford: Oxford University Press, 2013), pp. 9–36.

World Economic Forum (ed.). *Industrial Internet of Things: Unleashing the Potential of Connected Products and Services,* online available at: <http://www3.weforum.org/docs/WEFUSA_IndustrialInternet_Report2015.pdf>; last accessed January 29, 2019.

CHAPTER 3

# Soy Expansions

## *China, the USA and Brazil in Comparison*

*Ernst Langthaler*

## 1 Introduction

From a world-systemic point of view, globalization can be conceived of as the worldwide expansion of commodity chains since the "long sixteenth century." The concept of a *commodity chain*, defined by Hopkins and Wallerstein as "a network of labor and production processes whose end result is a finished commodity,"[1] has been a pillar of world-systems analysis. Since its introduction in the 1970s and its reconceptualization as global commodity chain and global value chain,[2] this approach has met some criticism: first, as a world-systemic concept, it tends to disregard the negotiations between social actors on regional and local scales;[3] second, as a social-science concept, it tends to disregard the environmental relations of capitalist societies, i.e. the exploitation of nature in addition to labor.[4]

The concept of *commodity frontier* offers solutions to these problems. It goes far beyond Turner's classical "frontier thesis", arguing that the frontier experience shaped collective identity in nineteenth-century North America.[5] As "a zone beyond which further expansion is possible,"[6] the commodity frontier directs our attention, first, to the more or less contested places of incorporation into the space of the capitalist world-system and, second, to the intersection of society and nature in the accumulation of value along the commodity chain. Since capitalism depends on growth, frontier expansion is thus inherent to capitalist development, as emphasized by Moore: "the extension of capitalist power to new, uncommodified spaces became the lifeblood of capitalism."[7]

1 Hopkins and Wallerstein, "Commodity Chains in the World-Economy Prior to 1800," p. 159.
2 See Bair, *Frontiers of Commodity Chain Research*.
3 See Hall, "Puzzles in the Comparative Study of Frontiers."
4 See Moore, *Capitalism in the Web of Life*, pp. 13–38.
5 See Turner, *The Frontier in American History*.
6 Moore, "Sugar and the Expansion of the Early Modern World-Economy," p. 412.
7 Moore, *Capitalism in the Web of Life*, p. 51.

 | DOI:10.1163/9789004448049_004

After the colonization of the last non-incorporated territories in the "Golden Age of Resource-Based Development" (1870–1914), global capitalism shifted from extensive to more intensive forms of incorporation.[8] Thus we may distinguish between *external* frontiers as zones of the extensive incorporation ("broadening") of new spaces (e.g. the conversion of grasslands into fields) and *internal* frontiers as zones of the more intensive incorporation ("deepening") of already commodified spaces (e.g. technological innovations).[9]

This chapter traces the expansion (and, if so, contraction) of frontiers of global agro-food chains in different world-historical contexts through the lens of a particular commodity – soy. Even though regularly undervalued, the importance of soy and its products for globalization cannot be overestimated: "shaping our world in multiple ways, while largely hidden or ignored."[10] This chapter concentrates on the domain of food production, while largely disregarding processing, trading and consumption.[11] Soybean production involves, among other things, the occupation of land, the mobilization of labor and the application of technology (including knowledge) as well as the governance of these activities by different actors situated along the commodity chain. In the following, the ways in which the corresponding modes of farming[12] contributed to expansions of the soy frontier is discussed in three different contexts: the northeast of China (Manchuria) from the 1900s to the 1940s, the US Midwest since the 1930s, and the Brazilian savannah and rainforest area since the 1970s. The comparison of these regional cases highlights the similarities and differences of soy expansions.

## 2 Soy as a Versatile Crop

The soybean, *Glycine max*, is a cultigen that apparently does not exist outside of human cultivation. Possible origins of the soybean are depicted in many legends, although it is known that the trial-and-error process of soybean domestication in northeastern China did not fully succeed until the eleventh century BCE. Through migration and trade, the soybean spread to other parts of East, Southeast, and South Asia in the following centuries and became a commonly

8 See Barbier, *Scarcity and Frontiers*, p. 2.
9 See Carlson, "Broadening and Deepening"; Komlosy, "Kapitalismus als frontier."
10 Du Bois, *The Story of Soy*, p. 8.
11 On the distribution and consumption of soy, see Langthaler, "The Soy Paradox"; Langthaler, "Gemüse oder Ölfrucht?"
12 See van der Ploeg, *The New Peasantries*, p. 114.

used ingredient in regional food cultures. In the twentieth century, the bulk of soybean cultivation shifted to the Americas. The US soy expansion took off in the 1930s, followed by another expansion in South America (Brazil, Argentina, Paraguay, etc.) from the 1970s onwards. Through this transfer from East to West in the twentieth century, soy was converted from a food crop into a cash crop with a multitude of commercial uses.[13]

The soybean plant, seen as a living organism, has specific characteristics that both enable and limit its interaction with other species, including humans. The plant's maturation is highly sensitive to day length. This phenomenon, which is known as photoperiodicity, as well as soy's vulnerability to frost means that each location may require a different variety of soy for optimal growth. However, under the right conditions, any given variety of soy is a reliable crop, which can grow in moderate, sub-tropical, and tropical climates and can tolerate poorer soils. The symbiosis between the soy plant and *Rhizobium* bacteria on its roots causes the bean's high protein content, and the bacteria itself plays a role in the renewal of soil fertility by tying up nitrogen. During the vegetative growth phase, the rather slow-maturing plant competes hard with other plants for sunlight, water, and nutrients. Thus, it requires effective weed control, either mechanically or chemically, by its cultivators. Asian-style, labor-intensive farming with mechanical weed control through hoeing has given way to Western-style capital-intensive farming, including the growing use of large-scale machinery, agrochemicals, and herbicide-resistant transgenic seeds. During the following reproductive growth phase, the plant requires pest control and, depending on the location, irrigation. The harvested bean consists of 25 to 45 percent protein and 15 to 20 percent fats, depending on the variety and farming conditions. In addition, the soybean is high in amino acids and vitamins. In comparison to other vegetal crops, it is strikingly complete as a human food.[14]

Due to its richness in protein and fats, soy serves as a multipurpose crop. Therefore, soy-related commodity chains are widely spread.[15] The bean has traditionally been used for a variety of foodstuffs in its non-fermented (tofu, soy milk, okara, etc.) and fermented forms (soy paste, soy sauce, natto, etc.), as practiced in East Asian food cultures for centuries. In the modern era, the processing of soy has shifted to bean crushing in order to allow extraction of the oil with chemical solvents (which takes place primarily at large-scale extraction plants, mostly run by transnational companies) or screw presses

13 See Du Bois and Mintz, "Soy"; Sorosiak, "Soybean."

14 *Ibid.*

15 See van Gelder and Dros, *Corporate Actors in the South American Soy Production Chain.*

(more frequently used at smaller extraction plants). The oils are then refined, bleached, and deodorized to be used for food (margarine, mayonnaise, cooking oil, etc.) or for industrial purposes. The residual cake is mainly used as protein-rich animal feed by the livestock industry.[16] The soybean resists any singular definition, instead combining features of a *pulse*, due to its high protein content, and an *oilseed*, due to its high oil content. Thus, the most appropriate definition is determined not by soy's biological features but by society's appropriation of this crop.[17]

## 3 The Chinese Soy Expansion

Manchuria, the region the Chinese call *Dongbei* or "the Northeast," comprising the three provinces of Liaoning, Jilin, and Heilongjiang, ranked first among the incorporated territories of the Chinese empire until the nineteenth century. In political terms, the region at the intersection of China, Russia, Korea, and Japan was conceived of as the "cockpit of Asia." In economic terms, it emerged as Beijing's breadbasket due to the rich quantity and quality of land reserves and the favorable monsoon climate (warm, wet summers and cold, dry winters) in the Manchurian plain. Nonetheless, Manchuria's rise to political and economic importance has been an issue of historiographical debate. While some authors adopt Turner's classical "frontier thesis," arguing that the transformation of wilderness into civilization in the periphery by the core shaped Chinese collective identity as a whole, others conceive of the region as a "middle ground", where the interaction of various social groups and landscapes shaped a new borderland culture. Reardon-Anderson rejects both interpretations by arguing that Manchuria was incorporated by the "transplantation of institutions and practices previously established in China proper," thus resulting in "growth without development." Accordingly, the tension between the densely populated, land-short heartland of China and the sparsely populated, land-rich borderland of Manchuria pulled people from the south towards land in the north, thereby transplanting the conventional way of life beyond the Great Wall.[18]

In the mid-nineteenth century, the Qing dynasty began to promote the settlement of Han-Chinese people as well as the reclamation and cultivation of land in their homeland Manchuria where immigration was formerly prohibited. For

16 See Huang, "Early Uses of Soybeans in Chinese History"; Du Bois and Mintz, "Soy"; Sorosiak, "Soybean"; Clay, *World Agriculture and the Environment*, pp. 173–202.

17 See Langthaler, "Gemüse oder Ölfrucht?"

18 See Reardon-Anderson, *Reluctant Pioneers*, pp. 2–10.

this purpose, the Manchu rulers abandoned the manorial system and offered land for lease and sale. This decision was taken with two goals: to raise imperial revenues to finance rising military efforts through the lease and sale of public land and the taxation of privatized farmland; and to strengthen the empire's defense against Russian (and later also Japanese) claims by settling a larger and more permanent population on the borders.[19] After the turn of the century, the colonization of Manchuria accelerated due to political and economic drivers. As debts and threats worsened, the government reinforced the reclamation and cultivation of land in the northeast provinces with the "New Policies" of 1902. This initiative coincided with the opening of railroads through Manchuria in 1903 – most importantly, the Chinese Eastern Railway, running east to west from Siberia via Harbin to Vladivostok, and the South Manchuria Railway, connecting north and south from Harbin via Changchun to Dairen. While initially both lines were in Russian hands, the track section between Changchun and Dairen came under Japanese control following the Russo-Japanese War of 1904/05. Consequently, the exploitation of Manchuria's rich resources was increasingly shaped by foreign imperialist powers and commercial enterprises, culminating in the Japanese occupation of 1931 (the "Manchurian Incident"). As famine and warlordism spread throughout China in the late 1920s, voluntary migrants to Manchuria, primarily male, were joined by refugees, many of them women and children, forced to search for a safer home.[20]

The Great Migration to northeastern China was equal to simultaneous mass migrations in other parts of the world. From 1891 to 1942, 25.4 million people migrated from northern China to Manchuria, 16.7 million returned, leaving a net transfer of 8.7 million. Most of the Han-Chinese settlements were created along rivers and railroads, which facilitated bringing migrants in and shipping produce out, thereby linking these areas to market exchange. The young men who left their villages in northern China to make their way through Manchuria to the outer edges of settlement, initially expecting to earn money and return home to their families, became tied to social networks that channeled them to towns, villages, and farms. Rather than adapting to the world around them, the new villages became extensions of the old ones, bound together by the values of family and the peasant community. Serial migration from south to north

19 See Reardon-Anderson, *Reluctant Pioneers*, pp. 71–84; Reardon-Anderson, "Land Use and Society in Manchuria and Inner Mongolia during the Qing Dynasty."

20 See Gottschang and Lary, *Swallows and Settlers*, 87, p. 38; Gottschang, "Economic Change, Disasters, and Migration"; Sun, *The Economic Development of Manchuria in the First Half of the Twentieth Century*, pp. 19–41; Chao, *The Economic Development of Manchuria*, 43, pp. 1–21; Reardon-Anderson, *Reluctant Pioneers*, pp. 147–159, 208–209.

enabled upward social mobility, as former laborers and tenants invested their earnings to become land owners and found families.[21]

With the state-driven reclamation and cultivation of land by Han-Chinese settlers, the production of soybeans in Manchuria expanded rapidly from the 1900s to the 1920s, before political turmoil, economic crisis and ecological adversities terminated this boom in the 1930s (Figure 3.1). The Manchurian soy expansion resulted solely from the enlargement of cultivated land, since yields per unit of land, amounting to 1,300 kilograms per hectare in 1930, tended to decline in the long run. Throughout this period, soybeans occupied a central place in Manchuria, accounting for 70 to 80 percent of total exports.[22] The supply of soybeans met a growing demand on national and international markets. From the late nineteenth century onwards, beancake was carried by carts and junks to the port of Newchwang and shipped to Japan, where it served as a fertilizer on paddy rice fields. Oil, commonly treated as a by-product, was sold mainly to China proper. In the early twentieth century, a supply crisis of vegetable oils in Europe due to adverse weather conditions and wartime shortages raised international demand for soybean oil as lubricant and raw material for industrial products (e.g. soap). As the world's leading supplier of soybeans, Manchuria was connected to international trade, organized by Japanese companies that marketed soybeans via the port of Dairen and Vladivostok mainly to the United Kingdom, Germany, and Denmark. The frontier region had thus become incorporated in a global commodity chain, connecting East Asian suppliers and Western European buyers.[23]

Manchurian soybeans were usually planted once within a three- or four-year cycle of crop rotation.[24] They were cultivated "almost entirely by hand methods," as outlined by contemporary descriptions: The soil was broken in April, using a single-handled, steel-tipped plough, drawn by a mixed team of oxen, mules or donkeys. The seed was sown and covered by hand, and fertilized, if at all, with a compost of manure and soil. Since the plant matured very slowly and fertilizer was in short supply, the weeds had to be removed several times by carefully turning and breaking the ground with a heavy hoe. The beans were harvested in September by pulling the plants up by the roots or cutting them with a sickle before they had fully ripened. After drying, the seeds were separated from the pods using a stone roller, dragged by a mule. Winnowing was done by throwing the mixture of beans and chaff against the

21 See Reardon-Anderson, *Reluctant Pioneers*, pp. 127–146.
22 See Reardon-Anderson, *Reluctant Pioneers*, pp. 226–229.
23 See Prodöhl, "Die Dynamiken globaler Vernetzung."
24 See Reardon-Anderson, *Reluctant Pioneers*, pp. 179–183, 240–241.

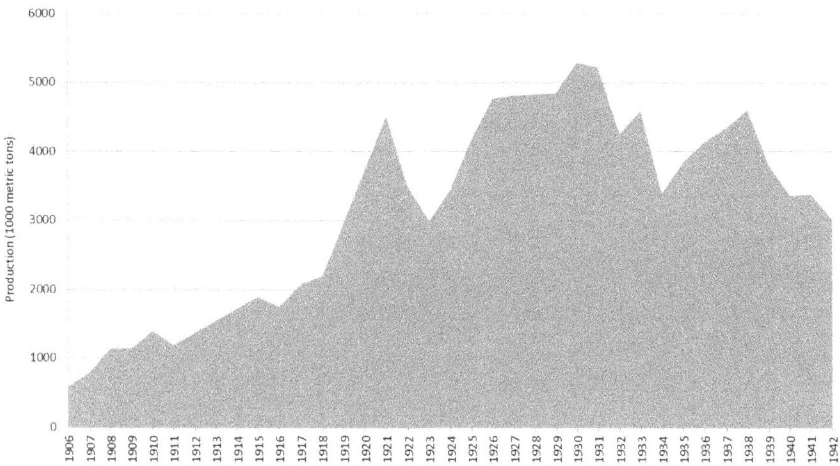


FIGURE 3.1 Soy expansion in Manchuria, 1906–1942
SOURCE: LANGENBERG, *DIE BEDEUTUNG DER SOJABOHNE IN DER WELTWIRTSCHAFT*, P. 20; STEWART, "THE SOYA BEAN AND MANCHURIA," PP. 221–226; DEASY, "THE SOYA BEAN IN MANCHURIA," PP. 303–310; CHAO, *THE ECONOMIC DEVELOPMENT OF MANCHURIA*, P. 44

wind. Once dried and separated, the beans were ready for sale as a whole or for pressing to produce oil and beancake.[25]

According to the Kotoku surveys of the mid-1930s, landed property in Manchuria was highly concentrated, with a gradient running from the more equal south to the more unequal north. On average, the property of the biggest owners was tenfold the property of the others. However, leasing of nearly half of the landed property by the biggest owners alleviated the inequality. With the land rents paid by the tenants, the biggest owners hired twice the amount of labor capacity provided by their own family members. The wage laborers came from the households of landless workers, which made up 30 percent of the total households of the villages covered by the surveys. The other owners relied predominantly on family labor, while the tenants ran pure family farms. One striking feature concerns the weight of soybean production: While crop selection showed some differences by household class, the share of the acreage sown with soybeans was similar at one fifth of the cultivated land. Although big landowners had enough revenues to specialize in soybean cash crop production with advanced technology, they did not do so; instead, they used their land the same way as the others (Table 3.1).

25 See Imperial Maritime Customs, *The Soya Bean of Manchuria*, pp. 4–5.

TABLE 3.1 Agricultural land, labor and capital per household in Manchuria, 1935/36

| | Biggest owners (N =74) | Other owners (N = 793) | Tenants (N = 376) | Total (N = 1,243) |
|---|---|---|---|---|
| Land owned (ha) | 56.8 | 5.3 | 0.0 | 6,8 |
| Land cultivated (ha) | 33.9 | 4.6 | 6.2 | 6.8 |
| Family labor (man-days/year) | 963 | 642 | 699 | 679 |
| Total labor (man-days/year) | 2,726 | 741 | 714 | 851 |
| Draft animals (pcs) | 10.4 | 1.7 | 1.5 | 2.1 |
| Ploughs (pcs) | 3.3 | 0.8 | 0.8 | 0.9 |
| Cultivated land sown in soybeans (%) | 21.9 | 18.3 | 21.6 | 20.3 |
| Land productivity (*piculs*/ha) | 9.1 | 8.6 | 8.6 | 8.7 |
| Labor productivity (*piculs*/1,000 man-days) | 113 | 53 | 75 | 70 |

SOURCE: REARDON-ANDERSON, *RELUCTANT PIONEERS*, PP. 220–233

Reardon-Anderson's explanation for the uniformity of land use draws on social and cultural aspects: Chinese farmers – like other pioneers at the Manchurian frontier –, regardless of farm size, were reluctant to change due to their risk-averse habitus, which was in turn informed by the traditional values of family and peasant community: they all "used simple, traditional technologies, favored small organizations with small financing, and moved their investments among various business activities based on a preference for short-term profits and low risks."[26] However, the uniformity of land use can also be explained by economic interdependencies: Since soybean production relied on simple technology, large farmers did not enjoy advantages due to economies of scale. The basic equipment, comprising two draft animals and a plough, was commonly available on medium and even on small farms as well. Indeed, the reverse was the case: medium and small family farms with rather intrinsically motivated laborers enjoyed a cost advantage over large farms, where rather extrinsically

26 Reardon-Anderson, *Reluctant Pioneers*, p. 196.

motivated wage laborers had to be monitored to ensure the quantity and quality of work (e.g. weeding the soybean fields as carefully as possible).[27] This was probably the reason why the pure family farms of tenants gained more yield per labor unit than the mixed family-wage work farms of most landowners. Only the big owners more than compensated their disadvantage – obviously not through more productive technology, but through more exploitive labor relations: on the one hand, they had considerable leverage over wage laborers due to the enormous number of landless people; on the other hand, landless households sent their most efficient members – usually young men – to wage work on large holdings in order to maximize earnings.[28]

## 4 The US Soy Expansion

The "American frontier," expanding from east to west and, according to Turner, shaping collective identity,[29] had already been closed as soy entered US agriculture. From the mid-nineteenth century onwards, the Corn Belt, centered on the states of Ohio, Indiana, Illinois, Iowa, and Missouri, had emerged as a specialized region of commercial corn-livestock production. The region is characterized by a mid-continental climate with cold winters and warm summers as well as former grassland soils rich in nutrients.[30] However, declining corn yields after the turn of the century, due to overexploitation and depressed commodity prices in the interwar period due to overproduction, plunged the region's farming community into a fundamental crisis. Approaches to solving the ecological and economic crisis resulted in two crop innovations that became pillars of Corn Belt agriculture from the 1930s onwards: one solution was the introduction of high-yielding varieties of hybrid corn as part of the technological package of American-style capital-intensive farming (commercial fertilizers, pesticides, motorized machinery, etc.). The other solution was the introduction of a neophyte deriving from Asian-style labor-intensive farming – soy.[31]

While previously known only to natural scientists, religious minorities, and Asian immigrants, the exotic plant caught the attention of the US Department of Agriculture (USDA) at the turn of the century. The official closing of the US

27 See Allen and Lueck, "Agricultural Contracts," pp. 479–480.
28 See Reardon-Anderson, *Reluctant Pioneers*, pp. 226–229.
29 See Turner, *The Frontier in American History*.
30 See Loomis, Connor and Cassman, *Crop Ecology*, pp. 459–470.
31 See Hudson, *Making the Corn Belt*, pp. 151–172.

frontier in 1890 had reoriented agricultural research and development from the areal extension of European-style farming, based on nutrient mining on former prairie grasslands, to more intensive and sustainable land uses. In the following decades, the USDA commissioned a series of expeditions to East Asia (e.g. the Dorsett-Morse expedition from 1929 to 1931) in order to search for soy varieties adapted to the climate, soil, and latitude of North America. Among several thousands of collected soy samples, 41 were selected as US cultivars and crossbred to be adapted to particular conditions. In the meantime, farmers in the Mississippi Valley and Corn Belt had begun to plant soybeans, in correspondence with the opening of oilseed mills. Henry Ford's obsession with soy as a raw material for the automobile industry caused a sensation in the mass media, but never proceeded far beyond the experimental stage. Despite these administrative and commercial efforts, soy farming and processing remained a niche business.[32]

Soy's transition from niche to mainstream took off only in the mid-1930s, driven by both institutional and technological developments. At the institutional level, the federal state began to regulate soy commodity chains in several steps: first, the New Deal administration managed the economic and ecological crisis through setting-aside corn and other price-depressed crops as well as introducing soil-enriching plants on eroded fields, thereby opening a window of opportunity for soy as an alternative. Second, the wartime government successfully encouraged US farmers to plant price-subsidized oilseeds such as soybeans for food purposes in order to save scarce tropical oils for military use. Third, the continuation of favorable commodity prices after the war led to soybean surpluses, which were used, for one, as oil in the manufacturing of food stuffs such as margarine and, for another, as cake in the livestock feeding complex, both at home and abroad (Western Europe and Japan).[33]

At the technological level, the transition to capital-intensive farming based on fossil fuels accelerated soy's integration into the cropping system of the Corn Belt in multiple ways: first, due to the replacement of draft animals by tractors, acreage formerly used for feed crops (e.g. oats) became available for cash crops (e.g. soybeans). Second, since combines for corn harvesting and threshing were also appropriate for soybeans, no special machinery had to be purchased. Third, crop rotation of nitrogen-mining corn and nitrogen-fixing soybeans accrued ecological and economic advantages by saving commercial fertilizer. Within a few decades, the soy frontier had expanded deeply into the

32 See Du Bois, *The Story of Soy*, pp. 53–69.

33 See Prodöhl, "From Dinner to Dynamite"; Patel, *Stuffed and Starved*, pp. 169–173; Du Bois, "Social Context and Diet," pp. 209–214.

Corn Belt, thus shaping the agrarian landscape of the Midwest. Already in the mid-1950s, the region was officially labeled the "Corn-Soy Belt."[34]

Soy's success in the agro-food chain is reflected by the expansion of production: After its take-off in the 1930s and acceleration in the 1940s, soybean production grew strongly from the 1950s to the 1970s and, after stagnation during the farm debt crisis of the 1980s, continued to grow from the 1990s onwards. The expansion of production resulted mainly from the extension of cultivated land devoted to soybeans: Compared to the level of 1924, the area had increased twofold in 1930, fivefold in 1939, tenfold in 1952, twentyfold in 1964, and fiftyfold in 2014. Soybeans increasingly displaced small grains such as oats, barley, and wheat in the Corn Belt. The intensification of land use played an important role in the US soy expansion as well: yields per hectare had multiplied twofold in 1937, fivefold in 1946, and tenfold in 1979. The USA as a soy powerhouse dominated world trade until the 1970s, before new competitors entered the market (Figure 3.2).

As technological change progressed in the Corn Belt from the mid-1930s onwards, soybean cultivation required less manual labor and more farm machinery, as depicted by the instructional film *Soybeans for Farm and Industry* from about 1940. It demonstrates the application of a multitude of tractor-drawn machines: soil preparation with the disc harrow, fertilizing with the manure distributor, sowing with the seed drill, weeding with the rotary hoe, weeder, and cultivator, cutting for hay with the mower, harvesting and threshing for beans with the combine, and so on. The only person who appears on the field is the tractor driver.[35] This notion of a fully-mechanized one-man farm was exaggerated by the film, since neither family labor nor hired labor disappeared: in Iowa, a typical Corn Belt state, the average number of hired laborers per family farm even rose from 1.2 in 1950 to 1.4 in 1964, reflecting farm growth from 68 to 89 hectares.[36] However, the film did accurately forecast the vanishing point of the already ongoing transition from labor-intensive to capital-intensive farming. With the advent of large-scale machinery such as self-propelled combines, soybean farming, along with corn cropping, faced economies of scale. Iowa in the mid-1960s provides a telling case: although the percentage of the acreage covered by soybeans was slightly below or above one fifth for all classes (except for the smallest farms), the percentage of farms planting soybeans positively correlated with farm size. Conversely, the number of combines per 1,000 acres

34 See Anderson, *Industrializing the Corn Belt*, pp. 152–167; Haystead and Fite, *The Agricultural Regions of the United States*, p. 140.

35 See International Harvester Company, *Soybeans for Farm and Industry*.

36 See USDA, *US Census of Agriculture 1964, Iowa*, pp. 7, 11.

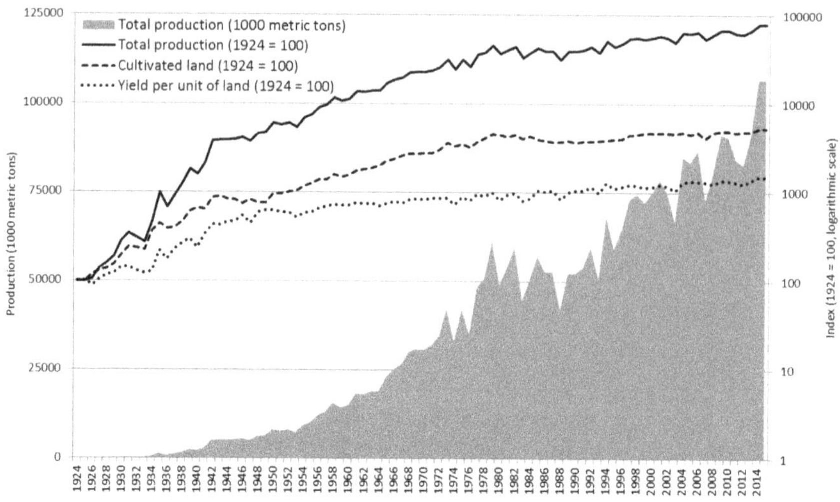


FIGURE 3.2 Soy expansion in the USA, 1924–2015
SOURCE: USDA, *NATIONAL AGRICULTURAL STATISTICS SERVICE* (AUTHOR'S CALCULATIONS)

of cropland negatively correlated with farm size, thus indicating scale effects to the advantage of larger farms (Figure 3.3). According to Anderson's regional study on Iowa, saving labor and money were the farming families' main motives for purchasing or renting machines. Their success in doing so required some creativity: "But the willingness of farmers to experiment, on the faith that sooner or later the new machines would help them harvest with greater financial and labor savings, was the most influential factor in their acceptance of the combine."[37]

The mechanization of Corn Belt farms was closely intertwined with the social relations of farming families. On the one hand, the decision to invest in farm equipment arose not only from operational calculations, but also reflected the priorities of family life. Apart from the families' general motive of reducing bodily strain, farm women were especially thankful for machines which reduced the need to engage seasonal workers. For instance, corn pickers were paid by the bushel and provided room and board for the duration of the harvest. Unlike permanent workers who did other farm-work in case of unfavorable weather, corn pickers waited inside the house for conditions to improve – and had to be served by the farm women. On the other hand, farm mechanization changed the gendered division of labor within the family.

37 Anderson, *Industrializing the Corn Belt*, p. 158.

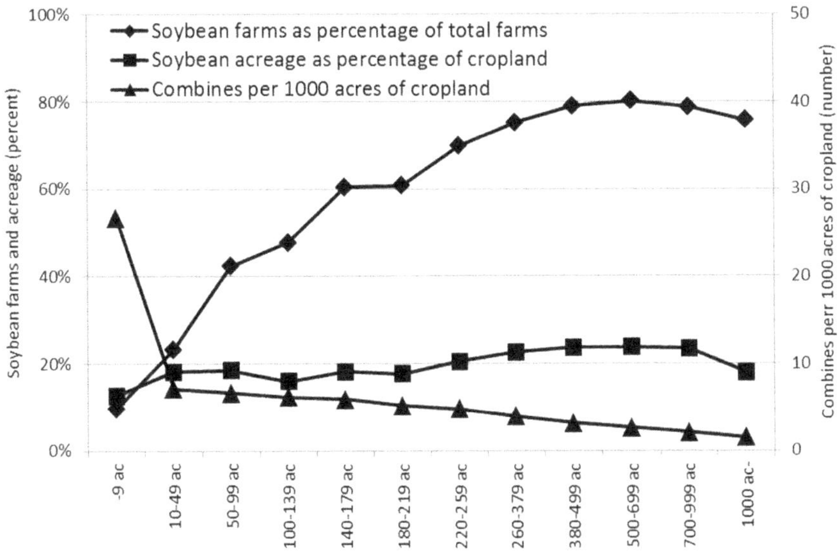


FIGURE 3.3 Soybean cropping and mechanization by farm size in Iowa, 1964
SOURCE: U.S. BUREAU OF THE CENSUS, *CENSUS OF AGRICULTURE 1964 – IOWA*, PP. 74–87 (AUTHOR'S CALCULATIONS)

Contrary to the women's multiple roles in previous agricultural production, the adoption of the fully-mechanized farm model, framing the male farmer as "master" of the machinery, increasingly relegated the farmer's wife to household work. Thereby, the farm enterprise and household became more separated, but were still integrated through the mode of entrepreneurial family farming.[38]

While the above-mentioned film highlighted mechanical innovations, the US soy expansion also relied on agrochemicals, i.e. commercial fertilizer and pesticides. Initially, agricultural scientists, extension professionals, and farm journalists discouraged farmers from fertilizing the nitrogen-fixing soybean crop, since the benefits were unlikely to outweigh the costs. However, Corn Belt farmers challenged the received wisdom by applying commercial fertilizers to soybeans in the same way as they did to corn. While this trial-and-error method proved to be more or less effective, the application of pesticides, especially herbicides, to soybean fields achieved far-reaching effects. Herbicides promised an effective response to weeds as a severe challenge during the

38 See Adams, *The Transformation of Rural Life*, pp. 243–253; Anderson, *Industrializing the Corn Belt*, p. 169–171.

soybean's growth cycle. In a sense, the postwar battle against weeds continued the battle against the axis powers during the war: the herbicide 2,4-D, which the University of Chicago had experimented with as a weapon for biological warfare, was an effective growth regulator, causing the plant to literally grow itself to death.[39]

After 1945, 2,4-D was adopted as a simple and cheap tool for eliminating weeds in the Corn Belt and elsewhere. Exciting success stories, distributed among the farming community, overshadowed the experts' advice to balance chemical and mechanical practices. In fact, farmers' excessive application of 2,4-D effectively eliminated broadleaf weeds, but simultaneously created a niche for other weeds tolerant of this herbicide, thereby aggravating rather than alleviating the problem. Corn Belt farmers consequently saw themselves forced to apply ever more 2,4-D as well as alternative herbicides developed by the chemical industry, thus rendering weed control more complex and expensive. By the 1960s, corn and soybean farmers were caught in the vicious cycle of their intended actions to manage the agroecosystem and its unintended reactions. However, they embraced herbicides and experimented from day to day to shape their use, since they tried to avoid the labor and expenses associated with mechanical cultivation.[40] From 1996 onwards, the rapid diffusion of the herbicide glyphosate in combination with glyphosate-resistant transgenic seeds initiated a new phase of the struggle between farmers and weeds in the expansion of the soy frontier, in both North and South America.[41]

## 5 The Brazilian Soy Expansion

The soybean, which had been adopted as a crop in Rio Grande do Sul in the very south of Brazil in the 1920s, did not play a significant role in agriculture before its expansion took off in the 1970s. Initially, soy varieties from the USA and Japan were grown under moderate climate on mixed peasant farms for hay and, from the 1940s onwards, for beans to extract cooking oil and animal feed for the domestic market. In the course of only a few decades, however, soy gained not only national but global importance due to political, economic, and environmental impacts. First, after the Brazilian army had seized power in 1964, the military dictatorship implemented a high-modernist program of agro-industrial development to fix several problems at once: creating jobs for

39 See Anderson, *Industrializing the Corn Belt*, pp. 33–50, 62–63.
40 See Anderson, *Industrializing the Corn Belt*, pp. 33–50.
41 See Lapegna, *Soybeans and Power*, pp. 3–5.

the rural poor who had been disadvantaged by urban-centered Import Substitution Industrialization; securing cheap food for the urban poor who had moved to the cities from the countryside; counterbalancing the country's negative trade balance through agricultural exports; and colonizing "empty" landscapes in the vast territory of the country.[42]

Second, a supply crisis of North American soy due to years of bad harvests, massive purchases by the USSR, and a subsequent US trade embargo stacked against Japan and Europe in 1973 culminated in shortages of soy's key substitutes as animal feed, Peruvian fishmeal and West African peanuts, due to an El Niño Southern Oscillation. The resulting spike of soy prices in the 1970s not only offered incentives to domestic commercial farmers to expand soy cropping, but also to Japanese and Europeans to invest in Brazil's transport and processing facilities to reduce dependency on US exports.[43]

Third, the Brazilian soy expansion was further accelerated in the 1990s by Mad Cow Disease in the UK and other parts of Europe, as well as China's growing appetite for meat, as both developments raised demand for soy as animal feed. Consequently, China joined international investors in Brazil's growing soy complex. Soy's northward expansion involved US knowledge transfer for breeding varieties adapted to the abysmal soils, tropical climate, and smaller latitude of the savannah region (*cerrados*).[44]

Fourth, Brazil's hyperinflation in the 1980s, accompanied by the resignation of the military dictatorship, permitted foreign multinationals such as Archer Daniels Midland, Bunge, and Cargill to buy large parts of the state-sponsored soy industry. The republican government supported its agro-industrial power houses by an aggressive program of trade liberalization in the frameworks of the Mercosur agreement and the World Trade Organization. Vested interests of multinational corporations were thereby represented as those of the whole nation.[45]

Brazil's soybean expansion unfolded in two bursts of growth: the first one from the 1960s to the 1970s, driven by state-led development and international supply crisis, and the second one from the 1990s onwards, reflecting the shifts

42 See Schönardie, *Bäuerliche Landwirtschaft im Süden Brasiliens*, pp. 236–247; Patel, *Stuffed and Starved*, pp. 173–181; Du Bois, *The Story of Soy*, pp. 116–133; de Sousa and Busch, "Networks and Agricultural Development"; Turzi, *The Political Economy of Agricultural Booms*, pp. 83–85.

43 See Patel, *Stuffed and Starved*, pp. 181–187; Du Bois, *The Story of Soy*, pp. 116–133.

44 See de Sousa and de Cássia Milagres Teixera Vieira, "Soybeans and Soyfoods in Brazil, with Notes on Argentina"; Patel, *Stuffed and Starved*, pp. 181–187; Du Bois, *The Story of Soy*, pp. 116–133.

45 See Patel, *Stuffed and Starved*, pp. 181–187; Vorley, *Food, Inc.*, p. 44.

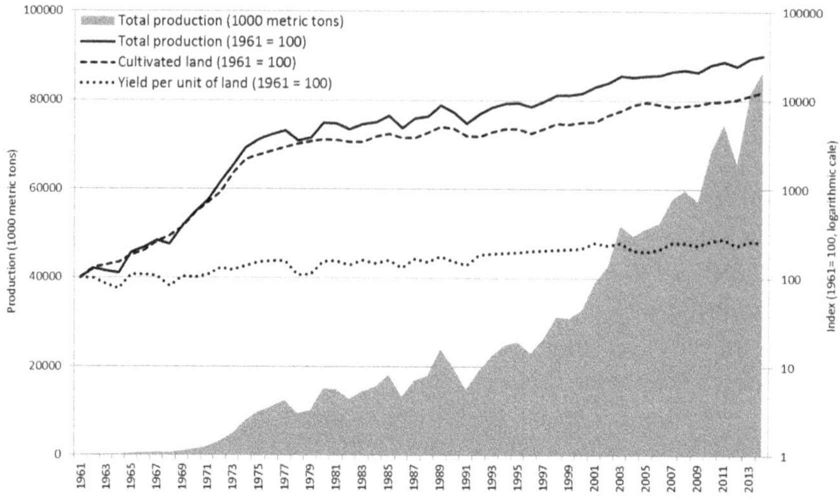


FIGURE 3.4 Soy expansion in Brazil, 1961–2014
SOURCE: FAO, *FAOSTAT* (AUTHOR'S CALCULATIONS)

of corporate power as well as European and Chinese demand.[46] The expansion of production almost completely resulted from the extension of the cultivated land devoted to soybeans: Compared to the level of 1961, the area had increased tenfold in 1972, twentyfold in 1974, fiftyfold in 1989 and hundredfold in 2012. The intensification of land use played a minor role: since yields per hectare increased slowly throughout this period, they had only doubled in the mid-1990, before showing signs of acceleration in the mid-2000s (Figure 3.4).

The Brazilian soy frontier crossed natural boundaries between the moderate south and the tropical north, moving from the state of Rio Grande do Sul though Paraná, Mato Grosso do Sul, and Goiás to Mato Grosso. Since unused or only extensively used land in the savannah and rainforest areas was incorporated, the expansion of Brazilian soy farming resembled the expansion of European-style farming at the US frontier one century earlier. In short, Brazil's "Wild West" lay in the north.[47] This pattern of soy expansion corresponded to the farmers' "frontier mentality", much like the mindset of the European settlers in nineteenth-century North America, driven by the obsession to replace wilderness by civilization. Accordingly, values such as conquering nature, securing income, and achieving progress became hegemonic in public

46 See Soskin, *Non-Traditional Agriculture and Economic Development*; Warnken, *The Development and Growth of the Soybean Industry in Brazil.*

47 See Du Bois, *The Story of Soy*, p. 118; Loomis, Connor and Cassman, *Crop Ecology*, pp. 476–482.

discourses on soy farming, as institutionalized by the congressional rural bloc (*bancada ruralista*).[48]

The Brazilian soy expansion relied on large-scale machinery both directly, through the application of mechanical inputs (e.g. combines), and indirectly, through devices for applying chemical inputs (e.g. sprayers). The extent to which the moto-mechanization of Brazilian soy farming involved economies of scale is revealed by the agricultural census of 2006: both the percentage of farms growing soybeans and the percentage of the acreage covered by soybeans positively correlated with farm size. In short, the bigger the farm, the heavier the soy's weight. Conversely, the number of combines per 1,000 hectares of cropland negatively correlated with size on farms larger than 100 hectares. Medium owners probably used their combines not only on their own 20 to 100 hectares of farmland, but also rented them to smaller farms lacking such large-scale devices (Figure 3.5). This economic driver was reinforced by government policies, directing green-revolution technologies towards large-scale farms.[49]

Application of mechanical and chemical high-technology, most notably pesticides, on Brazilian soy fields went hand in hand. Soy's general vulnerability to weeds during its early growth phase was especially pronounced in the savannah region: monocultures and soy-grain rotations as well as the tropical climate opened up a niche for weeds. Therefore, farmers were forced to apply more and stronger herbicides to the fields by sprayers and crop dusters than elsewhere. Since many herbicides kill not only weeds but also crops, farmers found proper application quite difficult – hence their unreserved welcoming of the herbicide-tolerant soy variety introduced by the US company Monsanto in 1996. Through genetic engineering (GE), Monsanto's Roundup-Ready soy was made resistant to glyphosate, marketed under the label Roundup by the same company. Glyphosate is an efficient plant killer which soon breaks down into quite harmless substances and, hence, is less toxic to animals and humans than many other herbicides. Applied in combination with glyphosate-tolerant seeds, glyphosate thus simplified and cheapened soy cultivation. Since the Brazilian government only legalized GE soy in 2005, transgenic seeds were illegally imported from Argentina, where they had already been approved in 1996, and other neighboring countries. By 2014, 93 percent of the soybeans planted in Brazil were glyphosate-tolerant.[50]

48 See Turzi, *The Political Economy of Agricultural Booms*, pp. 85–91.

49 See Turzi, *The Political Economy of Agricultural Booms*, p. 84.

50 See Du Bois, *The Story of Soy*, p. 161; de Sousa and Du Bois, "Genetically Engineered Soy."

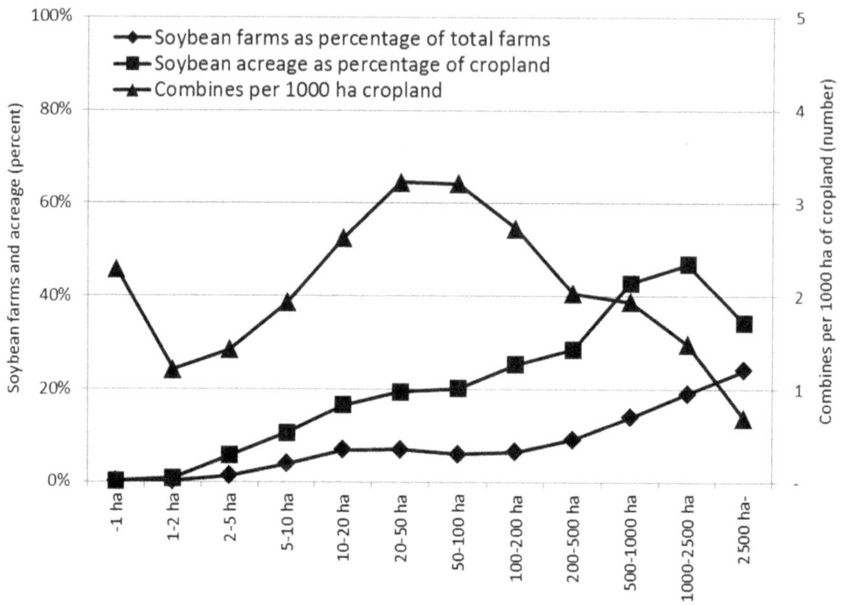


FIGURE 3.5 Soybean cropping and mechanization by farm size in Brazil, 2006
SOURCE: IBGE, *CENSO AGROPECUÁRIO 2006*, TAB. 1.2.14, 1.2.23, 1.6.73 (AUTHOR'S CALCULATIONS)

Instead of slowing down the vicious cycle of high-tech farming, the application of transgenic soy accelerated the rift between human actions and environmental reactions. Some years after the introduction of the transgenic soy, what worried farmers most was the appearance of glyphosate-tolerant weeds on their fields. "Superweeds," created through genetic and epigenetic mutations due to strong selection pressure, resisted normal doses of glyphosate. Farmers tried to combat them through the application of more and stronger herbicides, thereby making soy cultivation more troublesome and costly. The agrochemical industry soon reacted to this demand by supplying mixtures of glyphosate and 2,4-D, to eliminate conventional weeds and "superweeds," respectively. All in all, the application of herbicides, especially glyphosate, has skyrocketed since the introduction of GE soy.[51]

Brazil's soy expansion was not only a burden on the environment, with regard to degraded biodiversity, soil health, and water purity; it disorganized rural society as well. The market-driven and state-supported expansion of commercial soy farms, often run by white farmers of European or US descent, threatened

51 See Lapegna, *Soybeans and Power*, pp. 37–45; Du Bois, *The Story of Soy*, pp. 163–166.

peasant communities, including indigenous people, by both illegal and legal means. Most importantly, the ongoing struggle for land disrupted rural livelihoods. Where landed property rights were insecure, peasant families were often displaced through brute violence, including murder, by large landowners and their henchmen. For instance, 390 Indians were killed in Mato Grosso do Sul between 2003 and 2014. Where land titles prevailed, rising prices led smallholders to sell their landed property in order to make a living elsewhere. The state promoted the marketization of land through regulatory measures. For instance, in a recent Ecological Economic Zoning Plan for the highway BR-163, lands occupied by peasant and indigenous landholders were designated for soy expansion and extractive industries. Land sales were also driven by the collateral damages of soy expansion. Small landholders enclosed by expanding soy farms saw themselves cut off from their personal networks, and therefore abandoned their farms. Besides the loss of social capital, soy expansion also undermined the peasantry's natural resource base. Most disastrous were the agrochemical drifts due to large-scale spraying of herbicides on fields planted with GE soy, harming neighboring people as well as their livestock and non-GE crops. As a consequence of illegal and legal land transfers, concentration of farm size, and hence income inequality, progressed faster than in other branches of agriculture.[52]

The "accumulation by dispossession" of land led to large-scale displacement of the peasant population. In 2002, 5 million landless families were registered in Brazil. Many of the displaced people resorted to rural-urban migration to make a living, either through formal occupation in the manufacturing and service sectors or through informal work in the crowded slums of megacities. Some flocked to the self-organized communities of the Landless Rural Workers Movement (MST) which was reclaiming large tracts of land lacking a "social function" according to the 1988 constitution. Those who stayed in the nearby countryside, often lacking a roof over their heads, hired themselves out as wage workers in the labor-intensive branches of export-oriented agriculture such as sugarcane production and cattle ranching. They often got roped into the vicious cycle of unfree labor (*trabalho escravo*), forcing them to amortize their (mostly unjustified) debts through work under slave-like conditions in peripheral regions. Between 2003 and 2012, 63,417 cases of enslaved rural laborers and 2,569 landowners accused of serious labor code violations were officially registered.[53]

52 See Lapegna, *Soybeans and Power*, 84–114; Turzi, *The Political Economy of Agricultural Booms*, pp. 91–97; Ofstehage, "Farming is Easy, Becoming Brazilian is Hard"; Baletti, "Ordenamento Territorial"; Garrett and Rausch, "Green for Gold," p. 472–473.

53 See Patel, *Stuffed and Starved*, pp. 204–212; Carstensen, " 'Modern Slave Labor' in Brazil at the Intersection of Production, Migration and Resistance Networks"; Costa, *Fighting*

The most important impact of the Brazilian soy expansion on labor relations was quantitative, i.e. the reduction of on-farm work through adoption of the labor-saving technological package of agro-industrial farming. Between 1985 and 2004, a period in which production nearly tripled, employment on soy farms fell by 80 percent, from 1.7 million to 335,000 workers. Most employment opportunities in the soy complex arise off farm, in related agribusiness such as transportation, processing and services. However, job-hunting residents are often unable to acquire the new positions created by agribusiness due to lack of adequate skills; these new jobs are often taken by immigrants from southern Brazil, leading to conflict with the residing population and outmigration.[54]

Soy expansion also had qualitative impacts on working conditions. The labor force in agricultural frontier regions such as Mato Grosso has been segmented into a majority of underpaid and unskilled helpers for laying out fields on the one hand and a minority of well-paid and skilled crafters for operating the mechanical and chemical facilities on the other hand. While many employees in the upper segment only work at the farm and live with their families in nearby cities with good infrastructure, workers in the lower segment regularly face dire conditions: hard work, low wages, bad food, dirty dwellings, social isolation, etc. Wages amount to only 2.6 percent of total costs of soy production in Brazil, compared to 5.0 percent in the USA. However, there are relatively few opportunities for unfree labor in soy farming compared to sugarcane production or cattle ranching. This is not only due to the labor-extensive nature of agro-industrial farming, but also to regulatory measures such as the "dirty list of slave labor," published by the President's Secretary of Human Rights. Employers included on this list are barred from accessing public financing such as subsidized rural credit, on which the soy industry heavily depends. In 2014 only 10 out of 583 of the listed farms produced soy. Thus, soy expansion brings about unfree labor indirectly, through substituting technology for labor, rather than directly, through exploiting enslaved workers.[55]

---

*Forced Labour*; Harnoncourt, *Unfreie Arbeit*, pp. 48–87; Robles and Veltmeyer, *The Politics of Agrarian Reform in Brazil*, pp. 189–195; Cáceres, "Accumulation by Dispossession and Socio-Environmental Conflicts Caused by the Expansion of Agribusiness in Argentina."

54 See Pérez, Wise and Schlesinger, *The Promise and the Perils of Agricultural Trade Liberalization*, p. 12; Garrett and Rausch, 'Green for Gold', p. 475.

55 See Patel, *Stuffed and Starved*, pp. 188–194; Costa, *Fighting Forced Labour*; Carstensen, "'Modern Slave Labor' in Brazil at the Intersection of Production, Migration and Resistance Networks"; Turzi, *The Political Economy of Agricultural Booms*, p. 96; Garrett and Rausch, "Green for Gold", p. 475.

## 6 Conclusion

Although the soy expansions in Manchuria, the US Corn Belt, and the Brazilian savannah were time- and space-bound, they can be compared with regard to similarities and differences. A comparative framework for these specific cases – and, perhaps, for incorporation into capitalist spheres in general – is provided by two dimensions of frontier shifts: extensive incorporation at external frontiers ("widening") and intensive incorporation at internal frontiers ("deepening").[56] The positions of the above-discussed cases along these dimensions correspond to different modes of farming, as outlined by van der Ploeg: the *peasant* mode, involving the co-production of society and environment through application of self-controlled resources; the *entrepreneurial* mode, oriented towards flows of inputs (e.g. high technology) and outputs (e.g. industrial raw products) via factor and product markets; and the *capitalist* mode, organized by the sole principle of profit-maximization, regardless of the exploitation of labor and nature.[57]

The Chinese soy expansion resulted almost exclusively from shifts of the external frontier through the expansion of cultivated land, especially after the construction of railroads in Manchuria around 1900. The widening of the soy frontier was connected to the peasant mode of Han-Chinese farming: at the material level, it involved family labor, polyculture with crop rotation, and simple technology. At the ideational level, the families and communities were guided by the conservative mindset of "reluctant pioneers" rather than by a progressive "frontier mentality."

The US soy expansion resulted mainly from shifts of the internal frontier, i.e. the replacement of feed grains and other forage crops by soybeans on already cultivated fields of family farms. The deepening of the soy frontier was guided by the entrepreneurial mode of Corn Belt farming: at the material level, it involved family and wage labor, corn-soy bi-culture with crop rotation, and the technological package of machinery and agrochemicals. From the 1990s onwards, the internal frontier shifted further through the application of transgenic seeds. At the ideational level, the farming families followed the logic of enhancing their own standards of living through saving labor and money.

The Brazilian soy expansion initially resulted from extreme shifts of the external frontier, especially after the neoliberal turn in the 1980s, before the internal frontier also moved forward through adoption of biotechnology in the

56 See Carlson, "Broadening and Deepening."

57 See van der Ploeg, *The New Peasantries*, pp. 114.

1990s. The widening and deepening of the soy frontier was driven by the capitalist mode of high-tech farming: At the material level, it involved wage and forced labor, monoculture without crop rotation, and the technological package of machinery, agrochemicals, and transgenic seeds. At the ideational level, it adopted the colonialist attitude of "frontier mentality" towards indigenous societies and near-natural environments.

Shifts of commodity frontiers are often disruptive and, hence, contested among the actors involved. From these contests, counter-forces to soy expansion emerge. The case of Brazil shows these struggles most clearly: social disruptions, such as dispossession of smallholders, low wage levels or forms of unfree labor, have led to the emergence of the landless movement as a counter-force to soy expansion at the external frontier. Environmental disruptions, such as the large-scale application of agrochemicals, have led to the emergence of herbicide-resistant "superweeds" as a counter-force to soy expansion at the internal frontier. While these social and environmental counter-forces have partially slowed down the expansion or even contracted soy commodity chains, food regime scholars seem to be very optimistic about a fundamental transition to a socially and environmentally sustainable regime.[58] In-depth case studies suggest more pessimism, however, since these counter-forces run the danger of being overridden by well-established political and corporate powers, as revealed for instance by the struggles over transgenic soy in Argentina.[59] The degree to which the global boom of capitalist soy farming and its severe social and environmental burden over past decades can be countered by forces envisioning a more sustainable future remains to be seen.

## Bibliography

Adams, Jane. *The Transformation of Rural Life. Southern Illinois, 1890–1990* (Chapel Hill and London: University of North Carolina Press, 1994).

Allen, Douglas W., and Dean Lueck. "Agricultural Contracts," in Claude Ménard and Mary M. Shirley (eds), *Handbook of New Institutional Economics* (Berlin and Heidelberg: Springer, 2008), pp. 465–490.

Anderson, Joseph Leslie. *Industrializing the Corn Belt: Agriculture, Technology, and Environment, 1945–1972* (DeKalb, Illinois: Northern Illinois University Press, 2009).

58 See McMichael, *Food Regimes and Agrarian Questions*, pp. 131–156.
59 See Lapegna, *Soybeans and Power*.

Bair, Jennifer (ed.), *Frontiers of Commodity Chain Research* (Stanford, California: Stanford University Press, 2009).

Baletti, Brenda. "Ordenamento Territorial. Neo-developmentalism and the Struggle for Territory in the Lower Brazilian Amazon," *Journal of Peasant Studies*, 39, 2 (2012), pp. 573–598.

Barbier, Edward. *Scarcity and Frontiers: How Economies Have Developed Through Natural Resource Exploitation* (Cambridge: Cambridge University Press, 2011).

Cáceres, Daniel M. "Accumulation by Dispossession and Socio-Environmental Conflicts Caused by the Expansion of Agribusiness in Argentina," *Journal of Agrarian Change*, 15, 1 (2015), pp. 116–147.

Carlson, Jon D. "Broadening and Deepening. Systemic Expansion, Incorporation and the Zone of Ignorance," *Journal of World-Systems Research*, 7, 2 (2001), pp. 225–263.

Carstensen, Lisa. " 'Modern Slave Labor' in Brazil at the Intersection of Production, Migration and Resistance Networks," in Marcel van der Linden and Magaly Rodríguez García (eds), *On Coerced Labor. Work and Compulsion after Chattel Slavery* (Leiden, Boston: Brill, 2016), pp. 267–290.

Chao, Kang. *The Economic Development of Manchuria: The Rise of a Frontier Economy* (Ann Arbor, Michigan: University of Michigan Press, 1982).

Clay, Jason W. *World Agriculture and the Environment: A Commodity-by-commodity Guide to Impacts and Practices* (Washington, DC: Island Press, 2010).

Costa, Patricía Trindade Maranhão. *Fighting Forced Labour: The Example of Brazil* (Geneva: International Labour Office, 2009).

de Sousa, Ivan Sergio Freire, and Lawrence Busch. "Networks and Agricultural Development. The Case of Soyhean Production and Consumption in Brazil," *Rural Sociology*, 63, 3 (1998), pp. 349–371.

de Sousa, Ivan Sergio Freire, and Rita de Cássia Milagres Teixera Vieira. "Soybeans and Soyfoods in Brazil, with Notes on Argentina. Sketch of an Expanding World Commodity," in Christine M. Du Bois, Chee-Beng Tan, and Sidney Mintz (eds), *The World of Soy* (Urbana: University of Illinois Press, 2008), pp. 234–256.

de Sousa, Ivan Sergio Freire, and Christine M. Du Bois. "Genetically Engineered Soy," in Christine M. Du Bois, Chee-Beng Tan, and Sidney Mintz (eds), *The World of Soy* (Urbana: University of Illinois Press, 2008), pp. 74–96.

Deasy, G. F. "The Soya Bean in Manchuria," *Economic Geography*, 15, 3 (1939), pp. 303–310.

Du Bois, Christine M., "Social Context and Diet. Changing Soy Production and Consumption in the United States," in Christine M. Du Bois, Chee-Beng Tan, and Sidney Mintz (eds), *The World of Soy* (Urbana: University of Illinois Press, 2008), pp. 208–233.

Du Bois, Christine M. *The Story of Soy* (London: Reaktion Books, 2018).

Du Bois, Christine M., and Sidney Mintz. "Soy," in Solomon H. Katz (ed.), *Encyclopedia of Food and Culture*. Volume 3 (New York: Scribner, 2003), pp. 322–326.

FAO (Food and Agriculture Organization). FAOSTAT, online available at: http://www.fao.org/faostat/en; last accessed: September 1, 2018.

Garrett, Rachael D. and Lisa L. Rausch. "Green for Gold: Social and Ecological Tradeoffs Influencing the Sustainability of the Brazilian Soy Industry," *The Journal of Peasant Studies*, 43, 2 (2016), pp. 461–493.

Gottschang, Thomas R. "Economic Change, Disasters, and Migration. The Historical Case of Manchuria," *Economic Development and Cultural Change*, 35, 3 (1987), pp. 461–490.

Gottschang, Thomas R., and Diana Lary. *Swallows and Settlers: The Great Migration from North China to Manchuria* (Ann Arbor, Michigan: University of Michigan, 2000).

Hall, Thomas D. "Puzzles in the Comparative Study of Frontiers. Problems, Some Solutions, and Methodological Implications," *Journal of World-Systems Research*, 15, 1 (2009), pp. 25–47.

Harnoncourt, Julia. *Unfreie Arbeit. Trabalho escravo in der brasilianischen Landwirtschaft* (Vienna: Promedia, 2018).

Haystead, Ladd, and Gilbert C. Fite. *The Agricultural Regions of the United States* (London: Methuen & Co., 1955).

Hopkins, Terence K., and Immanuel Wallerstein. "Commodity Chains in the World-Economy Prior to 1800," *Review: A Journal of the Fernand Braudel Center*, 10, 1 (1986), pp. 157–170.

Huang, H. T. "Early Uses of Soybeans in Chinese History," in Christine M. Du Bois, Chee-Beng Tan, and Sidney Mintz (eds), *The World of Soy* (Urbana: University of Illinois Press, 2008), pp. 45–55.

Hudson, John C. *Making the Corn Belt: A Geographical History of Middle-Western Agriculture* (Bloomington, Indiana: Indiana University Press, 1994).

IBGE (Instituto Brasileiro de Geografia e Estatística). *Censo Agropecuário 2006* (Rio de Janeiro: IBGE, 2012).

Imperial Maritime Customs. *The Soya Bean of Manchuria* (Shanghai: Inspectorate General of Customs, 1911).

International Harvester Company. *Soybeans for Farm and Industry*, 1935, Wisconsin Historical Society, International Harvester Company Film Collection, AC 741, online available at: http://archive.org/details/0914_Soybeans_for_Farm_and_Industry_00_21_44_29 (1.10.2019).

Komlosy, Andrea. "Kapitalismus als frontier. Die Verwandlung von Kulturen in Rohstofflieferanten," in Karin Fischer, Johannes Jäger, and Lukas Schmidt (eds), *Rohstoffe und Entwicklung. Aktuelle Auseinandersetzungen im historischen Kontext* (Vienna: New Academic Press, 2016), pp. 36–51.

Langenberg, Johannes. *Die Bedeutung der Sojabohne in der Weltwirtschaft*, Inaugural-Dissertation zur Erlangung der Doktorwürde der Wirtschafts- und Sozialwissenschaftlichen Fakultät der Universität Köln, 1929.

Langthaler, Ernst. "Gemüse oder Ölfrucht? Die Weltkarriere der Sojabohne im 20. Jahrhundert," in Cornelia Reiher and Sarah Ruth Sippel (eds), *Umkämpftes Essen. Produktion, Handel und Konsum von Lebensmitteln in globalen Kontexten* (Göttingen: Vandenhoeck & Ruprecht, 2015), pp. 41–66.

Langthaler, Ernst. "The Soy Paradox. The Western Nutrition Transition Revisited, 1950–2010," *Global Environment*, 11, 1 (2018), pp. 79–104.

Lapegna, Pablo. *Soybeans and Power: Genetically Modified Crops, Environmental Politics, and Social Movements in Argentina* (Oxford: Oxford University Press, 2016).

Loomis, R. S., D. J. Connor, and Kenneth G. Cassman. *Crop Ecology: Productivity and Management in Agricultural Systems* (Cambridge: Cambridge University Press, 2011).

McMichael, Philip. *Food Regimes and Agrarian Questions* (Rugby: Practical Action Publishing, 2013).

Moore, Jason W. "Sugar and the Expansion of the Early Modern World-Economy. Commodity Frontiers, Ecological Transformation, and Industrialization," *Review: A Journal of the Fernand Braudel Center*, 23, 3 (2000), pp. 409–433.

Moore, Jason W. *Capitalism in the Web of Life: Ecology and the Accumulation of Capital* (London, New York: Verso, 2015).

Ofstehage, Andrew. " 'Farming is Easy, Becoming Brazilian is Hard. North American Soy Farmers' Social Values of Production, Work and Land in Soylandia," *The Journal of Peasant Studies*, 43, 2 (2015), pp. 442–460.

Patel, Raj. *Stuffed and Starved: Markets, Power and the Hidden Battle for the World Food System* (London: Portobello Books, 2008).

Pérez, Mamerto, Timothy A. Wise, and Sergio Schlesinger (eds), *The Promise and the Perils of Agricultural Trade Liberalization: Lessons from Latin America* (Washington DC and Medford, MA: Washington Office on Latin America and Global Development and Environment Institute, 2008).

Prodöhl, Ines. "Die Dynamiken globaler Vernetzung. Mandschurische Sojabohnen auf dem Weltmarkt," *Zeitschrift für Agrargeschichte und Agrarsoziologie*, 61 (2013), pp. 75–89.

Prodöhl, Ines. "From Dinner to Dynamite. Fats and Oils in Wartime America," *Global Food History*, 2, 1 (2016), pp. 31–50.

Reardon-Anderson, James. "Land Use and Society in Manchuria and Inner Mongolia during the Qing Dynasty," *Environmental History*, 5, 4 (2000), pp. 503–530.

Reardon-Anderson, James. *Reluctant Pioneers: China's Expansion Northward, 1644–1937* (Stanford, California: Stanford University Press, 2005).

Robles, Wilder, and Henry Veltmeyer. *The Politics of Agrarian Reform in Brazil: The Landless Rural Workers Movement* (New York, NY: Palgrave Macmillan, 2015).

Schönardie, Paulo Alfredo. *Bäuerliche Landwirtschaft im Süden Brasiliens: Historische, theoretische und empirische Studie zu Ernährungssouveränität, Modernisierung, Wiederbelebung und Staatsfunktion* (München: Oekom Verlag, 2013).

Sorosiak, Thomas, "Soybean," in Kenneth F. Kiple and Kriemhild Coneè Ornelas (eds), *The Cambridge World History of Food.* Volume 1 (Cambridge: Cambridge University Press, 2000), pp. 422–427.

Soskin, A. B. *Non-Traditional Agriculture and Economic Development: The Brazilian Soybean Expansion, 1964–1982* (New York: Praeger, 1988).

Stewart, John R. "The Soya Bean and Manchuria", *Far Eastern Survey* 5, 21 (1936), pp. 221–226.

Sun, K. C. *The Economic Development of Manchuria in the First Half of the Twentieth Century* (Harvard, MA: Harvard University Press, 1969).

Turner, Frederick Jackson. *The Frontier in American History* (Newburyport: Dover Publications, 2012).

Turzi, Mariano. *The Political Economy of Agricultural Booms: Managing Soybean Production in Argentina, Brazil, and Paraguay* (Cham: Palgrave Macmillan, 2017).

US Bureau of the Census. *Census of Agriculture 1964 – Iowa* (Washington, DC: US Government Printing Office, 1967).

USDA (US Department of Agriculture). National Agricultural Statistics Service, online available at: https://www.nass.usda.gov; last accessed on September 1, 2018.

van der Ploeg, Jan Douwe. *The New Peasantries: Struggles for Autonomy and Sustainability in an Era of Empire and Globalization* (London: Earthscan, 2009).

van Gelder, Jan Willem, and Jan Maarten Dros. *Corporate Actors in the South American Soy Production Chain* (Castricum, Amsterdam, 2002).

Vorley, Bill. Food, Inc.: *Corporate Concentration from Farm to Consumer* (London: International Institute for Environment and Development, 2003).

Warnken, Philip F. *The Development and Growth of the Soybean Industry in Brazil* (Ames: Iowa State Univ. Press, 1999).

CHAPTER 4

# Who's Upgrading? Class Differentiation and Labor Relations in Argentinian Agribusiness

*Christin Bernhold*

*Together we add value.* This is a catchphrase of Amplio,[1] one of the leading agribusiness groups in Argentina. The company refers to itself as the nucleus of an innovative and knowledge-based network of partners who act collectively. Its president, Santiago, is a figurehead in this South American country for having restructured its agriculture from a system based on family farming to a highly technologized, network-like industry, and for carrying out investments all along the value chain, from raw material production to commercialization, (bio)technology development, service provision, and industrial processing. Amplio's agro-industrial chain development mirrors the dominant understanding of grain production and processing in Argentina. According to the governmental Agribusiness Strategic Plan 2010–2020 (PEA), for instance, the vitality of farming is based on "a complex network of agents connected to each other by a variety of contracts,"[2] and value added in situ stretches along the whole value chain and provides the possibility of "boosting the (…) development of our country."[3]

Undeniably, agriculture in Argentina's farming heartland (the Pampean region) has undergone far-reaching changes throughout the past decades. The soy industry in particular has grown in significance. Principally exported as animal feed, soy production has more than quintupled to 58.8 million tons between 1990 and 2016, whereas the area under cultivation has quadrupled to nearly 20 million ha in the same period.[4] The oilseed and its derivatives alone accounted for 30 percent of all exports leaving the country in 2016, compared

1 The names of companies and persons referred to in this chapter are pseudonyms; the author translated all interview-quotes from Spanish.

2 MAGyP, *Argentina Agribusiness*, p. 43.

3 *Ibid.*, p. 65.

4 Own calculations, based on FAOSTAT, available at: <http://www.fao.org/faostat/en/#data>; last accessed October 9, 2017. Soy is highlighted here, because it is the emblematic commodity in Argentinian agribusiness. Yet the analyzed relations of production also apply for other grains.

 | DOI:10.1163/9789004448049_005

to 15 percent in 2000.[5] As regards the processing industry, Argentina has become the world's top exporter of soybean oil and meal.[6]

These developments can be interpreted as a successful example of upgrading, as it is generally defined by global value chain (GVC) scholars. A common definition of various forms of upgrading includes:

> *process upgrading*, which transforms inputs into outputs more efficiently by reorganizing the production system or introducing superior technology; *product upgrading*, or moving into more sophisticated product lines; *functional upgrading*, which entails acquiring new functions (…) to increase the overall skill content of the activities; and *chain* or *inter-sectoral upgrading*, where firms move into new but often related industries.[7]

The overall argument is that firms or regions shift to higher profit activities "within or between industries through organizational learning facilitated by networks."[8] In Argentina, it is not only the global competitiveness of the processing industry that provides an example of upgrading as defined by mainstream GVC scholars. As I will show in detail below, this also applies to organizational changes and productivity gains within primary production.

In contrast to the origins of chain research in a critical world-systems perspective (see Komlosy in this volume), much of today's literature concentrates on upgrading as a "new paradigm for development."[9] Particularly policy-oriented studies increasingly regard upgrading as a tool for enhancing the economic situation of firms and the social situation of workers. This inheres the implicit assumption that social problems are inherited by underdevelopment from the past and can be remedied by economic modernization. In a similar vein, Argentinian scholars have argued that agro-industrial chain development has the potential to spawn a globally competitive industry based on domestic value added, and to create jobs.[10] Business actors, for example the Argentinian Soy Chain Association (ACSOJA) and its pendant for wheat, ArgenTrigo, have also taken up the value chain metaphor. They have argued that a capital-driven development of (organizational) processes and technologies has created high

5 Own calculations, based on UN Comtrade, available at: <https://comtrade.un.org/data>; last accessed 16 November, 2017.

6 USDA, *Oilseeds*, p. 13.

7 Gereffi et al., *Skills for Upgrading*, p. 4.

8 Werner, "Beyond upgrading," p. 403.

9 Gereffi and Fernandez-Stark, *Global Value Chain*, p. 24; for a critique see Werner et al., "Linking Up."

10 Anlló et al., *Cambios estructurales*; Llach et al., *La generación*.

quality employment along the grain chains and eventually led to the replacement of pre-modern agriculture by modern production to the benefit of all actors involved.[11]

Based on a case study, this chapter challenges the idea that firm-level upgrading leads to a rising tide that lifts all boats; companies can upgrade to core-activities without improving the conditions for achieving social equality in situ. I do not dispute that (social) upgrading is possible. Rather, I propose to take a closer look at processes on the ground and to analyze class dynamics and labor relations to understand how, why, and for whom economic upgrading may entail benefits and for whom it merely brings different forms of exploitation. To this end, I focus on the interplay of upgrading strategies in a production network controlled by Amplio and the concurrent shaping of class relations. I show how capital has reorganized the labor process and the combination of means of production and labor power in agriculture, and how these developments have been accompanied by a process of class differentiation to the benefit of capital. In particular, the relations between Amplio, intermediate classes and qualified labor tend to be concealed as co-equal network-partnership, whereas poorly paid, physical, rural labor is outsourced to labor contractors. The company's upgrading strategies and the corresponding organization of the labor process rely essentially on a perpetuation of exploitative class relations – not *despite*, but in the wake of upgrading.

My analysis draws from in-depth interviews with representatives of Amplio, petty capitalist partners –including labor service providers–, and unionists conducted in Argentina between 2014 and 2016. Additionally, it uses data provided by the Argentine National Statistics Institute (INDEC) and the Ministry of Labor (MTEySS).

## 1 Commodity Chains, Class and Labor

A rich body of literature critically discusses the impacts of capital-led agrarian change in Argentina. Topics include violent displacements, environmental and health effects,[12] economic concentration, as well as the growing influence of finance capital and large agribusiness corporations in primary production, reinforced by state politics.[13] Importantly for this chapter, scholars have also

11 Interviews with different agribusiness associations, 2016.

12 Cáceres, "Accumulation"; GER, "Desalojos"; Lapegna, "The Expansion"; Leguizamón, "Modifying Argentina"; Pengue, "Transgenic Crops."

13 Fernández, "Sojización"; Gras and Sosa Varotti, "megaempresas agropecuarias."

analyzed job losses in an increasingly capital-intensive agriculture, and pointed to the growing relevance of poorly paid temporary and subcontracted rural labor.[14] Yet these debates have been evolving largely independent of chain and network discourses.

Globally, scholars have formulated sound criticism of the GVC framework, among other things for its neglect of labor relations and the treatment of labor as a mere input factor. Selwyn and Campling, for example, have recently pointed to the need to conceptualize exploitation, and to take property relations and class dynamics into account more generally.[15] In this light, studies have questioned GVC scholars' often all too optimistic beliefs in companies or states as providers of social upgrading,[16] which tend to neglect both capitalist imperatives of profit-maximization[17] and the problem that workers cannot "simply impose their demands on capital without the latter responding in kind."[18] To address these limitations, studies have proposed to pay greater attention to the shaping of capital-labor relations.[19] This would require elucidating shifting patterns of exploitation that accompany firm's strategies, but also showing which conditions are possibly influenced by labor.[20]

The present chapter ties into these discussions. I agree that class relations "are constitutive of development processes and central to understanding inequality."[21] In addition, I suggest that a class analytical perspective[22] can enrich commodity chain research as a tool for analyzing not only capital-labor relations but also intra-capital relations and the role of intermediate classes in commodity chains. The sometimes complex ways in which means of production and labor power are combined in production networks –not necessarily under the roof of single capitals– can play an important role in capital's strategies for gaining power.

---

14 Neiman, "Los estudios"; Villulla, *Las cosechas*.

15 Selwyn, *Workers, state and development*; Campling et al., "Class dynamics."

16 Studies have defined social upgrading as improvements in labor conditions, gender equality, wages, economic security, and other benefits of workers in GVC s, including their right to organizing. See, Barrientos et al., "Economic and social upgrading"; Milberg and Winkler, "Economic and social upgrading."

17 Taylor et al., "Putting Labour in its Place," p. 12.

18 Selwyn, *Workers, state and development*, p. 7; Anner, "Social downgrading," p.154.

19 Bair and Werner, "Global Production," p. 131; Smith et al., „Networks," p. 42.

20 Werner, "Beyond Upgrading," p. 403; Selwyn, "Social upgrading"; Selwyn, "The struggle"; Taylor et al., "Putting Labour in its Place."

21 Campling et al., "Class dynamics," p. 1745.

22 See for example, PKA, *Materialien*. For this chapter, Bernstein's work on class differentiation in agriculture is helpful: Bernstein, *Class Dynamics*.

Drawing on Marx's *Capital*, I thus begin with the assumption that the valorization of value is *necessarily* based on social relations of exploitation. Marx argued that value is a social characteristic attributed to commodities when they are exchanged and therefore are implicitly related to each other as equals. Importantly, however, value production is not only characterized by market, but also by *class* relations. From a Marxist perspective, class is, thus, a relational concept. It defines actors' positions in the social relations of production (their control over the means of production), and concurrently in the distribution of the produced value.[23] In capitalism, the relations of production are aligned for continuous accumulation, based on the appropriation of surplus value. The latter is defined by the value produced in the labor time that exceeds the working hours socially necessary to secure a worker's reproduction. (However, the value of the labor power is historically and geographically specific – a question of class struggle.)

Compared to this view, mainstream GVC scholarship tends to reduce value added to money capture *between* capitals,[24] and to understand surplus value as arising from returns on innovation or from "barriers to entry (that is, scarcity)."[25] In other words, differentials among firms in commodity chains result from an unequal exchange based on power and entry barriers. Although this is not wrong, what gets lost here is that the uneven relations between actors in commodity chains are not merely exchange- but also class relations.

Importantly, capitalist production and circulation is a dynamic process, and development in time and space includes changing forms of class differentiation. Clearly for Marx and Engels, "similarity of reproduction – the repetition of reproduction under the same conditions does not exist. Productivity itself changes and changes the conditions [of production]."[26] This means that systematic efforts to increase the extraction of surplus value, driven by competition among capitals, include ongoing qualitative transformations of production systems[27] through the development of the productive forces. In this context, Marx has comprehensively analyzed, how the growing relevance

23 Carchedi, "Classes," p. 117; Campling et al., "Class dynamics," p. 1746; Bernstein, *Class dynamics*, p. 101.
24 Quentin and Campling, "Global Inequality," p. 36.
25 Kaplinsky, "Globalisation," p. 122.
26 Marx, *Theories of surplus value*.
27 Altvater, "Wertgesetz," p. 149; Selwyn, *Workers, state and development*, pp. 23 ff.; In the words of the communist manifesto, "[t]he bourgeoisie cannot exist without constantly revolutionizing the instruments of production, and thereby the relations of production, and with them the whole relations of society." Marx and Engels, *Manifesto of the Communist Party*.

of constant capital inherently entails a tendency towards the concentration and centralization of capital. But the development of the productive forces, as well as constant struggles over production also imply changing forms of the *organization* of production, including the ways in which capitals, intermediate classes, and labor are related to one another (and labor power and means of production are combined in production networks).

As for changing social relations in capitalist agriculture, Henry Bernstein has convincingly argued that, rather than assuming an ever-ongoing existence of farmers as a homogenous social group, research should analyze the class dynamics of agrarian change.[28]

In my case, these dynamics have brought forth a social structure that is not easy to see through. First, capitals of different scales, functions, and forms of appropriating surplus value[29] within the analyzed productive network are related to one another in a complex way. Second, there are intermediate actors, including a diverse class of petty capitalist producers,[30] who (depending on the amount of capital they possess) may be either emergent capitalists or hardly able to bear the costs of capitalist farming and thus rather resemble remunerated service providers. The social boundaries to qualified labor may also be fluid. Notably, the role of managers is important in this instance. Depending on their specific functions, they can be qualified workers or solely direct representatives of capital.[31] Third, the diverse forms of organizing capitalist production include socioeconomic, historical/spatial, and work process-related differentiations among the exploited. For instance, this concerns the inclusion in the reproduction of capital as qualified or unqualified workers, unequal salaries and working conditions, social and spatial segmentation,[32] and the degree of oppression and informality.[33]

In sum, capitalist development is essentially based on the exploitation of labor. Concurrently, it implies diverse and at times complex ways of relating class representatives to one another in production and circulation. However, since capital is a social and not a natural relation, the actual historical and

28 Bernstein, *Class Dynamics*, p. 4. Such an account needs to exit the logic of juxtaposing agriculture and industry. See also the special issue "The Political Economy of Agrarian Change", edited by Campling and Lerche.

29 This regards productive capital, which makes industrial profits, and capitals that participate thereof in form of interest or ground rent, or as commercial capital; PKA, *Materialien*, pp. 180 ff.

30 *Ibid.*, p. 177; Bernstein, *Class dynamics*, p. 103.

31 Marx, *Theories of surplus value*.

32 Campling et al., "Class dynamics," p. 1752.

33 Werner, *Global Displacements*.

geographical outcomes of these tendencies essentially depend on how firms organize the labor process, and on whether or how such strategies are resisted. Yet inequality and exploitation are not *automatically* followed by resistance. In line with Gramsci's concept of (active or passive) consensus,[34] social groups and classes may also cooperate in the reproduction of existing structures of exploitation and domination, or at least not oppose them. In this chapter, I show how the class dynamics of upgrading Argentinian agribusiness are organized in a way that facilitates a harmonious appearance of production as a collective effort by partners: *Together we add value*.

## 2 Upgrading Pampean Agriculture

A much-discussed issue in Argentina is the decreasing viability of so-called *chacareros*, a romanticized figure that dominated the Pampean agriculture until the late twentieth century. *Chacareros* have been described as traditional farmers, characterized by a confluence of landownership, the possession of means of production, and a strong participation of family labor in direct production for both the market and subsistence.[35] Their existence was tightly connected to a series of state regulations, including price control mechanisms.[36] The Pampean agro-industry has changed profoundly during the past several decades. This happened in the context of neoliberal transformations of the Argentinian political economy, and of a concurrently increasing orientation towards agro-industrial exports, and was connected to growing (transnational) finance capital interests in investing in soy production.[37] Among these changes are the development of the productive forces including a massive incorporation of the latest agricultural software technology and machinery, no-till farming, and, above all, bioengineering, accompanied by an enormous expenditure of agro-toxics. This not only massively increased labor productivity, but also the resulting necessity to increasingly invest in constant capital. One result is the profitability of primary production only on large scales, which has led to a process of capital concentration.[38]

34 Gramsci, *Gefängnishefte*, p. 411.
35 Archetti and Stölen, *Explotación familiar*; Balsa, *El desvanecimiento*.
36 Giarracca and Teubal, "Del desarrollo."
37 Gras and Hernández, "El modelo agribusiness," pp. 20–22.
38 For a detailed empirical account of capital concentration in the Pampean agriculture, see Fernández, "Sojización."

In the past years, there have been a few large corporations in the country producing on 200,000 ha or more, including Amplio.[39] Assuming the GVC-understanding of upgrading as defined above, this development of the productive forces can be considered as process upgrading via the introduction of new technologies that leads to a better economic performance, and, as mentioned above, to a high international market participation. In line with this shift, companies like Amplio have also increased their efficiency by reorganizing the production system. More precisely, the ways in which the labor process is organized have changed and tasks in the agro-industrial commodity chains have been rearranged. This includes the fact that today, Amplio and similar companies in Argentina do not own large parts of the constant capital and of the land necessary for primary production. Rather, in what Amplio calls its network, the firm leases land short-term, often from former *chacareros*, and outsources physical rural labor to *contratistas*, the local name for labor contractors. In Pampean grain production, most of them are petty capitalist producers who, according to Marxist class analysis, own means of production but also participate in the productive labor process.[40] However, the diversity within the class of petty capitalists in some cases makes it difficult to empirically differentiate them from remunerated service sellers, since they may own a firm and employ workers, or rather just own some tools and mainly work self-exploitatively. It is broadly considered that the lower an actor is positioned in this hierarchical order, the more she/he resembles a salaried service provider.[41]

With these differences, the degree of domination and subordination exercised by capital may also change. The Pampean *contratistas* normally own one or two machines, hire wageworkers, and work themselves in order to sell sowing, fumigation, harvesting or transport services. By subcontracting labor to them, large firms manage to control primary production without having to sink too much capital in land and machinery and without having equity relations of any kind with the *contratistas*. The strategy of outsourcing labor to *contratistas* had already been adopted in the 1970s. Yet during the 1990s, it started to gain more importance in Argentinian agribusiness (see the analysis of rural labor below). Many of these labor contractors used to be *chacareros* who owned the means of production for crop production.

---

39 Apart from primary production, agro-industrial development in Argentina also entails an outstanding market power of highly monopolized seed, agrochemical and trading companies. See Gras and Hernandez, "El modelo agribusiness."

40 PKA, *Materialien*, p. 177; Bernstein, *Class Dynamics*, p. 103.

41 PKA, *Materialien*, p. 269.

For production in today's scales, they instead only have the capital to invest in some machinery and to be included in the production process in a more complex way.

Hence, some of the actors who have been driven out of the market as independent farmers have now become rentiers or *contratistas*.[42] Others started producing in association with companies like Amplio. There are many variants of these associations. For example, they can be established with former *chacareros* who contribute land and a part of the necessary labor power (but do not have further capital to invest), while Amplio provides seeds, agrochemicals, and agricultural consulting services, while someone else is assigned as the production manager, and so on. In the end, all associates receive a share of the harvest agreed upon beforehand. The company thus ensures that a part of the labor process and the accompanying risk entailed by agriculture production is outsourced to associates that are often petty capitalists: "I mean, this way it does not happen that you lease land and put the labor and the inputs and then when the harvest isn't good it goes wrong only for you."[43] In such a context, management tasks and different services have become increasingly important and a centerpiece of Amplio's upgrading strategies, as I will show in the next section.

Overall, we can say that in the case of Argentinian agribusiness, process upgrading and capital concentration at the point of primary production have not necessarily led to a simultaneous concentration of the labor process under the roof of single capitals. Rather, we can observe the simultaneity of cooperation (necessary for production on large scales without capital having to own the majority of land and machinery) and individual capital's strategy to compete for the produced surplus value.[44] It is in this context that Amplio has managed to upgrade not only primary production, but also to accumulate capital to a degree that allows the firm to invest in several different activities in agro-industrial commodity chains. Besides process upgrading in primary production, Amplio has therewith been able to upgrade its products and functions. As I will depict in the following, from a class analytical perspective, this also represents a diversification of capital functions within the company, which allows it to appropriate surplus value, produced by workers, at different points of production and circulation. Afterwards, I will take a

---

42 See also Craviotti and Gras, "De Desafiliaciones y Desligamientos."

43 Interview Emilia, Commercial Manager of Amplio, formally employed.

44 The fact that cooperation along GCCs does not necessarily take place under the auspices of a single firm has also been a key insight of the debate on global commodity chains as developed by Gereffi and Korzeniewicz, *Commodity chains*.

cutout of its network as an example, and look at how the particular labor process and social fabric has been constructed according to Amplio's accumulation interest.

## 3 Amplio: A Case of Upgrading and Capital Diversification

Capital is not only differentiated by the scale of production and by its competitive position. Capitals, too, have different functions and related forms of appropriating surplus value.[45] Productive capital appropriates industrial profits based on the production of surplus value. As interest bearing finance capital, commercial capital, or in the form of landownership (ground rent), capital is not involved in the creation of new value. Rather, it participates in and competes over the surplus value generated in production. In the wake of the outlined agribusiness development, Amplio has managed to diversify its investments in several branches, all related to agribusiness, both upstream and downstream, to represent all these forms of capital. Therefore, it acts across class-analytical differentiations: a strategy that avowedly enhanced its accumulation capacity by diversifying its possibilities of surplus capture. While it started as a family business in agriculture and storage some decades ago, throughout the past years, it has grown into a company with an annual turnover of more than a billion USD. Yet it does not employ more than 800 people directly (mainly office and industrial-processing workers), since according to Amplio president Santiago, accumulation works best with a knowledge-based network strategy. Describing his strategy as asset-light, Santiago has even compared his company to landless people. And yet in contrast to the latter, Amplio was able to invest an equivalent of around 450 million USD in 2015. Furthermore, while its primary production section has long been based on land leasing, the owner family possesses over 10,000 ha of land, which is rented out to the company.[46] Thus, while capital concentration in Pampean agribusiness works relatively independent of land ownership, it is not entirely separable.

In its function as productive capital, in addition to primary production, the group today has upgraded its products and functions e.g. by running wheat mills. It also produces seeds and agrochemicals and develops biotechnology and software for precision farming. Furthermore, Amplio sells various

---

45 PKA, *Materialien*, pp. 180 ff.

46 Interview with Emilia.

agro-related services. According to manager María, this amplification of activities was part of a strategy to lower risks.

> The margins [primary production] were narrowing, the business is not giving as we would like it to be, so I think that opening new roads to other services or other activities, I think that's a pretty clear vision. (…) the idea is to participate in all these chain links.[47]

According to company information, the share of primary production in its gross profits has actually decreased to only 9 percent in 2018 from 18 percent in previous years. In the 2009–10 season, the company produced grains and oilseeds on over 250,000 ha in Argentina and neighboring countries; in the 2015–16 season, it had gone back down to around 50,000 ha. After 2015, production went up again to around 100,000 ha. It is important for the company not to entirely withdraw from this division. Its whole business strategy is built around agriculture and its presence on the ground secures Amplio good contacts with clients. According to company managers, the commercial capital activities are currently the most profitable ones. In other words, as commercial capital, the company manages to appropriate a good share of the surplus originating in production. Besides storing crops and oilseeds, Amplio sells inputs such as seeds and agrochemicals, and it commercializes crops and oilseeds. Today, the company also functions as finance capital through a company-owned Reciprocal Guarantee Society (RGS). It provides bank guarantees against counter-guarantees and low interest. The hereby obtained bank receivables are used by the clients, for instance, to buy seeds or machinery. The RGS has a risk fund that today mainly consists of capital from Amplio's owner family. This capital is re-invested in other businesses: "[I]t generates a rent for the guarantors […] we buy bonds, shares, stock …"[48] Yet the main economic importance of the RGS still resides in its capacity to attract and maintain clients for the commercial section. RGS clients normally agree to buy inputs from and sell crops to the company, hence securing it the appropriation of an additional part of the produced surplus value. The diversity of Amplio's points of value capture encompasses the existence of relations with a myriad of actors.

The following analysis concentrates on tasks within the agro-industrial chain, which are more closely related to primary production, and on the respective actors and labor relations.

---

47 Interview María, Manager of Amplio's RGS, formally employed, 2016.

48 *Ibid.*

## 4 "You oversee your own things ..."

Amplio is connected to smaller capitals and many forms of petty capitalist producers who pursue different activities, produce on different scales and have different forms of income. The corresponding form of organizing production benefits big capital through a variety of mechanisms. This includes control over primary production without risky investments in constant capital, access to qualified labor without expensively including it in terms of permanent employment, and the outsourcing of rural labor. It also includes a close relationship to customers of the commercial section that secures loyalty and the appearance of this whole construct as a network of co-equal partners. Importantly, however, it is highly unlikely for the latter to climb the value chain the way Amplio did. All this is part of Amplio's upgrading basis, which I will now analyze by means of examples.

Some of the related actors can be analyzed as smaller capitalists who run farming businesses on their own and are related to Amplio mainly as clients, buying financial or other services, seeds and agrochemicals, or selling their crops to the company. This is the case, for instance, for Martina, who employs several workers, sells fumigation services to Amplio with her own aircraft, and controls production on 5,300 ha of leased land. Others do own land and/or some agriculture machinery but they produce exclusively in association with Amplio, or they sell services as *contratistas*. Mateo, for example, manages the belongings of his family, including 878 ha of land, which are constantly leased-out to Amplio. One ha in this zone may be worth several thousand USD today, and still – absurdly enough – this is not to say that Mateo's family owns the capital necessary for profitable *and* independent production. In addition to the rent income, they own some farming machinery and sell labor services to Amplio. They hire a salaried tractor driver.[49] Lorenzo more clearly adopts an intermediary position in the capital-labor relation. He sells fumigation services to Amplio with a machine he runs himself, since he does not have the capital to hire someone. In addition, he co-manages the production of crops on 200 ha of leased land. Thanks to his academic education, his job is agronomic consultancy.[50] Not being formally employed (he sells fumigation services to Amplio rather than his labor power), Lorenzo is an empiric example of the fluid boundaries between petty capitalists and salaried service providers. Yet while most of the work he does is for Amplio and while he could not

49 Interview with Mateo, lessor and *contratista*, 2016.

50 Interview with Lorenzo, petty commodity producer and *contratista*, 2016.

raise the capital necessary to produce independently, he explicitly perceives himself as a partner, though one without future prospects that resemble those of Amplio. All of these actors are clients of Amplio's RGS. But the differences among them clearly affect the degree of influence exercised by the company. In the case of actors like Lorenzo, self-exploitation entangles with being directed by capital, and his de facto independence is quite narrow. However, despite class differences among them, all these actors consider themselves network-partners.[51]

With regard to relations of qualified labor, it is worth taking a closer look at those actors who are included as managers, yet often without being directly employed by the company. Only some of them (in the case of my interviewees María and Emilia) have a formal employment contract. Instead of being paid a fixed salary, others receive forms of wages, which tend to mystify the labor relation, such as a previously determined share of the harvest.[52] Thus, necessary labor time is only paid insofar as it is successfully embodied in a commodity. One example is Felipe, who does not only sell transport services to Amplio, but also works as a sales manager. He charges a commission for the crops he buys for the company and for the inputs he sells. Similarly, Germán, production manager, charges the company a previously fixed part of the harvest for providing it with land for lease. As he describes, "I am part of the staff but [...] I am not waged; I get a percentage of the production [...] I'm outside the company and inside the company."[53]

Germán is financed by the RGS. He uses this financial service to advance the leases for the land on which Amplio controls production. He considers himself a managing partner (though without possessing capital) rather than a waged qualified worker, since he co-invests, even though this is only made possible through the RGS. Amplio, in turn, benefits from the accumulation process without having to advance capital in the lease of land, and even earns interest via the RGS. Germán also has a younger partner, Pedro, who helps him manage production, even though these two do not have any formal labor relation either. Pedro, therefore, considers that "we are all part of the business."[54] Thus, Amplio avoids fixed salaries for qualified labor and diminishes the risk

51 Elsewhere, we have analyzed more in depth how Amplio manages to unequally benefit from these relations and how this fosters concentration tendencies. Bernhold and Palmisano, "Relaciones sociales."

52 Compare Marx's analysis of piece wages: *Capital*, pp. 692 ff.

53 Interview with Germán, local manager of Amplio's agriculture production, no formal employment.

54 Interview with Pedro, Germán's colleague, no formal employment.

of having to pay it if the harvest is bad. Furthermore, the firm keeps the flexibility to spontaneously decide over the quantity of hectares to produce on in function of commodity prices, without having a fixed staff. Importantly for consensus-building, in times of good harvests, this particular relation between capital and qualified labor also increases the material concessions received by actors like Germán. Here, the win-win discourse has some truth in it. However, the well-being of its associates is also in Amplio's economic interest; without solvent clients, it would lose its economic base as finance- and commercial capital. Or as Martina puts it:

> It is not useful to have partners who are crashing, whom you squeeze so much that the poor guy does not survive. [...] If we both win, the business relation sustains itself over time [...] because it benefits the business, not because you're good.[55]

Amplio's economic power is accompanied by cultural-ideological power. Many of my interviewees consider this network a "love-love partnership," despite obvious class differences.[56] This is not only due to material concessions, but also to Amplio president Santiago's capacity to generalize his ideas of network reciprocity. Santiago is often described as someone who helped my interviewees recapture the prospect of advancement after severe crises during the 1990s, as in the case of Felipe:

> [Santiago told me] I see that you want to progress. I won't employ you. Let's make a partnership. Bring me crops and I'll pay you a commission. You oversee your own things.[57]

Elsewhere, we have analyzed how these trajectories and ideological rationalizations, plus the fact that the technical managers are not 'merely' employed, but rather motivated to run their own business as partners, are among the reasons why they feel so committed to Amplio such that they even do some of the work without asking for remuneration.[58] As he is not a mere employee, Germán, for instance, considers some jobs that involve lengthy travel "like

55 Interview with Martina, local manager of Amplio's production, *contratista*, petty commodity producer.

56 Interview with Agustín, petty commodity producer.

57 Interview with Felipe, local manager of Amplio's agriculture production, no formal employment.

58 Bernhold and Palmisano, "Relaciones sociales."

participating in an NGO *ad honorem*". Others feel obliged to transfer a greater part of the produced value to the company than necessary.

> I told them that I was morally or ethically obliged to sell them my cereals. I could not take money [from the RGS] (...) and then go sell my cereals somewhere else. (...) You know, this does not seem right.[59]

The simultaneity of cooperation and competition – while Amplio concentrates capital, most of its partners remain in simple reproduction – and the strategy of organizing qualified labor keep a variety of actors from falling out of the system. Yet at the same time, it shapes their practices to Amplio's benefit. While these relations are fundamental to Amplio's accumulation strategies, the different actors mentioned tend to establish themselves within this status quo. Self-employed managers and petty capitalist producers like Germán are rather Amplio's allies (in the sense of a Gramscian consensus) than people likely to develop sympathies with struggles from below.

The following section focuses on the labor relations and conditions of those who do seeding, fumigating, or harvesting labor in the field. Since these tasks are outsourced, the respective workers are not directly related to Amplio. My focus here shifts to rural labor in Argentinian agribusiness more generally, on which Amplio's primary production section also relies.

## 5 (Scattered) Rural Wage Labor and Contratistas

In a book titled *Las cosechas son ajenas* ("The harvests are alien"), sociologist Juan Manuel Villulla explains how the class-based exploitation of rural workers is rendered invisible in hegemonic discourses, which describe modern agro-industries as "the countryside," where "producers" work together as partners.[60] This "invisibilization" is an expression of both actual labor relations and the refusal of the responsible union of rural workers (UATRE) to engage in class struggles, despite the fact that the salaries of rural laborers are particularly poor in national comparison, as will be discussed in the following. In fact, while workers in other Argentinian agriculture branches are rather combative,

59 Interview with Agustín.
60 Villulla, *Las cosechas son ajenas*, p. 2.

there have not been any organized labor disputes in grain production in the past decades.[61]

The first important aspect regarding rural labor is that census data provided by INDEC indicates a process of relative proletarianization in the Pampean region. The percentage of wage labor from all tasks (in agriculture, hunting, and forestry)[62] grew from 47 percent in 1990 to 59 percent in 2010, the remaining share consisting mainly of petty capitalist producers, family labor, and roughly 7 percent *patrones* (employers).[63] Clearly, a mayor part of the labor objectified in agriculture produce was and is growingly done by workers who do not own means of production and who produce a surplus value that does not remain in their own hands. This rural wage labor is directly linked to the strategy of outsourcing labor to *contratistas*.

In quantitative terms, data by the Ministry of Economy show that between the harvest season of 2001–2002 and that of 2013–2014 the number of hectares worked by *contratistas* grew by 58 percent to 24.4 million in the province of Buenos Aires, which is part of the Pampean heartland.[64] Critical voices have analyzed the outsourcing of rural labor to *contratistas* as a strategy of labor flexibilization that allows capital to reduce costs and risks.[65] Villulla, in particular, has looked at the implications for capital-labor relations and concludes that this form of brokering tends to conceal exploitation, for it defines capital and labor without them being in direct contact with one another.[66] Rather, the *contratistas*, mostly petty capitalists, appear as the direct exploiters. Meanwhile, companies like Amplio apparently only relate to *contratistas* as partners, hence facilitating a network-driven narrative in which accumulation is not based on the exploitation of labor power. Amplio can thus control the production process, without having to employ workers directly. Concurrently, the company avoids the risk of sinking capital in means of production with long amortization rates, as the *contratistas* are the ones who invest in the farming machinery. On this matter, Villulla and Chen have shown that the tariffs paid to *contratistas* for labor services over the past years have increased less than their

61 An in-depth analysis of absent organized labor struggles and UATRE's support of neoliberal politics is beyond the scope of this chapter. Readers may refer to Villulla, *Las cosejas*. The author also analyzes individual forms of workers' protest which, however, could not counter capital's strategies.
62 There is no way to further disaggregate census data.
63 Own calculations based on INDEC/National Census data.
64 See Bernhold and Palmisano, "Relaciones sociales."
65 Neiman, "Los estudios"; Quaranta, "Estructura ocupacional."
66 Villulla, "Intermediacion laboral," p. 65; Villulla, *Las cosechas*, pp. 68–74.

costs of increasingly expensive machinery.[67] Companies like Amplio, whose profits are based on agriculture (be it as industrial profit, rent, interest, or commercial profit) therefore benefit from productivity increases while its costs are outsourced. They shorten the turnover time of capital and release it for other kinds of investments. Secondly, capital thereby circumvents the problem in agriculture that production time exceeds the labor time (the labor process is paused during the plant's growth). Third, it does not have to pay labor in off seasons. Finally, this way, capital avoids being in direct contact with the workers and, hence, with potential conflicts, for instance, over salaries. Subcontracting thereby has "deleterious impacts on labor's terms and conditions and the exercise of effective agency,"[68] as it creates obstacles for workers to organizing. This concerns the analyzed way in which the specific social relations of agribusiness tend to conceal their exploitative character. Concurrently, in contrast to other industries, agribusiness workers are not only spatially scattered but also socially dispersed in terms of whom they work for. The fact that rural wageworkers are not directly related to the same capitalist, but rather work for petty capitalists, who are often personal acquaintances from the village, and with whom they share the physical work, further blurs class differences both objectively and subjectively.[69]

The development of the productive forces and the high level of mechanization in grain production have furthermore made parts of the labor process less physically demanding compared to other agriculture activities.[70] For instance, from the standpoint of immediate material conditions, working in a harvesting cabin or driving a tractor is more comfortable (but also more individualizing and isolating) than manual labor in horticulture. Yet working conditions comprise more than that. Countering the invisibilization of the direct producers, Villulla has offered an in-depth qualitative analysis of their conditions of life and labor on the fields. One of his findings is that mechanization has not shortened the working days of those who seed, fumigate, and harvest (see below). Furthermore, while the work in the field as such is monotonous, the rural

67 Villulla and Chen, "Costos y tarifas."

68 Taylor et al., "Putting labour in its place," p. 11. As Coe and Jordhus-Lier put it for other cases, labor contractors are not just neutral intermediaries: Coe and Jordhus Lier, "Constrained agency?", p. 226.

69 See Villulla, "Intermediación laboral," p. 74.

70 A description of working conditions that considers the various tasks of the entire production process is beyond the scope of this chapter. Suffice to say that while large parts of grain production are mechanized, there is still legwork done by workers who assist machinists and manual labor continues, for instance, in the production of hybrid seeds. See, Villulla, *Las cosechas son ajenas*, p. 140.

proletariat is required to be flexible in terms of territorial mobility, especially in the case of the transitory workers, who spend most of their time away from home during working seasons. Many of them report associated family problems and emotional effects. In addition, they are constantly exposed to glyphosate and other agrochemicals.[71]

A further important point is economic insecurity. Many rural workers are a part-time "reserve army." Data shows that the replacement of permanent jobs with transitional ones is a trend accompanying modernized agribusiness. According to a survey held by the MTEySS in 2014, only 44 percent of the surveyed rural wageworkers had permanent employment that year. It also reveals that permanent employment is rather related to those who have worked in agriculture for a long time. 57 percent of those who started working before 1990 declared that they have spent most of their working years in permanent jobs. Of those who started after 2014, only 27 percent have permanent contracts.[72] Accordingly, workers who started at the higher levels of upgrading agribusiness face the least stable conditions. Seasonal underemployment leads to a de facto competition among workers and further weakens their position to struggle for benefits that they themselves could gain from upgrading. Furthermore, rural labor is characterized by a high degree of informality. An article published by the Labor Ministry indicates that the rate of non-registered labor in crop and oilseed production was 66 percent in 2010.[73] Fittingly, according to the MTySS, only 44 percent of all surveyed workers' jobs included any form of social security. In the case of temporary workers, it was only 17 percent.

Salaries at the point of primary production are the lowest when compared nationally. For 2014, permanent workers declared an average *annual* net income equaling approximately 6,000 USD (January) or 4,600 USD (December) of that year. For temporary workers, the annual income equaled only 2,300 USD (January) or 1,800 USD (December).[74] In comparison, the minimum wage in Argentina was the equivalent of approximately 500–600 USD *per month* in 2014.

71 For a comprehensive analysis that includes many more aspects of rural working life in the Argentinian Pampa see Villulla, *Las cosechas*.

72 MTEySS, *Encuesta sobre empleo*, p. 12. The survey includes different agricultural activities (grain and fruit production, livestock, and forestry). It is not possible to disaggregate grain production. But the survey suggests that temporary labor is more important here than, for instance, in horticulture production.

73 Ohaco, "Precariedad," p. 82.

74 Author's own currency conversions, data based on MTEySS, *Encuesta sobre empleo*, pp. 20–24. The monthly changes are due to inflation.

Villulla points out that the seasonal wages of qualified machinists are above these averages and can range up to approximately 8,000 USD (or 5,000 USD in the case of tractor drivers).[75] However, he opposes a discourse maintained by agribusiness actors according to which their workers earn "very well."[76] Especially when considering hourly wages, Villulla argues, workers in the grain fields earn three times less than their colleagues in other industries. They do not necessarily earn poor seasonal wages in absolute figures, but their pay is measured by work units, not by time units. Eight-hour working days would not allow them to afford the basic family basket. In fact, they often spend three or more months on the road, work up to 16 hours per day, and are disposable around the clock.[77]

In contrast, workers and employees in the soy processing industry are highly organized, and – based on eight-hour working days – earned considerably better annual salaries, namely the equivalent of 16-25,000 USD in 2014, according to the responsible trade union.[78] However, the union emphasized that they fought to receive this. "Last year we were on strike for 25 days in a row," one of the secretaries stressed in an interview.[79]

While crop and oilseed production is, above all, seasonal work, the majority of rural workers have to manage to live with the outlined salaries all year long, since according to the MTEySS, "other branches of the local economy do not show dynamism or the capacity to create jobs."[80] Consequently, there is a huge dependency on the existing jobs.

## 6 Conclusion

Agro-industrial chain development in the Pampean region, including the organizational and technical development of the productive forces, has made the Argentina's grain production and processing industry competitive on a global scale. This chapter has argued, however, that a class analytical view of such upgrading processes can help shed light on whom they may benefit and for whom they rather entail a perpetuation of exploitation. Furthermore, an

75 Villulla, *Las cosechas*, p. 111, own currency conversion.

76 Villulla, *Pergamino, Iowa y los salarios*, p. 71.

77 *Ibid.*, pp. 74–83.

78 Author's own currency conversion, data available at: <http://www.federacionaceitera.com.ar/viejo/conveniosaceiteros.html>; last accessed 9 October 2017.

79 Interview with Daniel Yofra, 2016.

80 MTEySS, *Encuesta sobre empleo*, p.10.

analysis of how means of production and labor power are combined among capital, intermediate classes, and labor in the wake of upgrading helps explain how such strategies may serve capital, above all, rather than improving the conditions for achieving social equalization. To expand on this question, I have concentrated on network-upgrading strategies and investment diversification led by a case company named Amplio, as well as on the concurrent shaping of class structures. Here, I have focused on those parts of the commodity chain that are directly related to primary production. However, this includes chain links such as services and commercialization.

The way that relations between capital, intermediate classes, and labor are organized provides benefits, mainly to Amplio. Yet, it also provides intermediate actors with material concessions that tend to prevent them from calling the currently prevalent agribusiness model into question. Simultaneously, the way in which the labors of different actors involved are related to each other tends to conceal the class character of these relations beneath a mask of a co-equal network-partnership. In particular, the inclusion of qualified management workers as partners rather than as qualified salaried workers, as well as the organization of physical rural labor through *contratistas,* play a crucial role. In one of the most dynamic branches of the Argentinian economy, poor salaries and working conditions among rural wage workers are essential to the conditions of accumulation pushed by Amplio. In other words, the described labor relations are part of the basis upon which Amplio's upgrading strategies are built. They are thus not best interpreted as a remnant of pre-modern agriculture to be overcome through further upgrading. Rather, they are part of exploitative class relations that are essential to the success achieved by upgrading companies like Amplio. Even though the company does not employ poorly paid fumigators directly, for instance, they benefit from their low salaries and working conditions: "The less well remunerated productive workers are, the greater the surplus available for appropriation in the entire system."[81]

Capital's interest first and foremost lies in accumulation, not in national social development, and material concessions are made when profits are abounding and capital has an interest in making these concessions – or when they are fought for. In Argentina, those who are willing to struggle face severe (though along the commodity chain differing) challenges, which must be discussed elsewhere. At any rate, unionists in the soy processing industry have started to think about how to connect their struggles to the problems faced in primary production, and small farmers' organizations from outside the

81 Quentin and Campling, "Global inequality chains," p. 11.

Pampean region have started to think about how to find a connection to organized labor struggles. Hopefully, this is a start.

## Acknowledgments

I wish to acknowledge C. Stache, C. Parnreiter and the economic geography unit at the University of Zurich for their comments during the development of this chapter. Particular thanks are due to T. Palmisano and J. M. Villulla, who helped me with my work in Argentina. Generous funding from the UZH-*Forschungskredit* has allowed me to extend my research time.

## Bibliography

Altvater, Elmar. "Wertgesetz und Monopolmacht," in Wolfgang Fritz Haug (ed.), *Zur Theorie des Monopols. Staat und Monopole (I)*, Argument Sonderbände AS6 (Berlin: Argument, 1975), pp. 129–198.

Anlló, Guillermo, Roberto Bisang and Guillermo Salvatierra (eds). *Cambios estructurales en las actividades agropecuarias. De lo primario a las cadenas globales de valor* (Buenos Aires: CEPAL, 2010).

Anner, Mark. "Social Downgrading and Worker Resistance in Apparel Global Value Chains," in Kirsty Newsome et al. (eds.), *Putting Labour in its Place: Labour Process Analysis and Global Value Chains* (London: Palgrave, 2015), pp. 152–170.

Archetti, Eduardo and Kristi Stölen. *Explotación familiar y acumulación de capital en el campo argentino* (Buenos Aires: Siglo XXI Editores, 1975).

Bair, Jennifer and Marion Werner. "Global Production and Uneven Development: When Bringing Labour in isn't Enough," in Kirsty Newsome et al. (eds.), *Putting Labour in its Place: Labour Process Analysis and Global Value Chains* (London: Palgrave, 2015), pp. 119–134.

Balsa, Javier. *El desvanecimiento del mundo chacarero. Transformaciones sociales en la agricultura bonaerense: 1937–1988* (Bernal: Universidad de Quilmes, 2007).

Barrientos, Stefanie, Gary Gereffi and Arianna Rossi. "Economic and social upgrading in global production networks: A new paradigm for a changing world," *International Labour Review*, 150 (2011), pp. 319–340.

Bernhold, Christin and Tomás Palmisano. "Relaciones sociales, concentración de capital y construcción de consenso en el agronegocio. Un caso de estudio." *Revista Interdisciplinaria de Estudios Agrarios*, 46 (2017), pp. 105–140.

Bernstein, Henry. *Class Dynamics of Agrarian Change. Agrarian Change and Peasant Studies* (Halifax and Winnipeg: Fernwood Publishing, 2010).

Cáceres, Daniel. "Accumulation by Dispossession and Socio-Environmental Conflicts Caused by the Expansion of Agribusiness in Argentina," *Journal of Agrarian Change*, 15 (2015), pp. 116–147.

Campling, Liam et al. "Class dynamics of development: a methodological note," *Third World Quarterly*, 37 (2016), pp. 1745–1767.

Campling, Liam and Jens Lerche. "Introduction to the Special Issue The Political Economy of Agrarian Change: Essays in Appreciation of Henry Bernstein," *Journal of Agrarian Change*, 16 (2016), pp. 365–369.

Carchedi, Guglielmo. "Classes and Class Analysis," in Edgar Olin Wright et al. (eds.), *The Debate on Classes* (London and New York: Verso, 1998).

Coe, Neil and David Jordhus-Lier. "Constrained agency? Re-evaluating the geographies of labour," *Progress in Human Geography*, 35 (2011), pp. 211–233.

Craviotti, Carla and Carla Gras. "De Desafiliaciones y Desligamientos: Trayectorias de Productores Familiares Expulsados de la Produccion en la Region Pampeana Argentina," *Desarrollo Economico*, 181 (2006), pp. 117–134.

Fernández, Diego. "Sojización del sector agropecuario y concentración de la producción: una historia a partir de los números a nivel de empresa," in Gabriela Martínez Dougnac (ed.), *De especie exótica a monocultivo. Estudios sobre la expansión de la soja en Argentina* (Buenos Aires: Imago Mundi, 2013), pp. 211–241.

GER (Grupo de Estudios Rurales). "Desalojos y arrinconamientos de campesinos y comunidades indígenas en la Argentin," *Realidad Económica*, 203 (2004), pp. 111–120.

Gereffi, Gary and Miguel Korzeniewicz. *Commodity Chains and Global Capitalism* (Westport: Praeger, 1994).

Gereffi, Gary and Karina Fernandez-Stark. *Global Value Chain Analysis: A Primer* (Duke University, Center on Globalization, Governance & Competitiveness, 2016).

Gereffi, Gary, Karina Fernandez-Stark and Phil Psilos. *Skills for Upgrading. Workforce Development and Global Value Chains in Developing Countries* (Duke University, Center on Globalization, Governance & Competitiveness, 2011).

Giarracca, Norma and Miguel Teubal. "Del desarrollo agroindustrial a la expansión del 'agronegocio': el caso argentine," in Mançano Fernandes, B. (ed), *Campesinato e agronegócio na América Latina: a questão agraria atual* (São Paulo: Expressão Popular, 2008).

Gramsci, Antonio. *Gefängnishefte, Band 3* (Hamburg: Argument, 2012 [1975]).

Gras, Carla and Andrea Sosa Varrotti. "El modelo de negocios de las principales megaempresas agropecuarias," in Carla Gras and Valeria Hernández (eds), *El Agro como Negocio. Producción, Sociedad y Territorios en la Globalización* (Buenos Aires: Editorial Biblos, 2013), pp. 215–236.

Gras, Carla and Valeria Hernández. "El modelo agribusiness y sus traducciones territoriales," in Carla Gras and Valeria Hernández (eds), *El Agro como Negocio. Producción,*

*Sociedad y Territorios en la Globalización* (Buenos Aires: Editorial Biblos, 2013), pp. 49–66.

Kaplinsky, Raphael. "Globalisation and Unequalisation: What can be learned from Value Chain Analysis?" *The Journal of Development Studies*, 37 (2000), pp. 117–146.

Lapegna, Pablo. "Notes from the Field. The Expansion of Transgenic Soybeans and the Killing of Indigenous Peasants in Argentina," *Societies Without Borders*, 8 (2013), pp. 291–308.

Leguizamón, Amalia. "Modifying Argentina: GM Soy and Socio-Environmental Change," *Geoforum*, 53 (2014), pp. 149–160.

Llach, Juan José, Marcela Harriague and Ernesto O'Connor. *La generación de empleo en las cadenas agroindustriales* (Buenos Aires: Fundación Producir Conservando, 2004).

Lódola, Agustin and Rafael Brigo. "Contratistas de servicio agropecuarios, difusión tecnológica y redes agroalimentarias: una larga y productiva relación," in Guillermo Anlló, Roberto Bisang and Mercedes Campi (eds), *Claves Para Repensar El Agro Argentino* (Buenos Aires: Eudeba, 2013), pp. 203–250.

MAGyP (Ministerio de Agricultura, Ganadería y Pesca). *Argentina Agribusiness Leader. Federal and Participative Agri-Food and Agribusiness Strategic Plan 2010–2020* (Buenos Aires, 2011).

Marx, Karl. *Theories of surplus value*, available at https://www.marxists.org/archive/marx/works/1863/theories-surplus-value/add3.htm; last accessed 28 November 2017.

Marx, Karl. *Capital, A Critique of Political Economy*, Volume 1 (London: Penguin Books, 1990 [1867]).

Marx, Karl and Friedrich Engels. *Manifesto of the Communist Party*, available at https://www.marxists.org/archive/marx/works/1848/communist-manifesto/ch01.htm; last accessed 28 November 2017.

Milberg, William and Deborah Winkler. "Economic and social upgrading in global production networks: Problems of theory and measurement," *International Labour Review*, 150 (2011), pp. 341–365.

MTEySS (Ministerio de Trabajo, Empleo y Seguridad Social). *Encuesta sobre empleo, protección social y condiciones de trabajo de los asalariados agrarios. Acceso a las políticas de protección y seguridad social de los asalariados agrarios* (Buenos Aires, 2014).

Neiman, Guillermo. "Los estudios sobre el trabajo agrario en la última década: una revisión para el caso argentino," *Mundo Agrario*, 10 (2010), pp. 1–19.

Pengue, Walter. A. "Transgenic Crops in Argentina: The Ecological and Social Debt," *Bulletin of Science, Technology & Society*, 25 (2005), pp. 314–22.

PKA (Projekt Klassenanalyse). *Materialien zur Klassenstruktur der BRD* (Berlin: VSA-Verlag, 1974).

Quaranta, German. "Estructura ocupacional, caracteristicas de la demanda y perfil de la oferta laboral en el agro argentino a principios de la década acutual," in Guillermo Neiman (ed.), *Estudio sobre la demanda de trabajo en el agro argentino* (Buenos Aires: CICCUS, 2010), pp. 13–49.

Quentin, David and Liam Campling. "Global inequality chains: integrating mechanisms of value distribution into analyses of global production," *Global Networks*, 18 (2018), pp. 33–56.

Selwyn, Ben. *Workers, state and development in Brazil. Powers of labour, chains of value* (New York: Manchester University Press, 2012).

Selwyn, Ben. "Social Upgrading and Labour in Global Production Networks: A Critique and an Alternative Conception," *Competition and Change*, 17 (2013), pp. 75–90.

Selwyn, Ben. *The struggle for Development* (Cambridge: Polity Press, 2017).

Smith, Adrian et al. "Networks of value, commodities and regions: reworking divisions of labour in macro-regional economies," *Progress in Human Geography*, 26 (2002), pp. 41–63.

Taylor, Phil et al. "Putting Labour in its Place: Labour Process Analysis and Global Value Chains," in Kirsty Newsome et al. (eds.), Putting Labour in its Place: Labour Process Analysis and Global Value Chains (London: Palgrave, 2015), pp. 1–26.

United States Department of Agriculture (USDA). *Oilseeds: World Markets and Trade* (Washington, 2017).

Villulla, Juan Manuel. *Las cosechas son ajenas. Historia de los trabajadores Rurales detras del Agronegocio* (Buenos Aires: Editorial Cienflores, 2015).

Villulla, Juan Manuel. "Intermediación laboral en la agricultura pampeana argentina: trabajadores asalariados y contratistas," EUTOPIA, 9 (2016), pp. 63–79.

Villulla, Juan Manuel. "Pergamino, Iowa y los salarios en la agricultura pampeana: viejos mitos y nuevas realidades," *Realidad Económica*, 316 (2018), pp. 69–97.

Villulla, Juan Manuel and Chen, Yi Erh. "Costos y tarifas de los contratistas de cosecha en la agricultura pampeana, 1991–2014," *Revista Interdisciplinaria de Estudios Agrarios*, 42 (2015), pp. 99–141.

Werner, Marion. "Beyond Upgrading: Gendered Labor and the Restructuring of Firms in the Dominican Republic," *Economic Geography*, 88 (2012), pp. 403–422.

Werner, Marion. *Global Displacements. The Making of Uneven Development in the Caribbean* (New Jersey: Wiley-Blackwell, 2016).

Werner, Marion, Jennifer Bair and Victor Ramiro Fernández. "Linking up to development? Global value chains and the making of a post-Washington consensus," *Development and Change*, 45 (2014), pp. 1219–1247.

# PART 2

## *Commodity Chains and Proto-industrialization in Early Modern Central Europe*

CHAPTER 5

# Grain, Flour, Beer, and Liquor

## *Commodity Chains, Labor Relations and Economic Development in Habsburg Galicia, 1772–1918*

*Klemens Kaps*

### 1 Introduction: Explaining a Region's Economic Development by Analyzing Its Position within Commodity Chains

This chapter addresses the relationship between commodity chains and labor relations through the lens of regional economic development. The issue of transnationally organized production processes has been studied from a variety of theoretical approaches, ranging from micro-level analysis of transnationally active companies and their production structure to macro-economic interpretation.[1] The differences of perspective notwithstanding, both approaches provide complementary analyses of imbalances in the creation of wealth at different points within the production chain, understood as the process that goes from the production of raw materials to the distribution or commercialization of the finished product, including: labor relations; the division of labor necessary for organizing the production process; the entanglement of production with both purchase and sale markets; the ownership of production means; and the regional location of production sites of the corresponding components necessary for conducting the production of the specific commodity. Usually commodity chains are considered as transnational, that is, stretching beyond regional and national economies. Here I want to apply the concept of commodity chains linked to the world-systemic approach to economic development. The world-system model argues that the hierarchies of capitalist production processes lead to an unequal division of labor, and that states and regions can be classified according to their position within the system, and, therefore, their economic profile: the classification distinguishes between cores, semi-peripheries and peripheries. Each step in the commodity chain is associated with a certain ideal position within the capitalist world-system; as such, in this ideal system, peripheries extract raw materials and

1 Fischer and Reiner, "Globale Warenketten", pp. 27–44, 28–29.

 | DOI:10.1163/9789004448049_006

foodstuffs, semi-peripheries produce intermediate components, and the core areas assemble these components to produce finished products. Based on the level of added value generated in each step of the chain, different regions and polities draw starkly differing profit, which explains the geographical imbalance in terms of economic development.[2]

Analyzing the commodity chains involved in the production of different products can reveal not only the transregional social and economic entanglements required by capitalist production, but also represents an important contribution to the deconstruction of methodological nationalism by acknowledging its analytical limitations. It is important to reconsider the processes of development undergone by regions and states from a commodity chains approach. In contrast with classical accounts of commodity chains, which undertake an analysis of globalization through the study of the production process of a single commodity, our approach analyses specific regions on the basis of their position within the system of transregional division of labor. Here it is important to underline that commodity chains need not stretch across regional and national boundaries, but that the production process of a given product, from raw materials extraction up to distributing the finished products to the consumers, could occur in an exclusively regional or national setting. Thus, in this chapter I will analyze, which steps of the commodity chain of a certain group of products took place in the chosen region in order to understand the impact the production of certain commodities had on regional economic development. This approach can go a long way in explaining regional differences; I will explore whether the region's role in the commodity chain led to the development of the regional economy and the generation of added value. Equally, I will examine what kind of labor relations production processes in the region relied on.

I will assume a *longue durée* perspective to the analysis of Habsburg Galicia in the long nineteenth century, including its labor relations and the origin and development over time of the relevant commodity chains, in order to examine the economic performance of one of the poorest areas in the Habsburg Empire. The chronological limits of this analysis will be the annexation of the province by the Habsburg Monarchy in the First Partition of Poland-Lithuania in 1772 and the end of the First World War in 1918.

In order to analyze the relationship between regional economic development, commodity chains and labor relations, I will focus on grain and some

2 *Ibid.*, pp. 27–29; Wallerstein and Hopkins, "Commodity Chains," pp. 221–233. For the world-system approach see e.g.: Hopkins and Wallerstein, "Grundzüge," pp. 151–200; Wallerstein, *Historical capitalism*.

of its semi-finished products, such as flour, as well as finished products, namely bread, beer, and liquor. This group of products played an important role in the largely agricultural Galician economy. In Galicia, the secondary sector was poorly developed, and it mainly consisted of the extraction of raw materials, and crafts or industrial activities related to agriculture, such as the production of food, alcohol and cigarettes. According to an estimate of the Gross Regional Product (GRP) on the eve of the First World War, the production of food and beverages, including tobacco and sugar, amounted to 29 percent of the added value generated by the secondary sector; in 1841 the share of this commodity group had amounted only 17 percent.[3] Beer and liquor were important commodities within this group: in 1913, liquor contributed to 15.8 percent of foodstuff added value, and beer to 19.8 percent, that is, over a third of overall foodstuff production added value just before the First World War.[4] These figures demonstrate not only the important role played by the production of alcohol in the regional economy, but also its increasing weight, in both absolute and relative terms during the second half of the nineteenth century.

The economic significance of grain agriculture was also high. While the overall share of the primary sector (agriculture and extractive industry) was barely above (30 percent) that of the secondary sector (27 percent) in 1913,[5] the proportion of value added generated by agriculture and stock-breeding amounted to 84 percent of the primary sector's output.[6] Within this heterogeneous group of commodities, grain was the most important single product, according to agricultural statistics: thus, in 1789 51.5 percent of agricultural production in Galicia consisted of cereals. This share diminished gradually over the course of the nineteenth century: it was 29.4 percent in 1841 and 19.5 percent between 1904 and 1913, although absolute production figures obviously increased. This tendency reflected above all the increasing diversification of crops in Galicia's farming over the course of the nineteenth century.[7] Taking into account that agricultural output (and its by-products), amounted to two-thirds of the overall output of the primary sector in 1913,[8] we can conclude that grain cultivation contributed more to Galicia's regional income than alcoholic beverages, while data on flour and bread are not available.

3 Kool, *Economic Development*, pp. 268, 298.
4 Author's own estimates after Kool: *Ibid.*, p. 295.
5 *Ibid.*, p. 275.
6 *Ibid.*, p. 272.
7 Own calculation according to data propvided by: Sandgruber, *Österreichische Agrarstatistik*, pp. 161–175.
8 Kool, *Economic Development*, p. 272.

The product group grain/flour/bread/alcohol, therefore, played a crucial role in the regional income of Galicia between 1772 and 1914, although internal structures, and the distribution of shares between the different products within the group, changed significantly during the period under investigation: while grain cultivation clearly was a major source of regional income throughout the period, it progressively lost relative importance owing to the growing diversification of Galicia's agriculture and of the economy in general. In turn, the contribution of flour, bread and alcohol was important, albeit secondary, for the income of large aristocratic estates in the late 18$^{th}$ century, while its share tended to increase over the course of the nineteenth century, especially after the abolition of serfdom in 1848, and the associated changes in productive structures. At the beginning of the period under consideration, the commodities considered here were produced within a feudal economic framework based on demesne lordship (*Gutsherrschaftt* in German, *folwark* in Polish), which involved the imposition of compulsory and forced labor on tenants. The formal abolition of the legal subordination of peasants to their aristocratic lords in 1848 was the death-knoll of the system, which swiftly collapsed. Although some relics of feudal bondage persisted for decades after this date, the organization of labor was characterized by a similar variety of legal regulations and social types. There was an overall tendency towards commodification, that is, the generalization of regulated wage-labor, most notably between 1848 and 1914.

In the following sections, I will assess continuities and transformations in the commodity chain of the grain/flour/bread/beer/liquor product group, its relationship to labor relations and its impact on the region's economic development between 1772 and 1918. In order to do so, I will begin by presenting a brief overview on Galicia's economic profile in order to put the economic activities and commodities under consideration into context. Then, I will follow by analyzing commodity chains and labor relations; three stages will be distinguished in both Galicia's overall economic development and the characteristics of commodity chains and labor relations.

## 2 Galicia: A Poverty-Stricken Province on the Outskirts of the Habsburg Monarchy

Galicia was formed by the merging of several voivodships (*województwa* in Polish) in the southern regions of the vanishing Polish-Lithuanian commonwealth. It was 81,900 km$^2$ in size, according to the partition treaty of 1772, signed by Prussia, Russia, and the Habsburg Monarchy, which was later confirmed by the Habsburg-Polish Treaty of 1773 and took its final shape with the definition of the borders in 1776. Later border changes, both external and within the Habsburg Monarchy, enlarged and reduced Galicia's territory, and after 1866, the territory under the Habsburgs was 77,630 km$^2$ in size (Map 5.1).[9]

The population of the new imperial province initially oscillated between 2.3 million inhabitants (1773) and 2.6 million (1774),[10] but rose quickly in the following decades. At any rate, imperfections in population register systems prior to the introduction of systematic censuses in 1857 must be taken into account. According to the official registers, the population of Galicia increased at an average annual rate of 0.89 percent between 1773 and 1869, and 0.95 percent from 1869 to the outbreak of the First World War.[11] This made Galicia the most populous region of Cisleithania, the "Western" or "Austrian" half of the double Monarchy of Austria-Hungary, in the constitutional period (1867–1918), reaching a peak in population of 8 million in 1910.[12] The productive profile of this border region, situated at the northeastern edge of the Habsburg Monarchy, was dominated by agriculture throughout the whole period under consideration. Rough estimations suggest that four-fifths of the workforce were engaged in the agricultural sector in the late eighteenth century and 88 percent by the mid-nineteenth, only decreasing slowly afterwards; in 1910, an overwhelming 74.2 percent of the Galician workforce were employed in agriculture. The sharpest reduction in the proportion of agricultural workers took place between 1850 and 1880, and it was followed by a period of much slower structural change.[13] The slow socioeconomic transformation of Galicia's labor structure is usually attributed to a combination of rapid demographical growth, the low number of industrial job opportunities and the partible inheritance law, which contributed to keep a vast proportion of Galicia's population in agriculture.[14]

While these figures demonstrate that industrialization did not occur on a large scale, the fact is that the proportion of the workforce employed in crafts and industry rose slightly in the late nineteenth century.[15] This phenomenon is

9 Haczynski, "Two Contributions," pp. 94–104, 95, 99; Pacholkiv, "Entstehung," pp. 167–197, 169, 172.
10 Mark, *Galizien*, p. 53.
11 Kaps, *Ungleiche Entwicklung*, p. 87.
12 Mark, *Galizien*, p. 70.
13 Sandgruber, *Agrarstatistik*, p. 222.
14 Rudolph, "The East European Peasant Household," pp. 365–368, 378.
15 Pietrzak-Pawłowska, "Przewrót przemysłowy," pp. 57–103, 95.

MAP 5.1 Map of Habsburg Galicia in the borders after 1846/66 according to Polish and Ukrainian names of district capital towns (with present day national border between Poland and Ukraine)
SOURCE: TORONTO UKRAINIAN GENEALOGY GROUP, HTTP://WWW.TORUGG.ORG/HISTORY/HISTORY_OF_GALICIA.HTML

matched by the fact that the industrial sector grew faster in Galicia than in the core areas of the Monarchy in the Austrian and Bohemian crownlands after the world economic crisis of 1873, except for the period in the wake of the 1912–1913 recession.[16] Accordingly, GDP data presents a phase of comparative prosperity for the region, and a rather spirited economic performance: between 1870 and 1910, Galicia grew on average between 0.85 percent and 1.52 percent per year, according to two different estimates. Both estimates are well above GDP annual growth in the Austrian heartlands of the empire, but below the aggregated average of the Austro-Hungarian Empire (1.10 and 2 percent respectively).[17] However, in general, Galicia's share of the Empire's wealth remained fairly stable, and small, throughout the period under consideration: a first rough estimate suggests that Galicia accumulated 15.8 percent of the wealth of the Cisleithanian half of the Monarchy in 1785, that is, before the incorporation of Dalmatia, to the south and Salzburg in the west; later GDP estimates from 1841 and 1911/13 indicate that this situation hardly changed during the period under

16 Kaps, *Ungleiche Entwicklung*, p. 73.

17 Good, "Economic Lag," p. 16; Schulze, "Regional Income," p. 25.

scrutiny (14.2 percent and 15.3 percent respectively).[18] These performance figures are matched by the fact that Galicia's industrial growth rates have been overstated, for since analyses have focused on basic industrial activities and the extraction and processing of raw materials and crops, which were strongly represented in Galicia. In any case, despite the significant rate of growth, Galicia did not seem to be catching up with the core regions of the western half of the Austro-Hungarian Empire.[19]

As the data demonstrates, Galicia was not only one of the poorest regions within the Habsburg Monarchy, but one where structural economic change not only developed at a slower rate than those of the core areas in Austria and Bohemia, but also the semi-peripheral Hungarian territories, which were closer in terms of economic development. Only Dalmatia, Bukovina and Croatia had a similar level of economic development.

The analysis of commodity chains might clarify some of the reasons behind the limited industrialization and growth. The analysis divides the period under examination into three periods. The first period ranges between the province's annexation in 1772 and the end of the post-Napoleonic crisis in 1825/30; the second spans from this crisis to the world economic crisis of 1873; the third brings us from this crisis to the end of the First World War and the demise of the Austro-Hungarian Empire.

## 3 1772–1830: Disintegration of Global Markets and a Precarious Internal Upgrade of Production

The commodities of the here analyzed group of goods shared one important characteristic: They were produced mainly in the rural sphere of the Galician landscape, whereas the processing was carried out under the leadership of both peasants and lords of noble, clerical, and royal background. Thereby a tight interrelation between peasant and demesne economies existed as the vast majority of the rural population were tenants of land owned by nobles, church institutions, and the state. Although there were important differences within Galicia according to topographical, institutional, and social conditions, in general noble land represented the vast majority of landed property followed by crown estates, while church property was of least significance. According to the Josephinian land cadastre, carried out between 1785 and 1787

---

18 Dickson, *Finance*, vol. 1, p. 134; Bachinger and Matis, "Österreichs industrielle Entwicklung," p. 148.

19 Kaps, *Ungleiche Entwicklung*, pp. 76, 459–460.

during the reign of Emperor Joseph II,[20] in the three Western Galician districts of Tarnów, Rzeszów and Sanok 71.3 percent of all landed property, including all types from fields over gardens and meadows to ponds, pastures and forests, was in the hands of the nobility, while crown estates (25 percent) and church demesnes (3.7 percent) followed at a great distance.[21]

In addition, both state and church property underwent important changes during the late eighteenth century, which the cadastre in part already reflected: On the one hand, many crown estates were sold from the beginning of Habsburg rule, mainly to noble buyers, but also to a few civil servants and bourgeois businessmen. On the other hand, due to the decrees of 1782/83, a quite large number of convents and monasteries including their important landed property of Galicia's three main Christian churches – Roman-Catholic, Greek-Catholic and Orthodox Church – were dissolved and put under state administration in the so-called religious fund. Property from religious fraternities and bishoprics was also expropriated. Out of these confiscated properties the vast majority was mainly sold to the nobility.[22]

In sum, 81 crown demesnes and 25 church estates across the whole of Galicia were sold before 1796, although not all buyers had paid the corresponding purchase price by then.[23] By 1816 only 45 crown estates and 19 confiscated religious fund demesnes remained under state administration – a dwindling number compared with 3,695 private estates across the whole province.[24] This important redistribution of landed property, that took place in the decades after 1772, and that was motivated by the state's desperate search for additional revenue, strengthened further aristocratic demesnes from an already strong position. This development should not nevertheless neglect the fact that a high degree of stratification within the nobility among whom the so called magnates, owners of latifundium demesnes consisting of several estates, were economically powerful, but a minority in absolute numbers, whereas the bulk of Galicia's nobility was made up of modest-income noble categories up to poor segments whose situation resembled those of peasants, regarding wealth and even sometimes legal status.[25]

---

20 Rozdolski, *Agrar- und Steuerreform*, pp. 39–41; Falniowska-Gradowska and Leśniak, *Struktura własności ziemskiej*.

21 Falniowska-Gradowska and Leśniak, *Struktura własności ziemskiej*, p. 30.

22 Ślusarek, "Dobra państwowe," pp. 189–191, 196. Kargol, Jewuła and Ślusarek, *Dwór*, p. 151.

23 Centralnyj deržavnyj istoryčnyj archiv Ukrajiny, m. L'viv (CDIAL), fond (f.) 187opys (op.) 1, sprava (spr.), 196, fol. 7–19.

24 Zakład Narodowy im. Ossolińskich we Wrocławiu, Wykazy polityczne [statystyczne] Królestw Galicyi y Lodomeryi w roku 1817, fol. 2–3, 6–7.

25 Ślusarek, *Drobna Szlachta*.

A high level of stratification occurred also regarding peasants, who on general terms provided a sophistically differentiated set of feudal dues to the manor in exchange for usufruct of their holdings. These obligations depended on the size of the plots leased by the peasants and ranged from direct taxes in kind (or sometimes also in money) to all sorts of labor services (corvée, robot) including agricultural and handicraft activities, but also services such as transport, trade or monitoring of fields and buildings as well as infrastructural works, such as the building and reconstruction of roads.[26] The church imposed – in addition to its role as landlord demanding the same kind of feudal dues as noble lords – special dues in terms of parishes, bishoprics, chapters and convents, such as the tithe, usually extracted in kind (*Zehent* in German, *dziesięcina wytyczna* in Polish) and all kinds of payments for church services, among which the due for celebrating a mass (*meszne* in Polish) stood out. A range of other payments was also illegally and abusively demanded by local priests.[27]

The extent of both dues and corvée depended on the property category of the rural population, although there were important regional variations: only 16 percent of Galicia's peasants living in bondage belonged to the category of full and half peasants, which referred to usufruct of a full holding, which was of varying size between 5.8 and 20.1 hectares. They often had to fulfil corvée that extended three days a week – such as in the Western Galician districts of Bochnia, Tarnów and Rzeszów where full peasants had to work five to six days weekly on estates, whereas in the central Carpathian districts this compulsion amounted to three to four days and in the outmost districts in the west it remained below this threshold. Most of Galicia's agricultural population only owned a house and a small garden (*Gärtler, zagrodnik*), a cottage (*Häusler, chałupnik*), or were landless (*Inleute, komornik*) and lived either in the house of other peasants or on demesne ground.[28] Apart from this coercive and extractive mechanism, subjected peasants depended on the demesnes in terms of mobility restrictions, jurisdictional subordination and limitation of property rights.[29]

26 Cerman, *Villagers und Lords*, pp. 70–72; Kargol, Jewuła and Ślusarek, *Dwór*, p. 79.

27 *Ibid.*, pp. 249, 257, 259–260, 262–264; Kargol, "Uposażenie," pp. 149, 153–161.

28 Kargol, Jewuła and Ślusarek, *Dwór*, p. 79; Glassl, *Einrichtungswerk*, p. 164; Dinklage, "Die landwirtschaftliche Entwicklung", pp. 403–451, 407; Rychlikowa, "Realizacja", pp. 91–131, 93. For the size of full tenant see: Ślusarek, *Drobna Szlachta*, p. 98. HHStA (Haus-, Hof- und Staatsarchiv), KA (Kabinettssarchiv), Nachlass Baldacci, box 4 (2. Bochnia: Num 5. Unterthans Gegenstände, without fol.).

29 Cerman, *Villagers and Lord*, pp. 22–31.

These relationships were, however, not constant. While in the later Galician territory, as in overall Poland-Lithuania, many additional obligations to their demesnes were increased after 1750,[30] the Habsburg authorities extended their policy protecting peasants to the newly acquired province after 1772 and went on to curtail on demesne privileges in the 1780s. The state reduced some of their dues in kind, but especially the burden of corvée. The state's target was to increase the economic output and, therefore, the tax-base of peasant economies. A maximum of three robot days per week was imposed in 1781, and restated in a later decree, passed in 1784, although this measure remained limited to full peasants, thus leaving out the vast majority of the rural population as well as those peasants living on demesne land (so called *Dominikalisten.*) Still, many other regulations contributed to improve the peasants' lot. The Josephinian reforms, instigated during Emperor Joseph II's reign, between 1780 and 1790, strengthened the peasants' property rights over their land, although plans to entitle tenants to inherit their land-rights failed. The reformers also tried, unsuccessfully, to enforce the conversion of all dues in labor and kind into monetary values, however linking it to a fiscal reform that would have supposed important cuts on lords' incomes. While studies of single demesnes show that the reforms were implemented with great accuracy, this last step evoked wide resistance among noble landowners.[31]

Monetized feudal dues were especially common in the Carpathian Mountains and foothills, among other regions, where the infertility of the soil fostered the peasants' involvement in market-practices – such as carrying trade or textile production – from which income the subjected rural population paid monetized feudal dues.[32] An outstanding example for this pattern demonstrates the economic vitality of the Andrychów estate, especially the central village of Andrychów and a couple of smaller villages, to the southwest of Cracow. There, the production of a range of high-quality linen textiles, which were sold on interregional markets and exported to Europe's colonies in the Americas, was based on the peasants' hereditary rights over their land (*zakupieństwo*) and the monetization of feudal dues. The peasants used their land as a source of raw materials for their own craft production, although they also acquired raw materials and semi-finished products, such as flax yarn, from other

30 Baranowski, "Zmiany," p. 96.

31 Rutkowski, *Historia gospodarcza*, pp. 290–293; Rosdolsky, *Untertan und Staat*, pp. 69, 72, 82–84, 125–128, 186–190, 192, 205–207; Rychlikowa, "Realizacja."

32 Falniowska-Gradowska, "Some remarks"; Bobińska, "Niektóre przesłanki," pp. 361–375, 365–367.

Galician districts, for instance the area around Przeworsk und Łańcut, in the center of the province.[33]

The failure of the Josephinian agrarian tax reform and of the conversion of robot services into money dues in 1789/90 reflected the persisting constraints to transform a peripheral labor regime from above without the necessary socioeconomic changes having taken place. For redistributive policies empowering peasants, this failure translated into a setback when in the context of questioning the Josephinian reforms after the Emperor's death and in the midst of social upheaval, led by revolting landlords, protection of peasants after 1790 was weakened. In 1798 the conversion of dues in kind into money was made to depend on the voluntary bilateral agreement between lords and tenants to be approved by the district authorities.[34] In addition, lords circumvented legal restrictions by extending the working day or by introducing auxiliary robot services for the whole year, and thus creating, in practice, an increasingly severe standard robot system. In any case, and independently from the legal framework, the lords' robot-based privileges increased in the long term, as a consequence of demographic growth and the illegal, but widely practiced, division of peasant land (*Rustikalland*). However, diminishing plot size also limited the extent of corvée per holding.[35]

For producing the here analyzed commodities, the structure of property ownership, as well as labor relations, had a decisive impact resulting in a complex division of labor between the socially highly stratified producers: While peasants and demesnes were both engaged in grain cultivation, the further processing of crops, first to flour and then to bread, as well as to liquor and beer, took place exclusively on estates which were huge and diversified economic complexes engaging in various kinds of businesses, from agriculture to crafts including a role in marketing their commodities. This was a fairly common characteristic of East Central and Eastern European economies in the early modern age.[36]

In order to describe the production process adequately, we must point out the differences in the commodity chains of the different products belonging to the group. Concerning bread, at the turn of the nineteenth century, peasant populations predominately used barley, oats and buckwheat, rather than the classical cereals, wheat and rye. This is explained by the fact that wheat was

33 Kulczykowski, *Andrychowski ośrodek płócienniczy*, pp. 53–54, 57–58, 74–75, 77–78, 87.

34 Link, *Emancipation*, pp. 150–151, 166–168.

35 Rosdolsky, *Untertan und Staat*, pp. 251–254; Kai Struve, *Bauern und Nation*, pp. 72–73; Blum, *Noble Landowners*, p. 181.

36 Cerman, *Villagers und Lords*, pp. 87–92.

mainly cultivated on estates, rather than peasant holdings. As a result, the facilities set up by newly arrived German-speaking bakers, which specialized in the production of white bread, did not fit the consumption patterns of most of the rural population.[37] The use of barley, oats and buckwheat for bread reflected not only the precarious living-standards of the rural population, but also the varying quality of agricultural soil: while in the river valleys of the Vistula, San, Dunajec, Poprad, and Bug, fields were highly fertile, in the sub-Carpathian area soils were poorer, and in the mountainous area that stretched across the southern part of the province, arable ground was particularly meager and productivity was low.[38] While it is unclear to what extent noble estates produced wheat and rye bread for their own consumption or for sale, beer and hard liquor in aristocratic establishments was predominantly processed from barley (and sometimes also wheat and, in very specific territories, oats) and rye (and sometimes buckwheat).[39]

According to the Josephinian land cadastre the usufruct of overall landed property in the whole province was fairly equally divided between peasant holdings (51.3 percent of plots) and demesnes (48.7 percent of landed property).[40] However, the single categories of landed property were divided in an unbalanced way: While peasants had a higher share in using fields for crop cultivation, meadows, gardens and pastures, demesnes in turn dominated the property of forests and ponds.[41]

Accordingly, peasant economies dominated the production of grain: Two-thirds of overall crop production between 1785 and 1787, consisting mainly of all sorts of grain, were harvested on peasant land. In turn, the remaining third of grain output was contributed by demesne fields (*Dominikalland*).[42] Nevertheless, these figures say more about repartition of land tenure than about productivity: Thus, demesnes gathered basically the same income from crop harvests per fields (4.1 florins per yoke) as peasant economies (3.8 florins per yoke).[43] Moving beyond this static picture, production growth is difficult

37 Rychlikowa, *Produkcja zbożowa*, pp. 60, 62, 81; Idem., *Studia*, p.61.

38 Madurowicz and Podraza, "Próba rejonizacji," pp. 65, 68–69, 73–74; Fierich, "Kultury rolnicze".

39 Rychlikowa, *Studia*, p. 77.

40 Own calculation according to the data of the Josephinian cadastre provided by: Rozdolski, *Stosunki poddańczy*, vol.II, pp. 402–403, tables 19a and 19b.

41 *Ibid.*

42 Own calculation according to Rozdolski, *Stosunki poddańczy*, vol.II, pp. 402–403, tables 19a and 19b.

43 Own calculation according to the data on division of field holdings and monetary income from crop harvests deriving from the Josephinian cadastre and provided by: Rozdolski, *Stosunki poddańczy*, vol.II, pp. 402–403, tables 19a and 19b.

to measure due to scarce and hardly reliable data. Nevertheless, data of the cadastre and subsequently compiled official statistics show a slim growth in grain production between 1785/87 and 1830/50 from 1258.5 to 1307.2 thousand tons (Table 5.1). Within grain production, there was a fairly balanced division between the output of rye, barley, and oats, whereas wheat was a minority option for producers, both in 1785/87 and in 1841. Between these two benchmark years, shares of the four main grain sorts were slightly diminished mainly due to the introduction of potato cultivation.[44]

While there was a solid regional base of raw materials for producing bread, liquor, and beer in this period, it is more difficult to understand the extent and growth of these three commodities' output. While production data for this period is largely lacking, and where numbers are available they have to be treated with corresponding care, the different population censuses carried out by the authorities give some information on outlets on demesnes for turning grain into consumables bread, liquor, and beer. The number of mills decreased from 5,380 in 1773 to 2,519 three decades later, while numbers of distilleries and breweries are only available for 1803, when they amounted to 2,734 and 209 respectively.[45] This dominance of liquor production against brewing of beer is also confirmed by the division of the tax on the consumption of alcoholic beverages in the district of Stryj in the southeastern part of the province in 1809, when 91.5 percent of the overall tax revenue (64,788.2 florins) was collected for the consumption of liquor, with beer (6.7 percent) and mead (1.8 percent) lagging far behind.[46] Overall levels of the alcohol consumption tax, which rose from 288,352.4 florins in 1782 to 413,349 florins in 1803, suggest a substantial output growth of liquor and beer between 1782 and 1803, although slight changes in taxation as well as heavy inflation at the turn from the eighteenth to the nineteenth century have to be taken into account.[47]

---

44 Own calculations according to data provided by: Sandgruber, *Agrarstatistik*, pp. 75, 163–175.

45 Ślusarek, "Bevölkerung und Wirtschaft ", p. 73. For 1803 own calculation according to the district-wide data in: HHStA, KA, Nachlass Baldacci, box 3 (Biała), box 4 (Lemberg: fol. 12; Bochnia: without fol.; Tarnów: fol. 28, 37); box 5 (4. Rzeszów: fol. 13–16, 23–29, 125–126; 5. Przemyśl: without fol.), box 6 (7.Żółkiew without fol.; 9. Zloczów without fol.;10. Brzeżany: fol. 23–24, 34–37), box 7 (8. Zamość: fol. 31–32, 95–97, 346; 11. Tarnopol: fol. 17–18, 23–25, 146), box 8 (15. Sambor: fol. 6, 51–59, 75–76, 82–89, 160; 13. Stanisławów: without fol.; 12. Zaleszczyki, fol. 55–56, 91–94, 301), box 9 (16. Sanok: fol. 54, 162; 17. Jasło: without fol.)

46 Own calculation according to the data provided by the conscription of 1809 for the district of Stryj: CDIAL, f. 146, op.7, spr. 402, fol. 105.

47 Own calculations according to the data of the censuses of 1782 and 1803: L'vivs'ka Nacional'na Naukova Biblioteka Ukrajiny imeni V. Stefanyka, Oddział Rękopisów, Zespół (fond) 141: Zbiór Aleksandra Czołowskiego. Dział (opis) I, 2351: Wykazy konskrypcyjne

TABLE 5.1 Grain harvests in the Western regions of the Habsburg Monarchy 1770–1904/13 (in 100 tons)

| | 1770* | 1789 | 1830/50 | 1851 | 1857 | 1869/75 | 1876/85 | 1886/95 | 1895/04 | 1904/13 |
|---|---|---|---|---|---|---|---|---|---|---|
| Lower Austria | 246,3 | 291,7 | 467,1 | 474,2 | 638,9 | 510,1 | 534 | 664,1 | 719,1 | 755,3 |
| Upper Austria | 107,8 | 191,7 | 244,9 | 249,5 | 344,9 | 275,1 | 287,6 | 344,3 | 317,1 | 340,8 |
| Salzburg | | | 33,7 | 33,9 | 41,9 | 34,7 | 37,1 | 30,3 | 31,7 | 34,3 |
| Styria | 132,8 | 116,1 | 244,3 | 340,5 | 435,4 | 278,4 | 391, | 294,3 | 275,2 | 293,4 |
| Carinthia | 56,3 | 62,8 | 81,8 | 82,7 | 103,7 | 114,7 | 121,6 | 108,8 | 88,9 | 101,7 |
| Tyrol | 71,5 | 42,5 | 105,6 | 89 | 123,9 | 102,6 | 99,4 | 91,2 | 84,3 | 98,3 |
| Bohemia | 581,7 | 912,5 | 1526,8 | 1459,8 | 1656 | 1503,3 | 1714,8 | 1961,5 | 2025,9 | 2620,1 |
| Moravia | 288,1 | 493,2 | 717,8 | 539,6 | 992,4 | 595,3 | 714,4 | 785,1 | 925,4 | 1096,2 |
| Silesia | 31,8 | 75,8 | 136,8 | 77,5 | 190,4 | 115,9 | 126,2 | 138,3 | 149,5 | 172,1 |
| **Galicia** | **517,5** | **1258,5** | **1307,2** | **1253** | **948,3** | **1459,9** | **1562,7** | **1649,7** | **1682,5** | **2479,2** |
| Bukovina | | ** | ** | 97,3 | 90,3 | 180,4 | 168,3 | 219,8 | 233 | 251,4 |
| Carniola | 44,2 | 58 | 61,4 | 65,3 | 81,3 | 70,7 | 70,5 | 81,7 | 78,7 | 73,2 |
| Littoral | | 9,3 | 44,1 | 48 | 73,2 | 62,5 | 65,2 | 76,9 | 49,4 | 59,4 |
| Dalmatia | | | 36,3 | 34,6 | 66 | 72,7 | 110,3 | 94,6 | 61,5 | 111,4 |

SOURCE: SANDGRUBER, *AGRARSTATISTIK*, P. 162
* GALICIA REGISTERED AT FIRST IN 1774; ** REGISTERED TOGETHER WITH GALICIA

Hereby, production seemed to grow at least in grain and alcohol, while data for flour and bread are lacking, yet the development of productivity in this phase can only be analyzed for crop output: Average yields per hectare for grain seem to have fallen (from 860 kg per hectare in 1789 to 810 in 1830/50), while they clearly grew in most other Habsburg provinces in the west, apart from the Adriatic Littoral and Carniola, where setbacks were even more pronounced.[48] This drop in soil productivity was largely the result of the lack of innovations (such as the use of manure or complex crop-rotation systems) until the 1820s, which became ever more pertinent as, with the expansion of arable fields, marginal land came to be cultivated.[49]

obwodów Galicji z 1782 r. / Оссолінські Колекції Czolowski Fond 141, 2351. HHStA, KA, Nachlass Baldacci, boxes 3–9.

48 Sandgruber, *Agrarstatistik*, p. 177.

49 *Ibid.*, 146–147. Idem., "Agrarrevolution in Österreich," p. 224. Kaps, *Ungleiche Entwicklung*, pp. 225–228.

The organization of production was closely linked to property structure, labor relations and, thus, feudal prerogatives. The production figures obscure the fact that peasants were involved in grain cultivation both on their own holdings as well as on demesne lands, while a part of the considerable level of corvée was used to operate mills, distilleries and breweries.[50] At the same time, an important share of the peasantry's output had to be handed over to the manors; apart from meat or linen yarn, these transfers included precisely grain.[51] Although dues from fields and grain amounted only to 6.55 percent of overall income on both noble and crown demesnes, according to an estimate of demesnes' income by Galicia's first governor, Johann Anton Count Pergen, in 1772,[52] these transfers in kind represented the raw materials' base for producing flour, bread, beer, and liquor on demesnes. This raw materials base was completed by purchases on regional and external markets, including their own tenants who were compelled to offer grain for sale to the manor first, before the rest eventually went to the market beyond the single estates.[53] Thereby the output of estates in terms of consumable commodities directly reflects the feudal property relations and the associated labor regime. Moreover, demesnes made further profits from compulsory mechanisms and legally imposed productive privileges: Thus, peasants were forced to use the mills of the manor they legally belonged to, for turning grain into flour and had to pay for it, at least until the abolition of manorial milling monopolies by the Imperial Court.[54]

Since production and labor processes have now been analyzed largely focusing on the intra-regional developments and realities, it will now be explored to what degree these commodities were integrated into interregional and international commodity chains: In fact, 50 percent of Galicia's exports consisted of raw materials, according to the trade statistics in 1784/87[55] whereas the region's trade, both within the Habsburg Monarchy and on an international level, amounted approximately 12.4 percent of regional incomes (and this is, likely as not, an overestimation).[56] However, the raw material of the here analyzed product group – different sorts of grain – made up a marginal

50 Rychlikowa, *Produkcja zbożowa*, p. 46.

51 Rychlikowa, *Studia,* p. 86; Kulczykowski, *Andrychowski ośrodek płócienniczy*, p. 12. Kargol, "Uposażenie," pp.153–154, 156.

52 HHStA, Polen III 13, fol. 13.

53 Rychlikowa, *Produkcja zbożowa*, p. 86; Daniel Stone, *Polish-Lithuanian State*, p. 299.

54 Brawer, *Galizien*, p. 48; Rychlikowa, *Produkcja zbożowa*, p. 195.

55 For details on calculating the trade structure see: Kaps, *Ungleiche Entwicklung*, pp. 473–474.

56 Author's own calculation after Dickson, *Finance*, vol.I, p. 137; HHStA, KA, Nachlass Zinzendorf, Handschriften, vol.118, pp. 200–201.

3.1 percent of overall exports, being mainly directed to Poland and the trading city of Brody at the region's eastern border, whereas Hungary, Transylvania, the Bohemian and Austrian provinces, the Ottoman Empire, and Prussia received marginal deliveries. The other semi-finished and finished commodities of the group were even less important in Galicia's exports: Liquor was the relatively important one (0.2 percent) and was followed by flour (0.1 percent) and beer (0.04 percent) whereas bread was not exported at all.[57] These figures point to the fact that the product group was hardly connected to interregional and international markets by the mid-1780s and that thus commodity chains were largely organized regionally. Only pipes and kettles for distilling liquor and brewing beer were imported from Hungary as well as through the port of Gdańsk, on the Baltic coast, to the north, which was by then still part of the remaining Polish state before being annexed by Prussia in the Second Partition in 1793.[58] In some years, for instance between 1788 and 1791, grain had to be imported from Poland (understood as the rest of the Polish-Lithuanian Commonwealth before being partitioned completely in 1793 and 1795 respectively), Hungary and Transylvania, for which reason custom duties were even temporally lifted.[59]

These imports were due to local production shortages in the wake of climatic events (such as rainfalls and floods), a short-term dearth of workforce (due to a reduction of labor services by the state and the unwillingness of peasants to work on the noble estates, even for a wage) and the subsequent emergence of monetized production costs that estate economies had not faced before.[60] In the long term, however, the structurally stagnating soil productivity of arable fields had a much more significant impact on production, as described above.

The figures presented here speak of an already high, nearly an absolute regional control of the raw materials' base for producing flour, bread, liquor, and beer. This was far from being a long-term structural characteristic of Galicia's agriculture. The famous Polish-Lithuanian grain exports, mainly wheat and rye but also barley and oats, from Gdańsk to Amsterdam and France between the sixteenth and the eighteenth centuries (although the crisis of the seventeenth

57 *Ibid.*, pp. 523–590; Österreichiches Staatsarchiv (ÖStA), Finanz- und Hofkammerarchiv (FHKA), Neue Hofkammer (NHK), Bankale Nr. 2982, fol. 33–110. Shares are author's own calculation.

58 Kasperek, *Gospodarka folwarczna*, p. 154; Adamczyk, "Spław zboża," p. 194.

59 ÖStA, FHKA, NHK, Bankale Akten Bankaldirektion 2968, Bankaldirektionsakten Galizien, Getreideeinfuhr (1788–1791), especially: 41362/101, Ad 10875 § 307, 148/80, 1972/162, 10525/966, 7702/772.

60 Kaps, *Ungleiche Entwicklung*, pp. 223–224.

century witnessed a slight decrease in these exports),[61] also involved some of the districts later to be conflated into Galicia. Thus, 17.7 percent of the Polish-Lithuanian grain shipped through the toll station of Włocławek, at the Vistula River, in 1546, came from Little Poland (*Małopolska*), whereas the Ruthenian voivodship (*województwo ruskie*) contributed only 1.3 percent. In 1556 the Ruthenian share was considerably higher, amounting to 12.5 percent, while the contribution of Little Poland remained fairly stable; in 1568, Little Poland contributed 17% and Ruthenia 10% to the rye export through Gdańsk, while the Ruthenian share dropped dramatically to 3.5 percent in 1575, and Little Poland could now increase its share by contributing a substantial 22.8 percent.[62] This underlines that the later Galician territories were integrated at a modest scale in the export trade, especially of rye, but also of wheat through Gdańsk and the Baltic Sea to Western Europe.

Not all of Little Poland was situated within the newly drawn borders of Galicia after 1772/76. Still, some estates in the former southern Cracow voivodship, such as the estate of Nowy Sącz, to the west of Cracow, owned by the Polish Crown, shipped its grain for Gdańsk down the Vistula before 1772.[63] Similarly, many estates in the central and eastern sectors of the fertile valley belt that originated in Oświęcim/Auschwitz and stretched via Przemyśl and L'viv further east to Podolia, right above the rather meager Carpathian mountain districts, cultivated grain for export through the Vistula, which connected other rivers such as the San, the Poprad and the Dunajec with Gdańsk. In the 1760s, many magnate estates were still heavily involved in grain exports to Poland-Lithuania's main Baltic port city.[64] No consensus exists concerning how much grain estate owners managed to export to international markets. Estimates range between 5 and 10–15 percent of overall grain harvests,[65] and 25–30 percent of the overall marketed production during the sixteenth century.[66] While the impact of this export trade and the associated participation in interregional commodity chains on the overall economic activity was rather low, it was highly significant for the commercialized sectors of the economy.[67] Correspondingly, estate economies were heavily dependent on the income they

61 Rusiński, "Role of Polish Territories"; Pach, "The Role of East-Central Europe", p. 220; Stone, *Polish-Lithuanian State*, pp. 289–291, 300.

62 Adamczyk, *Stellung Polens*, p. 172; Guzowski, "Influence", p. 321.

63 Madurowicz and Podraza, "Próba rejonizacji", p. 76.

64 Rychlikowa, *Studia*, pp. 67–68. Kazusek, "Związki gospodarcze", pp. 243–248, 250–253.

65 Topolski, *Narodziny kapitalizmu*, p. 185. Kula, *Economic Theory*, pp. 89–91, 95.

66 Adamczyk, *Stellung Polens*, p. 172.

67 *Ibid.*, pp. 40, 45–46, 51, 53, 138–139, 153–154.

reaped from the grain export trade: only 25 percent of estate incomes derived from activities that were unrelated to grain production, and in the eighteenth century between 20 and 40 percent of grain was sold on the market.[68]

After 1772, the political economies involved in this exchange pattern changed, as Prussia introduced heavy import tolls on the Vistula, before the city of Gdańsk, in 1775 (up to 30 to 40 percent increasing them three- up to tenfold according to the single products), severely increasing transaction costs for grain exports.[69] This was compounded by the mentioned, state-enforced restriction of forced labor in 1775 and again in 1786, especially the so-called 'fare-away cartloads' (*weite Fuhren*), a kind of compulsory labor service commonly used by noble estates to transport grain to the Baltic coast. To begin with, the Court Chancery established a monetary compensation for journeys that lasted longer than a day; also, all expenses had to be compensated, and the service had to be deducted from other robot services. The distance that could be covered by subservient peasants was limited to four miles a day in the first half of the year and to three miles a day in the second half of the year. In 1786, the Chancery limited this service to a maximum of 20 miles in total, which increased transport costs massively, although infringements of the regulations up to that date had frequently occurred.[70] Further obstacles for grain sales at the Gdańsk market were imposed by the trade policy pursued by the Habsburg Monarchy in connection with Galicia's integration into the Bohemian-Austrian customs union in 1784:[71] grain exports were partially affected by the implementation of a protectionist trade policy in 1784 and 1787/88, which consisted of increased custom duties of both imports and exports, apart from import bans for a range of commodities.[72] In addition, since at least 1778, the custom administration repeatedly imposed temporary export bans on Galicia's grain. Sometimes, for instance in 1778 and in 1788, these legislative measures aimed to guarantee the food supply for the Galician population,[73] while in the early 1790s and in 1807, these export bans should provide the necessary rations for the imperial army.[74]

---

68 *Ibid.*, p.51. Baranowski, „Zmiany," p.106.

69 Cieślak, "The influence," pp. 205–209; Drozdowski, "Traktaty handlowe," p. 99.

70 Rosdolsky, *Untertan und Staat*, pp. 69–70, 72, 178; Glassl, *Einrichtungswerk*, p. 175.

71 Grossmann, *Österreichs Handelspolitik*, pp. 288, 384.

72 *Ibid.*, p.371; Beer, "Handelspolitik", pp. 116–119.

73 ÖStA, FHKA, NHK, Kamerale Ö Akten Fasz. 7 G – Mautwesen in Galizien, box 211, Nr. 30, 212; ÖStA, FHKA, NHK, Bankale Akten Bankaldirektion 2968, Bankaldirektionsakten Galizien, Getreideeinfuhr (1788–1791), Nr. 3368/310.

74 ÖStA, FHKA, NHK, Kommerz U Akten 1569, Ungarn und Galizien Fasz. 57, Die zum Königreich Ungarn revindizierten Provinzen Polens, Galizien und Lodomerien,

As such, the political economy of the grain trade increased export transaction costs for estate owners, so that many of them stopped sending their grain down the Vistula and the San. In sum, Galicia's grain exports decreased from 274,200 florins in 1783 to 195,365 florins four years later, when, to Gdańsk, only a tiny amount (202.8 florins) of a special type of barley (*Almengerste*) was delivered.[75] This unraveling of the Galician grain export sector, which especially affected demesnes and the Gdańsk export market, hit rye first, while wheat held its position in interregional commodity chains for some years; eventually, however, wheat exports to Western Europe through the Baltic ports also decreased. Even if grain exports were possible in some years, in particular after Prussia annexed Gdańsk after the second Partition of Poland in 1793, making it a more attractive proposition to some estates than producing alcohol, this opportunity was only open to a limited number of estates. A range of circumstances, such as the custom tolls imposed on the new state borders between the areas of partitioned Poland at the turn of the nineteenth century, precipitated the departure of most Galician grain producers from international markets, even if contact from the Gdańsk export market was not completely severed: it is estimated that approximately 10 percent of the grain shipped across the Baltic Sea came from Galicia.[76]

Exports were replaced by an increase in beer and liquor production, a business that many estates had embraced on a large scale since the seventeenth-century crisis. The crisis was severed through wars blocking access to the grain export, and competitors from Western European and the Russian Empire who marginalized Polish-Lithuanian grain on international markets.[77] From the 1770s onwards, alcohol production expanded even more rapidly. The so-called *propinacja*, the estate privilege to produce and sell alcohol exclusively to its serfs by way of leased inns and taverns represented the background to this practice where lords' extra-economic coercive power allowed them to create closed local markets that they dominated in an already asymmetric relationship.[78] The proportion of estate incomes from *propinacja* steadily rose: on the western Galician estates, it increased from 33.3 percent in 1764 to 40 percent in 1789; on the estate of the Zamoyski family, in Zamość (Eastern Galicia) it grew

Auschwitz, Zator, Kommerz in Ost- und Westgalizien, Teil 14, 1807, 7 ex Octobri 1807, Fol. 524–527.

75 HHStA, KA, Nachlass Zinzendorf, vol. 118, pp. 198–199; ÖStA, FHKA, NHK, Bankale 2982.

76 Kasperek, *Gospodarka folwarczna*, p. 163; Rychlikowa, *Studia*, pp. 64, 66–68, 174–175, 179, 203.

77 Rychlikowa, *Studia*, pp. 74–76; Kasperek, *Gospodarka folwarczna*, p. 146; Stone, *Polish-Lithuanian State*, p. 290.

78 Cerman, *Villagers and Lords*, pp. 87–88.

from 16 percent in the late 1760s to 30 percent after 1772; by the 1780s, this proportion had risen to 40 percent. As much as two-thirds or four-fifths of all the grain available to the estates, either grown on the estates themselves or handed over by the peasants in concept of feudal dues, was turned into alcohol.[79]

Thus, the partial disintegration of international commodity chains, not only strengthened intra-regional commodity chains, but also upgraded the region's position within commodity chains, thus augmenting the share of production processes conducted within the region: Raw materials were now being turned into consumer products within Galicia itself, and the consumption of the finished products in question was forcefully encouraged by the privileges of the agrarian system and the estate economy, which seem to have persisted in spite of the measures adopted by the Court Chamber in 1775 and 1786. In this way, estate owners could even increase their income, as they were at liberty to fix alcohol sale prices while demand remained stable, as peasants were forced to buy a certain amount of liquor and beer from the demesne. This system, therefore, combined market mechanisms with coercion. As such, the *propinacja* can be considered a kind of feudal due by which income was diverted from peasants to landlords. However, this production pattern not only resulted in widespread alcoholism among peasants, but also created the basis for social conflicts to be defined by inter-ethnic divisions between 'Christians' and 'Jews' as often estates and taverns were run by Jewish managers; this perception began appearing in elite discourses in the late eighteenth century, and was to have an enormous impact much later on.[80] It has to be stressed that the comparatively low degree of commercialization of Galicia's agriculture and rural economy due to the high degree of subsistence production of peasant households was a severe constraint to pursuing this compensation strategy of strengthening the regional market in replacement of transregional entanglements. This means that the shift from international and trans-regional markets towards regional economic circuits was not equally possible for other branches of Galicia's economy, although, in any case, grain-driven agriculture was one of the main economic activities in the region.

The transformation of commodity chains in the late eighteenth and early nineteenth centuries had further consequences for Galicia's productive structure: many estates started to change their cultivation strategies, by reducing the cultivation of wheat and focusing on rye, barley, and oats, in order to

79 Hundert, *Jews in Poland-Lithuania*, p. 37; Kasperek, *Gospodarka folwarczna*, p. 163; Rychlikowa, *Studia*, pp. 106–107.

80 Hundert, *Jews in Poland-Lithuania*, pp. 36–38: Levine, *Economic Origins*, pp. 9–10, 12; Kargol, Jewuła and Ślusarek, *Dwór*, pp. 306–308; Tokarz, *Galicya*, pp. 165–166, 168–169.

produce, not only liquor, but also beer, with which to offset their lost income, after the unraveling of the grain trade.[81] This was the only alternative open for the demesnes, as the redirection of grain sales to other destinations, such as the Black Sea, or to Polish markets were rather exceptional, such as the small amount of grain demonstrates that could be exported to what remained of the Polish-Lithuanian Commonwealth, under King Stanisław II August Poniatowski in 1793 and 1794.[82] After the Polish state eventually vanished from the political map the following year, new custom borders made export there difficult. In particular, the Habsburg Empire itself was not a viable option for most estates, owing to high transport and transaction costs, since rivers or canals were absent on this route. Due to costly land transport the high price differentials between Galicia and the markets in the remaining Habsburg dominions could not be exploited for redirecting regional grain surpluses south- and westwards.[83] According to the trade statistics of the Bohemian-Austrian customs union, Galician exports of grain amounted to an extra-tiny amount of 947 florins in 1783, which further decreased to 207.5 florins the following year.[84] Only on exceptional occasions, grain exports to the Hereditary Lands were possible, such as the 200,000 or 300,000 bushels sold to the imperial army, stationed in Bohemia, in 1813.[85] The persistent price differentials between Galicia and the western Habsburg provinces between 1774 and 1815 for the four main grain sorts is an outspoken indicator that Galicia did not integrate with grain markets in the Habsburg Monarchy of the time[86] and, thus, maybe represented an exception to the integration of grain markets on a European and even transatlantic level during that time, mainly due to the institutional factors described above.[87]

In conclusion, while the mobilization of labor for production of raw materials and foodstuffs, a significant proportion of which was sold on the regional and local markets, was based on severe peasant subjection, the robot reforms implemented by the state in the 1770s and 1780s were incompatible with the

81 Rychlikowa, *Studia*, pp. 194, 198; Idem., *Produkcja zbożowa*, pp. 68–74; Lipelt et al., *Życie gospodarcze*, p. 59.

82 Kazusek, "Handel", p. 58.

83 Kasperek, *Gospodarka folwarczna*, p. 148; Morawski, *Dzieje gospodarcze Polski*, p. 122; Kaps, *Ungleiche Entwicklung*, p. 266.

84 HHStA, KA, Nachlass Zinzendorf, Handschrift vol. 118, pp. 321–377, 523–590.

85 Andre, *Neueste geographisch-statistische Beschreibung*, p. 232.

86 Zamoyski, "Ceny zbóż".

87 Dobado-González, García-Hiernaux and Guerrero, "Integration of Grain Markets"; Federico, Schulze and Volckart, "European goods market integration"; Persson, *Grain Markets*.

simultaneously occurring disintegration of international markets and, eventually, an unreformed economic system. The elsewhere-exposed hypothesis that the demesne economy in early-modern Poland-Lithuania tackled market failures such as the high level of uncertainty and limited market access might be a case in point.[88]

The here analyzed Galician case corresponds to that finding insofar as deteriorating market access and partial disintegration at least led to a mid-term reinforcement of feudal prerogatives in order to check the crisis effects. Also, this happened although an external variable, that is state policy, attempted to push for a dismantling of feudal dues and especially corvée: The state reforms, which limited both labor services and dues (in kind and monetary), forced noble estates to employ a higher number of wage laborers to complement the ongoing labor services. However, and as a reaction to the state regulations many demesnes reconverted monetized feudal dues back into robot services in order to relieve labor shortages and rising labor costs – a trend that ran against the declared objectives of the Crown's reforms. The requirements of new ordinances and laws imposed by the authorities in Vienna, parallel to the complex processes of reshuffling of Galicia's transregional market and trade relations, made it even harder for the noble estates to compensate losses in income derived from the crisis in the grain trade: The most common reaction of landlords to vanishing export markets for their grain was to process their grain locally into liquor (and sometimes also to beer and mead) and to sell this self-produced alcohol locally to their subjects, thus creating a closed local business circuit. All this strategy precipitated in a rise, rather than a fall, of labor demand. The legal limitation of coercive access to subjected labor thus created a problem of labor shortages and rising production costs in a time of crisis. This led to obstacles when estates tried to find strategies to compensate for the losses of disintegration off international markets, as precarious as these attempts might have been: Thus, some demesnes were compelled to divert brewery and distillery workers to the fields, to plug the shortages in labor.[89]

This explains the fierce opposition posed by estate owners and leaseholders to the government's plans to transform the peripheral labor system by commercializing the rural economy. As mentioned above, the successful commodification of Galicia's rural labor force would have resulted in additional substantial losses in nobles' income by raising labor costs.[90] This indicates that serfdom or peasant subjection was a system that precisely was reinforced not

88 Malinowski, "Serfs and the city."

89 Rychlikowa, *Produkcja zbożowa*, pp. 28–29, 46–47, 55, 57, 111: Idem., *Studia*, p. 169.

90 Kaps, *Ungleiche Entwicklung*, pp. 219–220.

with intensifying market integration, but when access to trans-regional and international markets was hindered or even collapsed. This means that the property owners of Galicia's peripheral economy could not compensate all production costs arising for the production of grain and its derivate commodities. This also demonstrates that a substantial part of the consequences of Galicia's post-annexation crisis were to be paid by the subaltern strata of the regional society – the subjected peasants. According to the lords, the disintegration of the international grain trade should be compensated by extra feudal prerogatives, which allowed demesnes to mobilize labor resources at a low cost in order to produce goods to be mostly consumed by the tenants themselves (mainly liquor and beer). This productive model was based on a largely untrained labor force, whose poor levels of education were criticized by reforming bureaucrats, but which fitted the persistence of aristocratic landowners in pursuing extensive production. Production was based on simple agricultural techniques, such as the three-field-system, mediocre ploughs and harrows, and the limited application of manure and eventually led to shrinking productivity.[91] Moreover, forced labor fitted Galicia's focus on raw materials and foodstuff for the local and, to a lesser extent, the interregional markets. In the end, the upgrade of the commodity chains in this sector was not a strategy for long-term development, but a contingency strategy used by property owners who based their income on maintaining social inequality and a precarious economic structure.

## 4 1830–1873: Galicia's Return to International Commodity Chains

In the second phase, the spatial arrangement of commodity chains was affected by two key factors: first, the construction of railways, which began in the 1840s and whose impact became particularly noticeable in the 1860s and early 1870s; second, the shift away from protectionist to liberal foreign trade policies.[92] Therefore, technological innovation, mainly in transport, and policy changes led to a decrease in transaction costs at the interregional (within the Habsburg Monarchy) and the international levels. This significantly contributed to a closer integration of Galicia into transregional commodity chains.

This integration occurred on different levels of the commodity chain. First, it involved the export of raw materials – cereals, mainly wheat and rye, whose presence in the international markets had decreased dramatically in the first

91 *Ibid.*, pp. 225–228, 234.

92 Bachinger, "Verkehrswesen", pp. 278–279, 281–282, 285, 287–288; Turnock, *Economy of East Central Europe*, p. 128.

phase. In this second phase, international markets were reopened for Galician grain; during the 1830s and 1840s only little grain was exported to the Baltic Sea, with a peak of 30,540 tons in 1839. From the 1860s onwards exports began to rise again, until they reached a new peak in 1864 with 82,608.5 tons, which left Galicia by railway.[93] Galicia's reintegration into international grain markets, therefore, benefitted significantly from the construction of railways, but also from the custom reforms of 1852 and 1854 in the Habsburg Monarchy, which abolished previous protectionist barriers. This early liberalization of trade policy was further strengtehend by the trade agreement concluded between the Habsburg Empire and Prussia in 1853, to which the other members of the German Customs Union (*Deutscher Zollverein*), created in 1834, adhered to consecutively. This treaty abolished all custom barriers for grain in the German Confederation (*Deutscher Bund*) beyond the Habsburg dominions, and thus also reopened Gdańsk to Galician grain.[94]

This improved access to international markets, however, was met at first with a decrease in absolute outputs between the 1830s and the late 1850s, when the amount of grain harvested shrank from 1307.2 thousand tons in 1830/50, to over 1253 in 1851 and a minimum of 948.3 in 1857, and was thus far smaller than in the late eighteenth century. Growth only returned in the 1860s, with an annual average of 1459.9 thousand tons between 1869 and 1875 (Table 5.1). The decline witnessed by the 1850s was not an isolated phenomenon, affecting many Habsburg provinces in the course of the revolution of 1848/49 and the abolition of serfdom. However, the effects of this crisis were especially severe and long lasting in Galicia, due to unfavorable climatic conditions, diseases (for instance the cholera epidemic of 1854/55), and the fact that agriculture in the province had depended on peasant subjection far more than elsewhere.[95]

The integration of grain into international commodity chains precipitated a shift to the cultivation of wheat and rye, whose share among the four main cereals being grown rose from 10 percent to 17 percent and from 25 percent to 30 percent respectively between 1830/50 and 1869/75.[96] At the same time, rising grain export in times of stagnating or even decreasing harvests was only possible via changes in the liquor commodity chain. From the 1820s onwards,

93 *Bericht der von dem Landtage*, p. 60; Lipp, *Verkehrs- und Handelsverhältnisse*, p. 14; CDIAL, f.146, op.80, spr.263, Z.21641, Fol. 100, 106.

94 Huertas, *Economic Growth*, pp. 26–35; Koch, "Österreich und der Deutsche Zollverein," pp. 537, 545.

95 Sandgruber, *Agrarstatistik*, p. 162; Stauter-Halsted, *Nation*, pp. 24–26; Ślusarek, *Uwłaszczenie chłopów*, pp. 117, 173–175.

96 Author's own estimates after Sandgruber, *Agrarstatistik*, pp. 163–167.

this heavily alcoholic beverage was increasingly produced from potatoes rather than grain, a shift in production which sometimes took decades, for instance in the Sanok area in south Central Galicia, where the cultivation of potatoes only increased after 1850.[97] In 1847, 40 percent of the potato harvests across the whole Habsburg Empire was used to make liquor. Only in the early 1840s, after the potato harvest failed due to flooding caused by heavy rain, Galicia's distilleries switched temporarily back to grain.[98]

The reshuffling of the liquor commodity chains helped cereals to return to international commodity chains, while liquor remained organized as a predominately regional commodity chain. Like in the first phase, technical equipment was imported from abroad. Technological imports grew in size with the mechanization of distilleriesas steam machines were installed starting in the 1830s and accelerating from the 1850s onwards.[99] This allowed distilleries to increase their output, but a dramatic decrease in the number of distilleries – from 3,926 in 1836, to 2,034 five years later and a minimum of 628 in 1858 – meant that overall output shrank. This phenomenon was triggered by the introduction of the excise duty in 1835 (although this tax was somewhat compensated by custom refunds for sales in Hungary). The 1844/47 potato blight plunged liquor production even further into crisis; production took an upward turn from the revolution onwards, but was to remain at a low level until 1873.[100] These factors were compounded with the abolition of serfdom and the difficulties faced by noble estates when confronting the sudden loss of forced laborers and the end of the peasants' obligation to buy a certain amount of alcohol; lords still maintained the exclusive right to produce and sell alcohol.[101] While the rapid population growth increased internal demand, exports rose significantly from the 1860s onwards, embedding products that had been produced and processed within Galicia even more firmly into transregional markets.[102]

Concerning flour, similar processes can be detected, as technological components from abroad, or from other regions of the empire, were also needed.

97 Rychlikowa, *Produkcja zbożowa*, p. 111; Lipelt et al., *Życie gospodarcze*, p. 74.

98 Blum, *Noble Landowners*, p. 110; CDIAL, f.146, op.80, spr.267, Fol. 44; CDIAL, f.146, op.68, spr.31, Nr.1548, Fol. 62.

99 *Kunst- und Industrie-Ausstellung zum Humoristen* 11 (11.3.1837), 41–42; 12 (18.3.1837), 45–46, quoted according to: Marinelli-König, *Polen und Ruthenen*, p. 559; Stauter-Halsted, *Nation*, p. 30.

100 Michalewicz, *Przemysł gorzelnialny*, pp. 69, 93–95, 139; Rutkowski, *Historia gospodarcza*, p. 360; CDIAL, f.146, op.80, spr.254, Fol. 1–32.

101 Ślusarek, "Czy dochody", pp. 291, 294; Stauter-Halsted, *Nation*, pp. 29–30; Hryniuk, "Peasant and Alcohol," p. 75.

102 *Rocznik Statystyki Galicyi*, II, Lwów 1889, p. 202.

Already in the late 1830s and early 1840s, new grain steam mills were installed on some estates, a tendency which, in principle, should have accelerated after the abolition of peasant subjection. Then aristocratic landowners sought to cut labor costs, although they were severely hindered by the lack of monetized capital. Accordingly, only a small number of mills were run by steam power, with most mills being driven by water power. The machines were manufactured in Vienna, Prague, and abroad,[103] for example France (these were traded by a Belgium agent, starting in 1838).[104] As with liquor, partial and selective integration into international commodity chains allowed Galicia's economy to continue processing grain to flour within the region and meet a substantial proportion of internal demand. At any rate, flour imports during the 1860s demonstrate that internal demand outstripped regional output, while exports of flour, mainly to the German Customs Union, occurred on a modest scale, even if the trade agreement of 1853 significantly lowered custom duties. In this regard, there was significant continuity with regard to the first phase.[105]

The production of beer also faced a similar phenomenon, with a reduction in the number of breweries, although this decrease was much less sharp than with distilleries; the number fell from 430 in 1841 to 373 six years later and 315 in 1858. Output increased staggeringly during the 1840s, but decreased again after 1850, before entering a phase of stagnation that lasted until the early 1870s.[106] While the concentration process undergone by the sector in the 1840s reflected some technological improvements, albeit still very limited, that pushed the output up,[107] the evolution of the sector after 1850 is harder to read. In this case, too many estates sought to reduce labor costs through mechanization, but the sort of capital that was needed for large-scale investment was lacking. Further technological innovations were only introduced in breweries in the late 1860s.[108] Owing to these technological shortcomings, only small amounts of raw materials were imported from extra-regional markets; these imports included barley, used for the production of high-quality beer, which was brought from Moravia and the Russian-controlled Kingdom of Poland but mainly only directed to the western districts of Galicia. Barley and hops imports aimed to complement local production.[109] As such, the commodity chain was still almost

103 Kramarz, "Młynarze," pp. 295–317, 310–311.

104 Archiwum Państwowe w Przemyślu (APP), 1307/6: Fol. 3–6, 27–31.

105 Lipp, *Verkehrs- und Handelsverhältnisse*, pp. 21–31; Huertas, *Economic Growth*, pp. 34–35.

106 *Tafeln für Statistik* 1841; Spyra, *Browarnictwo*, pp. 29, 34.

107 Lipelt et al., *Życie gospodarcze*, p. 74.

108 Spyra, *Browarnictwo*, p. 62.

109 Lipelt et al., *Życie gospodarcze*, p. 74; Lipp, *Verkehrs- und Handelsverhältnisse*, pp. 16, 53.

entirely regional, and faced a consumption pattern that we have already seen with other products after 1848 – forced consumption by peasants was abolished, but overall consumption increased owing to demographic growth, first campaigns against excessive alcohol consumption notwithstanding. However, in the 1860s, beer exports rose and overtook those of hard liquor.[110]

Concerning labor relations, the abolition of serfdom in 1848 was a decisive turning point. Robot was the key variable of Galicia's serfdom system; in 1845, 83.2 percent of all peasant dues were rendered in labor, while only 10.8 percent were delivered in kind and 6 percent in money.[111] These figures underline the fact that lords fully mobilized the available workforce for labor-intensive agricultural processes and industrial activities (for instance in distilleries, breweries, iron works, potash factories, and mills). Since the 1820s, peasants became significantly less willing to meet these compulsory labor requirements: there were 97 peasant rebellions between 1822 and 1847, with the main uprising taking place in 1846, only two years before the abolition of serfdom.[112] After the revolution of 1848, the new law fostered the emergence of a new landless class of peasants, who were forced to work for money or kind on the aristocratic estates out of mere economic necessity, but without legal or other extra-legal compulsion.[113]

Even peasants who owned land had to resort to additional wage-labor activities or look for other alternative sources of income, as the average plot size decreased during this phase – from 5 hectares in 1859 and 1868 to 3 hectares in 1880. The number of peasant holdings that may be regarded as not economically viable, under 5 ha, increased markedly: while in 1819 these properties amounted to an already high 60.8 percent of the total, their proportion rose to 69 percent in 1859.[114] This went hand in hand with an increasing concentration of landed property in the hands of noble landowners. While the abolition of serfdom was a strong push towards the commodification of agricultural labor, low salaries in the wake of rapid population growth, unequal land distribution, and compensation payments for a period of 40 years, guaranteed the privileged economic status of noble estates, as the high level of indebtedness of peasant economies translated traditional bondage into new economic dependencies channeled through the market. The gradual commodification of agricultural labor ran in parallel to the growing integration of the region in the

110 Lipp, *Verkehrs- und Handelsverhältnisse*, pp. 236, 241–242.
111 Himka, *Galician villagers*, p. 2.
112 Struve, *Bauern und Nation*, pp. 72–74.
113 Berger, *Landwirtschaft in Galizien*, pp. 40, 101.
114 Ibid., pp. 50–51.

trans-regional and international commodity chains of grain, liquor, and beer. However, many relics of the feudal economy remained in place: peasants were taxed more heavily than aristocrats, and paid labor services to noble estates in exchange for tools and equipment, the lease of meadows and the use of forests that the peasants had previously lost in court, after the enactment of the servitude law of 1853, and finally as interests for the loans that they took from aristocratic landowners. Sometimes, the wages of agricultural laborers were in kind or vouchers for the local tavern – a relic of the old obligation of peasants to consume the lord's alcohol.[115] In the end, the miserable situation of most peasants during this phase also implies that the regional purchasing power remained quite limited and that the subsistence economy of peasant households continued to remain strong, thus working against a complete commodification of the rural labor regime.

## 5 1873–1918: Interregional Versus International Commodity Chains

The international economic crisis of 1873 was another turning point for Galicia's economy: Critiques launched against the liberal economic model led to a return to protectionist trade policies in 1878, to growing state intervention, while the consequences of the crisis led to an inflow of capital in search of new assets in peripheral areas, where salaries were low and profit rates promised to be extraordinarily high. Railway construction, largely funded by the state, and a stronger degree of integration with transregional markets within the Habsburg Monarchy, despite the new protectionist wave, fostered Galicia's integration into transregional commodity chains, while the region's connections with international markets progressed on a much weaker scale.[116]

Tighter market integration within Austro-Hungary had a profound effect on Galicia's role in commodity chains of grain/bread/beer/liquor. The increasing commodification of agriculture and, in its wake, the intensification of agricultural practices, lifted some of the limitations on the production of raw materials that had characterized the two preceding periods, in which production had only grown on a modest scale. New production methods and techniques, such as: crop-rotation; animal husbandry; the introduction of new crops; better tools; machines and fertilizers predominantly natural but sometimes also chemical; converged to increase yields per hectare.[117] While noble estates took

115 Buszko, *Wandel*, pp. 8–9; Stauter-Halsted, *Nation*, p. 22.
116 Matis, "Sozioökonomische Aspekte", pp. 252–253, 258; Chonigsman, *Pronyknennja*, p. 48.
117 Franaszek, *Produkcja roślinna*, pp. 118–120, 122, 129–130; Sandgruber, *Agrarstatistik*, p. 177.

the lead in the diffusion of fertilizers and the use of machinery, peasant economies were also important innovators as they introduced crop-rotation, new crops, and better tools as early as the 1880s, to respond to the diminishing size of plots and increasing market integration.[118] Both processes were interlinked to a certain degree: The shrinking size of land per peasant economy led to the necessity to improve output and productivity in order to obtain rising incomes from market sales of their produce. This was also linked to the ever-bigger family sizes, which was precisely the reason for the diminishing size of peasant holdings. Average plot size decreased further to 3 and eventually to 2.5 hectares in 1880 and 1900 respectively, and the proportion of properties under 5 hectares rose to as much as 80 percent by 1900.[119] But there were also other mechanisms at play that forced peasants to get involved with market transactions to an increasing degree: This was the soaring debts of peasant households, largely caused by compensation payments, taxes, and the low prices of grain on the world market during the 1870s and 1880s, which had driven 36,549 peasant economies into ruin and compulsory auction between 1874 and 1889.[120] To be sure, this process was quite complex: Rising market transactions stretched from the local to the regional and trans-regional level, as dramatically falling transport costs, due to the construction of railway lines, laid down the basis for the entanglement of Galician rural markets with consumer markets in the western regions. Also, part of this process was the reinforcement of international market entanglements, such as with the agrarian exporters of the Atlantic economy. It was precisely these far-flung market ties that augmented competition within grain markets and exerted a downward pressure on grain prices – which were one important cause of the mentioned bankruptcies of thousands of Galicia's peasant economies. This also meant that the positive link between market integration and innovation-driven productivity gains was not a viable option for all peasant economies. The necessary facilities to implement innovative techniques already required a substantial degree of market integration, as peasants needed money to acquire seeds for new crops, tools, or literature and journals diffusing new knowledge. In fact, many innovations could only be implemented with the help of cooperatives and the gradual influx of capital sent by Galicians working abroad, mainly in the US and Canada, which was also used to buy land and thus somewhat offset the tendency of peasant land plots to shrink. This meant that the market mechanisms alone

118 Hryniuk, *Peasants with Promise*; Hauser, *Zur wirtschaftlichen Entwicklung*, pp. 61–67.

119 Hauser, *Zur wirtschaftlichen Entwicklung*, pp. 50–51.

120 Dinklage, "Die landwirtschaftliche Entwicklung", p. 423; Berger, *Landwirtschaft in Galizien*, pp. 61, 75, 84; Pilch, "Migrations", p. 91.

had to be supplemented by forms of strategic institutional planning in order to be able to translate competitive pressure into welfare gains.

That increasing output and productivity were linked to deepening market integration can be demonstrated by trade figures. The exports of agricultural products grew at breath-taking speed: between 1869 and 1883, grain (including pulses) exports by railway increased from 392,000 to 2.6 million metric hundredweight. Exports of flour rose from 20,000 to an impressive 150,000 metric hundredweight. However, at the top end of the commodity chain there were setbacks, for instance, liquor sales in the interregional markets dropped from 58,000 to 50,000 metric hundredweight. The following years witnessed sharply different tendencies. According to the railway statistics for 1890/92, exports of grain, flour and beer were lower than imports, although both grain (increase to 1.1 million metric hundredweight) and liquor (935,270 metric hundredweight) yielded rising export figures, while flour exports shrank massively (to 47,330 metric hundredweight) (Table 5.2). Beer, which was not mentioned in the earlier statistics, now features with a slim 15,827 metric hundredweight of gross exports and a negative trade balance. Liquor was the only commodity of these four that presented a positive trade balance (9,352.7 tons gross export and 8,063 tons net export).[121] More than two decades later, when Galicia's agriculture plunged into a recession on the eve of the First World War,[122] grain exports, which were by then limited to wheat, shrank further to 610,621 metric hundredweight, while imports were necessary to meet the regional demand. In contrast, transregional sale of flour (523,718 metric hundredweight), liquor (550,869 metric hundredweight) and beer (184,117 metric hundredweight) rose briskly and held a strengthened position in extra-regional markets.[123]

This already suggests an increasing interregional competitiveness in the semi-finished (flour) and finished products (beer, liquor) markets within the agricultural commodity chains that we selected as a proxy for the examination of Galicia's economic development. The increasing significance of external sale markets was, in the case of liquor and beer, also due to the eventual conversion of the noble alcohol production monopoly into a state-wide organized prerogative in 1889, and the increasing pressure from the Christian-Social-influenced cooperative movement to restrict alcohol consumption by peasants.[124] Conversely to exports, raw materials for these commodities had to be imported in increasing quantities. This development, however,

121 Biegeleisen, *Stan ekonomiczny Małopolski*, pp. 273–274.

122 Kaps, *Ungleiche Entwicklung*, p. 68.

123 Pączewski, "Bilans handlowy," vol.2, pp. 385–386.

124 Morawski, *Dzieje gospodarcze*, p. 121.

TABLE 5.2 Exports of grain, flour and liquor by railway from Galicia to trans-regional and international markets, 1869–1890/92 (in metric hundredweights)

| | 1869 | 1883 | 1890-92 |
|---|---|---|---|
| Grain and pulses | 392000 | 2600000 | 1016620 |
| Oilseed cake, corn flour | 20000 | 150000 | 47330 |
| Liquor | 58000 | 50000 | 935270 |

SOURCE: SZCZEPANOWSKI, *NĘDZA GALICYI*, P. 46; BIEGELEISEN, *STAN EKONOMICZNY MAŁOPOLSKI*, PP. 273–274

only affected our limited set of goods, and cannot be regarded as representative of the whole of the Galician economy. The railway transport statistics of 1890/92 and 1913 clearly demonstrate that, overall, Galicia's role as a provider of raw materials (their export share rose from 57.8 percent in 1890/92 to an incredible high 84.8 percent in 1913) and an importer of finished products (the ratio was 53.5 percent in 1890/92 and grew rapidly to 73.3 percent in 1913), consolidated.[125] Despite the generalized downgrading of industrial and proto-industrial production, caused by the ever tighter integration into transregional commodity chains, the processing of grain and potatoes into flour, beer, and liquor grew at a fast pace: beer output increased from 459,824 to 1,304,324 hectolitres between 1873 and 1913, the production of liquor rose somewhat less steeply from 200,463.5 to 585,939 hectolitres between 1872/73 and 1913/14. However, productivity seemingly increased more in breweries, whose numbers dwindled from 211 to 84, while the number of distilleries grew from 598 to 889.[126]

These commodities benefitted from a tighter integration in transregional commodity chains. Many of the technological improvements in agriculture, such as machinery or fertilizers, were imported from abroad, as shown by trade statistics. This holds especially true for the machinery used for processing crops. Starting in the 1870s, the so-called 'American steam mills' were advertised in Galicia's specialized agricultural journals. The switch from water-powered mills to steam engines, which was largely made possible by the influx of external capital, was, however, very limited in its extent. The mechanization of mills mainly took place in large or mid-sized urban areas, and by

125 Author's own estimates after Biegeleisen, *Stan ekonomiczny*, pp. 273–274; Pączewski, "Bilans handlowy," pp. 385–386.

126 Michalewicz, *Przemysł gorzelnialny*, pp. 69, 93–96; Spyra, *Browarnictwo*, pp. 30–31, 34–35.

the end of the nineteenth century only 20 percent of all Galician mills had been mechanized – because of the large amount of capital required.[127] Similarly, new machines and equipment, which allowed breweries and distilleries to produce larger quantities and better products, were predominantly imported from within the Habsburg Monarchy.[128] In conclusion, it seems clear that Galician flour, beer, and liquor became, in this period, more entangled in transregional and, to a lesser extent, international, commodity chains than ever before.

The conservative swing in Austro-Hungarian policies after 1879, resulted in the passing of new crafts regulation which aimed to protect trades from external competition in 1882 and 1885. This regulation of industrial labor was complemented by the introduction of accident and health insurance in 1887–89, as well as by the creation of the first pension system for white-collar workers in 1906. Meanwhile, trade unions pressed for better working conditions, although salaries in Galicia remained low compared with other regions, both overall and specifically in agriculture.[129] This tendency to regulate and formalize labor had only limited effects in Galicia, where it mainly affected heavy industry workers, including the extraction of raw minerals – from coal to oil – and the few factories that produced iron and machinery, and the railways. In general, the professionalization of production with the incorporation of new technology required a skilled workforce, which was paid higher wages and benefitted from regulated working conditions. The basic literacy of the population of Galicia increased markedly around the turn of the century: literacy indexes for Cisleithania indicate that literacy increased in Galicia from 23 in 1880 to 67 in 1910, which is a significant improvement.[130] The salaries of this privileged sector of the workforce tended to converge with those in other regions of the Habsburg Monarchy, while landless laborers working on noble estates, but also petty artisans, seemed to benefit much less from these changes in labor regimes. The main reason for the persistent divergence between the Galician and the Austro-Hungarian economy at large (as the GDP figures demonstrate) lay in these socio-professional groups and their low wage levels.[131] In addition, the setbacks of proto-industrial activities in the countryside made things harder for peasant households that relied on the additional income provided by the

127 Kramarz, "Młynarze," pp. 310–312.

128 Michalewicz, *Przemysł gorzelnialny*, p. 151; Spyra, *Browarnictwo*, p. 62.

129 Herbert Matis, *Österreichs Wirtschaft*, pp. 444–445; Idem., "Sozioökonomische Aspekte", p. 258; Sandgruber, *Ökonomie und Politik*, pp. 301, 303; Buszko, *Wandel*, p. 21.

130 Kool, *Economic Development*, p. 192.

131 Kaps, *Ungleiche Entwicklung*, pp. 80–81, 83–85.

home production and sale of textiles, pottery, shoes, and the like.[132] Unsurprisingly, when these tendencies became manifest in the early 1870s in the Western Galician districts, emigration started. The exodus of Galician workers accelerated throughout the 1880s, 1890s and, in fact, up to the First World War. At first, emigration was mostly seasonal and directed mainly to relatively nearby destination such as East German agriculture, but soon permanent emigrants began leaving for other European countries, such as France, and, especially, the US and Canada.[133] Still, the over-abundance of the rural workforce, that in part emigrated to Galicia's cities and towns, left enough hands to continue a certain degree of subsistence production of simple consumer goods such as textiles, baskets and the like, although the integration of peasant households with consumer markets, both regional and trans-regional, increased rapidly at the turn from the nineteenth to the twentieth century thus broadening aggregate domestic purchasing power. Thus, it seems that peasant women, who were at most affected by the driving of the traditional proto-industrial activities off the market, found new economic roles, not only in subsistence production, but also increasingly in agricultural activities. In turn, mainly male workers outmigrated, thereby leaving women in managerial positions of peasant holdings.

## 6 Conclusion

Galicia's position in transregional and international commodity chains underwent a gradual change from a semi-peripheral to a peripheral position in the course of the long nineteenth century between 1772 and the end of the First World War. The product group under scrutiny, however, is a clear example of how Galicia's economy could, despite the less than unfavorable context, still make some structural progress. In the first phase, protectionism and interimperial competition between Prussia and the Habsburg Monarchy nearly drove Galicia's crop production off international and transregional markets; this led to some production processes being upgraded. These were, however, little more than contingency measures implemented by aristocrats to compensate for the lost grain trade by mobilizing and redirecting resources, thanks to their feudal prerogatives. The second phase brought only slight changes to the commodity chains that transformed grain into flour, bread, beer, and liquor. However, the structural progress made in the first phase received a new

132 Berger, *Landwirtschaft in Galizien*, p. 102; Kulczykowski, "Protoindustrializacja i deindustrializacja," p. 116.

133 Pilch, "Migrations", pp. 84–89.

boost from closer international market entanglement, which was the result of liberalizing trade policies. Further upgrades of production processes, however, were limited to isolated instances, which required the import of raw materials and technology. In the third phase, market integration advanced at a fast pace in the wake of the expansion of the railway network, while a return to protectionist policies acted as a stimulus for closer transregional connections (within Austro-Hungary) to the detriment of international integration (which advanced with a comparatively slower velocity). In this phase, production processes were upgraded systematically, largely following the adoption of technological innovations across the sector, from flour mills to breweries and distilleries.

The transformation of Galicia's labor structure was heavily determined by state economic policy. In broad terms, we can argue that some attempts were made to transform the labor regime in the late eighteenth century by redistributing resources and property rights from feudal landowners to peasants, but they were soon brought to a halt. The liberal reforms of the mid-nineteenth century abolished serfdom and liberalized crafts, before a new state-interventionist swing in the three decades that preceded the outbreak of the world war, increased workers' protection and formalized labor regimes, although this affected artisans and industrial much more than land laborers who largely were left out from social securities and protective labor legislation.

We can, therefore, speak of a period of liberalization squeezed between two periods of more or less close state interventionism. During these phases, the structure of the labor force in Galicia seems to have changed little between the late eighteenth century and 1850 – different estimates suggest that the proportion of the workforce engaged in agricultural activities remained pretty much the same throughout the period. Greater change occurred in the second half of the nineteenth century, when the share of agricultural labor decreased decisively, although not spectacularly. Much more important were the profound changes undergone by labor regimes in the wake of the 1848 and 1859 reforms. While the abolition of peasant subjection finally achieved the long-sought commodification of labor, and the substitution of wage labor for robot labor, at least in theory, the severe inequalities that characterized the countryside kept certain relics of serfdom alive, at least for landless laborers. In contrast, the liberalizing reform of the industrial code in 1859 opened up local markets to transregional and also intra-regional competition, which led to a drop in artisans' income. The renewed interventionist policies put forward in the 1880s not only limited transregional competition by re-introducing licenses for local artisans, but also improved the situation of heavy industry workers by introducing social security legislation, protecting the workers' health and limiting the length of the working day. It has to be stressed that different labor regimes coexisted throughout the period, both in agriculture as such and in grain-related industries from distilleries over breweries to bakeries, although serfdom-type forced labor and its residuals had finally disappeared in Galicia at the turn of the twentieth century.

Concerning the relationship between labor structure and commodity chains, it is striking that Galicia's lack of integration with international markets and, therefore, the disentanglement of the province's internal commodity chains, went hand in hand with maintaining and even reinforcing severe labor pressures and the widespread use of forced labor. This confirms the findings that the high degree of uncertainty and risk characterizing the exports markets for Polish-Lithuanian grain during the 17th and 18th centuries in contrast to the relatively stable phase in the 16th century had spurred the imposition of severe regimes of peasant subjections in the sixteenth and in particular in the seventeenth centuries.[134] The fact that Galicia's role was to supply rather simple products to international and local markets made the use of forced labor a profitable strategy for aristocratic landowners. In contrast, the reintegration of Galicia into international commodity chains after 1830, gave a boost to the commodification of the workforce. The agrarian transformation of the late nineteenth and early twentieth centuries would not have been possible without a free, land-holding peasantry. However, the commodification of labor, both in agriculture and industry, was not completed until the last quarter of the nineteenth and the early twentieth centuries and also faced countertendencies as the return of peasant women working in transregionally oriented proto-industry to subsistence production with pressure being exerted on traditional craft home production. The commodification of labor relations had a lot to do with the agricultural revolution, that is, the introduction of new crops and techniques. The need for a skilled and highly educated workforce, in particular in grain-related industries such as brewing and distilling, but also on peasant economies in order to acquire knowledge about innovations and their application, was the key factor that ultimately transformed Galicia's labor system, which for decades (not to say centuries) had relied on low-skilled workers producing simple commodities, either for export or for domestic consumption. It is, nevertheless, true that large parts of the rural workforce being hired on big noble estates participated less in this process as they fulfilled rather simple tasks and landowners saw their education as a potential threat to the maintenance of their socioeconomic position and productive model.

134 Malinowski, "Serfs and the city", p. 139; Guzowski, "Influence," p. 317.

The institutional mechanisms, such as social security and labor protection laws that led to better working conditions in some sectors, are an additional element in this process, but more a consequence than a cause of change. In any case, agricultural labourers and peasants were not included at all in these new reforms. In conclusion, the analysis of this product group demonstrates that while Galicia's status deteriorated gradually from a semi-periphery to a periphery in the trans-regional and international division of labor, some improvement in agricultural commodity chains occurred by an upgrading of production processes within the region and innovations in existing commodity chains, augmenting productivity, helping to stabilize the region's economic development, which, nevertheless, remained at a low level. State economic policies concerning agriculture, infrastructures and trade, had a decisive impact in regulating commodity chains. While lack of integration in international and transregional commodity chains facilitated structural improvements in the region's commodity chains during the first phase, with the accelerating pace of technological innovation and the increasing complexity of production processes later on, the economic framework of the peripheral Galician economy could not support further development in the flour- and alcohol-processing sectors. The integration into transregional and international commodity chains in the second half of the nineteenth century was the logical consequence of the limitations of the peripheral Galician economy, and brought prosperity to these economic sectors, although benefits obviously were unevenly spread between sectors and, in particular, social groups, both within property owners and the highly stratified workforce in the countryside and urban centers. The severe socioeconomic inequality and, in particular, the precariousness of the agricultural labor force and small producers over the whole period analyzed is the main factor of structural persistence characterizing the bundle of products, partially tied together in one commodity chain and sometimes split apart. Labor forms and personal rights certainly changed a lot between the late 18th and the early 20th centuries having an impact on living-standards – but the overall picture underlines the precarious situation of the vast majority of Galicia's agricultural workforce over the scrutinized period so that the modest upgrading effects did not lead to a clear and sustainable improvement of living-standards.

## Bibliography

Adamczyk, Stanisław. "Spław zboża z dóbr Ordynacji Myszkowskiej do Gdańska w drugiej połowie XVIII w.", *Zeszyty Naukowe Politechniki Świętokrzyskiej. Nauki Ekonomiczne* 24, Kielce 1986, pp. 188–198.

Adamczyk, Dariusz. *Zur Stellung Polens im modernen Weltsystem der frühen Neuzeit* (Schriftenreihe Studien zur Geschichtsforschung der Neuzeit, vol.21) (Hamburg: Kovač, 2001).

Andre, Christian Karl. *Neueste geographisch-statistische Beschreibung des Kaiserthums Österreich* (Weimar: Verlag des Geographischen Instituts, 1813).

Bachinger, Karl and Herbert Matis. "Österreichs industrielle Entwicklung," in Alois Brusatti (ed.), *Die Habsburgermonarchie 1848–1918, vol.I: Die wirtschaftliche Entwicklung* (Wien: Verlag der österreichischen Akademie der Wissenschaften, 1973), pp. 105–232.

Bachinger, Karl. "Das Verkehrswesen", in Alois Brusatti (ed.), *Die Habsburgermonarchie 1848–1918, vol.I: Die wirtschaftliche Entwicklung* (Wien: Verlag der österreichischen Akademie der Wissenschaften, 1973), pp. 278–322.

Baranowski, Bohdan. "Zmiany w stosunkach folwarczno-pańszczyźnianych w drugiej połowie XVIII w." in Bohdan Baranowski, *et al.* (eds), *Zarys historii gospodarstwa wiejskiego w Polsce*, vol.II, part 4: *Okres gospodarki folwarczno-pańszczyźnianej (od drugiej połowy XV do XVIII w.)* (Warszawa: Państwowe Wydawnictwo rolnicze i leśne, 1964), pp. 88–115.

Beer, Adolf. "Die österreichische Handelspolitik unter Maria Theresia und Joseph II." *Archiv für österreichische Geschichte* 86 (1899), pp. 1–204.

Berger, Andrea. *Landwirtschaft in Galizien 1848–1914. Mit einer Analyse anhand des Ökotypen-Systems* (Master Thesis University of Salzburg 1999).

*Bericht der von dem Landtage zur Ausarbeitung des Projectes einer Galizischen Eisenbahn bestellten Commission, welcher von derselben den versammelten Ständen im Monate September 1842 erstattet wurde* (Lemberg: Pillerische Schriften, 1842).

Biegeleisen, Leon Władysław. *Stan ekonomiczny Małopolski na podstawie bilansu handlowego* (Warszawa: Biuro prac kongresowych and Ministerstwo spraw zagranicznych, 1921).

Blum, Jerome. *Noble Landowners and Agriculture in Austria 1815–1848. A Study in the Origins of the Peasant Emancipation of 1848* (Baltimore: The John Hopkins Press, 1948).

Bobińska, Celina. "Niektóre przesłanki rozwoju rynku wewnętrznego w Małopolsce w XVIII wieku", in *Pamiętnik VIII Powszechnego Zjazdu Historyków Polskich w Krakowie*, vol.1, part 2 (Warszawa: Polskie Towarzystwo Historyczne, 1958), pp. 361–375.

Brawer, A.J. *Galizien wie es an Österreich kam. Eine historisch-statistische Studie über die inneren Verhältnisse des Landes im Jahre 1772* (Leipzig and Wien: Freytag and Tempsky, 1910).

Buszko, Józef. *Zum Wandel der Gesellschaftsstruktur in Galizien und in der Bukowina* (Wien: Verlag der österreichischen Akademie der Wissenschaften, 1978).

Cerman, Markus. *Villagers und Lords in Eastern Europe, 1300–1800* (Basingstoke and New York: Palgrave Macmillan, 2012).

Chonigsman, Jakiv Samuel. *Pronyknennja inozemnoho kapitalu v ekonomiku Zachidnoji Ukrajiny v epochu imperializmu (do 1918 r.)* (L'viv: Vydavnyctvo L'vivs'koho universytetu, 1971).

Cieślak, Edmund. "The influence of the first partition of Poland in the overseas trade of Gdańsk," in Heeres, W.G. *et al.* (eds), *From Dunkirk to Dantzig: Shipping and Trade in the North Sea and the Baltic, 1350–1850: Essays in honour of J.A. Faber* (Hilversum: Verloren Publishers, 1988), pp. 203–215.

Dickson, P.G.M. *Finance and Government under Maria Theresia 1740–1780*, 2 vols (Oxford: Oxford University Press, 1987).

Dinklage, Karl. "Die landwirtschaftliche Entwicklung," in Alois Brusatti (ed.), *Die Habsburgermonarchie 1848–1918, vol.I: Die wirtschaftliche Entwicklung* (Wien: Verlag der österreichischen Akademie der Wissenschaften, 1973), pp. 403–451.

Dobado-González, Rafael, Alfredo García-Hiernaux and David E. Guerrero, "The Integration of Grain Markets in the Eighteenth Century: Early Rise of Globalization in the West," *The Journal of Economic History* 72, 3 (September 2012), pp. 671–707.

Drozdowski, Marian. "Traktaty handlowe po pierwszym rozbiorze Polski a problem jedności gospodarczej ziem polskich," *Roczniki Historyczne* 37 (1971), pp. 85–110.

Falniowska-Gradowska, Alicja. "Some remarks on the rental system in southern Poland," *Studiae Historiae Oeconomicae* 10 (1975), pp. 173–175.

Falniowska-Gradowska, Alicja and Franciszek Leśniak, *Struktura własności ziemskiej i użytkowania gruntów w Galicji w cyrkułach rzeszowskim, sanockim i tarnowskim w świetle katastru józefińskiego (1785–1787)* (Toruń: Europejskie Centrum Edukacyjnie, 2009).

Federico, Giovanni, Max-Stephan Schulze and Oliver Volckart, "European goods market integration in the very long run: from the Black Death to the First World War," *Economic History Working Papers* 87184 (London School of Economics and Political Science, Department of Economic History) 2018.

Fierich, Jerzy. "Kultury rolnicze, zmianowania i zbiory w katastrze jozefinskim 1785/87", *Roczniki dziejów społecznych i gospodarczych* 12 (1950), pp. 25–66.

Fischer, Karin and Christian Reiner, "Globale Warenketten: Analysen zur Geographie der Wertschöpfung," Z. *Zeitschrift Marxistische Erneuerung* 23/89 (2012), pp. 27–44.

Franaszek, Piotr. *Produkcja roślinna Galicji w dobie autonomicznej* (Kraków: Nakład Uniwersytetu Jagiellońskiego, 1995).

Glassl, Horst. *Das Österreichische Einrichtungswerk im Galizien, 1772–1790* (Wiesbaden: Harrassowitz, 1975).

Good, David. "The Economic Lag of Central and Eastern Europe: Evidence from the Late Nineteenth-Century Habsburg Empire," *Working Papers in Austrian Studies*, 93–7, December 1993.

Grossmann, Henryk. *Österreichs Handelspolitik mit Bezug auf Galizien in der Reformperiode 1772–1790* (Studien zur Sozial-, Wirtschafts- und Verwaltungsgeschichte, vol. x, ed. by Karl Grünberg) (Wien: Konegen, 1914).

Guzowski, Piotr. "The influence of exports on grain production on Polish royal demesne farms in the second half of the sixteenth century," *Agricultural History Review* 59, 2 (2011), pp. 312–327.

Haczynski, Leo. "Two Contributions to the Problem of Galicia," *East European Quaterly* IV/1 (1970), pp. 94–104.

Hauser, Jochen. *Zur wirtschaftlichen Entwicklung der österreichischen Karpatenländer Galizien und der Bukowina 1848–1918* (Wien: unpubl. Diplomarbeit Universität Wien, 1997).

Himka, John-Paul. *Galician villagers and the Ukrainian national movement in the nineteenth century* (Basingstoke: Macmillan, 1988).

Hopkins, Terence K. and Immanuel Wallerstein, "Grundzüge der Entwicklung des modernen Weltsystems. Entwurf für ein Forschungsvorhaben, " in Dieter Senghaas (ed), *Kapitalistische Weltökonomie. Kontroversen über ihren Ursprung und ihre Entwicklungsdynamik* (Frankfurt/Main: Suhrkamp, 1979), pp. 151–200.

Huertas, Thomas, *Economic Growth and Economic Policy in a Multi-National Setting: The Habsburg Monarchy* (New York: Arno Press, 1977).

Hundert, Gershon David, *Jews in Poland-Lithuania in the Eighteenth Century. A Genealogy of Modernity* (Berkeley: University of California Press, 2004).

Hryniuk, Stella. "The Peasant and Alcohol in Eastern Galicia in the Late Nineteenth Century: a Note," *Journal of Ukrainian Studies* 11/1 (1986), pp. 75–85.

Hryniuk, Stella. *Peasants with Promise. Ukrainians in South-Eastern Galicia 1880–1900* (Edmonton: Canadian Institute of Ukrainian Studies, University of Alberta, 1991).

Kaps, Klemens. *Ungleiche Entwicklung in Zentraleuropa. Galizien zwischen überregionaler Verflechtung und imperialer Politik* (Wien: Böhlau, 2015).

Kargol, Tomasz, Łukasz Jewuła and Krzysztof Ślusarek. *Dwór, wieś i plebania w przestrzeni społecznej zachodniej Małopolski w latach 1772–1815* (Kraków: Towarzystwo Wydawnicze "Historia Iagellonica", 2015).

Kargol, Tomasz. "Uposażenie i gospodarka plebańska zawiślańskich (galicyjskich) parafii archidiakonatu sandomierskiego na przełomie XVIII i XIX w. Kontynuacja czy zmiana?" in Tomasz Kargol, Bohdan Petryszak and Krzysztof Ślusarek (eds), *Studia z dziejów wsi polskiej na przełomie XVIII i XIX wieku* (Kraków and Lwów: Towarzystwo Wydawnicze "Historia Iagellonica", 2015), pp. 147–186.

Kasperek, Józef. *Gospodarka folwarczna Ordynacji Zamojskiej w drugiej połowie XVIII w.* (Warszawa: Verlag der österreichischen Akademie der Wissenschaften, 1972).

Kazusek, Szymon. "Handel an der polnisch-österreichischen Grenze nach 1772 (bis 1815)," in Christoph Augustynowicz and Andreas Kappeler (eds), *Die galizische Grenze 1772–1867: Kommunikation oder Isolation?* (Europa Orientalis vol.4) (Wien: LIT, 2007), pp. 51–64.

Kazusek, Szymon. "Związki gospodarcze dóbr magnackich z Gdańskiem w połowie XVIII wieku," in Jadwiga Muszyńska, Szymon Kazusek and Jacek Pielas (eds),

*Folwark – Wieś – Latyfundium. Gospodarstwo wiejskie w Rzeczypospolitej w XVI-XVIII wieku* (Kielce: Wydawnictwo Uniwersytetu Humanistyczno-Przyrodniczego Jana Kochanowskiego, 2009), pp. 241–256.

Koch, Klaus. "Österreich und der Deutsche Zollverein (1848–1871)," in *Die Habsburgermonarchie 1848–1918, vol. 6/1: Die Habsburgermonarchie im System der internationalen Beziehungen* (Wien: Verlag der österreichischen Akademie der Wissenschaften, 1989), pp. 537–560.

Kool, Leslie. *Economic Development on the periphery. A case study of East Galicia* (Ph.D. Temple University Ann Arbour, Michigan 1994).

Kramarz, Henryka, "Młynarze i młynarstwo zbożowe w Galicji (Z problematyki uprzemysławiania rzemiosła chłopskiego)," in Krzysztof Ślusarek (ed.), *Polska i Polacy w XIX-XX wieku. Studia ofiarowane Profesorowi Mariuszowi Kulczyckowskiemu w 70. rocznicę Jego urodzin* (Kraków: Towarzystwo Wydawnicze "Historia Iagellonica", 2002), pp. 295–317.

Kula, Witold. *An Economic Theory of the Feudal System* (London: Verso, 1976).

Kulczykowski, Mariusz. *Andrychowski ośrodek płócienniczy w 18 i 19 wieku* (Wrocław, Warszawa, Kraków and Gdańsk: Zakład narodowy imienia Ossolińskich and Wydawnictwo Polskiej Akademii Nauk, 1972).

Kulczykowski, Mariusz. "Protoindustrializacja i deindustrializacja Galicji w latach 1772–1918. Problemy badawczy," *Roczniki Dziejów Społecznych i Gospodarczych* 50 (1989), pp. 105–118.

Levine, Hillel. *Economic Origins of Antisemitism. Poland and Its Jews in the Early Modern Period* (New Haven and London: Yale University Press, 1991).

Link, Edith Murr. *The Emancipation of the Austrian Peasant 1740–1798* (New York: Columbia University Press, 1949).

Lipelt, Robert et al. *Życie gospodarcze ziemi sanockiej od XVI do XX w.* (Sanok: Stowarzyszenie Inicjowania Przedsiębiorczości w Sanoku, 2004).

Lipp, Adolf. *Verkehrs- und Handelsverhältnisse in Galizien* (Prag: C.H. Hunger, 1870).

Madurowicz, Helena and Antoni Podraza, "Próba rejonizacji gospodarczej Małopolski zachodniej," in Celina Bobińska (ed.), *Studia z dziejów wsi małopolskich w drugiej połowie XVIII w.* (Warszawa: Książka i Wiedza, 1957), pp. 57–167.

Malinowski, Mikołaj, "Serfs and the city: market conditions, surplus extraction institutions, and urban growth in early modern Poland," *European Review of Economic History* 20 (2016), pp. 123–146.

Marinelli-König, Gertraud. *Polen und Ruthenen in den Wiener Zeitschriften und Almanachen des Vormärz. Versuch einer kritischen Bestandsaufnahme der Beiträge über Galizien, die Bukowina und das polnische Geistesleben insgesamt* (Wien: Verlag der österreichischen Akademie der Wissenschaften, 1992).

Mark, Rudolf A. *Galizien unter österreichischer Herrschaft. Verwaltung – Kirche – Bevölkerung* (Historische und landeskundliche Ostmitteleuropa-Studien vol. 13) (Marburg: Marburg. Herder-Institut, 1994).

Michalewicz, Jerzy. *Przemysł gorzelnialny Galicji doby autonomicznej. Między monopolem dworskim a monopolem państwowym* (Kraków: Nakład Uniwersytetu Jagiellońskiego, 1988).

Matis, Herbert. *Österreichs Wirtschaft 1848–1913. Konjunkturelle Dynamik und gesellschaftlicher Wandel im Zeitalter Franz Joseph I.* (Berlin: Duncker & Humblot, 1972).

Matis, Herbert. "Sozioökonomische Aspekte des Liberalismus in Österreich 1848–1918," in Hans-Ulrich Wehler (ed.), *Sozialgeschichte Heute* (Göttingen: Vandenhoeck & Ruprecht, 1974), pp. 243–265.

Morawski, Wojciech. *Dzieje gospodarcze Polski* (2nd edition, Warszawa: Difin, 2011).

Pach, Zsigmond Pál. "The Role of East-Central Europe in International Trade (16th and 17th centuries)," in *Idem.*, *Hungary and the European Economy in Early Modern Times* (Aldershot: Routledge, 1994), pp. 217–264.

Pacholkiv, Svjatoslav. "Entstehung, Überwachung und Überschreitung der galizischen Grenze 1772–1867," in Christoph Augustynowicz and Andreas Kappeler (eds), *Die galizische Grenze 1772–1867: Kommunikation oder Isolation?* (Europa Orientalis vol. 4) (Wien: LIT, 2007), pp. 167–197.

Pączewski, Leon. "Bilans handlowy Małopolski," in Stanisław Aleksander Kempner (ed.), *Dzieje Gospodarcze Polski Porozbiorowej w zarysie* (Warszawa: Drukarnie K. Kowalski, 1922) vol.2, pp. 372–391.

Persson, Karl Gunnar. *Grain Markets in Europe, 1500–1900. Integration and Deregulation* (2nd edition, Cambridge: Cambridge University Press, 2004).

Pilch, Andrzej. "Migrations of the Galician Populace at the turn of the nineteenth and twentieth centuries," in Celina Bobińska and Andrzej Pilch (eds), *Employment-seeking emigrations of the Poles world-wide XIX and XX c.* (Zeszyty naukowe Uniwersytetu Jagiellońskiego CCCCXVII, Prace Polonijne, Zeszyt 1) (Kraków: Państwowe Wydawnictwo Naukowe, 1975), pp. 77–101.

Pietrzak-Pawłowska, Irena. "Przewrót przemysłowy i warunki industrializacji do 1918 r." in *Idem* (ed.), *Uprzemysłowienie ziem polskich w XIX i XX wieku. Studia i materiały* (Wrocław, Warszawa and Kraków: Zakład narodowy imienia Ossolińskich and Wydawnictwo Polskiej Akademii Nauk, 1970) pp. 57–103.

*Rocznik Statystyki Galicyi*, II (Lwów: Krajowe Biuro Statystyczne, 1889).

Rosdolsky, Roman. *Untertan und Staat in Galizien. Die Reformen unter Maria Theresia und Joseph II.* (Mainz: von Zabern, 1992).

Rozdolski, Roman. *Die große Agrar- und Steuerreform Josephs II. Ein Kapitel zur österreichischen Wirtschaftsgeschichte* (Warszawa: Państwowe Wydawnictwo Naukowe, 1961).

Rozdolski, Roman. *Stosunki poddańczy w dawnej Galicji*, 2 vols. (Warszawa: Wydawnictwo Naukowe, 1962).

Rudolph, Richard L. "The East European Peasant Household and the Beginnings of Industry: East Galicia, 1786–1914," in I.S. Koropeckyj (ed.), *Ukrainian Economic History. Interpretative Essays* (Cambridge, Mass.: Cambridge University Press, 1991), pp. 339–382.

Rusiński, Władysław. "The Role of Polish Territories in the European Trade in the Seventeenth and Eighteenth Centuries," *Studiae Historiae Oeconomicae* 2 (1967), pp. 115–134.

Rutkowski, Jan. *Historia gospodarcza Polski do 1864 r.* (Warszawa: Książka i Wiedza, 1953).

Rychlikowa, Irena. "Realizacja społeczno-gospodarczych reform terezjańsko-józefińskich w Galicji," *Roczniki Dziejów Społecznych i Gospodarczych* 19 (1957), pp. 91–131.

Rychlikowa, Irena. *Produkcja zbożowa wielkiej własności w Małopolsce w latach 1764–1805* (Warszawa: Państwowe Wydawnicto Naukowe, 1967).

Rychlikowa, Irena. *Studia nad towarową produkcją wielkiej własności w Małopolsce w latach 1764–1805*, part 1 (Wrocław, Warszawa and Kraków: Zakład narodowy imienia Ossolińskich and Wydawnictwo Polskiej Akademii Nauk, 1966).

Sandgruber, Roman. *Österreichische Agrarstatistik 1750–1918* (Wirtschafts und Sozialstatistik Österreich-Ungarns, Teil 2) (Wien: Verlag für Geschichte und Politik, 1978).

Sandgruber, Roman. "Die Agrarrevolution in Österreich, " in Alfred Hoffmann (ed.), *Österreich-Ungarn als Agrarstaat. Wirtschaftliches Wachstum und Agrarverhältnisse in Österreich im 19. Jahrhundert* (Wien: Verlag für Geschichte und Politik, 1978), pp. 195–271.

Sandgruber, Roman. *Ökonomie und Politik. Österreichische Wirtschaftsgeschichte vom Mittelalter bis zur Gegenwart* (Wien: Ueberreuter, 1994).

Schulze, Max-Stephan. "Regional Income Dispersion and Market Potential in the Late Nineteenth Century Hapsburg Empire," *Working Papers* No. 106/07.

Spyra, Adam. *Browarnictwo Galicji doby autonomicznej* (Kraków: Księgarnia Akademicka, 1994).

Stauter-Halsted, Keely. *The Nation in the Village. The Genesis of Peasant National Identity in Austrian Poland, 1848–1914* (Ithaca and London: Cornell University Press, 2001).

Stone, Daniel. *The Polish-Lithuanian State* (Seattle and Washington: University of Washington Press, 2001).

Struve, Kai. *Bauern und Nation in Galizien. Über Zugehörigkeit und soziale Emanzipation im 19. Jahrhundert* (Göttingen: Vandenhoeck & Ruprecht, 2005).

Szczepanowski, Stanisław. *Nędza Galicyi w cyfrach i program energicznego rozwoju gospodarstwa krajowego* (Lwów: Gubrinowicz i Schmidt, 1888).

Ślusarek, Krzysztof. *Drobna Szlachta w Galicji 1772–1848* (Kraków: Księgarnia Akademicka, 1994).

Ślusarek, Krzysztof. *Uwłaszczenie chłopów w Galicji zachodniej* (Kraków: Towarzystwo Wydawnicze "Historia Iagellonica", 2002).

Ślusarek, Krzysztof. "Czy dochody z propinacji, czyli produkcji wódki i piwa, uratowały galicyjskich ziemian przed bankructwem?" in *Idem.* (ed.), *Polska i Polacy w XIX-XX wieku. Studia ofiarowane Profesorowi Mariuszowi Kulczyckowskiemu w 70. rocznicę*

*Jego urodzin* (Kraków: Towarzystwo Wydawnicze "Historia Iagellonica", 2002), pp. 285–294.

Ślusarek, Krzysztof, "Bevölkerung und Wirtschaft Galiziens im Jahre 1773," in Christoph Augustynowicz and Andreas Kappeler (eds), *Die galizische Grenze 1772–1867: Kommunikation oder Isolation?* (Europa Orientalis herausgegeben vom Institut für Osteuropäische Geschichte an der Universität Wien, vol.4) (Wien: LIT, 2007), pp. 65–81.

Ślusarek, Krzysztof. "Dobra państwowe w Galicji w końcu XVIII wieku. Część I. Galicja zachodnia," in Tomasz Kargol, Bohdan Petryszak and Krzysztof Ślusarek (eds), *Studia z dziejów wsi polskiej na przełomie XVIII i XIX wieku* (Kraków and Lwów: Towarzystwo Wydawnicze "Historia Iagellonica", 2015), pp. 187–216.

Tokarz, Wacław. *Galicya w początkach ery józefińskiej w świetle ankiety urzędowej z roku 1783* (Kraków: Akademia umiejętności, 1909).

Topolski, Jerzy. *Narodziny kapitalizmu w Europie XIV-XVII wieku* (3rd edition, Poznań: Wydawnictwo Poznańskie, 2003).

Turnock, David. *The Economy of East Central Europe, 1815–1989. Stages of Transformation in a peripheral region* (London and New York: Routledge, 2006).

Wallerstein, Immanuel and Terence K.Hopkins. "Commodity Chains in the World-Economy Prior to 1800," in Immanuel Wallerstein (ed.), *The Essential Wallerstein* (New York: New Press, 2000), pp. 221–233.

Wallerstein, Immanuel. *Historical capitalism* (London: Verso, 1984).

Zamoyski, Grzegorz. "Ceny zbóż w Austrii i Galicji w latach 1775–1815," in Tomasz Kargol, Bohdan Petryszak and Krzysztof Ślusarek (eds.), *Studia z dziejów wsi polskiej na przełomie XVIII i XIX wieku* (Kraków and Lwów: Towarzystwo Wydawnicze „Historia Iagellonica", 2015), pp. 237–257.

CHAPTER 6

# Global Commodity Chains and Labor Relations in the Distribution of Central European Copper in the Eighteenth Century

*Miroslav Lacko*

## 1 Introduction

The production of copper in Central Europe attained a global dimension in the Early Modern Age, as copper products were exported not only to European markets but also those in Africa and Asia. During the eighteenth century, Central European copper production was concentrated in several mining production centers of the Habsburg Monarchy under state administration and the region became one of the largest copper producing hubs in the world at that time.[1] Copper production and processing in the Habsburg Monarchy had been realized in the four most essential mining centers as follows:

(1) The Upper Hungarian (Spiš and Gemer – present-day East Slovakia) mining district, under the administration of the Chief Inspectorate in Smolník (*Schmöllnitz*), together with the state copper enterprise and many private mining plants, which would become the largest copper producer in the whole empire.

(2) The Lower Hungarian mining district, with state copper mining and metallurgical plants administered by the Mining Chamber in Banská Bystrica (*Neusohl*) (present-day Central Slovakia).[2]

(3) The state copper works in the Banat, administered by the Mining Inspectorate and the Office of the Chief Mining Master in Oraviţa (*Orawitza*) (present-day Romania).

(4) Tyrolean state copper plants under the administration of the State Commercial Office in Schwaz (Austria).

Nearly all the copper production and processing in the Habsburg Monarchy was managed by the state government, a practice that was gradually introduced

1 Cf. Blanchard, *Russia's 'Age of Silver': Precious-Metal Production and Economic Growth in the Eighteenth Century*, pp. 32–43.

2 See Map 6.1: The most important centers of copper production in the Early Modern Habsburg Monarchy.

 | DOI:10.1163/9789004448049_007

in the individual production centers during the seventeenth century. In the Hungarian Kingdom, the state copper monopoly had been successively introduced, especially as a new form of state dominance in copper mining and production. Active state enterprise commenced in the field of mining, metallurgy and trade for all-important raw materials such as copper, quicksilver, iron, and others. Under Ferdinand II, the redemption (repurchase) of copper (*Kupfereinlösung*) was introduced foremost through Act No. 42 of 1625, as well as the restriction of copper export by private subjects. The origin of the intensive state regulation in copper production could be characterized by this act.

Copper trading on the internal market was permitted by Act No. 65 of 1638. The Mining Chamber in Banská Bystrica (*Neusohl*), as the only state office, had to secure the observance of both of the above acts, and therefore the mentioned acts from 1625 and 1638 could not be applied throughout the whole kingdom. Therefore, this regulation was only introduced in the Lower Hungarian mining district (present-day Central Slovakia).

The normal legal establishment of the state copper monopoly finally came in 1655 through Act No. 28 under Ferdinand III's rule. On the basis of this act, the Mining Chamber in Banská Bystrica (*Neusohl*) was charged with the copper redemption in Lower Hungary (present-day Central Slovakia) and the private export of copper from the Hungarian Kingdom was prohibited. The legal basis was derived from the reasoning that copper had been used for monetization as one of the coinage metals.[3]

Copper production in the Upper Hungarian mining district and in the Banat had been monopolized by the state administration in the late seventeenth century, after the defeat of the Ottoman Empire and the resumption of the south and south-east lands of the Hungarian Kingdom. Tyrolean copper production was concentrated under the mining authority in Schwaz. By stabilizing the state government in the above-mentioned lands, the Habsburg state established control over the largest copper production centers throughout the Monarchy. A new type of cooperation and capital commitments with private Western European banks and merchants began to take place, in contrast to the previous so-called "*Appaltzeit*", when state companies were directly leased to private enterprisers.[4] The copper and tobacco monopolies, established during

3 See Lacko, "Zwischen Regulierung und Liberalisierung: Staatliche Wirtschaftspolitik in der Habsburgermonarchie und das Eisenhüttenwesen in der ersten Hälfte des 18. Jahrhunderts," pp. 47–48.

4 For the problem of "*Appaltzeit*", i.e. the era of leasing mining and metallurgical plants to private subjects, see: Srbik, *Der staatliche Exporthandel Österreichs von Leopold I. bis Maria Theresia*, pp. 3–65.

MAP 6.1 The most important centers of copper production in the early modern Habsburg Monarchy
ELABORATED BY M. LACKO

the last years of the seventeenth century, could be described as new state monopolies with the clear aim of increasing the state's revenues.

The relationship between the private copper producers and the state government became strained during the war years as payments for copper redemption were seriously delayed and the producers were discontented with the state-fixed redemption prices of copper. In the first half of the eighteenth century, the state-fixed redemption price reached 27 fl. 30 kr.[5] for one Viennese cent of copper.[6] Mostly, the state administration set the redemption prices on an individual basis with the private producers for a period of three years (from 31 fl. to 37 fl. 30 kr. for one cent of copper).[7] A characteristic ambivalent relationship of the state and private producers persisted from the introduction of a state copper monopoly at the end of the seventeenth century until its dissolution in the mid-nineteenth century. The representatives of the state chamber and the mining administration reflected the needs of the producers, but state

5 1 fl./Gulden = 60 kr./Kreuzer.

6 1 Viennese cent = 100 lb/pounds = 56.12 kg.

7 Cf. Lacko, "Gewerken und Staat im protoindustriellen Bergbau. Die Gründung der Oberungarischen Waldbürgerschaft im Jahr 1748 in unbekannten Zusammenhängen," pp. 182–186, Table 1.

interests had priority, especially the current power-political and military demands of the Monarchy.

The real profit of the state from mining therefore constituted the so-called "copper loans" – debts that the copper fund (*Kupferfundum*) and state mining enterprises recorded as liabilities, which commercial partners (mostly the creditors – bankers and merchants from Hamburg, Frankfurt am Main, Amsterdam, or London) regularly provided to the state as loan capital.[8] These loans were secured on revenues from copper production in the Habsburg Empire, which was an assurance of repayment. The quicksilver fund was similarly exploited within an amortization of the state debt, and it was exactly this indebtedness through borrowed capital that generated a net profit for the state. The Habsburg Monarchy, as a typical Early Modern fiscal-military state, derived significant profit from the loans secured on mining revenues, especially on the copper and quicksilver production administrated by the state government. If these loans could not be repaid by the state administration with financial capital, the state had to repay the loans from foreign creditors secured on mining revenues with semi-finished copper or refined mercury. For example, in May 1712 the debt charged on the copper fund reached 3,000,000 Dutch Gulden, i.e. 2,453,000 fl. of Viennese currency that was allowed by the Dutch creditors in the early eighteenth century. The so-called "Dutch security" on copper production remained until 1735.[9]

Payment of such debts represented one of the main external problems of the state mining enterprise, while the maintenance of the state copper monopoly, with its redemption from private producers, where the debts also gradually increased, formed a further, internal problem in state enterprise. As an example, in the period of the War of the Austrian Succession (1740–1748), these two factors seriously affected the development of copper production as a whole in the Habsburg Monarchy. The managing officials had to find a strategic partner for the marketing of copper – such a partner could only be the foreign banking houses.[10] In 1748, the debt of the copper fund and the aforementioned financial demands of the private copper producers represented the largest part of the total debt held by the state mining and metallurgy sector. Within a new system represented by the financial contributions to the state debt service, effective from 1 November 1748, the sector of state mining and metallurgy was obliged to contribute to the debt service annually to the amount of more than

8 Dickson, *Finance and Government under Maria Theresia (1740–1780)*, II, pp. 300–310.

9 Srbik, *Der staatliche Exporthandel Österreichs von Leopold I. bis Maria Theresia*, pp. 362–363.

10 See Lacko, "Ungarisches Kupfer und das Staatsfinanzwesen der Habsburgermonarchie in der Zeit des Österreichischen Erbfolgekriegs (1740–1748)," pp. 109–145.

700,000 fl. (fl. = Austrian Gulden), which accounted for 21 percent of debt-service revenues. These debt-service revenues constituted the annual incomes that were associated with paying off a state debt.[11]

In this regard, the state's interest in proto-industrial copper mining and production is generally not surprising. The growth and spread of state dominance in the mining and metallurgy of the eighteenth century was perceived as an obvious trend in the Habsburg Monarchy as a fiscal-military state. This occurred due to the necessity of higher state revenues to meet military needs and as a result of a cameralistic policy to establish the state's supremacy in the economy of the Empire as legitimate. This chapter therefore discusses the commodity chains in the proto-industrial copper production and how they were essentially affected by the enterprising of the fiscal-military state, but it also analyses labor relations found inside these chains. This analysis should represent a first attempt at comprehensively reviewing the problems of labor relations in Central European copper mining and production under the terms of the estates-based society.

The labor relations in proto-industrial manufacturing, formed through the estates-based society, were partly based on an improvement of profitability through the extra-economic enforcement of labor in the form of servitude or corvée – "robot" – labor services for landlords. Milan Myška demonstrated in his research on proto-industrial iron-making in the Bohemian lands that the Bohemian landlords, as private entrepreneurs in iron production, markedly exploited forced labor in their ironworks. The enterprisers represented by the Bohemian nobility disposed of their large domains in favor of the iron manufactories where the labor services of serfs were intensively used. According to Myška, salaried coerced labor was the most pervasive form of forced labor on the aristocratic estates.[12] This chapter will illuminate the conditions in the

---

11 For more information about the above-mentioned problems with state finance and mining enterprise, see Lacko, "Bergbau und Staatsfinanzen der Habsburgermonarchie in der Zeit der Staatsreformen 1748–1749," pp. 362–384. Dickson, *Finance and Government under Maria Theresia (1740–1780)*, II, pp. 95–98.

12 Myška covers the economic development of the Bohemian iron manufactories in the era from the turn of the sixteenth and seventeenth centuries until the 1820s. This represents a period of their growth during which the labor services of serfs and forced labor were often utilized due to an underdeveloped labor market in their lands. This labor service of serfs or salaried forced labor improved the profitability of private iron manufactories in the lordships and was utilized for ancillary work operations. See Myška, "Pre-Industrial Iron-Making in the Czech Lands: The Labour Force and Production Relations circa 1350–circa 1840," pp. 44–72. Myška, "Protoindustriální železářství v českých zemích: Robota a jiné formy nucené práce v železářských manufakturách," pp. 143–162.

state copper mining industry and metallurgical plants, which were of central importance for the state finance of the Habsburg Monarchy and compare them with the research results of Milan Myška. Categories of workers, their labor relationship with the state enterprise and the recruiting of laborers for the state plants are examined within the two following sections on the copper commodity and production chain.

## 2 Labor Relations in Copper Mining

The first segment of the global commodity chain in copper production and marketing was represented by ore mining and beneficiation, including the final production of semi-finished copper products. The primary resource of this commodity chain was obtained by underground ore mining in the above-mentioned mining regions of the Habsburg Monarchy. Workers were organized into many categories, formed in relation to workload. The individual production subdivisions and phases of copper processing were reflected in a stock of the work. The mineworkers, who were represented by very numerous groups within the crew, were divided into several salaried classes according to the type of position and wages as follows:

(a) The so-called "ore miners" (*Erzhäuer*/*Häuer*) mined the ore that was bought by the state mining administration. Valuation of the copper ore was fixed depending upon the metal content within. Ore miners had to separate the ore from the mullock directly underground and their wages depended on the metal content in the stopped-out ore. The mining assayers were obliged to ascertain the level of metal content in one mine car[13] as a volume measure (*Pahr*, *Paar*) or in one cent.[14] The volume of these measures differed substantially across individual mining districts. Changing the ore valuation could induce social conflict among the mineworkers. A possible modification of the ore valuation, according to the mining officials, would lead to greater efficiency of the state enterprise, evidenced by, for an example, Bartholomäus Ludwig Hechengartner's (1702–1773)[15]

13 For example, in the Upper Hungarian mining district, one mine car (*Pahr*) contained 106 liters = 3 cents = 168 kg. Cf. Lacko, "K transferu inovácií v stredoeurópskom hutníctve: Bartolomej Ľudovít Hechengartner (1702–1773) a zhutňovanie medi na Spiši v prvej polovici 18. storočia," pp. 167–168.

14 1 Viennese cent = 56.12 kg.

15 Bartholomäus Ludwig Hechengartner (1702–1773) was a prominent mining expert of the Habsburg state administration in the mid-eighteenth century who was descended as a mineworker from the Tyrolean Oberndorf. He worked until 1747 as a chief mining master

TABLE 6.1 The valuation of purchased ore from the ore miners in the Upper Hungarian state copper mines in Smolník (*Schmöllnitz*), valid from 1741 to 1747, and the Hechengartner's ore valuation approved in January 1747 (1 mine car "*Pahr*" = 106 liters = 3 cents = 168 kg; 1 Viennese cent = 100 lb/pounds = 56.12 kg; 1 fl./Gulden = 60 kr./Kreuzer)

| **The valuation of purchased copper ore, valid from 1741 to 1747** | | **Hechengartner's ore valuation, approved in January 1747** | |
|---|---|---|---|
| **Metal content in 1 *Pahr*** | **Redemption price** | **Metal content in 1 cent** | **Redemption price** |
| from 1 lb | 12 kr. | 3–4.5 lb | 15 kr. |
| from 2 to 2.5 lb | 22.5 kr. | 5–6.5 lb | 18 kr. |
| from 2.5 to 3 lb | 24 kr. | 7–10.5 lb | 20 kr. |
| from 3 to 7.5 lb | 30 kr. | 11–13.5 lb | 25 kr. |
| from 8 to 11.5 lb | 40 kr. | 14–18.5 lb | 30 kr. |
| from 12 lb | 1 fl. | 19–20.5 lb | 40 kr. |
| – | – | 21–23.5 lb | 50 kr. |
| – | – | 24 lb and more | 1 fl. |

(ÖSTERREICHISCHES STAATSARCHIV WIEN, FINANZ- UND HOFKAMMERARCHIV – NEUE HOFKAMMER, MÜNZ- UND BERGWESEN, ROTE NR. 10, CAR. 19, ACT FROM 29 JANUARY 1747)

proposal for the Upper Hungarian state mines in 1747 that was approved by the Court Chamber in Vienna in that same year. The new ore valuation of Hechengartner was intended to motivate the miners to greater exactness when unloading the raw ore. Hechengartner divided the categories of ore valuation valid at the time by the metal content in one *Pahr*, which weighed three cents in the case of poorer ores and four cents in the case of richer ores, into many new categories, but also by the metal content, in one Viennese cent (Table 6.1).

According to the Court Commission for Coinage and Mining of 1747, the miners of the Upper Hungarian state mines should cover the costs for candles, blasting powder, and for smithy works to maintain their working tools, at their

in Oraviţa (Banat) and after 1747 as a chamber vice-count in Banská Štiavnica (*Schemnitz* in then Lower Hungary, present-day Central Slovakia). In 1749, he was ennobled with the noble predicate "von Hechengarten". See Lacko, "K transferu inovácií v stredoeurópskom hutníctve," pp. 165–166.

own expense.[16] Later, in the 1760s, for example, the ore miners and piecework-miners in Špania Dolina (*Herrengrund*) under the Mining Chamber in Banská Bystrica (*Neusohl* in then Lower Hungary, present-day Central Slovakia) had to cover the costs for tallow, supplied by the state mining administration. Other categories of workers received tallow for the lamps free of charge.[17]

**(b)** The piecework-miners (*Gedinghäuer*) were paid according to the *klafter* (unit of length) which was stopped out in the drift mine. They were tasked with drifting the adits (horizontal passages), break-troughs, shafts, drifts, and other workings. Their wages depended on the performed work, i.e. per *klafter* or for one mine car of stopped-out ore (*Pahr*). This category of mineworkers was very numerous in the state copper mines and their incomes varied between the individual mining centers through the years. For an example, the piecework-miners in the Upper Hungarian copper mines of the late seventeenth century earned from 4 fl. to 14 fl. (fl. = Austrian Gulden) or more for one *klafter*, or from 1 fl. to 1 fl. and 36 denarii for one mine car of ore (*Pahr*), depending on the volume of the ore deposits or on the needfulness of the mine working. In the case of the extremely hard rock, the miners could obtain a price per *klafter* of up to 60 fl. and more without being charged for the blasting powder.[18] In the Lower Hungarian mines, the piecework-miners had to pay for the blasting powder used.[19] The conditions in the Tyrolean and Banat copper mines were very similar, whereby the miners in South Tyrol were usually paid their salary on a weekly basis (for shift work), but a category of the piecework-miners subsisted too.[20]

**(c)** Shift workers: Not only miners were employed as shift workers, but also other categories of workers, such as machine minders, water wheel pump watchers, timbermen (*Zimmerleute*), tipplers (*Stürtzer*), who unloaded the raw ore from the mine cars, water scoopers, winch workers (*Haspelzieher*), mine car pushers (*Hundstösser*), cagers (*Anschläger*), cleaners (*Sauberjungen*) and drifting supervisors. The widely varying salaries of shift workers were paid out weekly.[21]

16 Österreichisches Staatsarchiv Wien [hereafter, ÖStA], Finanz- und Hofkammerarchiv – Neue Hofkammer [hereafter, FHKA NKH], Münz- und Bergwesen [hereafter, MBW], rote No. 10, car. 19, act from 29 January 1747.

17 See Vozár, *Das Goldene Bergbuch*, pp. 224–225.

18 ÖStA, FHKA – Handschriftensammlung, HS 1008, report from 1695, fo. 1v–14v.

19 Vozár, *Das Goldene Bergbuch*, p. 225.

20 See Tasser, *Das Bergwerk am Südtiroler Schneeberg*, pp. 34–40.

21 ÖStA, FHKA – Handschriftensammlung, HS 1008, report from 1695, fo. 14r–16v. Tasser, *Das Bergwerk am Südtiroler Schneeberg*, pp. 36–38.

**(d)** The mining and metallurgical officials belonged to a permanent clerical staff of the state mining administration in the Habsburg Monarchy. The number and workload of the mining officials was directly dependent on the structure and organization of the chief mining departments in the empire that in this case represented the Mining Chamber in Banská Bystrica (*Neusohl*), the Chief Inspectorate in Smolník (*Schmöllnitz*), the Mining Inspectorate in Oraviţa (*Orawitza*) and State Commercial Office in Schwaz. In addition to the wages, the officials had obtained various allowances, including the housebote, oats, hay for the horses, and additional charges for the office supplies. The wood played a very important role at that time in the heating of the official houses and flats. In the milieu of the state administration during the eighteenth century, the mining officialdom was highly professionalized and managed mainly independently of the estates-based social background, which may have marked it as a very progressive element of the reigning society. The transfer of knowledge and innovation among individual mining areas was carried out by means of the social mobility of the chief officials – experienced mining experts in the state mining administration. The chief clerks were real innovators who possessed practical know-how and whose abilities and knowledge played a key role in dealing with the technological challenges of daily life in mining and metallurgy.[22]

## 3 Labor Relations in Copper Processing and Metallurgy

Labor relations in this section of the copper commodity chain were in some ways different from the conditions in the mines. When dealing with copper processing, it is necessary to comprehend the beneficiation and enrichment of the raw copper ore as well as the processes of roasting and smelting in the smelters. Sorting and separation of the stopped-out ore was carried out at the dumps of raw ore and waste rock at the active mines, where workers, including women, widows, children, and often orphans, had been employed. Also, many washing plants were in operation at the dumps. In 1746, up to 300 persons were engaged in the sorting and washing of raw ore in the Upper Hungarian state copper enterprise in Smolník (*Schmöllnitz*), whereupon a controller

22 Cf. Lacko, "Príspevok k archontológii Vrchného inšpektorského úradu v Smolníku do roku 1788," pp. 94–195. See also Lacko, "Bergbau und Staatsfinanzen der Habsburgermonarchie," pp. 377–384.

of cementation and sulphur production supervised.[23] At the Lower Hungarian mines in Špania Dolina (*Herrengrund*), the sorted and washed-up ore was bought from the workers. In the second half of the eighteenth century, the valuation of purchased, sorted and washed ore had been fixed by these mines every year and the overseers in Špania Dolina were paid according to the number of processed and handed-over cents of ore. These overseers paid the sorters and washers in relation to the quantity of processed ore; perhaps these workers could even be salaried depending on the working shifts.

Workers such as lumberjacks, charcoal burners, hammer-smiths, and carters were paid according to the carried-out work on the basis of the various fixed price lists. The hammer-smiths earned in terms of priced products such as nails, iron chains, tools, components of pump machines, bores, wedges and the like. In the case of factory hammer-smiths, they made their living from about 50 types of products or work operations.[24] The lumberjacks and charcoal burners were paid by similar means. The services of lumberjacks were much needed due to the high charcoal consumption in the state copper smelters. From these services, the forest departments developed within the state mining administration. As an example, in the mid-eighteenth century, approximately 10,000 to 15,000 cartloads of charcoal were consumed per year by the Upper Hungarian state copper smelters alone.[25]

The metallurgists in the smelting plants had been paid out according to the precisely fixed prices for the working operations done in one of the manufacturing stages. Within the scope of copper smelting, the smelter workers could be paid out by the one-time melting charges for a defined volume or by an entire week's work in the smelters. Each of the melting stages, such as raw smelting, roasting, smelting of roasted copper-based alloy and refining of so-called royal copper, required special categories of workers. In the case of argentiferous copper,[26] it was necessary to extract the silver from the copper-based alloys through a complicated process of liquation and drying (*Saigern*).[27] This

---

23 Slovenský národný archív – Slovenský banský archív in Banská Štiavnica [hereafter, SNA – SBA], Vrchný inšpektorský úrad v Smolníku [hereafter, IS], act 15 from 16 March 1746 [register No. 261] and act 28 from 22 April 1746 [register No. 271].

24 ÖStA, FHKA – Handschriftensammlung, HS 1008, report from 1695, fo. 17r–18v.

25 1 cartload of charcoal in the Upper Hungarian mining district = cca 2.5 m$^3$. ÖStA, FHKA NKH, MBW, rote Nr. 4, car. 7, protocol from 25 June 1745 and report from 12 May 1745 with attachments.

26 The argentiferous (silver-bearing) copper was described in contemporaneous sources as a black copper.

27 Cf. L'Héritier and Téreygeol, "From copper to silver: Understanding the *saigerprozess* through experimental liquation and drying," pp. 136–152.

liquation process had been used within the "Habsburg" mining districts mainly in the Lower Hungarian state copper smelteries under the Mining Chamber in Banská Bystrica (*Neusohl*), in the smelting plants in Tajov and Moštenica (present-day Central Slovakia), as well as in the Upper Hungarian state smelteries (from the mid-eighteenth century).[28] At these operations, the smelter workers and clerks had to be very experienced in the technology of copper smelting and were therefore adequately salaried.

Copper-based physical commodities were produced in the state hammer smithies, in which coppersmiths hammered diverse products such as copper plates, various dishes, pots, cookers and laminae. Here, in these hammer smithies, copper from private producers was also bought under the state copper monopoly, according to the state-fixed prices. The copper plates (sheets) were made in several forms, known as foursquare copper plates, "rosette" copper, "Prussian" copper, forged copper or granulated copper to use for coinage. Coppersmiths formed the plates by their repeated reheating and forming until the pots and cookers had a required size and profile. By then, the copper hammer smithy in Banská Bystrica (*Neusohl*) employed a wire-drawing mill too. This copper wire was used to produce needles and strainers.[29]

A part of the produced copper was used in the brass works that operated especially in the Austrian lands such as, for example, in Frauental (Styria) from 1752 as a state factory, in Annaberg at Lilienfeld (1767–1773), Möllbrücke (1762–1775), Achenrain (Tyrol) from 1725, Lienz (Tyrol) and in Nadelburg near Wiener Neustadt from the mid-nineteenth century.[30] The Hungarian copper, which was suitable for brass production, was exported not only to the Austrian brass works but also – mainly in the first half of the eighteenth century until the War of the Austrian Succession (1740–1748) – to the Upper Silesian brass factory in Kotlarnia (*Jakobswalde*, present-day Poland) owned by the counts von Hoym.[31]

28 For detailed information, see Vozár, *Das Goldene Bergbuch*, pp. 231–240. Lacko, "Technológia zhutňovania medi," pp. 93–99. ÖStA, FHKA – Handschriftensammlung, HS 1008, report from 1695, fo. 24r–29v.

29 Vozár, *Das Goldene Bergbuch*, pp. 241–243. Lacko, "Technológia zhutňovania medi," pp. 97–98.

30 See Ucik, "Messing in Österreich: Die Herrstellung und die wirtschaftliche Bedeutung unter besonderer Berücksichtigung der ehemaligen Messinghütte Möllbrücke," pp. 161–188. ÖStA, FHKA – Handschriftensammlung, HS 346, book of accounts from 1780, pp. 177–178, 249–252.

31 ÖStA, FHKA – Alte Hofkammer [hereafter, AHK], Ungarisches Münz- und Bergwesen [hereafter, UMB], rote Nr. 95, act from 16 March 1739, fo. 40r–43r; rote No. 96, act from 30 July 1739, fo. 204r–218v.

## 4 Recruitment of Laborers for Copper Mining and Processing

Each production stage required numerous laborers including thousands of people throughout the Habsburg Empire. Due to a shortage of manpower, forced labor or corvée (*robot*) was used in the private iron manufactories of the Bohemian landlords, which is known on the basis of Milan Myška's studies, though its prevalence among all the work outputs in these iron manufactories gradually descended during the eighteenth century. Lastly, this forced labor was exploited only for the ancillary works within carriages, preparation of charcoal or for physically heavy work.[32] In this regard, the situation in the copper mining and metallurgical plants was different from the conditions in the private iron manufactories of the Bohemian landlords, because the labor relations in the state enterprises were strictly capitalistic and consistently salaried, which was a ubiquitous concept in the Austrian and Hungarian state mines and smelteries.

However, one aspect of both was similar: when a shortage of manpower occurred, the state also used the labor services of the serfs. These cases are known from the Banat mining district from the time after the Treaty of Belgrade of 1739, when an acute shortage of labor affected the state mines. The state administration had to exploit the services of serfs from 15 villages in the Banat for manual labor, woodcutting, and carriage. About 100 persons were utilized as *robot*-serfs from that time until the 1770s by some works. In the Banat copper mines as a whole, between 500 and 600 laborers, including serfs, were employed in the second half of the eighteenth century.[33] Due to a shortage of manpower, the state administration organized the migration of workers within the empire at that time. The laborers from the stagnant Tyrolean mining district were relocated into the Banat. Likewise, the miners and officials from Upper Hungary were moved into the Banat, which also caused a lack of laborers in the Upper Hungarian mining district.[34]

The state administration used an authority of state government when relocating the workers and officials into the Upper Hungarian mining area and the relocating was ordered to be carried out by the subordinated mining offices. As an example, on 23 June 1712, the Court Chamber in Vienna asked the Bohemian Chamber to relocate workers from the Bohemian mining districts to the state copper works in Smolník (*Schmöllnitz*) in Upper Hungary. The Court Chamber

32 Cf. Myška, "Protoindustriální železářství v českých zemích," pp. 156–158.

33 See Wessely, *Der Banater Bergbau von 1717–1780 und seine bevölkerungspolitische Bedeutung*, pp. 95–99 and Table 11 in the appendix.

34 Wessely, *Der Banater Bergbau*, pp. 17–21.

referred to an acute shortage of labor in Smolník (*Schmöllnitz*), which were decimated by a pestilence in the previous years.[35] At that time, many incomers were arriving into the Upper Hungarian mining district, which was the largest copper producer in the Monarchy, from the Polish Kingdom and other mining districts in the Habsburg Monarchy. Indeed, the number of workers in the Upper Hungarian state copper enterprise increased from 398 workers in September 1689 to 1,853 in December 1769.[36] The structure of workers who were directly employed by the state enterprises in 1769 is analyzed in Table 6.2.[37] The casual laborers such as, for example, the carters are not counted in these figures; therefore, the real number of workers was even higher. According to these figures, it might be ascertained that the state mining and metallurgical enterprises were big companies at the time, comparable to modern corporations. This is a testimony to the attractiveness of labor in the state works, though the migration movements among the Central European mining districts have not been processed in the historiography yet.

Labor recruitment was carried out by the chamber or mining offices that were established in the so-called chamber (state) domains. These domains were confiscated from the aristocracy in the second half of the seventeenth century as a response to aristocratic rebellions. They represented an important phenomenon, especially in the Hungarian Kingdom. The chamber domains were meant to improve the profitability of the state enterprise, but these domains were managed as self-contained economic units within the state administration of the chambers or mining departments. The aforementioned chamber domains played a very important role in supplying the mining districts with agricultural products such as corn, meat, wine, and beer. The inhabitants of the state dominions worked as salaried laborers partly in the state mining and metallurgical plants, but mainly through carriage, woodcutting or charcoal burning. Many of the serfs on these domains earned their living as peasants and produced rural products.

For example, the largest revenues of the Lower Hungarian state domain Ľupča (*Lipsch*), which existed under the Mining Chamber in Banská Bystrica (*Neusohl*), came from selling corn, beer, and wine.[38] These financial yields were

35 Národní archiv Praha (Czech Republic), Vrchní horní úřad Jáchymov, inventory No. 268, car. 8, act from 23 June 1712.

36 ÖStA, FHKA AHK, Vermischte ungarische Gegenstände [hereafter, VUG], rote Nr. 15/B, fo. 246r–273v. Cf. Miroslav Lacko, "Kontakty a transfer inovácií medzi českými banskými revírmi a spišsko-gemerskou banskou oblasťou v prvej polovici 18. storočia," pp. 171–181.

37 SNA – SBA, IS, act 6 from 19 January 1770.

38 SNA – SBA, Hlavný komorsko-grófsky úrad v Banskej Štiavnici [hereafter, HKG], inventory No. 1867, car. 5991, summary report of chamber domain Ľupča (*Lipsch*) from 1738 to 1747.

TABLE 6.2 The number of workers in the Upper Hungarian state copper enterprise on 31 December, 1769

| Plant | Number of employees |
|---|---|
| State mines in Smolník (*Schmöllnitz*) | 465 |
| Washing plants | 202 |
| Stamping mills in Smolník | 13 |
| State mines in Gelnica (*Göllnitz*) – Schlossgrund | 66 |
| State mines in Gelnica – The Holy Trinity | 81 |
| State mines in Gelnica – Wasch's and Roll's mines | 43 |
| Smelteries in Smolník | 149 |
| Liquation and drying works | 11 |
| Smelteries in Švedlár/*Schwedler* (Stará Voda/*Altwasser*) | 32 |
| Smelteries in Opátka | 57 |
| Smelteries in Stratená | 42 |
| Smelteries in Zlatá Idka | 23 |
| Copper hammer smithies in Smolník | 50 |
| Ironworks in Štós (*Stoss*) | 1 |
| Cementation of copper in Smolník | 40 |
| Sulphur production | 5 |
| Forest administration | 573 |
| Overall | 1,853 |

SLOVENSKÝ NÁRODNÝ ARCHÍV – SLOVENSKÝ BANSKÝ ARCHÍV IN BANSKÁ ŠTIAVNICA, VRCHNÝ INŠPEKTORSKÝ ÚRAD V SMOLNÍKU, ACT 6 FROM 19 JANUARY 1770

transferred to the account of the state mining administration, though profits from the state domains represented only supplementary income among all the revenues of state enterprise in ore mining and metal production. The *robot*-serfs, living in the Ľupča (*Lipsch*) domain, also carried out labor services for the chamber administration such as agricultural labor (through tilling, seeding, harvesting or skiving) and carriage (of wood and products). However, the labor in mining and metallurgy was salaried.[39] The problems of labor management,

39 Cf. Tomeček, "Robotné povinnosti poddaných panstva v čase tereziánskej urbárskej regulácie," pp. 106–107.

financing and labor relations are yet to be examined by more in-depth historical studies.

Outside of Banat, workers had positive motivation to labor for state mining enterprises, i.e. primarily financial motivation or employment with the opportunity for social rise in the structure of the state mining administration. The attractiveness of this labor increased thanks to the social security and healthcare that were an integral part of the state mining enterprising in the Early Modern Age. In the Upper Hungarian mining district, e.g. within the state copper enterprise in Smolník (*Schmöllnitz*), one surgeon provided healthcare for the employees as early as the first half of the eighteenth century with an annual salary 30 fl. from the copper enterprise and 96 fl. from the local fraternal treasury.[40] The surgeon was reimbursed for all the medicines, bought from the local pharmacist, and the medical operations carried out.

For that reason, all the workers from the state copper works as well as from the private plants contributed to the fraternal treasury. In the event of illness, the fraternal treasury paid them 6 kr. daily. The workers that could not be employed due to old age were to receive 2 Rhine fl. monthly and widows, according to the number of dependent children, were to obtain from 1 to 3 fl. monthly, with one half coming from the state mining office and the other half from the fraternal treasury. The state mining clerks and other residents had to cover the costs for all the medicines at their own expense, paid to the fraternal treasury, and for medical operations to the state surgeon. At that time, there was a mining hospital in the Smolník district. A new hospital was built after the reform of the Upper Hungarian Chief Inspectorate in 1747.[41] Similar social welfare and healthcare also existed with other state copper enterprises in the Monarchy.

## 5 Copper Marketing: Private Financiers versus State Administration

After the monopolization of Hungarian copper production in the late seventeenth century, the state could not ensure the sale of copper on the foreign

40 The fraternal treasuries represented self-supporting institutions of social security and solidarity that subsisted in the many early modern mining centres. Within the frame of state mining and metallurgical plants, these fraternal treasuries were subordinated to the state mining administration. Initially, in the Late Middle Ages, these institutions subsisted as the religious fraternities. See Jankovič, "Počiatky pomocných bratských pokladníc v stredoslovenských banských mestách," pp. 103–109.

41 ÖStA, FHKA NKH, MBW, rote Nr. 10, car. 19, act from 29 January 1747, Hechengartner's report from 17 January 1747; rote Nr. 14, car. 26, decree from 9 May 1747.

markets. For that reason, the so-called administration for copper as well as for quicksilver was founded by the Court Chamber in Vienna at the time. According to the instruction from 2 July 1699 for the copper administrator Matthias Mittermayer von Waffenberg, the copper administrator should oversee the transport of copper, keep a record and communicate with the chamber clerks. The distribution of semi-finished copper products was to be realized through two repositories, namely Vienna (for the Lower Hungarian copper from Banská Bystrica/*Neusohl*) and Wrocław (for the Upper Hungarian copper from Smolník/*Schmöllnitz*). The administrators had to follow the prices of competitors, especially those of Swedish and Ottoman copper. Depending on the market condition, the administrator was to regulate the price of Hungarian copper. Periodically (at least once a quarter), he was to submit the income and expense statements and he could receive a sales commission to the amount of 1.3 percent. In addition, 900 fl. were paid out annually to the copper administrator; whereof he had to hold commission agents – so-called factors – in Vienna, Bratislava (*Pressburg*), and in Racibórz (present-day Poland) as well as one accountant, Johann Pupfhueber von Triebenpath, in 1699.[42]

The specific position of copper administrator, with a set of competences between those of a state official and of a private businessman, was staffed mainly by persons from the field of trade and finance. In the long period of the so-called Dutch monopoly, when copper production was subordinated to Dutch creditors, Christian Gottfried von Schreyvogel performed this function until the full amortization of the Dutch credits in the 1730s.[43] After 1744, the function of the copper administrator was replaced by the Office for Copper and Quicksilver in Vienna, established as an office for commerce with both of these goods and for financing the mining production and metallurgical processing under the Court Chamber in Vienna. This office was to coordinate the copper production, its financing, transport and primarily the copper marketing on the foreign markets.[44] From 1759, a new office known as the Sales Directorate for Mining Products under the supervision of Johann von Fries (1719–1785) – one of the most important Austrian bankers of the Early Modern Age, assumed all

42 See Schmidt, *Chronologisch-systematische Sammlung der Berggesetze der Königreiche: Ungarn, Kroatien, Dalmatien, Slavonien und des Großfürstenthumes Siebenbürgen*, V, No. 393, pp. 594–602; No. 394, pp. 602–610.

43 Schreyvogel performed this function in 1712–1733. Cf. Srbik, *Der staatliche Exporthandel Österreichs von Leopold I. bis Maria Theresia*, pp. 364–398.

44 Kallbrunner and Winkler, "Die Zeit des Directoriums in publicis et cameralibus (Vorstadien 1743–1749, das Directorium 1749–1760)," II, No. 62, pp. 1–11.

competences in the marketing of copper and other metals that were produced within the Habsburg Monarchy.[45]

The copper administrators and chamber officials from the Office for Copper and Quicksilver did not work alone, but also in collaboration with the State Commercial Office in Schwaz and with many commission agents in the important commercial centers of Europe. These commission agents coordinated the transport of copper deliveries by carts on the overland trade routes or on navigable rivers such as the Oder, Danube or Tisa, as well as their distribution from several repositories. The copper was traded in a semi-finished form (copper sheets) or in the form of finished copper-based commodities as described above. In the 1740s, the network of commission agents was represented by the officials and merchants as follows:

(1) **Stará Ľubovňa** (*Lublau*): officials of the Customs Office,
(2) **Ružomberok** (*Rosenberg*): officials of the Salt Office,
(3) **Bratislava** (*Pressburg*): Franz Anton Schröfl von Mannsberg,
(4) **Ljubljana** (*Laibach*): Franz Sigmund Kappus,
(5) **Těšín** (*Teschen*): Nicolaus Anton Grossmayer,
(6) **Wrocław** (*Breslau*): Samuel Hirlscher and son,
(7) **Ancona**: Samuel Cagli,
(8) **Regensburg**: Elias Ritter and Philipp Peter Elers,
(9) **Trieste** (*Triest*): Paul Tribitsch,
(10) **Venezia**: Benedict Hermann,
(11) **Hamburg**: Philipp Heinrich Stenglin and son.[46]

For an example of copper marketing during the eighteenth century, the sales areas in 1739 have been summarized in Table 6.3, at the time under the copper administration of brothers Franz Gottlieb von Palm (1691–1749) and Leopold Karl von Palm (1701–1776), who managed the copper marketing from 1735 to 1743.[47] Under the administration of the brothers von Palm, the export sales of Hungarian and Banat copper rose in all the important European seaports. This export culminated in the years before the War of the Austrian Succession (1740–1748), especially in 1739 and 1740.[48] At that time, the English subsidies that the creditors from London had paid out to the Habsburg Monarchy within

45 For more information, see Matis, "Die Grafen von Fries: Aufstieg und Untergang einer Unternehmerfamilie," pp. 484–496. Mentschl and Otruba, *Österreichische Industrielle und Bankiers*, pp. 39–46.

46 ÖStA, FHKA NKH, MBW, rote Nr. 8, car. 15, act from 26 October 1746. Cf. Lacko, "Ungarisches Kupfer und das Staatsfinanzwesen der Habsburgermonarchie," pp. 109–145.

47 ÖStA, FHKA AHK, VUG, rote Nr. 8/C, fo. 1713r–1718v. Cf. Kollmer, *Die Familie Palm: Soziale Mobilität in ständischer Gesellschaft*, pp. 5–11, 54–61.

48 ÖStA, FHKA AHK, VUG, rote Nr. 8/C, fo. 1792v–1793r.

TABLE 6.3 Marketing of Hungarian copper in 1739 under the administration of brothers Franz Gottlieb von Palm (1691–1749) and Leopold Karl von Palm (1701–1776) by types of semi-finished copper products and marketplaces (1 Viennese cent = 100 lb/pounds = 56.12 kg)

| Location | "Prussian" copper from the copper enterprise in Banská Bystrica (*Neusohl*) | | Copper plates from the copper enterprise in Banská Bystrica (*Neusohl*) | | Copper plates from the copper enterprise in Smolník (*Schmöllnitz*), Upper Hungary | | "Rosette" copper from the copper enterprise in Smolník, Upper Hungary | | Copper plates from the Spišská Nová Ves (*Zipser Neudorf*) mining area, Upper Hungary | |
|---|---|---|---|---|---|---|---|---|---|---|
| | Cent | lb | Cent | lb | Cent | lb | Cent | lb | Cent | lb |
| Ancona | – | – | – | – | 177 | 91 ½ | – | – | – | – |
| Belgrade | – | – | – | – | 31 | 45 | – | – | – | – |
| Bratislava | – | – | 161 | 69 ½ | – | – | – | – | – | – |
| Cádiz | – | – | – | – | – | – | – | – | – | – |
| Civitavecchia | – | – | – | – | – | – | – | – | – | – |
| Frankfurt am Main | – | – | – | 96 7/8 | 232 | 51 | – | – | – | – |
| Gdańsk | – | – | – | – | 605 | 98 ½ | – | – | – | – |
| Genoa | 2 | 46 | – | – | 16 | 35 ½ | – | – | – | – |
| Hamburg | – | – | 377 | 15 | 401 | 85 ½ | – | – | – | – |
| La Rochelle | – | – | – | – | – | – | – | – | – | – |
| Livorno | – | – | – | – | 12 | 77 ½ | – | – | – | – |
| Ljubljana | – | – | – | – | 215 | 80 ½ | – | – | – | – |
| Marseille | – | – | – | – | – | – | – | – | – | – |
| Messina | – | – | – | – | – | – | – | – | – | – |
| Ostende | – | – | – | – | 6 | 10 | 3 | 42 | – | – |
| Racibórz | – | – | 345 | 85 ¼ | – | – | 8 | – | 20 | 77 |
| Regensburg | 16 | 13 | 289 | 31 | 397 | 11 | 31 | 16 ¾ | – | – |
| Stará Ľubovňa | – | – | – | – | 489 | 94 | – | – | – | – |
| Trieste | 12 | 69 ½ | 21 | 96 ½ | 1,261 | 58 ½ | 3 | 47 ½ | – | – |
| Ulm | 10 | | 166 | 54 | 40 | 32 | – | – | – | – |
| Vienna | 50 | 18 | 250 | 84 | 2,060 | 59 ¼ | – | – | – | – |
| Warsaw | – | – | – | – | 16 | 6 ½ | – | – | – | – |
| Wrocław | – | – | 1,648 | 1 | – | – | 18 | – | 142 | 43 ¼ |

TABLE 6.3 Marketing of Hungarian copper in 1739 under the administration of brothers Franz Gottlieb von Palm (1691–1749) and Leopold Karl von Palm (1701–1776) by types of semi-finished copper products and marketplaces (1 Viennese cent = 100 lb/pounds = 56.12 kg) (*cont.*)

| Location | "Prussian" copper from the copper enterprise in Banská Bystrica (*Neusohl*) | | Copper plates from the copper enterprise in Banská Bystrica (*Neusohl*) | | Copper plates from the copper enterprise in Smolník (*Schmöllnitz*), Upper Hungary | | "Rosette" copper from the copper enterprise in Smolník, Upper Hungary | | Copper plates from the Spišská Nová Ves (*Zipser Neudorf*) mining area, Upper Hungary | |
|---|---|---|---|---|---|---|---|---|---|---|
| | Cent | lb | Cent | lb | Cent | lb | Cent | lb | Cent | lb |
| Žilina | – | – | – | – | – | – | 247 | 54 ½ | – | – |
| Total | 91 | 46 ½ | 3,262 | 33 1/8 | 5,966 | 36 ¼ | 311 | 60 ¾ | 163 | 20 ¼ |

| Location | Copper plates from the Banat (*Temeswar*) | | "Rosette" copper from the Banat (*Temeswar*) | | Forged copper | | Total | |
|---|---|---|---|---|---|---|---|---|
| | Cent | lb | Cent | lb | Cent | lb | Cent | lb |
| Ancona | – | – | – | – | 25 | 67 5/8 | 203 | 59 1/8 |
| Belgrade | – | – | – | – | – | – | 31 | 45 |
| Bratislava | – | – | – | – | – | – | 161 | 69 ½ |
| Cádiz | – | – | – | – | 18 | 13 ½ | 18 | 13 ½ |
| Civitavecchia | – | – | – | – | 8 | 33 | 8 | 33 |
| Cádiz | – | – | – | – | 18 | 13 ½ | 18 | 13 ½ |
| Frankfurt am Main | – | – | 20 | 36 | – | – | 253 | 83 7/8 |
| Gdańsk | – | – | – | – | – | – | 605 | 98 ½ |
| Genoa | – | – | – | – | 47 | 96 | 66 | 77 ½ |
| Hamburg | – | – | – | – | – | – | 779 | ½ |
| La Rochelle | – | – | – | – | 3 | 47 | 3 | 47 |
| Livorno | – | – | – | – | 3 | 19 ½ | 15 | 97 |
| Ljubljana | – | – | – | – | 1 | – | 216 | 80 ½ |

TABLE 6.3 Marketing of Hungarian copper in 1739 under the administration of brothers Franz Gottlieb von Palm (1691–1749) and Leopold Karl von Palm (1701–1776) by types of semi-finished copper products and marketplaces (1 Viennese cent = 100 lb/pounds = 56.12 kg) (*cont.*)

| Location | Copper plates from the Banat (*Temeswar*) | | "Rosette" copper from the Banat (*Temeswar*) | | Forged copper | | Total | |
|---|---|---|---|---|---|---|---|---|
| | Cent | lb | Cent | lb | Cent | lb | Cent | lb |
| Marseille | – | – | – | – | 23 | 63 ½ | 23 | 63 ½ |
| Messina | – | – | – | – | 105 | 84 ½ | 105 | 84 ½ |
| Ostende | – | – | – | – | 8 | 67 | 18 | 19 |
| Racibórz | – | – | – | – | – | – | 374 | 62 ¼ |
| Regensburg | – | – | 197 | 14 | – | – | 930 | 85 ¾ |
| Stará Ľubovňa | – | – | – | – | 6 | 35 ¼ | 496 | 29 ¼ |
| Trieste | – | – | 129 | 10 | 472 | 52 3/8 | 1,901 | 34 3/8 |
| Ulm | – | – | – | – | – | – | 216 | 86 |
| Vienna | 15 | 82 | 372 | 92 | 152 | 36 ¾ | 2,902 | 72 |
| Warsaw | – | – | – | – | – | – | 16 | 6 ½ |
| Wrocław | – | – | – | – | – | – | 1,808 | 44 ¼ |
| Žilina | – | – | – | – | – | – | 247 | 54 ½ |
| Total | 15 | 82 | 719 | 52 | 877 | 16 | 11,407 | 46 7/8 |

(ÖSTERREICHISCHES STAATSARCHIV WIEN, FINANZ- UND HOFKAMMERARCHIV – ALTE HOFKAMMER, VERMISCHTE UNGARISCHE GEGENSTÄNDE, ROTE NR. 8/C, FO. 1782R–1783V)

the European political alliances were repaid, partly through Hungarian copper. This copper was exported into the seaport in Trieste and from there to London, where the aforementioned copper was sold through John Bance or John Gore to the East India Company. Thereafter, the East India Company exported the copper from the Habsburg Monarchy to African and Asian markets (Map 6.2). As an example, 2,000 Hungarian copper plates (998 Viennese cents) were exported from Trieste to London by the ship "Le Crowe" in June 1739 and sold mostly to the East India Company.[49]

49 ÖStA, FHKA AHK, VUG, rote Nr. 8/C, fo. 1800r–1847r.

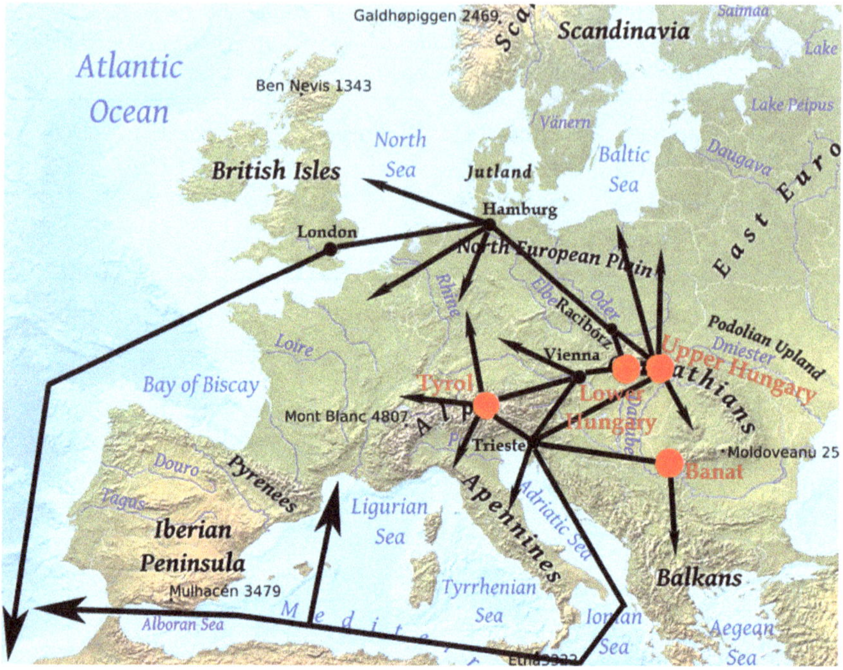


MAP 6.2 Dominant routes of copper export from the Habsburg Monarchy during the eighteenth century
ELABORATED BY M. LACKO

## 6 Conclusion

In this chapter, several research questions have been opened that need to be explored by future research. The research focus in early modern social and economic history should be aimed at the highly complex processes of proto-industrial state entrepreneurship. Within the actual research results presented, it has been shown that the labor relations in state copper mining and processing during the eighteenth century were defined by a capitalistic foundation, existing in the paradigm of an estates-based society. The whole commodity chain of copper production and marketing proved very heterogeneous in terms of labor relations, and that was despite substantial state regulation. The state used different types of labor relations, such as those depending on the work performed (e.g. piecework), on the metal content in the stoped-out ore, on the working of shifts, etc. In spite of the state control, the private producers and merchants were an important part of these commodity chains, though their private enterprises, mines and smelteries were subject to the state copper monopoly; perhaps even the traders, who were mostly foreign, had to collaborate with the Habsburg state administration.

All laborers in this one analyzed commodity chain had to be especially flexible with regard to the dynamic changes in the markets, prices, and production practices. There is a need to investigate the exact role of the recruitment practices that were based on feudal relations, in particular coerced labor and serf labor, in the profitability of state mining and metallurgy, though its share of all yields seems, on the basis of the data submitted in this chapter, negligible. This paradigm is in contrast to the economy of the private iron manufactories in the Bohemian lands at that time, which were marked by extra-economic, i.e. feudal, relationships, as shown by Milan Myška.[50] The social security of all mentioned workers in the state mining enterprises of the day was not present at that time in other production sectors that had been shaped by the estates-based society.

During the eighteenth century, the examined commodity chain of state-controlled copper production reached a global size. This commodity chain consisted of several basic segments and could be summarized as follows:

(1) Production of copper ore in state and private mines by salaried mine-workers: a) in Upper Hungary (with the center in Smolník), b) in Lower Hungary (with the center in Banská Bystrica), c) in Tyrol (with the center in Schwaz) and d) in Banat (with the center in Oraviţa).
(2) Processing of copper ore, redemption of copper from private producers and production of semi-finished copper in state smelting plants.
(3) Production of finished copper-based commodities in state hammer smithies and brass works, and eventually in the private brass works that cooperated with the state administration.
(4) Transportation of copper-based commodities by salaried carters and rafters from the production centers to the European repositories.
(5) Distribution and marketing of copper-based commodities through the commission agents from the European repositories on the European markets and on the overseas markets outside of Europe: in Africa, Asia, etc. This last segment of the analyzed commodity chain was dependent upon cooperation with foreign private merchants and business companies.

Additionally, the topic of migration movements among the proto-industrial mining districts in Central Europe is among the important intended targets of historical research. These movements played, as proven here, a key role in the recruitment of labor and were related to the various economic booms or

50 See Myška, "Pre-Industrial Iron-Making," pp. 44–72. Myška, "Protoindustriální železářství v českých zemích," pp. 143–162.

problems in the Early Modern mining areas. The questions of living standard, social security, and the potential social rise of proto-industrial workers still call for continued analytical archive investigations. Answers to these questions would currently be welcome indeed, as the modern state and the patterns of modern society, including the industrial revolution, emanate from the above-mentioned proto-industrial production, labor, and administrative relations.

## Bibliography

Blanchard, Ian. *Russia's 'Age of Silver': Precious-Metal Production and Economic Growth in the Eighteenth Century* (New York: Routledge, 1989).

Dickson, Peter George Muir. *Finance and Government under Maria Theresia (1740–1780)*, 2 vols (New York: Oxford University Press, 1987).

Jankovič, Vendelín. "Počiatky pomocných bratských pokladníc v stredoslovenských banských mestách", in Richard Marsina (ed.), *Banské mestá na Slovensku* (Martin: Osveta, 1990), pp. 103–109.

Kallbrunner, Joseph and Melitta Winkler. "Die Zeit des Directoriums in publicis et cameralibus (Vorstadien 1743–1749, das Directorium 1749–1760)," in Heinrich Kretschmayr (ed.), *Die österreichische Zentralverwaltung, II. Abteilung: Von der Vereinigung der österreichischen und böhmischen Hofkanzlei bis zur Einrichtung der Ministerialverfassung, 1749–1848* (Wien: Adolf Holzhausen, 1925), II, pp. 1–11.

Kollmer, Gert. *Die Familie Palm: Soziale Mobilität in ständischer Gesellschaft* (Ostfildern: Scripta Mercaturae Verlag, 1983).

L'Héritier, Maxime and Florian Téreygeol. "From copper to silver: Understanding the *saigerprozess* through experimental liquation and drying," *Historical Metallurgy*, 44, 2 (2010), pp. 136–152.

Lacko, Miroslav. "Príspevok k archontológii Vrchného inšpektorského úradu v Smolníku do roku 1788," *Montánna história*, 3 (2010), pp. 94–195.

Lacko, Miroslav. "Technológia zhutňovania medi na Spiši koncom 17. storočia," *Z dějin hutnictví – Rozpravy Národního technického muzea v Praze*, 42 (2012), pp. 93–99.

Lacko, Miroslav. "Ungarisches Kupfer und das Staatsfinanzwesen der Habsburgermonarchie in der Zeit des Österreichischen Erbfolgekriegs (1740–1748)," in Wolfgang Ingenhaeff and Johann Bair (eds), *Bergbau und Krieg: 12. Internationaler Montanhistorischer Kongress* (Wattens: Berenkamp Buch- und Kunstverlag, 2014), pp. 109–145.

Lacko, Miroslav. "Kontakty a transfer inovácií medzi českými banskými revírmi a spišsko-gemerskou banskou oblasťou v prvej polovici 18. storočia," *Acta rerum naturalium*, 16 (2014), pp. 171–181.

Lacko, Miroslav. "K transferu inovácií v stredoeurópskom hutníctve: Bartolomej Ľudovít Hechengartner (1702–1773) a zhutňovanie medi na Spiši v prvej polovici 18. storočia," *Montánna história*, 7 (2014), pp. 162–199.

Lacko, Miroslav. "Gewerken und Staat im protoindustriellen Bergbau. Die Gründung der Oberungarischen Waldbürgerschaft im Jahr 1748 in unbekannten Zusammenhängen," in Wolfgang Ingenhaeff and Johann Bair (eds), *Bergbau und Persönlichkeiten: 13. Internationaler Montanhistorischer Kongress* (Wattens: Berenkamp Buch- und Kunstverlag, 2015), pp. 177–208.

Lacko, Miroslav. "Zwischen Regulierung und Liberalisierung: Staatliche Wirtschaftspolitik in der Habsburgermonarchie und das Eisenhüttenwesen in der ersten Hälfte des 18. Jahrhunderts," *Montánna história*, 8–9 (2015–2016), pp. 38–65.

Lacko, Miroslav. "Bergbau und Staatsfinanzen der Habsburgermonarchie in der Zeit der Staatsreformen 1748–1749," *Mitteilungen des Instituts für Österreichische Geschichtsforschung*, 125, 2 (2017), pp. 362–384.

Matis, Herbert. "Die Grafen von Fries: Aufstieg und Untergang einer Unternehmerfamilie," *Tradition: Zeitschrift für Firmengeschichte und Unternehmerbiographie*, 12 (1967), pp. 484–496.

Mentschl, Josef and Gustav Otruba. *Österreichische Industrielle und Bankiers* (Wien: Bergland Verlag, 1965).

Myška, Milan. "Pre-Industrial Iron-Making in the Czech Lands: The Labour Force and Production Relations circa 1350–circa 1840," *Past and Present: A Journal of Historical Studies*, 82 (1979), pp. 44–72.

Myška, Milan. "Protoindustriální železářství v českých zemích: Robota a jiné formy nucené práce v železářských manufakturách," in Aleš Zářický (ed.), *Milan Myška: Z díla hospodářského historika* (Ostrava: Filozofická fakulta Ostravské univerzity, 2010), pp. 127–180.

Schmidt, Franz Anton (ed.). *Chronologisch-systematische Sammlung der Berggesetze der Königreiche: Ungarn, Kroatien, Dalmatien, Slavonien und des Großfürstenthumes Siebenbürgen*, 25 vols (Wien: Hof- und Staats-Aerarial-Druckerey, 1835).

Srbik, Heinrich von. *Der staatliche Exporthandel Österreichs von Leopold I. bis Maria Theresia: Untersuchungen zur Wirtschaftsgeschichte Österreichs im Zeitalter des Merkantilismus* (Wien and Leipzig: Wilhelm Braumüller, 1907).

Tasser, Rudolf. *Das Bergwerk am Südtiroler Schneeberg* (Bozen: Athesia, 1994).

Tomeček, Oto. "Robotné povinnosti poddaných panstva v čase tereziánskej urbárskej regulácie," in Vladimír Homola and Oto Tomeček (eds), *Hrad Ľupča: Klenot Pohronia vo svetle vekov* (Podbrezová: Železiarne Podbrezová a. s., 2017).

Ucik, Friedrich Hans. "Messing in Österreich: Die Herrstellung und die wirtschaftliche Bedeutung unter besonderer Berücksichtigung der ehemaligen Messinghütte Möllbrücke," *Carinthia II*, 112 (2002), pp. 161–188.

Vozár, Jozef (ed.). *Das Goldene Bergbuch/Zlatá kniha banícka* (Košice: Banská agentúra, 2000).

Wessely, Johann. *Der Banater Bergbau von 1717–1780 und seine bevölkerungspolitische Bedeutung* (diss., Universität Wien, Wien, 1937).

# PART 3

## *Commodity Chains in (Post-)Colonial Settings*

CHAPTER 7

# Labor as a Bottleneck

## *Entangled Commodity Chains of Sugar in Hawaii and California in the Late Nineteenth Century*

*Uwe Spiekermann*

Four years ago, *Alexander & Baldwin*, Hawaii's last sugar plantation, announced "that it would phase out growing sugar by 2016, marking the end of sugar's dominance in the state's economy."[1] With this, a constitutive element of modern Hawaiian history came to an end. Sugar production laid the foundations of Hawaii's economic strength today, its colonization by the U.S., its complex ecological and rural structures and its multi-ethnic social composition. From the late 1870s, industrialized cane sugar production transformed the former mixture of small sugar plantations and traditional Hawaiian taro and fruit farming into export-orientated monocultures, only partly accompanied by investments in military and tourism, today's backbones of the state's economy. Efficient sugar cane production enforced new systems of land cultivation and water management, of pest control and fertilization. The incursions of white missionaries, settlers, and investors from the western powers initiated the import of the Portuguese, Chinese, Japanese, and Philippine majority of today's state and were accompanied by an immense decline of the native Hawaiian population to only one tenth of its size during the nineteenth century. Although local sugar interests weren't decisive in ending the independent Hawaiian Kingdom in 1893 and its transition into an U.S. territory in 1900, the close economic ties to the North American mainland and the economic and strategic prospects of the islands had already forecasted U.S. dominance by the late nineteenth century.

The story of King Sugar in Hawaii has been told several times and from different perspectives – and in 2015, two compelling books paralleled *Alexander & Baldwin*'s decision to end Hawaii's history of large-scale sugar plantation.[2]

1 Olivia Lowenberg, "Why sugar, once a big business in Hawaii, is now disappearing," *Christian Science Monitor*, January 8, 2016.

2 MacLennan, *Sovereign Sugar*; Jones and Osgood, *From King Cane*. On political history cf. Haley, *Captive Paradise*. On individual plantations see: Dorrance and Morgan, *Sugar Islands*, while Abbott, *Sugar* puts Hawaii into the global production system of sugar.

 | DOI:10.1163/9789004448049_008

Historical research is shaped by the economic and political control of the Sandwich Islands by the "Big Five," a group of interconnected Hawaiian companies that owned the plantations and a large portion of associated businesses, and which dominated politics until the Second World War. From a deeper historical point of view, however, this is quite a questionable perspective, because this oligopoly was not established before 1898 and more than two additional decades were necessary to establish a firm grip on the islands. In contrast, this chapter argues that the transformation of Hawaii to sugar islands can't be explained properly without a precise analysis of the investments of large-scale investor and first mover Claus Spreckels and the Californian background of his endeavors. His establishment of the *Hawaiian Sugar Company* on Maui in 1878 functioned as a model for modern industrialized sugar-cane production, for engineering nature, for vertically integrated agribusiness structures and political influence. Although the Spreckels family lost control of this firm in 1898, it still maintained an economic hand in Hawaii's sugar business until 1948. Spreckels established a learning base[3] for the "Big Five's" modernization and the successful handling of agribusiness at the periphery of the sugar world market, and it was his dominant position in refinery, transport and finance, which incurred the opposition of formerly small and isolated planters, who built up their business to overcome the reign of "King Spreckels" and to replace it by the reign of the "Big Five." This transition became possible, because Spreckels saw even better economic chances in the establishment of a domestic large-scale U.S. beet sugar production in California. This, however, was based on the experiences made in the Pacific periphery. Hawaii became a learning base for the rise of an immensely profitable new agri-business in the American mainland and the import of an ethnic labor force, necessary to run the "factories in the fields".

## 1 Towards the Spreckels Sugar Empire: Irrigation and the Industrialized Plantation Economy on Maui

The Spreckels family was already an economic power in California in the 1870s. Claus Spreckels (1828–1908) was an immigrant entrepreneur, one of many, who were crucial for America's transition to global economic power in the nineteenth century.[4] Similar to several neighbors and relatives, Spreckels left his

3 The concept of the learning base was developed by Chandler, *Inventing the Electronic Century*.

4 Cf. Berghoff and Spiekermann, "Immigrant Entrepreneurship," pp. 5–15. I am following my argumentation in Spiekermann, "Expanding the Frontier(s)," pp. 171–194.

northern German home village of Lamstedt in 1846 to find a better life in the United States.[5] Born the son of cottagers he started working as a clerk and retailer in Charleston, South Carolina and continued his career in dry goods and alcohol trade, first in New York City and, from 1856 on, in San Francisco. Integrated into a family network of several brothers and many relatives, he invested his profits first in beer brewing and later in sugar refining. The *Bay Sugar Refining Company*, incorporated in 1864, and the 1867 *California Sugar Refinery Company* were key elements of an immensely profitable business career, which set Claus Spreckels in a monopolistic position in sugar production in the American West from the mid-1870s. Naturalized in 1855, he was a leading representative of German-Americans in California. He also crossed the borders of the ethnic niche community and was proud of being a Californian and an American. Spreckels's dual or even triple identity was not only a personal pride but also functional for business. He could act as an intermediate, linking German, Californian and American business interests and production regimes.

This became important when the Reciprocity Treaty between the independent Kingdom of Hawaii and the U.S. opened new horizons from 1876.[6] After at first having fiercely fought against this trade agreement, he sent his eldest son, John D. Spreckels (1853–1925), to the Sandwich Islands to explore business prospects. Trained in chemistry and mechanical engineering at the Polytechnic School in Hanover, John D. Spreckels had become superintendent of the *California Sugar Refinery* in 1873 and received additional business training during a brief apprenticeship at the Bremish trade house *Hackfeld & Co.* in Honolulu in 1876, at that time the largest merchant house and leading sugar planter in Hawaii.[7] Based on his son's pilot surveys, Claus Spreckels went to Hawaii in 1876. The Reciprocity Treaty gave high incentives for investments into sugar cultivation, because every pound of sugar exported from the islands to the U.S. was subsidized with two cents by the American taxpayer – the retail price was eight cents. Spreckels bought several smaller sugar plantations on Oahu and the Big Island, purchased the vast majority of the Hawaiian crop and established his San Francisco refinery as the center to convert Hawaiian raw sugar into granulated white and brown sugar.[8]

---

5 Spiekermann, "Claus Spreckels."

6 For a strategic perspective cf. Pletcher, *The Diplomacy of Involvement*, pp. 46–65 and Tate, *Hawaii: Reciprocity or Annexation* for political aspects.

7 *San Francisco Directory*, p. 620; "Claus Spreckels, the Sugar King, is Dead," *Hawaiian Gazette*, December 29, 1908, p.3. On Hackfeld, see: Hawkins, "Hackfeld, Heinrich," available at: <http://www.immigrantentrepreneurship.org/entry.php?rec=285> last accessed 17 July 2018.

8 *San Francisco News Letter*, 29, July 27, 1878/79, p. 20; *Pacific Commercial Advertiser*, April 29, 1879, p. 2; *Pacific Commercial Advertiser*, September 6, 1879, p. 3; *The Planters' Monthly*, 1,

When Spreckels arrived in Hawaii, the islands were already shaped by sugar cultivation. Located in the center of the Pacific, the archipelago had changed rapidly following explorer James Cook's (1728–1778) arrival in 1778. Based on European military technology, the eight main islands were united as the Kingdom of Hawaii in 1795. They functioned as a supply point for merchant ships and whaling. At that time, native Hawaiians had already established a highly developed agriculture, including advanced irrigation systems and cane sugar production for self-supply. Trade contacts were first accompanied by settlers and protestant missionaries from the U.S., several of them with European roots. At first, they changed Hawaii indirectly, through pathogenic germs, new animals, and cash crops. Infectious diseases caused most of Hawaii's native population decline from nearly 300,000 around 1800 to less than 30,000 in 1900, which severely limited the labor-force.[9] Mammals, introduced from 1820, destroyed traditional forms of agricultural land use, enforced the use of fences, and pushed the commercialization of soil use and the establishment of property rights in the 1840s and 1850s. The supply of ships and settlers furthered the use of citrus fruits and vegetables, rice, corn, tobacco, and cotton, which shook the fragile ecological balance of the islands. Population decline went hand in hand with intensified livestock production and new ways of farming. Western missionaries and early settlers began cane sugar production in the 1830s. Inspired by the plantation economy of the Caribbean sugar islands, the Spanish Philippines, and Dutch East Indies, the missionary families established sugar as the main cash crop in the 1850s. The Hawaiian State supported such endeavors by offering land contracts and the establishment of a *Royal Hawaiian Agricultural Society* in 1850. Early steam mills were established, German merchant house *Hackfeld & Co.* hired first Chinese contract workers in 1852, and, four years later, a first small irrigation ditch was constructed.[10] Although the area of cane rose from 2,760 acres in 1857 to 10,130 acres in 1867, the early plantations remained relatively small and employed in total only 3,800 people in 1874. Located at the rainy western parts of the main islands they suffered from the lack of capital, labor, technology, and access to profitable markets. Setbacks and failures were quite common, when the Reciprocity Treaty attracted investments by Spreckels, who was by far more solvent than all the Hawaiian sugar cane producers put together.

1882, p. 134; Buckland, "Report of the Agent of the Boston Exhibition"; *Pacific Commercial Advertiser*, July 7, 1883, p. 3.

9 Schmitt, *Historical Statistics of Hawaii*, p. 7, 25.

10 Wilcox, *Sugar Water*, pp. 54–55.

But Spreckels did not add some already established sugar plantations to his property simply to guarantee a steady raw sugar supply of his San Francisco sugar refinery. His goal was the creation of a vertically integrated sugar business, combining production, transport, finance, manufacturing, and wholesale distribution. Spreckels practiced economies of scale and scope; and with this he integrated Hawaii into the global sugar market. In a period, when beet sugar production in Europe outcompeted traditional cane sugar production in parts of the Caribbean, Spreckels brought not only capital, but new technologies, new ways of production, and new ways of business organization to the Hawaiian Islands. "Follow or vanish" became the parole in the Hawaiian cane sugar business from the 1880s – and only with such a challenge could the relatively peripheral and small Pacific kingdom keep track with global competition.

Spreckels's main and most ambitious project was the conversion of Maui, the second largest island of the kingdom, into a sugar island.[11] With this, he not only set the standards for the rise of his own vertically integrated business empire but also established a new type of industrial plantation firm, the *Hawaiian Commercial Company*, incorporated in 1878 and reincorporated in 1882 as the *Hawaiian Commercial and Sugar Company*. Within a few years, it would become the largest cane sugar plantation in the Pacific.[12] Although the Hawaiian state, namely King Kalakaua (1836–1891), supported the potent investor, the first problem Spreckels faced was to buy sufficient land to secure the water supply of the new plantation ground. Maui's climate and geological structure offered the best chances for a profitable agribusiness, but most of its early plantation failed or went out of business.[13] The almighty dollar, robust business methods, and his close relationship to King Kalakaua allowed Spreckels to secure the plain crownlands of the island; but these were arid regions, as sufficient water was only available in Maui's volcanic sections. Irrigation was necessary to start large-scale cane sugar cultivation; and Spreckels managed this based on general plans, developed by him, his son, and some American business partners.[14]

The later sugar king of Hawaii could enlist the German-American hydraulic engineer, Hermann Schüssler (1842–1919), for engineering water. He arrived, together with Claus Spreckels and additional investors, in Honolulu in May

11 Spiekermann, "Das gekaufte Königreich," pp. 47–66, 49–53.

12 "Incorporations," *Sacramento Daily Union*, October 3, 1878, p. 3; "A Serious Mistake," *San Francisco Chronicle*, November 16, 1883, p. 3.

13 Jones and Osgood, *King Cane*, pp. 54–55.

14 Cf., although with some mistakes, Teisch, *Engineering Nature*, pp. 134–150, esp. 137–141.

1878 and began his work in Maui in June 1878.[15] He organized a surveying party, "consisting of an assistant, eight natives, a Japanese cook and a mule driver."[16] Schüssler took two weeks to carry out a survey of the canal and ditch routes, including the pipes, their strength, and the water reservoirs. He suggested the construction of a narrow-gauge railroad through the plantation with lateral branches. Steel, pipes, and additional material for use in construction of the ditch were brought from Pittsburgh and San Francisco to Maui in December 1878. By that time, Schüssler already directed a team of several managers and foremen, 400 workers (mostly Hawaiians), 100 head of oxen and 60 mules.[17] In total, 45 miles of canal and around 20 tunnels were built. Schüssler left the kingdom in early October 1879.[18]

The irrigation system was the cornerstone of the large-scale cane sugar cultivation by Spreckels's *Hawaiian Commercial and Sugar Company*, which used Maui's plains for cash crop production.[19] It was praised as a milestone for Maui: "The dry valley of a few years ago has become a mine of wealth, a bonanza, pouring out its ceaseless flood of treasure."[20] The monoculture around the newly founded company town, Spreckelsville, triggered one-sided economic growth, which until today is shaping the island's landscape, apart from beaches, resorts and tourist destinations. From an agro-economic point of view, irrigation denaturalized sugar production, made it independent from "atmospheric rainfall"[21] and transferred it into a quite steady and stable business. From the late 1870s, the green central lands of Maui became the largest plantation of the first vertically integrated sugar firm in the U.S., because Spreckels organized not only the production and manufacturing of cane sugar, but also transport and finance.

Starting with his Hawaiian sugar business, he financed the shipping line J. D. Spreckels & Bros. in 1879, which was incorporated as the *Oceanic Steamship Company* in 1881.[22] It was the first line to offer a regular service between Honolulu and San Francisco, and Claus Spreckels's sons, John D., Adolph

---

15 *Pacific Commercial Advertiser*, May 25, 1878, p. 2; *Pacific Commercial Advertiser*, June 1, 1878 p. 2.

16 "Mr. Spreckles [sic!] Projected Enterprise on Maui," *Pacific Commercial Advertiser*, October 12, 1878, p. 3.

17 Hittell, *The Commerce and Industries of the Pacific Coast*, p. 548.

18 *Pacific Commercial Advertiser*, October 4, 1879, p. 2.

19 "The Hawaiian Commercial and Sugar Company's Estate at Spreckelsville, Maui, H.I.," *The Planters' Monthly*, 8, 1889, pp. 68–75.

20 *Pacific Commercial Advertiser*, January 31, 1880, p. 2.

21 Paasche, *Zuckerindustrie und Zuckerhandel der Welt*, p. 198.

22 Adler, "The Oceanic Steamship Company," pp. 257–269.

B. (1857–1924) and Claus "Gus" Augustus (1859–1946), managed to reduce transport time immensely. While the sailing ship *Claus Spreckels* made a record run of less than ten days in 1879, the new steam vessel *Mariposa* needed less than six days in 1883. A fleet of a dozen sailing vessels, five large steamers, and many chartered ships with additional sugar from Hawaii, the Philippines and Java made the *Oceanic Steamship Company* the largest U.S. shipping company in the Pacific, and facilitated a precisely timed delivery of raw sugar to the San Francisco refinery. Although 2,400 miles apart, the individual units of Spreckels's sugar machinery were tied together by an assembly line of sugar vessels. This did not only result in a more efficient use of refinery capacities, but also gave Spreckels power over most Hawaiian planters. They could either opt for slower and often more expensive chartered vessels or accept the dominance of Spreckels in sugar transport. The family enterprise also controlled, from 1884, the mail service on the San Francisco-Honolulu stretch. In 1885, the steamer service was extended to New Zealand and Australia, and the *Oceanic Steamship Company* remained an important factor in developing the Pacific until it was sold in 1926 to the Matson line.

The banking house *Spreckels & Co.*, established in 1884 in Honolulu by Spreckels, his British-born agent William G. Irwin (1843–1914), and former Californian governor Frederick Low (1828–1894), was another important institution in the German-American's vertical integrated sugar corporation.[23] Only the second bank established in Hawaii, it was not only functional to finance the sugar business, to give credits to the Hawaiian state, King Kalakaua, and many planters, but also connected the islands with international financial markets. In 1897, *Spreckels & Co.* was acting as an agent of the *Nevada Bank* (San Francisco), *Union Bank* (London), *American Exchange National Bank* (New York), *Merchants National Bank* (Chicago), *Comptoir National d'Escompte de Paris*, *Dresdner Bank* (Berlin), *Hongkong and Shanghai Banking Corporation*, *Bank of New Zealand* and the *Bank of British North America*.[24]

The combination of land and water management, transport, finance, and refining established a flexible and modern organizational structure. This allowed the German-American "sugar king" to compete even with the *American Sugar Refining Company*, the so-called Sugar Trust, at that time the company with the second largest capitalization in the U.S., when they tried to buy-out Spreckels's sugar empire of the American west in the late 1880s. But industrialized cane sugar plantation was still dependent on and limited by the access to

23 *Daily Alta California*, October 8, 1884, p. 2; *Daily Alta California*, April 23, 1885, p. 7.

24 *Hawaiian Star*, November 6, 1897, p. 3.

cheap and sufficient labor. Spreckels, often accompanied by *Hackfeld & Co.*, set the path for establishing a multi-ethnic society in Hawaii.

## 2 The Need for Cheap Labor: Contract Work and Economic Multiculturalism

The sugaring of Maui, the Big Island, and Oahu was decisive in populating the Pacific region with Europeans, and the opening of the labor market to Chinese and later Japanese and Philippine contract workers.[25] Over two decades, the Spreckelsville Mill became the center of a network with several thousand contracted plantation workers and approximately 200 to 300 white specialists.[26] Spreckels's early investments set an end to the traditional system of crown lands and community properties.[27] A new legal system based on private property rights, the establishment of the cash nexus and the almighty dollar led to a rapid redistribution of land and water-rights to foreign investors and the often naturalized planter elite from former missionary families. Theoretically, this would have already been possible three decades ago, but Spreckels was the first who walked the walk.

Labor migration changed the ethnic structure of the Hawaiian Kingdom fundamentally – a kingdom with only 80,578 inhabitants in 1884 (including 17,934 Chinese) and a shrinking native population.[28] Labor was scarce and Spreckels first tried to attract "white" labor to work at his plantations, although this was more expensive: In 1879 he paid his 125 "white" employees at the *Hawaiian Commercial Sugar Company* 3–4 U.S. dollars per day, while the first 100 Chinese workers received only 10–12 dollars per month.[29] However, Spreckels realized that economic rationality had to be balanced with wide-spread prejudices against "yellow" immigrants both by the native population and "white" immigrants.[30] Engineering nature should be accompanied by engineering society.

25 Hawaiian Sugar Planters' Association (ed.), *The Story of Sugar in Hawaii*; Bechert, *Working in Hawaii*; Takaki, *Pau Hana*.

26 "Spreckelsville Plantation, Hawaiian Islands," *Northern Star*, July 26, 1882, p. 2; Adler, *Claus Spreckels*, pp. 69–79.

27 Van Dyke, *Who owns the Crown Lands of Hawai'i?*

28 Jennings (ed.), *Chronology and Documentary*, p. 9; Hoerder, *Cultures in Contact*, p. 394.

29 "What Claus Spreckels Says," *Pacific Commercial Advertiser*, December 6, 1879, suppl., p. 5.

30 "The Danger of Unrestricted Chinese Immigration," *Pacific Commercial Advertiser*, August 30, 1879, p. 3.

In January 1881, *Hackfeld & Co.* launched a first transport of 127 Germans, most of them from Thuringia, followed by a second tranche of 180 persons in June 1882. Additional ships were planned in 1883, according to an ad in the *Gothaer Tageblatt*, trying to attract up to 300 additional workers; but such contract work was harshly criticized by German newspapers, because they "actually degrade free-born Germans to the level of coolies and negroes, rendering them useless to the Fatherland they have left, turning them from men into merchandise and practically using them as human manure for the properties of the sugar planters."[31] Even the German parliament discussed the matter and lawmakers agreed that plantation work in Hawaii would degrade German labor and German laborers.[32] Nevertheless, Spreckels hired some of these workers – more than 700 arrived in Honolulu in 1883 – although it is not clear how many. Most of them, however, were promoted to more responsible positions in the hierarchical world of Pacific plantations.

Together with his partner William G. Irwin, also proprietor of some mid-sized plantations, Claus Spreckels also hired ca. 500 Norwegians in 1881, "but they were accustomed to northern climate only."[33] Most of them left the country after a short while. Portuguese immigrants from the volcanic islands of first Madeira and then the Azores seemed to be a working alternative, although the passage cost the planter about 100 U.S. dollars per person, while the contract workers had to agree to a three year employment with a salary of about 1 dollar per day.[34] This immigration was predominantly managed by the German-born merchant Abraham Hoffnung (1833–1908), who came to Hawaii via Canada, and eventually became a Hawaiian chargé d'affaires and settled in London.[35] The Spreckels used their own resources as well, for instance, when they chartered the steamer *City of Paris*, which brought 824 immigrants from Saint Michael to Honolulu in 1884.[36]

These workers, indeed, could be accustomed to the hard work in the cane fields. Based predominantly on Spreckels's experiences, the newly founded

31 "The Slave Traffic," *San Francisco Chronicle*, June 3, 1883, p. 8. Cf. Spiekermann, "Deutsche Kulis in der hawaiianischen Zuckerindustrie?" available at: <https://uwe-spiekermann.com/2019/04/04/deutsche-kulis-in-der-hawaiianischen-zuckerindustrie-hintergruende-einer-reichstagsdebatte-von-1883>; last accessed 26. February 2020.

32 *Stenographische Berichte über die Verhandlungen des Reichstages*, pp. 1496–1898 (Kapp).

33 "Hawaiian Sugar," *Chicago Daily Tribune*, November 13, 1882, p. 8.

34 For a more general perspective see: Marques, "Portuguese Immigration to Hawaiian Islands," pp. 74–78; Felix and Senecal, *The Portuguese in Hawaii*. Until 1887, nearly 11.000 Portuguese immigrants, mostly families, went to Hawaii.

35 Alexander, *Kalakaua's Reign*, p. 28; Tulchinsky, *Taking Root*, pp. 64–65.

36 *Der Deutsche Correspondent*, June 3, 1884, p. 3.

*Hawaiian Planters' Labor and Supply Company* encouraged "the further immigration of Portuguese and Chinese."[37] When Portuguese immigration was interrupted in early 1882, Claus Spreckels attempted to take up to 2,000 Japanese workers and offered "to represent the Hawaiian Government in Japan in immigration questions."[38] This, however, was not accepted and the tide turned in favor of Chinese immigrants. From 1884, Spreckels used ships from his own line to import them to Hawaii.[39] Like other planters, he did not accept restrictions by the Hawaiian state, which tried to limit the transport to 20 persons per month.[40] In 1891, 1,200 Chinese laborers were employed by the *Hawaiian Commercial and Sugar Company*, in addition to 600 workers from other nations. They were "imported from every part of the earth," among them also Japanese people, who arrived first in 1884.[41] In 1912, the *Kilauea Plantation Company*, owned by John D. Spreckels and his brother Adolph B. Spreckels, had a labor force of 385 Japanese, 97 Filipinos, 59 Portuguese, 41 Puerto Ricans, 29 Chinese, 18 Koreans, and 6 Hawaiians.[42] Claus Spreckels was definitely not the first planter to import coolie workers, but he surely became the largest buyer of cheap labor; and the sheer quantity changed the ethnic composition of the islands fundamentally.

## 3 Labor and the Public: Scandalizing Coolie Work in California

From the late 1870s, American newspapers had consistently criticized the Spreckels' imperialistic dominance and his successful political lobbying in Honolulu, Sacramento and Washington, DC. Already by the early 1880s, the Spreckels case pushed broader debates on the essence of a democratic society, which became harbingers of the later populist movement and anticipated the central reform ideas of *Progressivism*.[43]

In San Francisco's thriving media market, the *San Francisco Chronicle*, led by the Sephardic de Young family, headed public criticism. Since the late 1870s, this early representative of the Yellow Press had scandalized the conditions in

37 "Report of the Secretary of the Planters' Labor and Supply Company," *The Planters' Monthly*, 2, 1883, pp. 185–194, 192.

38 *The Planters' Monthly*, 1, 1882, pp. 141–142, 141; "Report of the Secretary of the Planter's Labor and Supply Company," *The Planters' Monthly*, 1, 1882, pp. 176–188.

39 *Daily Alta California*, January 6, 1884, p. 7.

40 "The Sandwich Islands," *Argus*, February 19, 1884, p. 10.

41 "Chinese Emigration to Hawaii," *North China Herald*, July 31, 1891, p. 9.

42 MacLennan, "Kilauea Sugar Plantation in 1912," pp. 1–34.

43 Cf. McGerr, *A Fierce Contest*.

Spreckels's Hawaiian empire.[44] This was described as a corruption regime, as a crime against customs and decency, as slave economics. It was, in short, un-American. This was also an answer to Spreckels's use of Asian contract work, which earned him enmity and even death threats, namely among Irish-born immigrants. The *San Francisco Chronicle*, however, focused on the coolie work of "white" and Christian Portuguese contract workers.[45] Most local newspapers concluded that the living conditions of migrant workers were acceptable and much better than in the Caribbean sugar belt – a position later backed by official investigations by the Portuguese and Norwegian governments. The accusation of inhuman enrichment, however, could not be eliminated.[46]

Public opinion did not calm down. Week by week, the *San Francisco Chronicle* published new scandal reports, and used them to torpedo the extension of the Reciprocity Treaty in 1883/84.[47] Many Midwest and especially East Coast newspapers took over this position: "If there were no other reasons for throwing the Hawaiian reciprocity treaty into the waste-basket the moment it expires, the corruptions and frauds growing out of Claus Spreckels's sugar interests would be sufficient."[48] Corruption and fraud were terms commonly applied to the political business and its representatives. Deselection and leaving office, however, seemed to be more adequate reprimands than the criminal law. Similarly, widespread public accusations against the "Robber Barons", a small group of ruthless millionaires, exploiting their economic power or monopolies without reference to the common good, aimed less at criminal consequences, but at moral discrediting and a more effective monopoly legislation.[49]

The Spreckels' case, however, demonstrates that the lines of conflict in such public debates were by no means clear. The *San Francisco Chronicle* was not only revealing and scandalizing real grievances, since more than 100 articles were funded with 50,000 dollars a year from the leading East Coast sugar

44 *The Wasp*, a satirical magazine, defended de Young's civil rights in 1885 but had written earlier: "For many years the San Francisco Chronicle has terrorized this town. Its history, written in the blood of men and the tears of women, is a history of rapacity, cruelty, ruin, indecency, falsehood and exaction." See, *The Wasp*, 7, 1881, p. 260.

45 Most notable was the field report "Slave or Starve," *Chicago Daily Tribune*, October 18, 1881, p. 5, first published by the *Chronicle* and reprinted in many newspapers.

46 Cf. "The Chronicle on Hawaii," *The Wasp*, 7, 1881, p. 277; *The Argonaut*, 9, October 22, 1881, p. 8; "The Attack on Claus Spreckels and its Motive," *San Francisco News Letter*, 32, October 29, 1881/82, p. 10. Examinations in Maui were reported by "The 'Chronicles' Crow and What it Amounts to," *San Francisco Merchant*, 14, July 17, 1885, p. 104.

47 Dozer, "The Opposition to Hawaiian Reciprocity," pp. 157–183.

48 "Claus Spreckels' Monopoly," *Chicago Daily Tribune*, January 9, 1883, p. 4.

49 John, "Robber Barons Redux," pp. 1–38.

producers. They sought to demoralize the Spreckels family to integrate their businesses into the scheme of a nationwide sugar trust, the later *American Sugar Refinery Company*. Labor conditions in the Hawaiian periphery became an element of economic struggles in the U.S. mainland, and offered a chance to weaken the Spreckels sugar monopoly in the West. The Spreckels family clan responded drastically. When in November 1884 Claus Spreckels's wife Anna became the target of public accusations, her son Adolph B. tried to protect her honor. He went to the office of the *San Francisco Chronicle*, and shot twice at publisher Michael de Young, who survived only by fortunate circumstances.[50] Four years earlier, his brother Charles de Young was murdered in a similar case of "honorable" intervention.[51]

Although Spreckels's attempt at murder seemed to be obvious, the Spreckels family was able to corrupt San Francisco's public opinion in their favor in 1884/85. At first, most people believed: "It is time that in California we should begin to punish our wealthy criminals,"[52] but when the trial was started in June and July of 1885, public opinion had changed considerably. The unpopular Jewish publisher, de Young, saw himself not as a plaintiff, but as a defendant. Virile self-help seemed legitimate against tabloid journalism and slander.[53] The honor of a white mother and a leading Californian family seemed more important than the legal rights of an outsider and the labor conditions in the Hawaiian kingdom. Claus Spreckels paid 25,000 dollars to publish the long speech for the defense of his son in nine leading newspapers and magazines as a supplement.[54] In it, the Hawaiian plantation regime was acknowledged as an achievement of western civilization. Wide-spread criticism was discussed and rejected. Spreckels's lawyer gave detailed insights into the sugar industry's labor conditions. Now, the arguments were reversed: The *Chronicle* had been bought by Spreckels's Yankee competitors and had discredited an honest entrepreneur for simple profit-seeking. This should pave the way for a nationwide monopoly of Eastern sugar producers and Wall Street bankers, to enter the Californian market.[55] While some newspaper articles had discussed the morality of buying "bloody" sugar from Hawaii, now the Spreckels family suggested that

50 "The Ready Revolver," *Daily Alta California*, November 20, 1884, p. 1; "Another Shooting Affair in the San Francisco 'Chronicle' Office," *Sacramento Daily Union*, November 20, 1884, p. 2.

51 McKee, "The Shooting of Charles de Young," pp. 271–284.

52 *The Argonaut* 15, November 22, 1884, p. 3.

53 "In Spreckels' Defense," *Daily Gazette* [Colorado Springs], November 27, 1884, p. 1.

54 "The Golden Gate," *Chicago Daily Tribune*, June 28, 1885, p. 8.

55 "The Spreckels Case: H.E. Highton's Brillant Address to the Jury," *The Wasp*, 15, 1885, 1, suppl.

higher sugar prices for the public would be the result if the Eastern investors were to succeed.[56] Finally, Adolph Spreckels was acquitted by the jury on the grounds of temporary mental insanity – and remained one of San Francisco's leading entrepreneurs and citizens. Golden Gate Park and the Art Museum of the Legion de Honor are examples of his dedication to the public.[57]

Nonetheless, the long public debate and the trial led to numerous inquiries. Entrepreneurial responsibilities for the conditions of production and the well-being of their laborers were discussed. The legitimacy of private influence was questioned and public criticism of the "Robber Barons" and ubiquitous corruption of the political machines and the "interests" intensified. This triggered public claims for political reform and fair labor conditions.[58]

## 4 From Periphery to the Center: The Establishment of California's Beet Sugar Industry

In this case, however, it was perhaps even more important that models of population and re-population practiced in Hawaii were also used in the Western mainland. This was highly risky because the beet sugar business had been "a series of disasters"[59] up to that time. First agricultural experiments had already started in 1855 and supported the idea of California as "a sugar country *par excellence*".[60] In the late 1860s and early 1870s, capital was no problem, and even the scarcity of labor could be solved. In 1871, the *Sacramento Beet Sugar Company*, incorporated in 1868, employed more than 650 men – 150 "white" in the factory and 500 "Chinese" in the fields. But changing weather conditions, the lack of professional knowledge in handling the complex combination of cultivating, transporting, storing, and manufacturing the beet crops, and illusionary expectations by investors resulted in the failure of most endeavors. Only the mid-sized *Alvarado Sugar Factory*, established in 1870, remained in business. Californians were still proud of having the only factory in the United States; but it was obvious that a new start needed a different business approach.

It was the immigrant entrepreneur Claus Spreckels who made the difference. As the "Sugar King of the West" Spreckels had an ambivalent position

56 Cf. "Sugar," *Chicago Daily Tribune*, February 7, 1882, p. 7.

57 Cf. Secrest, *California Feuds*, pp. 114–118; Fine Arts Museums of San Francisco (ed.), *Legion of Honor*.

58 Cf. Beatty, *Age of Betrayal*.

59 United States Department of Agriculture, *Progress of the Beet-Sugar Industry*, p. 83.

60 Ernst Th. Gennert, "The Sugar Industry," *Pacific Rural Press*, 1, 18, August 23, 1879, p. 8.

to the Californian beet sugar production: A network of domestic producers and refiners could challenge his dominant position in business.[61] However, the German immigrant did not fight the newcomers. Instead, he always argued in favor of governmental tariff protection for the new domestic industry, and he did not use the tactic of reducing the sugar price in the 1880s to destroy the small Alvarado mill.[62]

This was surprising for the public, especially for those who saw Claus Spreckels as a ruthless and greedy robber baron who used cheap labor and monopolized prices to build up an immense fortune. Those who were more familiar with his career were well aware of his early interest in the beet sugar industry. Spreckels had already studied beet sugar farming and manufacturing in Prussia between 1865 and 1867.[63] His brother, Peter Spreckels, was one of the early directors of the *Alvarado Beet Sugar Company*.[64] Claus Spreckels used his Aptos ranch, purchased in 1872, for the cultivation of sugar beets and established a small sugar manufactory – the *California Sugar Beet Company* in Capitola – where he produced small amounts of beet sugar from 1874 to 1879.[65] At that time, however, Spreckels was not willing to invest larger sums. In contrast to Germany and France, where beet sugar production was profitable because of cheap rural laborers and tenant farmers, Californian labor conditions were not favorable to the new agribusiness. For Spreckels, production costs were simply too high for a profitable industry.[66] The failure of the early ventures was proof of his judgment.

However, Spreckels perception changed in the mid-1880s due to five major reasons, all resulting from his experiences in Hawaii: First, economies of scale could change the production costs significantly. Large scale-production, successfully practiced on the Sandwich Islands, could reduce the costs per pound and guarantee some profit – although the price of granulated sugar declined during the 1880s. Second, the Hawaiian experience had taught Spreckels a fundamental lesson: sugar production needed some political support. The U.S. had paid a bounty of two cents per pound for the cane sugar imported to California from 1876, but in the late 1880s it was obvious that this subsidy

61 "Our Sugar Supply," *Pacific Rural Press*, 14, April 8, 1871.

62 "Kill the New Industry," *Pacific Rural Press*, 4, no 24, December 14, 1872; "California for Sugar," *Pacific Rural Press*, 29, 2, January 10, 1885.

63 Collins, *Rio Del Mar: A sedate residential community*. p. 7.

64 "Beetroot Sugar in California," *Australian Town and Country Journal*, February 11, 1871, p. 13.

65 "The Coast Countries," *Daily Alta California*, October 16, 1872, p. 1; "Our Beet Sugar Interest," *Pacific Rural Press*, 6, 11, September 13, 1873.

66 NN, "Claus Spreckels," pp. 3–10.

could not be maintained any longer. The McKinley tariff of 1890 removed tariffs on cane sugar, but due to the engaged intervention of local Californian interests and representatives of the Republican Party – where the Spreckels family were important players – sugar beet producers received a bounty of two cents per pound to protect the domestic industry. Third, during the late 1880s, Claus Spreckels's formerly dominant position in Hawaii was eroding. On the one hand, planters tried to find alternative channels for selling and refining their product. On the other hand, the dominant political influence of the "sugar king" ended 1886, when he broke with King Kalakaua, and reduced his personal engagement in Hawaiian cane sugar production. Additional beet sugar could broaden the resource basis of the Spreckels sugar refinery in San Francisco. Fourth, from 1887 Spreckels was engaged in an intense fight with the Eastern Sugar Trust. After he refused to enter the trust, a long war between the monopolist in the West and the up-coming quasi-monopolist in the East began. The immigrant entrepreneur was able to defend his Californian territory in a harsh price war and hit back when he erected the largest refinery in the U.S. in Philadelphia. Finally, in 1891, the sugar trust guaranteed Spreckels's monopoly in the West and bought the Philadelphia plant for much more than Spreckels's investment. During this struggle, diversification was crucial to guarantee the supply of sugar to his refineries and to broaden the resource basis of his sugar empire in the West.[67] Fifth, in the late 1880s, Spreckels believed that his gospel of rural wealth would convince Californian farmers to invest into beet sugar as a new rural industry. While grain prices declined, beet production seemed to be a profitable alternative. Labor shortages could be overcome with a combination of high guaranteed prices and a new educational approach.

The result of all these considerations was the incorporation of the *Western Beet Sugar Corporation* on October 18, 1887 with a capital stock of 500,000 dollars.[68] In contrast to most of the former beet sugar enterprises, Spreckels's venture was the result of careful preparation, a five-month journey to Germany, Bohemia, Belgium and France, and modern forms of public relations. Spreckels spent 250,000 marks on machines and patents in Cologne and Prague and purchased 25 tons of beet seeds in France and Germany.[69] Perhaps more important was his public campaign for beet sugar production in the new world.

The immigrant entrepreneur utilized both American pride and the lack of American experience with beet cultivation to attract farmers, politicians, and the public to beet sugar production. He presented himself as a strong leader

67 "Fighting a Trust," *Daily Alta California*, September 3, 1888.

68 "Beet Sugar Company," *Los Angeles Herald*, October 18, 1887, p. 2.

69 "Claus Spreckels' Sugar Scheme," *Chicago Daily Tribune*, September 16, 1887, p. 5.

who could change the future of the business and the country. One of his key arguments was that the beet sugar industry would help to keep the millions of dollars at home, which were currently paid to mainly German imports by American consumers.[70] Spreckels made clear that American mechanics could make some basic machinery but that they are "ignorant"[71] regarding the modern equipment of a beet sugar factory. He brought chemical experts and experienced practitioners from Germany to California but stressed that their main task would be to inform themselves on the local conditions to run his venture successfully.[72] In general, however, he presented the United States as a country that needed knowledge from abroad to be able to compete with the leading European nations. Such statements were directed to the public and to politicians involved in tariff debates.

More important were Spreckels's local and regional campaigns in California. First, he addressed his idea to local politicians and businessmen to receive the best local support for his company. The decision for establishing his first refinery at Watsonville, Santa Cruz county, was therefore not only a result of former beet sugar production at the Soquel and Capitola factories and the personal experience of the "sugar king", whose Aptos farm was close by. The decision was also based on the donation of the land for the factory by a local capitalist and the willingness of many farmers to sign contracts for the delivery of beets – beet supply and labor shortage remained the crucial bottlenecks. The San Francisco capitalist knew that the amount of beet sugar supplies and the quality of the harvest was crucial for any large-scale endeavor. Again, he used a two-fold strategy to attract and guide the farmers of the Pajaro Valley. On the one hand, he referred to the natural conditions of California as a major reason for success. The failure of the former enterprises was presented as a result of insufficient machinery and a lack of business experience. Now, the farmers would have a second chance for wealth and higher incomes than with grain production. On the other hand, Spreckels actively engaged himself in educating American farmers and workmen in planting and cultivating the new cash crop.[73] He positioned himself as a supporter of the farmers, as a capitalist with ideas but insufficient capabilities: "I must have the support of the farmers."[74] Spreckels preached the gospel of wealth for everyone willing to support him.

70 "Great Enterprise in Beet Sugar," *Pacific Rural Press*, October 29, 1887, p. 34.
71 "Beet Sugar," *Sacramento Daily Union*, September 27, 1887.
72 "Beet Sugar," *Pacific Rural Press*, 34, 18, October 29, 1887.
73 Compare his letter to the farmers in "Beet Sugar," Daily Alta California, December 23, 1887 and his later reflections in "To Fight the Sugar Trust," *New York Times*, April 25, 1889.
74 "Claus Spreckels on Beet Sugar," *Pacific Rural Press*, 34, 20, November 12, 1887.

Consequently, his Watsonville factory was based on the supply of beets from independent farmers, who would accept detailed delivery contracts. Spreckels purchased seeds, and, as his chemists and managers advised, pushed higher qualities of beets with a bonus system for beets with a higher saccharine content.

The Watsonville factory was a success from the beginning. Although the profits of the first season were less than 3,000 dollars, Spreckels produced nearly 1,500 tons of raw sugar and employed 135 men.[75] During the following campaigns the Watsonville factory raised both output and profit – and became a cash cow even in the dry late 1890s.[76] However, Claus Spreckels's vision was more ambitious than simply erecting one larger sugar mill. In the late 1880s, he tried to establish a huge network of decentralized beet-sugar factories. Although he was willing to invest up to 5,000,000 dollars, his plans failed due to the lack of farmers willing and able to cultivate labor-intense beet crops. Farmers complained about the heavy manual labor and the continuous need to deal with the hoe. Traditional grain cultivation was less labor-intense,[77] and rural workers were not yet available.

The Watsonville factory, however, remained a success.[78] From 1888 to 1897, the amount of manufactured beets grew from 15,000 to more than 110,000 tons, and nearly 15,000 tons of raw sugar was produced in contrast to 1,500 at the beginning. The venture was profitable during the whole decade and not only the investors benefitted: In 1897, the farmers received 43 dollars per acre with beets, having started at 34 dollars.[79] But labor conditions changed rapidly. Most farmers were not peasants, but growers. From the early 1890s more than two-thirds of the work was done by Chinese and Japanese contract workers.[80]

In the early 1890s, the California beet sugar industry was only growing slowly. Farmers were hesitant to convert their business and the floating tariff protection made any investment highly speculative. Claus Spreckels, convinced

75 "The Beet Sugar Experiment," *Australian Town and Country Journal*, February 28, 1889, p. 29.

76 "Commercial," *Los Angeles Times*, 1897, April 22.

77 Cf. Walker, *The Conquest of Bread.*

78 On the early beet sugar industry in California cf. Street, *Beasts in the Field.* pp. 307–333, although he only briefly discussed the Watsonville case (ibid., pp. 361–362).

79 "Ten Years of Beet sugar at Watsonville," *Pacific Rural Press*, 56, 26, December 24, 1898.

80 Adolph B. Spreckels stated "that 95 per cent of the labor of beet raising at Watsonville is done by American laborers" ("Japan Moderates its Demands," *Chicago Daily Tribune*, June 10, 1897, p. 3). An examination by the labor commissioner, however, stated that two third of the cultivation work was done by approximately 1000 Chinese and Japanese ("In Beet Fields," *Pacific Commercial Advertiser*, July 31, 1897, p. 2).

that only large-scale production could make a difference, pushed the industry with new investments, based on successful public relations and on political lobbying in Sacramento and Washington.

The "sugar king" launched a new public campaign in 1896 for erecting a huge centralized factory. Parallel to this, Spreckels purchased large areas of farmable ground in central California. If individual farmers were not willing to produce the immense amount of raw material for a large beet sugar factory, this land could be cultivated by temporarily hired "white" or "Asian" rural workers. But Spreckels still preferred "white" settler farmers, bound to his factory by long-term contracts. During the summer he again offered beet seeds to interested farmers and sent them a detailed pamphlet with information on the value of the beets for the soil, the benefits of crop rotation, and the encouraging prospects for individual wealth: "The more they grow the richer they will be. I can take all they can raise, and my scheme will be the salvation of the country, but there is much to do to ensure this end."[81] Spreckels presented himself as a realistic visionary. His investment would need guarantees for growing large amounts of beets. He asked for "some protection" of the nascent industry. He asked businessmen and farmers whether they were able to compete with Europeans. In his mind, Americans could achieve everything they wanted to achieve.

But Claus Spreckels would not have become the dominant figure in the Western sugar business simply by believing his own statements. Simultaneously, he intensified his purchase of beet sugar land. In late 1897, Spreckels already held 18,000 acres of beet sugar land; a number, which would rise to 66,000 acres, leased or operated in 1919.[82] While the Watsonville factory was based predominantly on beet supply from independent farmers, the new factory in the Salinas valley had a more paternalistic touch. A contract system offered chances for independent farmers, while on its own land a kind of estate structure was established. This land was leased to farmers and cultivated by rural contract workers, most of them of Asian descent.

Similar to his early attempts in Hawaii, he tried to attract "white" labor first. In cooperation with the Salvation Army he founded a settler community of 150 farmers of German origin at Fort Romie, near Soledad in Monterey County, in 1897.[83] This was a successful experiment "in colonizing the poor

81 "Detailed Plans of the Sugar King," *Chicago Daily Tribune*, July 3, 1896, p. 1. It took most farmers two to three years to become an efficient supplier.

82 "News of the Big Cities," *Chicago Daily Tribune*, December 9, 1897, p. 3.

83 "Rural Homestead Plan," *New York Times*, May 21, 1897; "To Colonize the West," *Ogden Standard Examiner*, August 28, 1897, p. 1; "The All-Absorbing Topic," *Sacramento Daily Union*, October 17, 1897.

of the great cities upon idle land."[84] Here, "white" workers found new homes and an advanced infrastructure for their daily life. The Spreckels company took care of nearly everything but expected loyalty and hard word. But such a small number of settlers was insufficient to fill the gaps for supplying by far the largest beet sugar factory in the U.S. While the neighborhood of the factory, namely the company town, Spreckels, was predominately "white", the farm work was overwhelmingly done by Japanese immigrants. A kind of "colonial economy" was established in California.[85] Economic models, developed in the Pacific periphery, shaped California's transition to a multicultural and multi-ethnic state.

Backed by local, governmental, and financial support, construction began in 1898. It was a 2,500,000 dollar investment, which changed a whole region. The *Spreckels Sugar Company* was incorporated in 1899, with a capital of 5,000,000 dollars. The new factory combined modern construction technology, namely a steel frame construction and the intense use of electricity with modern foreign machinery. It included a large laboratory, which focused not only on the examination of beets, but more and more on the examination of soil and quality control of sugar production. The factory was the center of a huge railroad network and an "intertwining network of roads, [...] dump stations, irrigation canals, wells and pumps, and pipelines."[86] The plant employed nearly 700 workers during the campaign. The daily water supply was 13,000,000 gallons – the same as the city of San Francisco. The consequent use of economies of scale reduced the production costs significantly. While the Alvarado factory spent 6 dollars per ton of beets in the late 1880s, the Salinas factory had cut this to 2 dollars.[87] Continuous production was based on an immense system of irrigation, a consequence from the severe draughts in the late 1890s, especially in 1898. Finally, Spreckels had taken care that all by-products of the beet sugar production were used: The pulp fed 600 cows, which was at that time quite exceptional.[88]

Spreckels's Salinas company was profitable from the beginning – and remained the largest American beet factory for decades. This "mammoth sugar company"[89] became the model for the American beet sugar industry. From

84 "Abolish the Poor," *Chicago Daily Tribune*, December 12, 1897, p. 35.
85 McWilliams, *Factories in the Field*, p. 88.
86 Breschini, Gudgel, and Haversat, *Spreckels*, p. 32.
87 "Local Benefits of the Beet Sugar Industry," *Pacific Rural Press*, 53, 4, January 23, 1897.
88 "To Produce Our Own Sugar," *Beet Sugar Gazette*, 3, 1901, p. 120.
89 "Wheels of the Mammoth Sugar Factory at Spreckels Begin to Turn," *San Francisco Call*, September 1, 1899.

1898 to 1913, a total of 86 beet sugar factories were built in the United States, half of them by 1903.[90]

## 5 Coup d'État, Annexation and the Rise of the "Big Five" in Hawaii

While Spreckels extended his business empire on the American mainland and, simultaneously, diversified into sectors such as railroads, real estate, and public, the *Hawaiian Commercial and Sugar Company* remained the by far the largest cane sugar plantation in the Pacific with a steady extension of cane land under cultivation.[91] Meanwhile, however, the Hawaiian Kingdom suffered a constitutional crisis. King Kalakaua's and Prime Minister Walter M. Gibson's (1822–1888) autocratic regime and rapidly growing state debts resulted in a revolt by most sugar planters. Widespread rumors that Claus Spreckels had supported or even initiated the coup were denied.[92] Already by November 1886, the by far largest taxpayer and credit-giver of the monarchy had broken with the king over the subject of additional state loans and the threat of state bankruptcy. After establishing a safe and profitable business structure, the return on investment was now threatened by a shaking Hawaiian state and the end of reciprocity subsidies. The 1887 planter's coup forced the king to sign a new constitution, which reduced his influence and gave additional power to the Hawaiian parliament, dominated by natives and naturalized sugar planters. Kalakaua died in San Francisco in 1891 and was succeeded by his sister, Queen Liliuokalani, who attempted to establish a revised and more autocratic constitution. Threatened by a monarchist coup d'état of natives, U.S.-American annexationists revolted again in 1893 and put American annexation of Hawaii on the political agenda.[93] The insurgent's position was clear: The U.S. government should guarantee the legal and institutional framework for a wealthy planter oligarchy, something a corrupt and selfish Hawaiian monarchy could not deliver. Private economic order should be supported by state dominance.

90 Leonhard J. Arrington, "Science, Government, and Enterprise in Economic Development," pp. 1–18.

91 Cf. "The Hawaiian Commercial and Sugar Company's Estate in Spreckelsville, Maui, H.I.," *The Planter's Monthly*, 8, 1889, pp. 68–75; Adler, "The Spreckelsville Plantation," pp. 33–48.

92 "What is Said," *Daily Alta California*, July 10, 1887, p. 1. On different rumors cf. "Hawaii's New Regime," *Boston Daily Globe*, July 11, 1887, p. 5; *"Die Revolution auf Hawaii," Der Deutsche Correspondent*, July 12, 1887, p. 1.

93 Until today, the history of annexation is causing manifold debates on Hawaii's historical identity and the colonial past of the U.S. Cf. Siler, *Lost Kingdom*.

Claus Spreckels became the main antipode of the annexationists, although he had shared the goal of a U.S. supported republic of planters in early 1893.[94] The labor problem was the main cause for his turnaround: Hawaii's colonization would have resulted into the use of U.S. laws, including the notorious 1882 Chinese Exclusion Act. Spreckels would have no longer been allowed to import Chinese contract workers and higher wages and lower profits would have been the consequence. Such arguments were shared by trading houses *Hackfeld & Co.* and *Davies & Co.* and it is surely no coincidence that those power-houses against annexation were attacked by the white planter elite, descendants of missionaries, which formed the core of the later "Big Five." Their prime goal was order, because order would strengthen their position, and relative losses of superior competitors such as Spreckels, Hackfeld, and even Davies were an additional argument for annexation.

Claus Spreckels went to Hawaii in 1893, fought the provisional oligarchic government and tried to restore Queen Liliuokalani's reign, but finally left the islands threatened by death for him and his family. His direct interventions in Washington, however, slowed down the imperialistic policy of the U.S. federal government.[95] Spreckels declared: "I am opposed to stealing and do not believe that might make right."[96] Finally, however, the strategic and economic interests of the emerging Pacific power and a partly American, partly Hawaiian born white planter elite prevailed: In 1900, the formerly independent Kingdom became a territory, a de facto colony of the U.S.

At the time, Claus Spreckels had already assigned his Hawaiian interests to his children. This inheritance, however, was overshadowed by a devastating split in the Spreckels family. While his two elder sons gained interests in seven efficient, but only mid-sized plantations, at Oahu and the Big Island, the center piece of Spreckels's Hawaiians investments, the *Hawaiian Commercial and Sugar Company* was lost to his two younger sons Gustav "Gus" Augustus and Rudolph (1872–1958) after a long and painful series of public court battles. The sons formed coalitions with the local planter elite and supported U.S. annexation from 1897.[97] This, however, did not prevent a hostile takeover in 1898 by middlemen of Alexander & Baldwin, now becoming a leading representative

94 "Leading Men Favor a Republic," *Chicago Daily Tribune*, April 4, 1893, p. 4; "A Waiting Game," *Sacramento Daily Union*, May 18, 1893, p. 6.

95 "Spreckels Will Protest," *San Francisco Morning Call*, August 19, 1893, p. 1.

96 "Spreckels on Annexation," *Chicago Daily Tribune*, October 23, 1893, p. 1.

97 *Salt Lake Tribune*, February 5, 1897, p. 2; *San Francisco Call*, February 6, 1897, p. 2.

of the "Big Five."[98] Following and perfecting Claus Spreckels's example they established their grip on the Hawaiian economy and state in the next decades.

## 6 Conclusion

This case study demonstrates how the Kingdom of Hawaii, a state in the Pacific periphery of the global economy, became an integrated part of modern commodity chains. The interaction between Hawaii and California/United States, however, did not follow simplistic periphery-center models and can't be characterized by common interpretations of a *histoire croisée*.[99] Instead, Hawaii became a blueprint model for the development of business structures, serving the interests of large-scale investors and a majority of American sugar consumers.

These early commodity chains were not only an empirical reality, part of typical capitalistic "exploitation". Monocultures, racism, and the morality of investments were also part of late nineteenth century media and public debates on economic intervention and commercial transition. Labor conditions were an important part of these public discussions. They triggered private and state examinations, established a kind of public sensibility, and queried the values of the west and the legitimacy of consumer behavior.

This case study emphasizes that capital, and in some way even soil, were not the core obstacles for developing large-scale sugar production in new regions of the global south. Labor scarcity was the core problem for investors, states, and even the native population, in integrating such regions into the global commodity chains, dominated by western investors.

In this particular case, one can analyze private capitalism in action. In Hawaii, and even in central California, entrepreneurs like Spreckels were substitutes of the state. This resulted in immense profits and learning processes about the relevance of labor. Spreckels gave incentives for a dual structure, based on well-paid and trained "white" academic experts, foremen, and skilled workers on the one hand, and a far larger number of unskilled workers, mostly from Asia, on the other. As an immigrant entrepreneur, he developed new markets with technology transferred from his German home country, from Europe,

98 "Cleared Three Millions," *Salt Lake Herald*, October 1, 1898, p. 4; "Gebrüder Spreckels übertrumpft," *Der Deutsche Correspondent*, 1898, October 2, p. 4; "A Forty Thousand Tons Sugar Estate," *The Planters' Monthly*, 17, (1898), pp. 440–441.

99 On Hawaiian labor export, see: Rosenthal, *Beyond Hawai'i*.

and the U.S. mainland, and it is perhaps more than coincidence that he, as a successful immigrant, became a gatekeeper for a more wealthy and multi-ethnic Hawaii and California.

## Bibliography

Abbott, Elizabeth. *Sugar. A Bittersweet History* (New York: Overlook Books, 2010).

Adler, Jacob. "The Oceanic Steamship Company: A Link in Claus Spreckels' Hawaiian Sugar Empire," *Pacific Historical Review*, 29 (1960), pp. 257–269.

Adler, Jacob. "The Spreckelsville Plantation: A chapter in Claus Spreckels' Hawaiian Career," *California Historical Society Quarterly*, 40 (1961), pp. 33–48.

Adler, Jacob. *Claus Spreckels: The Sugar King in Hawaii* (Honolulu: University of Hawaii Press, 1966).

Arrington, Leonhard J. "Science, Government, and Enterprise in Economic Development: The Western Beet Sugar Industry," *Agricultural History*, 41 (1967), pp. 1–18.

Beatty, Jack. *Age of Betrayal: The Triumph of Money in America, 1865–1900* (New York: Vintage Books, 2008).

Bechert, Edward. *Working in Hawaii: A Labor History* (Honolulu: University of Hawaii Press, 1985).

Berghoff, Hartmut and Uwe Spiekermann. "Immigrant Entrepreneurship as a Challenge for Historiography," in ibid. (eds), *Immigrant Entrepreneurship. The German-American Experience since 1700* (German Historical Institute: Washington, DC, 2016), pp. 5–15.

Breschini, Gary S., Mona Gudgel, and Trudy Haversat. *Spreckels* (Arcadia Pub.: Charleston, 2006).

Collins, Allen. *Rio Del Mar: A sedate residential community* (n.p., 1995).

Dorrance, William Henry and Francis Swanzy Morgan. *Sugar Islands. The 165-Year Story of Sugar in Hawai'i*, 2nd ed. (Honolulu: University of Hawaii Press, 2005).

Dozer, Donald Marquard. "The Opposition to Hawaiian Reciprocity, 1876–1888," *Pacific Historical Review*, 14 (1945), pp. 157–183.

Felix, John Henry and Peter F. Senecal. *The Portuguese in Hawaii* (Honolulu: University of Hawaii Press, 1978).

Fine Arts Museums of San Francisco (ed.). *Legion of Honor: Inside and Outside* (San Francisco: FAMSF Publications, 2013).

Haley, James L. *Captive Paradise. A History of Hawaii* (New York, 2014).

Hawaiian Sugar Planters' Association (ed.). *The Story of Sugar in Hawaii* (Honolulu: Hawaiian Sugar Planters' Association, 1926).

Hawkins, Richard. "Hackfeld, Heinrich" in William J. Hausman and GHI (eds), *Immigrant Entrepreneurship: German-American Business Biographies, 1720 to the*

*Present*, vol. 2. Online available at: http://www.immigrantentrepreneurship.org/entry.php?rec=285; last accessed 17 July 2018.

Hoerder, Dirk. *Cultures in Contact: World Migrations in the Second Millennium* (Durham and London: Duke University Press, 2002).

Jennings, Helen (ed.). *Chronology and Documentary Handbook of the State of Hawaii* (Dobby Ferry: Oceana Publications, 1978).

John, Richard R. "Robber Barons Redux: Antimonopoly Reconsidered," *Enterprise and Society*, 13 (2012), pp. 1–38.

Jones, Allan and Robert V. Osgood. *From King Cane to the Last Sugar Mill. Agricultural Technology and the Making of Hawai'i's Premier Crop* (Honolulu: University of Hawaii Press, 2015).

MacLennan, Carol. "Kilauea Sugar Plantation in 1912: A Snapshot," *Hawaiian Journal of History*, 41 (2007), pp. 1–34.

MacLennan, Carol A. *Sovereign Sugar. Industry and Environment in Hawai'i* (Honolulu: University of Hawaii Press, 2015).

McGerr, Michael. *A Fierce Contest: The Rise and Fall of the Progressive Movement in America* (Oxford and New York: Oxford University Press, 2005).

McWilliams, Carey. *Factories in the Field. The Story of Migratory Farm Labor in California* (Berkeley: University of California Press, 1999).

NN. "Claus Spreckels," in *San Francisco. Its Builders Past and Present*, vol. I (Chicago and San Francisco, 1913), pp. 3-10

Pletcher, David M. *The Diplomacy of Involvement. American Economic Expansion across the Pacific, 1784–1900* (Columbia and London: University of Missouri, 2001).

Rosenthal, Gregory. *Beyond Hawai'i: Native Labor in the Pacific World* (Oakland: University of California Press, 2018).

Schmitt, Robert C. *Historical Statistics of Hawaii* (Honolulu: University of Hawaii Press, 1977).

Secrest, William B. *California Feuds: Vengeance, Vendettas & Violence on the Old West Coast* (Quill Driver Books: Sanger, 2005).

Siler, Julia Flynn. *Lost Kingdom: Hawaii's Last Queen, the Sugar Kings, and America's First Imperial Adventure* (New York: Atlantic Monthly Press, 2012).

Spiekermann, Uwe. "Claus Spreckels: A Biographical Case Study of Nineteenth-Century American Immigrant Entrepreneurship," *Business and Economic History Online*, (2010). Online available at: http://www.thebhc.org/sites/default/files/spiekermann.pdf; last accessed 17 July 2018.

Spiekermann, Uwe. "Das gekaufte Königreich: Claus Spreckels, die Hawaiian Commercial Company und die Grenzen wirtschaftlicher Einflussnahme im Königtum Hawaii, 1875–1898," in Hartmut Berghoff, Cornelia Rauh, and Thomas Welskopp (eds), *Tatort Unternehmen. Zur Geschichte der Wirtschaftskriminalität im 20. und 21. Jahrhundert* (Berlin and Boston: De Gruyter, 2016), pp. 47–66.

Spiekermann, Uwe. "Deutsche Kulis in der hawaiianischen Zuckerindustrie?" Online available at: <https://uwe-spiekermann.com/2019/04/04/deutsche-kulis-in-der-hawaiianischen-zuckerindustrie-hintergruende-einer-reichstagsdebatte-von-1883>; last accessed 26. February 2020..

Spiekermann, Uwe. "Expanding the Frontier(s): The Spreckels Family and the German-American Penetration of the Pacific, 1870–1920," in Hartmut Berghoff, Frank Biess, and Ulrike Strasser (eds), Explorations and Entanglements. *Germans in Pacific Worlds from the Early Modern Period to World War I* (Oxford and New York: Berghahn Books, 2018), pp.171-194.

Street, Richard Steven. *Beasts in the Field: A Narrative History of California Farmworkers, 1769–1913* (Stanford: Stanford University Press, 2004).

Takaki, Ronald. *Pau Hana: Plantation Life and Labor in Hawaii, 1835–1920* (Honolulu: University of Hawaii Press, 1983).

Tate, Merze. *Hawaii: Reciprocity or Annexation* (East Lansing: Michigan State University Press, 1968).

Teisch, Jessica B. *Engineering Nature: Water, Development, & Global Spread of American Environmental Expertise* (Chapel Hill: University of North Carolina Press, 2011).

Tulchinsky, Gerald. *Taking Root: The Origins of the Canadian Jewish Community* (Hanover and London: University Press of New England, 1993).

Van Dyke, John M. *Who owns the Crown Lands of Hawai'i?* (Honolulu: University of Hawaii Press, 2008).

Walker, Richard A. *The Conquest of Bread. 150 Years of Agribusiness in California* (New York and London: New Press, 2004).

Wilcox, Carol. *Sugar Water. Hawaii's Plantation Ditches* (Honolulu: University of Hawaii Press, 1997).

CHAPTER 8

# Coolie Labor, Tea Planters, and Transport in Colonial India

*Santosh Hasnu*

Most scholarship on colonial labor regimes in Assam and Cachar tea plantations (located in present-day north-east India) has been preoccupied with various forms of labor recruitment. Apart from Ian J. Kerr's work,[1] there is little interest in looking at the connection between labor circulation and railway construction in colonial India.[2] Moreover, a comparative study of labor relations in railway construction has been conducted, looking at India, Portugal and Africa in the second half of the nineteenth century.[3] Transport systems remain a vehicle of historical dynamism by expanding and intensifying the traffic of commodities, labor, knowledge, and ideas across trading regions. Beginning in the early nineteenth century, British capital ventured into the tea plantations of Assam and Cachar. As capital investment poured into tea estates, planters began to feel an acute shortage of local labor supply. The planters were banking on the local laborers but failed to turn them into permanent wage workers. The local laborers were peasants who voluntarily worked as seasonal workers in the plantations if they found the wages attractive and they had a deep political will to agitate for better wages.[4] The recruited immigrant coolie labor usually worked in and out of season under indentured contract[5]

---

1 Kerr, *Building the Railways.*

2 Scholars have drawn attention to the unexpected and popular appropriation of modern railway lines by religious pilgrims in colonial India, see: Ahuja, *Pathways of Empire* and Kerr, "Reworking a Popular Religious Practice." Yet other students of railway history underline the modernity of railway technology and its economic impacts for colonial India, see: Derbyshire, "The Building of India's Railways" and Mukherjee, "Mukul. Railways and Their Economic Impact". For a recent work that focuses on the imprint of the modern railway on the emergent popular culture of colonial India, see: Prasad, *Tracks of Change.*

3 Kerr, Navarro and Pereira, "Labour Relations and Processes," pp. 321–342.

4 The Kachari tribal laborers of Assam, for instance, agitated for higher wages in 1848 and 1859. This led to a law and order problem for the colonial government. Because of the seasonal participation of local labor, the British developed the myth of the lazy native who refused to be permanently employed by the plantation. See, Guha, *Planter Raj to Swaraj*, p. 13; Sharma, "'Lazy Natives'," pp. 1287–1324.

5 Sharma, "'Lazy Natives'," pp. 1287–1324.

 | DOI:10.1163/9789004448049_009

and they accept wages lower than that of local laborers. At this point, defining the word coolie[6] may be helpful. According to Henry Yule and A.C. Burnell's Hobson-Jobson dictionary, *coolie* (cooly) has two meanings – first, immigrant labor in a colonial plantation, and secondly, unskilled workers from the lower class of laborers in the context of north India. Both these definitions happen to fit the historical usages in my case study.

The planters demanded that the shortage in local labor be supplemented by immigrant sources of disciplined labor workforces. This situation induced the British India Government to lean on the agency of numerous labor contractors from the mid-nineteenth century. Planters in the Caribbean colonies resorted to the same strategy of recruiting indentured labor from India as an alternative to local labor of freed slaves since 1838.[7] From the 1860s, the planters began to recruit indentured migrant laborers from areas outside Assam and Cachar. The supply came from various parts of the Indian subcontinent such as Central Provinces, Chota Nagpur region, Bihar, Madras and the North-Western Provinces (NWP).[8]

These tea laborers were first brought to Calcutta from their native region; and from here they were transported to tea gardens across Assam and Cachar by means of steamers and boats. Steamers plying along the Brahmaputra and the Surma-Barak rivers facilitated the movement of these new supplies of laborers. Until the construction of railways in the late nineteenth century, steamers and boats were the only means of connecting to the Calcutta port. Further, the exports of commodities such as tea and jute heavily depended on the river route. But this transport system was a seasonal one confined to the monsoons when steamers become temporarily operational. This communication constraint coincided with peak demand for labor by the British planters. Moreover, transportation of laborers to Assam and Cachar via steamers and boats was occasioned with a high mortality rate. This led the tea planters to look for an alternate mode of transport from the 1880s. The construction of the Assam-Bengal Railway line was proposed as a solution for the transport bottleneck that impeded the flow of commodities and labor. It resulted in the formation of the Assam-Bengal Railway Company Limited in 1892 with headquarters in Chittagong. The new infrastructure was to provide an outlet to the sea by connecting Assam and Cachar to the European markets via Chittagong port. This rail line was to become crucial for maintaining tea traffic and to overcome

6 The word *koli* first appeared in Hamilton's description of Hindostan (1820) to refer to a caste of western India.

7 Mohapatra, "'Following Custom'?", pp. 173–202.

8 Chatterjee and Gupta, "Tea-Labour in Assam", pp. 1862–67.

the problems of labor shortages. Besides offering a direct link to the seaport, the promoters of the railway line claimed that it would reduce the distance, travel time and, more importantly, the cost-effectiveness for importing labor and exporting tea-boxes. The steamer industry was obviously a rival to this proposed railway since the latter would divert the bulk of the traffic along the new railway line. With the coming of new transport technology (the steam engine), railway became the primary mode of transportation on land, connecting interior tea belts and seaports. Therefore, this article is an attempt to study the role of transport systems in the circulation of labor and processed tea. A focus on transport and circulation can alert us to the flow of people (labor) and commodities (tea). As Nitin Sinha emphasized in his recent work on colonial Bihar, a study on the impact of communication should be specific in terms of commodity production and distribution to illustrate the connected history of commodity production, transport, and communication.[9] Similarly, an example of tea plantation is taken up in this essay to demonstrate the connected history of tea, coolie labor and transport. In doing so, this chapter also investigates the story of how the needs of the planters led to the shift from waterway to railway that took place in the 1890s with the building of the Assam-Bengal Railway track.

## 1 High Mortality of Coolies in Transit Via Steamers

Mobilizing an adequate labor force was the major problem confronting the growing tea estates in Assam and Cachar. Ever since the introduction of tea cultivation began in the 1840s, the planters had pressed for a regular supply of labor. The existing riverine systems in the region played an important role in maintaining the communication networks. Many of these navigable river networks connected Assam and Cachar with the neighboring Bengal and Calcutta ports. The mighty river Brahmaputra, which intersected the valley of Assam, remained the main route of communication to Bengal. In fact, the Brahmaputra, along with many tributaries, had acted as the natural highway between Assam and Bengal for centuries. In Cachar, the river Surma and the Barak acted as a splendid water route with a heavy concentration of traffic.[10] These existing navigable riverine systems provided the main communication routes for maintaining increasing volumes of

---

9 Sinha, *Communication and Colonialism*, p. 227.

10 Deloche, *Transport and Communications in India*, p. 30.

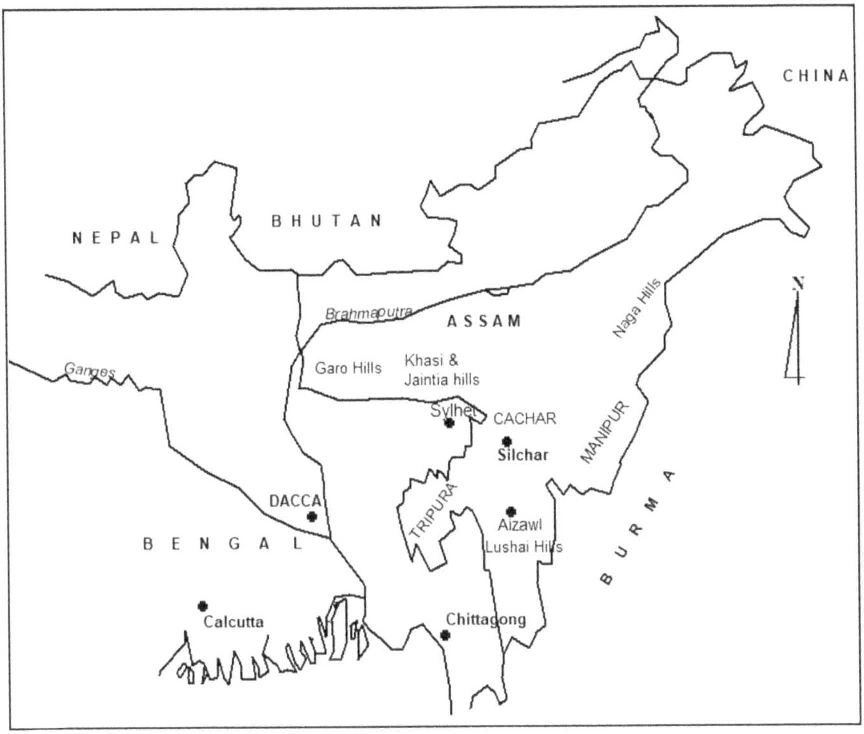


MAP 8.1 Assam during the nineteenth century
SOURCE: CREATED BY THE AUTHOR

commodities (processed tea) and people (import of labors) by the used of steamers and boats.

Formed in 1839 in London, the Assam Tea Company[11] was granted approval by the British East India Company[12] for the commercial production of tea in Assam. Soon, the Assam Tea Company established its headquarters in a place called Nazira, situated on the bank of the Dikhow river. To enhance their commercial interests, the Company began to make its own transport arrangements. The Assam Tea Company came to acquire many country boats of varying sizes from Calcutta and Dacca. Most of them were named after the rivers flowing across or into Assam such as the *Dibroo*, *Dehing*, *Dikhow*, *Brahmaputra*,

11 For the history on establishment and functioning of the Assam Tea Company, see: Antrobus, *A History of the Assam Company*.

12 EIC was not merely a commercial corporation, it exercised the role of a sovereign state in the colonies according to the monopoly charter granted by the British Crown. See, Stern, *The Company-State*.

*Dhunseri*, *Lohit* and *Tingri*. In 1842, the Company's steamer *Assam* was the first commercially owned steamer to ply the waterways of the Brahmaputra river.[13] By the year 1847, the British EIC Government too introduced steamers to the rivers of Assam. However, government steamers operated at irregular intervals, running only once a month or once every six weeks. The steamers were also mostly meant for transporting military troops and company officials.

By the 1860s, two private British firms started to operate weekly steamer services for both passengers and freight. In 1861, the India General Steam Navigation Company (IGSNC) started its service on the Brahmaputra river; making arrangements with planters for carrying coolies (laborers) into Assam tea gardens. By the year 1863, the IGSNC had expanded its service to Cachar. Their steamers reached up to Silchar (in Cachar) from Calcutta through the Surma-Barak river, taking five days in the summer and three days during the winter.[14] The steamer companies entered into arrangement directly with the Tea Company for the export of processed tea. For instance, in 1869 the River Steam Navigation Company (which started its steamer service in 1862) made a two-year agreement with the Jorhat Tea Company for carriage of its tea and stores at reduced rates, with the understanding that the whole of their goods were reserved for this company.[15] By the 1880s, the steamers from Calcutta could reach Dibrugarh (upper Assam) in six days and Guwahati (lower Assam) in three days.[16]

Steamers (and later trains) greatly facilitated the migration of tea coolies under indentured contracts to Assam and Cachar. First, recruited coolies were dispatched from their districts to Calcutta with the help of private recruiting agencies. These agencies took the services of native recruiters known as '*arkattis*' and garden *sardars* who operated in different districts of Eastern and Central India. From Calcutta, they were routed through a long, difficult journey by steamers, then via roads to Goalundo (in Bengal), and then transit to Dhubri (western most point of Assam). Dhubri had depots built that were owned by

13 Antrobus, *A History of the Assam Company*, p. 354.

14 Allen, *Assam District Gazetteers*, p. 107.

15 Medhi, *Transport System and Economic Development of Assam*, p. 21. In the mid-nineteenth century, when the Eastern-Bengal Railway was constructed, these steamer services connected to the nearest railhead at Khustia (160 kilometres north of Calcutta) which was located on the Assam-Bengal border. In 1863, the RSNC entered into an agreement with the Eastern-Bengal Railway for traffic to and fro between Assam and Khustia. The IGSNC entered into similar kind of agreement with the Eastern-Bengal Railway in 1869. But these agreements with both the Company were discontinued in 1871 and steamers again plied directly to Assam from Calcutta.

16 Sharma, *Empire's Garden*, p. 80.

recruiting agencies or contractors. From Dhubri, coolie laborers were transported to tea gardens in Assam by means of weekly or daily steamer services. Indentured coolie laborers travelling from Goalundo to Cachar were conveyed partly by steamer and partly by boat. From a point called Fenchuganj (Sylhet), the workers travelled almost entirely by small boats as the steamers could not operate due to shallow river water. These steamers were also used for importing rice to feed the coolies working in tea gardens. Thus, the planter communities in Cachar faced considerable expense when importing labor. The steamer services in Cachar were seasonal transport, as they couldn't get further than Fenchuganj (70 miles from Silchar) for five months of the year. The steamers were only able to reach Silchar (Cachar) during four months of the year, and since the steamers cannot get further than Fenchuganj during the five dry-weather months, Cachar was practically cut off from Bengal.

By the latter half of the nineteenth century, the transportation of people (coolie labor) via steamers incurred high mortality rates, and was thus marked as an unhealthy, undependable transport system. This led the British Government to monitor labor immigration into Assam and Cachar from 1861. To investigate the emigration of laborers to Assam and Cachar, the British Government set up a three members committee as early as 1861. A year later, the committee highlighted the harsh conditions that immigrant coolies had to suffer during steamer and boat journeys to Assam and Cachar. They pointed out that there was no proper accommodation for the coolies, nor any arrangements to secure cleanliness, insufficient and unsuitable food, over-crowding and inadequacy in medical attendance. The committee believed that this resulted in high mortality – reaching 10–12 percent during a month's voyage; sometimes even as high as 50 percent.[17]

These high mortality rates, both en route as well as on plantations, and large-scale desertions eventually forced the colonial state to intervene and regulate the recruitment process of the coolies. This resulted in the formulation of the Transport of Native Labourers Act of 1863 to control the emigration. Under the Act, recruiters and contractors were to be licensed and to present the emigrants before the magistrate of their own district for registration. After which, the emigrants were forwarded to the contractors depot where they were examined by a medical inspector to assess their fitness to work in the tea gardens. The Act also provided provision for the licensing of steamers and boats carrying coolies to the labor districts. However, the Act did not have provision

17 Assam State Archives (hereafter ASA), Guwahati, Report of Assam Labour Enquiry Committee, 1906, p. 136.

for the protection of the laborers after their arrival at the tea garden.[18] From 1863 onwards, the colonial state passed several laws to facilitate the recruitment and control of immigrant labor. Act VI of 1865 introduced a penal system punishing breach of contract (for three years) and stipulating minimum monthly wages, which were five rupees for men and four rupees for women.[19] However, these laws remained ineffective on the ground. The mortality rate in transit and death rates in the gardens were still high. When the British India Government passed the Labour Immigration Districts Emigration Act I in 1882 (which increased the term of indentured contracts to five years), it further deteriorated the working and living conditions with low wages, overwork, and undernourishment leading to high rates of mortality.[20]

Quantitative information on the demography of the labor force employed on Assam tea gardens was maintained annually in published official records titled as 'Report on Labour Immigration into Assam'. These reports included statistics on the mortality suffered en route and after reaching the tea gardens at Assam and Cachar. These annual labor reports kept statistics regarding migrants imported to Assam. The Chota Nagpur region and North West Provinces were the two major areas for importing laborers for Assam planters. The annual labor reports also highlighted the health concerns and mortality associated with steamer journey. For example, the total number of labor deaths in Dhubri and during the transit along the Brahmaputra river for 1895 remained at 248. In 1896, the number increased to 768; and it was 1,245 deaths in 1897.[21] Table 8.1 shows the total number of deaths (en route to Cachar and in hospital) from the year 1884 to 1891. These statistical records do not include the coolie mortality caused by the country boats as they rarely went through official depots. Due to their cost-effectiveness, many recruiters and native agents preferred to utilize country boats in conveying the coolies. Scholars working on the various forms of labor recruitment for tea plantations have already drawn our attention to deceitful recruitment and insanitary transportation leading to high mortality. For instance, R. Shlomowitz and L. Brennan investigated the mortality suffered by migrant laborers in Assam from 1865 to 1921.[22] These scholars draw our attention to the reluctance

18 The mortality rates in the gardens were also appalling. Between 1 May 1863 and 1 May 1866, a total of 84,915 laborers were brought to tea gardens, out of which it was reported that 30,000 had died by 30 June 1866. In addition, there were many cases of coolie desertions. See, ASA, Guwahati, Report of Assam Labour Enquiry Committee, 1906, p. 136.

19 Behl, "Power Structure Discipline and Labour," pp. 164–165.

20 *Ibid.*, p. 165.

21 ASA, Guwahati, Report of Labour Immigration into Assam, 1898. p. 8.

22 Shlomowitz and Brennan, "Mortality and Migrant Labour," pp. 313–30.

of planters to invest in sanitary provisions (causing cholera), which in turn contributed to high mortality of the labor force. Another reason for the increase in death rates was the low wages paid to the workers, leaving many of them undernourished. A link between steamer travel and labor mortality is captured nicely by a young British planter named John Carnegie when recounting what he saw during one of his journeys. He described the woes of steamer travel en route to Assam and bitterly complained of "mosquitoes ... and worse than all we have 500 coolies on board the dirtiest brutes in creation swarming with lice and one had cholera last night, what with coolies, mosquitoes and lice I shan't be sorry when this is at an end ..."[23] The kinds of conditions described by Carnegie clearly point to the poor conditions associated with steamer travel, resulting in severe mortality during transit. The impact on coolies of long and tedious journeys by steamer continues to inform more recent debates on labor historiography. More recently, Rana P. Behal's essay makes a comparative point that the coolies commuting to Assam by steamers on the Brahmaputra took longer than the passages of the 'coolie ships' to Mauritius.[24] Jayeeta Sharma's work on Assam tea gardens points out that even when facilities came to be improved for upper-class passengers due to an increase in trade traffic and profits; the coolie freight was left with hardly any upgrade.[25] Even in the context of extractive colonial forestry, Arupjyoti Saikia noted that "the subject of poor communications remained a major concern".[26] He further identified that the Public Works Department (PWD) and the tea planters often had mutual interests in either building roads or improving already existing ones.[27] Therefore, transport bottlenecks and mortality among immigrant laborers made a dent in the profit margins of capital investment. The tea planters felt the need for better logistics and ways of shipping out their cargoes and importing labor. Both Government and planters became concerned about the movements of labor. Steamers were regarded as an unsafe mode of transporting indentured laborers. Thus, it bolstered the case for constructing railways, in terms of efficiency. While pushing for railway construction, three concerns dominated amongst the British

23 Behal, "Coolie Drivers or Benevolent Paternalists?," pp. 29–51.

24 Behal, "Indian Migrant Labourers," p. 5. While Behal follows the transport of Indian indentured laborers into Assam, A.K. Mishra follows them into Mauritius where indentured workers found themselves under "a form of servitude, though not essentially a new system of slavery", see: Mishra, "Indian Indentured Labourers in Mauritius," p. 229.

25 Sharma, *Empire's Garden*, p. 81.

26 Saikia, *Forests and Ecological History of Assam*, p. 153.

27 *Ibid.*, p. 153.

TABLE 8.1 Number of deaths of the imported coolie labor to Cachar by steamer

| Year | Total number of laborers dispatched from Goalundo (in Bengal) | Deaths en route | Deaths in hospital | Total deaths |
|---|---|---|---|---|
| 1884 | 4,219 | 351 | 81 | 432 |
| 1885 | 2,793 | 110 | 35 | 145 |
| 1886 | 2,854 | 178 | 19 | 197 |
| 1887 | 2,385 | 79 | 22 | 101 |
| 1888 | 3,058 | 95 | 36 | 131 |
| 1889 | 2,899 | 117 | 61 | 178 |
| 1890 | 1,344 | 16 | 10 | 26 |
| 1891 (up to 14 November) | 2,940 | 39 | 20 | 59 |

SOURCE: FIGURES COMPILED FROM REPORT ON LABOUR IMMIGRATION INTO ASSAM, 1891

planters – the first concern was the economic export of tea consignments to the nearest sea-ports; secondly, safer and more economic modes of bringing coolie labor from outside Assam and; the thirdly, establishing a more economical way of supplying rice to feed the tea-workers.

The promoters of the railway projects (especially tea planters) used these official figures to underline the high-cost of relying on steamers. In contrast, it made their case for rail transport very attractive. By the early 1880s, railways were constructed in specific pockets in upper Assam. Two separate lines, namely, Dibru-Sadiya and the Jorhat Provincial State Railway line functioned merely as feeders to steamers plying along the Brahmaputra river, which connected to Calcutta. These railway lines were fragmented and disconnected; they didn't have a direct link with any sea outlet. During the same period, an ambitious idea was floated to construct an integrated railway connecting the farthest point of upper Assam to the Chittagong seaport in the Bay of Bengal. This proposed line aimed at easy movement of laborers and the ease of tea export. The line also promised to reduce travel time by bypassing the busy Calcutta port. The existing historiography does not give us a picture of the transition from river-borne transport based on steamers connected to the Calcutta port to a new and more efficient mode of transport based on Assam-Bengal Railway connected to the Chittagong port.

## 2 Building the Railways

The Assam-Bengal Railway project originated in June 1882, when Lieutenant-Governor of Bengal, Sir Rivers Thompson, suggested that a railway connection up to Chittagong port would open up the eastern districts of Bengal. He further advocated that the rail line could be expanded to Cachar and Assam. London pursued the proposal seriously to open up Cachar and Assam and sought the opinion of the Government of India.[28] As a result, the British India Government sanctioned surveys to be conducted, and under J.W. Buyers, a British official, such surveys were carried out across Cachar and Assam ahead of laying down the railway. The findings of the surveys were submitted in 1887, suggesting foregoing a rail line connection from Chittagong to the northern most part of Assam through Cachar. The survey report proposed creating a branch line (between Guwahati to Lumding) to connect with the Brahmaputra valley. Further, the survey report also pointed out that the Cachar-Surma valley was advantageous over the Brahmaputra valley as the most suitable line of railway.[29] The survey highlighted the need for expensive networks of communication, promising to connect and run through the major tea growing areas.

J.W. Buyers forwarded his idea of an integrated railway line citing the planters' interest. He wrote, at a public meeting of 117 planters held in Silchar (Cachar), that the planter community pressed the urgent need to connect Cachar with Chittagong port by railway. The planters pointed to the acute shortage in the supply of labor and expected that a railway would be the only effectual solution. The proposed Chittagong railway was expected to transfer laborers from the populated tracts of upper India to the tea estates of Assam. A tea planter named R. White opined that:

> By a railway alone can our labour wants be adequately met, and the health of the coolies provided for and any assistance afforded by dispatch steamers and such like is merely a move in proper direction. The help afforded by daily despatch boats has proved to be illusory when Fenchuaganj continues to be the terminus for the whole of the cold weather, so we must continue to clamour for the railway.[30]

28 National Archives of India (hereafter NAI), New Delhi, PWD Proceedings on Railway Construction, October 1893, Document Nos. 103–123.

29 NAI, New Delhi, Railway Construction A, December 1887, Nos. 224–261.

30 NAI, New Delhi, PWD Proceedings, Railway Construction, December 1887.

At another meeting of the Indian Tea Association held in Calcutta, the association brought their concerns to the British India Government that an ample supply of labor was required in the tea districts of Assam, and that to secure this supply a railway was needed. The planters begged the Government to undertake the construction work. The Association believed that, unlike steamers, a railway would reduce travel time, facilitate the transit of labor to the districts, and reduce the risk of mortality.[31]

Conversely, the Chief Commissioner of Assam, W.E. Ward, objected to the idea of connecting the tea gardens of upper Assam through Cachar. Instead, he advocated two independent systems of railway, one between Chittagong and Cachar and the other confined to the Brahmaputra valley between Guwahati and Fakirganj in Bengal, instead of one connected system, as Mr. J.W. Buyers suggested. These two lines were to be totally independent and disconnected.[32] The Chief Commissioner of Assam doubted whether the tea planters of upper Assam would use the railway communication to ship their tea direct to London through the Chittagong port. He was of the view that the direct link would disturb the existing arrangements for tea samples in Calcutta.

Tea gardens located in upper Assam had been using the services of the India General Steam Navigation Company at a contract rate of one point eight Rupees *maund* for the carriage of their tea to Calcutta. Those gardens with no contract with the Steamer Company paid a higher rate of three Rupees. The promoters of the railway line promised to make the rail freight direct outlet to seaport at much cheaper rate. In contrast, Mr. Ward contested the claimed made by the Railway Company and instead assured that the Steamer companies would be ready to reduce the freight for tea. In Cachar, planters complained about the high carriage cost demanded by the Steamer Company. In the late 1880s, a passage from Goalundo to Silchar costs eight to fourteen Rupees, while the fare by country boat cost only two.[33] Due to which, many of the employers preferred to utilize small, unlicensed country boats when importing the coolies. This resulted in numerous deaths en route to the Cachar tea gardens. Thus, regarding labor immigration, planters and commercial interests as a whole, the British Raj held that it would be better to confer the benefits of railway communication upon the fertile but completely landlocked tracts of Assam, which were then only served by steamer transport.[34]

31 NAI, New Delhi, PWD Proceedings, Railway Construction, September 1887, No. 225.

32 NAI, New Delhi, PWD Proceedings, Railway Construction, December 1887.

33 ASA, Guwahati, Report on Labour Immigration into Assam, 1888.

34 NAI, New Delhi, Railway Construction A, December 1887, Nos. 224–261.

By the early 1880s, the case for a railway line became favorable and close to feasible. The railway promoters made it clear that it was in the best interests of the province of Assam and Cachar to place it in direct communication with its nearest seaport, which was Chittagong. The steamers stood no chance against the proposed railway line. The case for the railway proposal boiled down to the question of difference of mileage between Calcutta and Chittagong. The great saving in time and vexation of long carriage along the Brahmaputra river turned the scale in favor of the railways connecting Chittagong.

However, this transport development did not materialize for a decade. The promoters in London were unable to obtain the capital. Finally, a financial house in London named Messrs. Sheppard Pellys, Scott & Co. raised the funds and submitted an application to undertake the construction of a railway. This led to the formation of the Assam-Bengal Railway Company Limited. Accordingly, on 26 April 1892, a contract was signed between the Secretary of State and the Assam-Bengal Railway Company Limited for a line of railway beginning at Chittagong via Badarpur to a terminus near Makum junction in upper Assam.[35] The contract guaranteed three percent interest to the railway company. In addition, the government also agreed to provide land free of cost for the purpose of the railway construction.

Considering the scarcity of labor that already existed in the tea plantation, where was the source of labor for constructing a new railway? How did the promoters get the railways built, and from what sources did they get the construction workers? As far as the colonial public works (such as road works) is concerned, as already noted in the beginning part of this chapter, the region had been characterized with a long history of local hill tribes' resistance against the British idea of conscription. Colonial authorities frequently complained about the desertion of local laborers from the work sites. Therefore, the labor supply for railway construction works had to come from outside Assam. The Assam-Bengal railway project found a new supply of labor from the Pathan community of North Western Provinces and Makran Coast. Recent work by Ian J. Kerr claimed that the construction of railway lines in Assam saw the recruitment of a large number of imported labor that included Pathan, Makranis, Khols, Santhals, Sylhetis, Nepalese and Punjabis. Kerr pointed out that,[36] elsewhere in colonial India, circulating labor contributed to a large unskilled segment of railway construction workers.[37] Not much is known about the physical movement of the circulating construction workers. When the Assam-Bengal

35 NAI, New Delhi, PWD, Railway Construction, August 1892, Nos. 18–40.
36 Kerr, *Engines of Change*, p. 66.
37 Kerr, *Building the Railways of the Raj*, p. 97.

Railway Company was finally approved in 1892, the railway authorities attempted to import labor through the agency of recruiting contractors. For that matter, J.W. Buyers (who was Chief Engineer of Assam-Bengal Railway) made arrangements with labor contractors who were willing to import labor.[38] Buyers reminded the railway engineers that arrangement with contractors were to be made before the working season, as the contractors refused to import unless they have the working season before them, as they were afraid of being unable to recover their advances.[39] The Railway Company was to work chiefly with contractors, leaving them to make their own arrangements for the importation of laborers. The workforces consisted of mainly skilled and unskilled laborers who came from outside Assam through contractors having a private arrangement with them and having advanced them money. Few of these workers came to seek work themselves without the mediation of a recruiting agent.[40] The colonial archive does reflect the various laborers employed in the construction of the Assam-Bengal Railway track. This workforce consisted almost entirely of Pathans, Makranies, Bengal Muslims from Sylhet, and only few from northern India. The Pathan workers (North-West frontier tribes) came by themselves. The Makranies (from the Makran Coast near Karachi and from Kabul) were all imported by native contractors. The Bengal Muslims from Sylhet worked off and on, returning to their homes when they had made a little money.[41] However, the laborers from northern India suffered much from the ill-effects of the climate than the better-fed Muslims of the North Western Provinces but the mortality even amongst the latter was great.[42] These men generally received advances from the contractors who would also feed them during the duration of active employment. Occasionally, planters protested against the railway authorities for attracting tea garden coolies to construction by offering higher wages.

By the year 1898, the Assam-Bengal Railway connected the plains of Cachar with the Chittagong port within the reach of Calcutta. However, the connections between the two valleys (Cachar and Assam) were finally complete in 1903. A branch line between Guwahati and Lumding was also constructed to accomplish the connection with the Brahmaputra valley. To cheapen the cost of local transport, tramways were constructed which operated as feeder lines connecting tea gardens to the Assam-Bengal Railway line. At times, road

38 NAI, New Delhi, PWD Proceedings, Railway Construction, June 1893, Nos. 298–301.

39 NAI, New Delhi, PWD Proceedings, Railway Construction, June 1893, Nos. 298–301.

40 ASA, Guwahati, Assam Secretariat Proceedings, Revenue – A, July 1897, Nos. 1–29.

41 ASA, Guwahati, Assam Secretariat Proceedings, Revenue – A, July 1897, Nos. 1–29.

42 NAI, New Delhi, PWD Proceedings, Railway Construction, October 1897, Nos. 218–250.

construction projects in tea gardens were taken up by planters. In the course of serving the interests of tea planters, railways connected to a growing web of communication networks that cut-across tea gardens, market centers and garrison towns. The military usage of the railways never diminished. In fact, initiated as a purely commercial venture, it was the strategic consideration that began to lend a note of urgency to the Assam-Bengal Railway project. The political disturbance that broke out in Manipur in early 1891 hastened the process of construction of the rail line.[43] The outbreak of this disturbance exposed the failure of the existing communication networks. Though the proposed Assam-Bengal railway line bypassed Manipur, it would add strategic weight by putting Dimapur on the railway map. To be connected by the shortest road, Imphal (Manipur) would then be within striking range from other garrison towns such as Guwahati, where British troops were stationed. Thus, the arrival of rail track put Assam and Cachar on the railway map of British India.

## 3 Travel, Migration and Transport Regulations

The coming of the Assam-Bengal Railway gave a great boost to the tea industry. Not only did it accelerate transportation, but it also provided direct access to Chittagong seaport, where planters shipped their tea-boxes straight to London. However, before the new mode of transportation could engage in the movement of migrant labor, the railway company needed to overcome a few legal hurdles. As per the Emigration Act of 1901, laborers and emigrants were to be imported to the Assam province only via steamer routes. The agent of the Assam-Bengal Railway Company requested that the local Assam Government permit the use of the railway routes for immigration by offering certain incentives on the travel and rates. In light of the improved transport system, the railway company submitted a proposition for the supply of cooked food to the coolies at halting stations.[44] In return, the Assam Chief Commissioner negotiated for an hour holding at one of the railway stations (Lumding) and

43 Since the First Anglo-Burmese War (1824–26), the Princely state of Manipur effectively came under indirect British rule even though the native Princes sovereignty was symbolically preserved. When the threat of the Burmese aggression had diminished by 1891, the native Prince began to resent the growing power of the colonial agent in the local court. The Prince conspired and murdered his guest (the Chief Commissioner of Assam) along with the rest of the British officers posted in Manipur. This is called the Palace Rebellion of Manipur, 1891.

44 ASA, Guwahati, Assam Secretariat Proceedings, Revenue – A, April, 1904, No. 120.

pressed for the arrangement of cooking facilities at railways stations (such as in Chandpur, Badarpur, Lumding and Tinsukia). Additionally, he requested 'ready prepared food and sweetmeats of the ordinary kinds sold to travellers on Indian railways should also be available at these places'.[45] The Railway Company agreed to the terms laid down by the Assam Chief Commissioner to provide the required facilities and supply of food for the coolies.[46] Accordingly, the Chief Commissioner issued an order for an amendment in the Assam Emigration Rules. The amended regulation read: "labourers, emigrants, and dependants shall travel through the province to the labor districts by either of the following routes –by the Eastern Bengal State Railway to Dhubri, and thence by steamer; by the Eastern Bengal State Railway to Dhubri, thence by steamer to Gauhati, and thence by rail; by rail from Chandpur [Assam-Bengal Railway]; by steamer or country boat from Goalundo."[47] All of this suggests that the coolie traffic would now be diverted towards railway transport. In one of his pioneering works, historian Ian J. Kerr describes that the arrival of the railways increased the mobility of people – such as the movement of construction workers, coolie labor, and including railway engineers who used rail travel in order to control labor costs and regulate the strength of labor at work sites.[48] Consequently, in 1898, the report on labor immigration to Assam indicated a reduction in the mortality rate among immigrants in transit to the Surma valley as a result of the diversion of coolie traffic to the Assam-Bengal Railway.[49] In 1901, the annual labor immigration report stated: out of 2,947 immigrants imported in Sylhet, 803 made used of the river transport and the remaining was conveyed by railway. Similarly, during the same year, Cachar imported a total of 2,512 immigrants, out of which 1,536 coolies were transported by railway and 976 by steamer.[50] Since this period, the railway's role in transporting the coolies to the tea gardens in Sylhet and Cachar became apparent and considerably increased in later years.

Soon, the Assam-Bengal Railway, in conjunction with the existing railway networks (such as Eastern-Bengal Railway & Bengal-Nagpur Railway), went onto tapped immigrant coolie routes. The official report of labour immigration into Assam for the year 1898 shows that the Chota Nagpur and Santhal *pargana* (administrative unit) became the top sources of labor supply, followed

45 ASA, Guwahati, Assam Secretariat Proceedings, Revenue – A, April, 1904, No. 123.
46 ASA, Guwahati, Assam Secretariat Proceedings, Revenue – A, April, 1904, No. 125.
47 ASA, Guwahati, Assam Secretariat Proceedings, Revenue – A, April, 1904, No. 129.
48 Kerr, *Building the Railways of the Raj*, p. 101.
49 ASA, Guwahati, Report of Labour Immigration into Assam for 1898, p. 9.
50 ASA, Guwahati, Report of Labour Immigration into Assam for 1901, p. 4.

by North West Province and Oudh.[51] This development is almost certainly a consequence of the completion of the new railway line in 1898. To promote, to tea planters, the desirability of the use of the railways to import coolies, the Assam-Bengal Railway Company introduced a 'credit note system' in 1906. In short, these credit notes served as railway passes (at the rate of one and a half pies per mile) aimed to ease the movement of laborers. Under this system, the tea garden *sardars* (overseers) were provided with a certain number of credit notes signed by the garden manager or superintendent. The garden *sardar* could get tickets issued and obtain transport for him and for each migrant laborer accompanying him by presenting this note at railway stations. Upon which, the railway authorities would make an arrangement for their journey from the recruiting districts to the tea gardens across Assam. Payments of fares were to be made by the garden manager or superintendent when the railway officials submitted the bill for the used credit notes.[52] Coolies returning home after the expiry of their contracts were also offered the same reduced rate for their journey. Further, railway conductors were instructed by the Company to travel with each train to look after the comfort of the emigrant workers and special carriages were provided for them. They were also instructed to consider that sanitary arrangements (such as latrine accommodations) were built. Food vendors in each immigrant carriage were made available where a coolie could make purchases at fixed prices or through food coupons (supplied by an agent of the Company). In fact, planters informed the Assam Labor Enquiry Committee (1906) that coolies disliked the river journey and that there was a strong preference for using rail lines. The report of the committee goes on to state that the railways proposed to introduced cheap return tickets (at reduced rate of one pie per mile) to coolies proceeding on leave to their homes. The ticket was to be valid for three months; after which they would have to travel at single fare of one and a half pies. The committee further recommended the adoption of the same reduced travel rate by the steamer services in the north of the Brahmaputra river in conjunction with the railway companies. As these portions of Assam were not tapped by the railways, here the export of tea and import of labor was still dominated by the steamer transport services. In fact, the steamer companies had initiated the giving out of concessions to garden

51 In 1895, Act and non-act coolies from Chota Nagpur and Santhal *pargana* recorded 13,709 and 4,660 respectively. And in 1898, Chota Nagpur and Santhal *pargana* recorded 15,465 act coolies and 3,129 non-act coolies. Those laborers which were contracted under the Labour Immigration were referred to as 'Act Coolies,' while the rest of the labor forces were termed as 'Non-Act Coolies'.

52 ASA, Guwahati, Report of the Assam Labour Enquiry Committee, 1906, p. 121.

*sardars* on their travel.[53] Scholars of transport history have cautioned against overemphasizing the effects of the railways as it prevents us from looking at other forms of networks that also contributed to the growth of commodity circulation.[54] This chapter, while proposing to assess the changes affected by the introduction of the railway does not intend to underplay the role of other means of transport (particularly steamer transport). It does, however, try to point out the effects on the older patterns of transport brought about with the advent of the new tool of steam technology.

The coming of the new transport infrastructure (*i.e.*, the Assam-Bengal Railway) also witnessed the diversion of the goods traffic in favor of railway transport. For instance, the bulk of jute export traffic from Naraingunge and Chandpur, which was earlier taken to Calcutta by the river companies, were now diverted towards Chittagong port by the railways. In 1904, Messrs. Kilburn & Company, a British company (based in Calcutta) for steamers complained about the diversion of goods traffic away from the waterways. In their letter to the Viceroy of India, they complained that the development of river navigation in India generally, and Assam in particular, was being hampered by the arrival of the railways, and that the railways attempted to draw trade away from the waterways, which are natural channels. The steamer company felt that they were in a position of an unfair competition whereby the state-aided railways charged unremunerated rates for traffic away from the steamer companies.[55] The complaint read as follows:

> Until recent years Assam has been entirely dependent for its communication with the outside world on its natural highways – the rivers – which have indeed created the Province; and the advent of a railway has introduced a new factor in its history, for weal or woe. In this connection what concern us, as it must concern all who have the interest of the Province at heart, is whether the railway is, unheeded, to be permitted to minimize the use of rivers that made the Province, by setting itself to draw away trade, the natural channel for which is the waterways, and in accomplishing this, to arrest all further progress in development of the rivers; or whether those responsible for the railway will respect the rights of the waterway and recognize that the railway's primary duty is to serve and develop tracts which cannot be directly served by the river, whilst

53 ASA, Guwahati, Report of the Assam Labour Enquiry Committee, 1906, p. 122.

54 Ahuja, *Pathways of Empire*, p. 6; Sinha, *Communication and Colonialism*, p. 207.

55 NAI, New Delhi, PWD, Railway Construction – A, April 1904, Nos. 302–318.

> indirectly aiding the development of the already established trade routes, to its own benefit.[56]

They presented their case by drawing parallels to the river development in Europe, America, and also on the Ganges river. They pointed out that the greatest railway systems in the United States had grown up alongside of the greatest internal waterway route – the Great Lakes. And that it was instructive to note that a former President of the New York Central railway always favored Erie Canal improvements on the grounds that the more traffic the canal carried the better it would be for the railways, notwithstanding that the two routes are parallel. Citing such examples, they were of the opinion that rail and river could exist in India side by side without injury to either interest.[57] In response to this complaint, C.W. Hodson (Officiating Secretary to the Government of India, PWD, Railways) argued that the contract entered into with the Assam-Bengal Railway Company for the construction of the railway had no condition that the river companies should be allowed the monopoly of the Assam trade. He pointed out that the railways were operating within their contract rights and that Messrs. Kilburn & Co. themselves cannot now expect to retain the monopoly of the traffic or to reap the same profits they had in the past. He concluded that the best solution seems to lie in the two parties – the River Companies and the Assam-Bengal railway – combining to prevent needless competition and loss.[58] Consequently, the displacement of the old pattern of transport by railway was not merely because of its ability to attract coolie traffic; it also included a range of others factors such as cost-effectiveness, easy and fast transportation of goods. This resulted in competition and contestation between the different modes of transport themselves.

The above case was not the first of its kind in which the river companies protested against the railway company. Earlier in 1900, managing agents of the India General Navigation Company, along with the Railway Company, had provided the capital for the construction of the Mymensingh-Jaggarnathgunge railway (a branch line of the Eastern Bengal State Railway). Messrs. Kilburn & Co. complained of the action of the Manager of the Eastern Bengal State Railway in endeavoring to keep the traffic of the Mymensingh-Jaggarnathgunge railway to the combined steamer and railway route as against the direct steamer route in Calcutta. In that instance, they argued that one of their reasons

---

56 Memorial of Messrs. Kilburn & Co. 4, Fairlie Place Calcutta, dated January 28, 1904. NAI, New Delhi, PWD, Railway Construction – A, April 1904, Nos. 302–318.

57 NAI, New Delhi, Railway Construction A, April 1904, Nos. 302–318.

58 NAI, New Delhi, Railway Construction A, April 1904, Nos. 302–318.

for investing capital in the branch railway was that railways tend to aid the development of the country, although they do, in some cases, deprive other carriers of business.[59] In fact, the Assam-Bengal Railway had the potential to monopolize trade in the region due to its competitive prices, their speed, and direct access to the sea outlet. Historian Anand A. Yang demonstrated how railways came to virtually monopolize the trade in the Gangetic Bihar – carrying 99.9 percent of the imports and 99.5 percent of exports from the year 1900 to 1905.[60]

The annual statistics on the rail and river-borne trade of the Assam province revealed a considerable diversion of goods traffic to the Chittagong port through the Assam-Bengal Railway. An official report from 1902–03 stated that tea became the most important article transported by the Assam-Bengal Railway to Chittagong. Other articles included jute, husked rice, gunny bags, iron and steel, till seed, stone, and lime.[61] The report also stated that Chittagong was expected to be the chief port for the shipment of tea in India as soon as the two valleys (Cachar and Assam) were connected by railway line. In 1903, when the two valleys were finally connected by one integrated rail line, the tea traffic increased substantially. The report on the administration of the province of Assam (1904–05) stated 'a considerable part of tea traffic of the upper Brahmaputra valley districts, which had previously been conveyed to Calcutta by the Steamer Companies' vessels now go via the hill section to the Chittagong port'.[62] The value of tea exported by the Assam-Bengal Railway to the Chittagong port increased from 2.50 lakh *maunds* in 1902–03 to 4.34 lakh *maunds* in 1904–05.[63] The efficient running of this railway played an important role in 1942 in maintaining refugee traffic from Burma (Myanmar). The rail track also added a strategic depth by becoming the main supply line of the Allied Forces against the Japanese during the course of the Second World War. After India's independence from the British colonial rule, the existing rail line underwent a series of changes. The drawing of political boundaries between the two newly independent states (India and East Pakistan) split the railway line. In this way, the railway tracks on the side of Assam lost access to its nearest sea outlet – the Chittagong port (which is in present-day Bangladesh).

59 NAI, New Delhi, Railway Construction A, April 1904, Nos. 302–318.

60 Yang, *Bazaar India*, p. 52.

61 ASA, Guwahati, Report on Rail & River Borne Trade of Province of Assam, 1902–03, p. 40.

62 ASA, Guwahati, Report on the Administration of the Province of Assam, 1904–05, p. 32.

63 Medhi, *Transport System and Economic Development of Assam*, p. 57.

## 4 Conclusion

So far studies on Assam tea have been limited within the framework of labor historiography. While the labor perspective is important, enquiring into the intersections of tea, labor and transport will be rewarding. Prior to the construction of railways, steamers and boats were the primary means of transport for commodities such as tea boxes and migrant workers. In colonial Assam and Cachar, the export of these commodities heavily depended on imported labor. But the facility for steamer transport was seasonal in nature – confined to the monsoon season when the rivers became navigable. The tea boom from the mid-nineteenth century triggered a demand for migrant labor dramatically; but the transport bottleneck remained unsolved. Apart from the seasonal constraint of steamers, this mode of transport was associated with high rates of mortality among coolies in transit. Given this circumstances, the planters' community searched for a safer and cheaper alternative to steamer transport. Construction of a railway was proposed as a solution to the crisis that impeded the flow of tea-boxes and coolie labor. The new infrastructure was to overcome the problems of labor shortages and would become crucial for maintaining tea traffic as it provided an outlet to the sea by connecting Assam and Cachar to the European markets via the Chittagong port. With this new project, the railway became the primary mode of transportation and circulation on land connecting coolie-recruiting districts of Central and Eastern India, tea belts of British Assam, and seaports of Bengal.

## Bibliography

Ahuja, Ravi. *Pathways of Empire, Circulation, 'Public Work' and Social Space in Colonial Orissa, c. 1780–1914* (Hyderabad: Orient Blackswan, 2009).

Allen, B.C. *Assam District Gazetteers*, Volume 1 (Calcutta: Baptist Mission Press, 1905).

Antrobus, H.A. *A History of the Assam Company 1839–1953*, (Edinburgh: T. and A. Constable Ltd., 1957).

Behal, Rana P. "Coolie Drivers or Benevolent Paternalists? British Tea Planters in Assam and the Indenture Labour System," *Modern Asian Studies*, 44, 1, January 2010, pp. 29–51.

Behal, Rana P. "Indian Migrant Labourers in South-east Asian and Assam Plantations under the British Imperial System," NLI Research Studies Series, 127 (Noida: V.V. Giri National Labour Institute, 2017).

Behl, Rana P. "Power Structure Discipline and Labour in Assam Tea Plantations during Colonial Rule", in Rana, P. Behl & Marcel van der Linden (eds) *Coolies, Capital and*

*Colonialism: Studies in Indian Labour History* (Cambridge: Cambridge University Press, 2006).

Deloche, Jean. *Transport and Communications in India Prior to Steam Locomotion: Water Transport*, Volume II (New Delhi: Oxford University Press, 1993).

Derbyshire, Ian. "The Building of India's Railways: The application of Western Technology in the colonial periphery, 1850–1920," in Roy Macleod and Deepak Kumar (eds), *Technology and the Raj* (New Delhi: Sage, 1995), pp.179–83.

Guha, Amalendu, *Planter Raj to Swaraj: Freedom Structure & Electoral Politics in Assam, 1826–1947* (New Delhi: Tulika Books, 2006).

Kerr, Ian J. *Building the Railways of the Raj 1850–1990* (New Delhi: Oxford University Press, 1997).

Kerr, Ian J. "Reworking a Popular Religious Practice: The Effects of Railways on Pilgrimage in 19th and 20th Century South Asia," in Ian J. Kerr (ed.) *Railways in Modern India* (New Delhi: Oxford University Press, New Delhi, 2001), pp. 304–327.

Kerr, Ian. J., Bruno J. Navarro and Hugo Silveira Pereira, "Labour Relations and Processes of railway construction in Portugal, India and Africa," in Anne Mccants, Eduardo Beira, José M. Lopes Cordeiro, Paulo Lourenco (eds) *Railroads in Historical Context: Construction, Costs and Consequences* (V.N. Gaia: Inovatec, Portugal, 2011), pp. 321–342.

Kerr, Ian. J. *Engines of Change: The Railroads That Made India* (Hyderabad: Orient Blackswan, 2012).

Medhi, Shyam Bhadra. *Transport System and Economic Development of Assam* (Guwahati: Assam Publication Board, 1978).

Mishra, Amit Kumar, "Indian Indentured Labourers in Mauritius," *Studies in History*, 25, 2 (2009), pp. 229–251.

Mohapatra, Prabhu P. "'Following Custom'? Representations of Community among Indian Immigrant Labour in the West Indies, 1880–1920," in Rana P. Behal & Marcel van der Linden (eds) *India's Labouring Poor: Historical Studies c.1600-c.2000* (New Delhi: Cambridge University Press India, 2007), pp. 173–202.

Mukherjee, Mukul. "Railways and Their Economic Impact on Bengal's Economy, 1870–1920". *Indian Economic and Social History Review*, 17, 2 (1980), pp. 191–209.

Prasad, Ritika. *Tracks of Change: Railways and Everyday Life in Colonial India* (Delhi: Cambridge University Press India, 2015).

Saikia, Arupjyoti. *Forests and Ecological History of Assam, 1826–2000* (New Delhi: Oxford University Press, 2011).

Sharma, Jayeeta. " 'Lazy Natives', Coolie Labour, and the Assam Tea Industry," *Modern Asian Studies*, 43, 6 (November 2009), pp. 1287–1324.

Sharma, Jayeeta. *Empire's Garden: Assam and the making of India* (Ranikhet: Permanent Black, 2012).

Shlomowitz, R. and Brennan, L. "Mortality and Migrant Labour en Route to Assam, 1863–1924," *Indian Economic Social History Review*, 27, 3 (July-Sept. 1990), pp. 313–330.

Sinha, Nitin. *Communication and Colonialism in Eastern India: Bihar, 1760s-1880s* (London: Anthem Press, 2012).

Stern, Philip. J. *The Company-State: Corporate Sovereignty and the Early Modern Foundations of the British Empire in India* (Oxford: Oxford University Press, 2011).

Suranjan, Chatterjee and Ratan, Das Gupta. "Tea-Labour in Assam: Recruitment and Governmental Policy, 1840–80," *Economic and Political Weekly*, XVI, 44–46 (November 1981), pp. 1862–67.

Yang, Anand A. *Bazaar India: Markets, Society, and the Colonial State in Bihar* (California: University of California Press, 1999).

CHAPTER 9

# Analyzing Structural Change and Labor Relations in Global Commodity Chains

*The Ethiopian Leather Industry*

*Jan Grumiller*

## 1 Introduction

Various theoretical perspectives[1] have used chain and network approaches to analyze changing global production patterns and upgrading processes, but the role of the state and labor in shaping these processes have long been neglected or undertheorized.[2] This is because the most commonly employed chain framework, developed by Gereffi,[3] overemphasized the role of governance and thus the coordination and power relations between lead and supplier firms in shaping Global Commodity Chains (GCCs) or Global Value Chains (GVCs), downplaying the role of institutions, the state, labor, and other actors. More recently, the role of the state, industrial policy, and labor in shaping the dynamics of global production chains or networks has been increasingly acknowledged,[4] but in particular industrial and labor relations in the context of GCCs in Sub-Saharan Africa remain under-researched. The conceptual framework of this paper employs the GCC approach to assess capital-labor relations through the concepts of bargaining, structural and associational power of labor,[5] as suggested by Selwyn.[6] The framework is also enriched by the developmental

1 Bair, "Global Capitalism and Commodity Chains"; Bair, "Analysing global economic organization."

2 Horner and Alford, "The roles of the state in global value chains"; Selwyn, "Beyond firm-centrism"; Smith, "The state, institutional frameworks and the dynamics of capital in global production networks".

3 Gereffi, "The Organization of Buyer-Driven Global Commodity Chains"; Gereffi, "Global Production Systems and Third World Development."

4 Horner and Alford, "The roles of the state in global value chains"; Selwyn, "Beyond firm-centrism"; Smith, "The state, institutional frameworks and the dynamics of capital in global production networks."

5 Wright, "Working-class power, capitalist-class interests, and class compromise."

6 Selwyn, "Beyond firm-centrism."

 | DOI:10.1163/9789004448049_010

regime approach[7] in order to better capture the state's role in promoting industrialization processes and shaping industrial and labor relations through industrial policy.

This chapter will therefore outline the transformation of Ethiopia's leather industry during the twentieth and early twenty-first century in the context of different industrial policy regimes and the leather GCC. The discussion of industrial and labor relations will particularly focus on the leather manufacturing segment of the industry. A key finding of this chapter is that the structural power of labor in the contemporary leather industry differs depending on the market integration and strategies of different groups of manufacturing firms, which explains the large diversity of labor relations in the industry. In particular, workers in some groups of export-oriented firms have a comparatively high (but nevertheless limited) degree of structural power. However, Ethiopia's developmental regime is characterized by the relative marginalization of labor in the context of an export-oriented industrialization strategy and a hierarchical and centralized approach to industrial relations,[8] limiting the workers' ability to transform their structural power to associational power.

Methodologically, this chapter is based on data analysis and semi-structured interviews. The 51 interviews were mostly conducted during two field research trips to Ethiopia (July–October 2018) and included 19 local firms, 13 sector experts, and 12 representatives of state institutions, business associations, and labor unions. At the firm level, the interviews were conducted with managers and represent a varied sample, based on differences in geographic location, ownership, size, production activities, end-market orientation, and degree of vertical integration.[9] Some of the interviews, in particular with global buyers (seven) and sector experts, were conducted by phone before and after the field research. The interviews were complemented by trade, national, and international sector data, including aggregate statistics from UN Comtrade (WITS) and the Ethiopian Leather Industry Institute (LIDI).

The chapter is structured as follows: Section 2 provides an overview of the conceptual framework that is employed to analyze industrial and labor

7 Pempel, "The developmental regime in a changing world economy"; Wylde, *Latin America after neoliberalism*; Wylde, *Emerging Markets and the State: Developmentalism in the 21st Century;* Grumiller, "A Strategic-Relational Approach to Analyzing Industrial Policy Regimes within Global Production Networks."

8 Hardy and Hauge, "Labour Challenges in Ethiopia's Textile and Leather Industries," p. 724.

9 The interviews with managers are particular important to shed light on different groups of firms' dynamics, for example regarding GVC integration, labor turnover, and wage levels. These interviews, however, were only of limited use for an analysis of firm-level labor relations in its full complexity.

relations in the network that links the leather GCC and Ethiopia's developmental regime. Section 3 gives a brief overview of the leather GCC dynamics that are relevant to understand the development of the Ethiopian leather industry in the following sections. Section 4 presents a historical contextualization of Ethiopia's industrialization process since the early twentieth century, with a particular focus on the industrial policy regime since the 1990s. The section concludes by giving a brief overview of the contemporary leather manufacturing industry. Section 5 presents an analysis of the industrial and labor relations of Ethiopia's leather manufacturing industry by taking into account Ethiopia's developmental regime and GCC dynamics based on the conceptual framework presented in section 2. Section 6 concludes.

## 2 Analyzing Industrial Relations in (Global) Commodity Chains

The early literature employing chain and network approaches largely neglected the role of the state and labor in shaping the dynamics of and developmental outcomes of participating in GCCs. More recently, however, a growing body of literature has acknowledged the importance of broadening the theoretical framework and empirical focus of chain and network research. The literature initially focused on how globalization and GCCs influence labor, failing to acknowledge the agency of workers.[10] In an attempt to better capture the agency of labor in GCCs, researchers increasingly analyzed the role and bargaining power of collective actors such as farmer cooperatives or labor unions. The theoretical framework, in addition, was broadened with concepts including "social upgrading" or "decent work", but most authors failed to theorize and analyze class relations in a deeper sense.[11] Similarly, even though the GCC literature increasingly incorporated the state as an important actor, the framework continues to lack a theorization of the state.[12]

This chapter is informed by a strategic-relational perspective that analyzes social phenomena in terms of social relations through a dialectical analysis of structure and agency, acknowledging that institutions privilege some actors and strategies over others and strategies structure institutions.[13] The strategic

10 Selwyn, "Beyond firm-centrism," p. 206.

11 Ibid.

12 Neilson, Pritchard, Yeung, "Global value chains and global production networks in the changing international political economy."

13 Jessop, "The Strategic Selectivity of the State"; Jessop, "Institutional Re(turns) and the Strategic – Relational Approach"; Grumiller, "A Strategic-Relational Approach to Analyzing Industrial Policy Regimes within Global Production Networks."

relational perspective is firmly rooted in materialistic state theory,[14] which emphasizes that societies are constituted of different classes with contradicting and competing materialistic interests that are connected to their role in the productive system of an economy (e.g., labor, landlords, industrial or financial capital). The state is thus understood as a social relation and not as neutral terrain for the articulation of social interests. The specific configuration of the state must therefore be considered as a result of historical social struggles between social forces; that is, as a "material condensation of a relationship of forces".[15]

The analysis of the industrial relations and industrialization processes roots in the developmental regime approach[16] that goes beyond Evans's[17] embedded autonomy[18] conceptualization to assess the emergence and effectiveness of developmental or industrial policy by employing the concepts of relative autonomy and state capacity. From a relative autonomy perspective, the state needs different degrees of autonomy vis-à-vis social forces opposing and supporting industrial policy, and a certain degree of autonomy needs to be sustained so that the industrial policies are not diluted. Within these contexts, state capacities that implement specific sets of industrial policy can be created and protected until power relations change.[19]

In addition to the political elite, different fractions of capital, and other actors, labor is a crucial force in the network relations that link developmental regimes and GCCs. Selwyn[20] argues that class relations are at the heart of GCCs and outlines a framework that more fully takes into account the state's role in guaranteeing the reproduction of capital-labor relations, the process of working class formation, and workers' structural and associational power. This framework can easily be linked to developmental regime perspective outlined above since both conceptualize the state from a strategic-relational

14 Poulantzas, *State, Power, Socialism.*

15 Ibid., p. 129, 136.

16 Pempel, "The developmental regime in a changing world economy"; Wylde, *Latin America after neoliberalism*; Wylde, *Emerging Markets and the State: Developmentalism in the 21st Century;* Grumiller, "A Strategic-Relational Approach to Analyzing Industrial Policy Regimes within Global Production Networks."

17 Evans, *Embedded autonomy.*

18 The embeddedness of the state reflects a connection "to particular social groups with whom the state shares a joint project of transformation," while the autonomy allows the state to act with some independence in relation to particularistic societal pressures (ibid. p. 59).

19 Grumiller and Raza, "Towards an Institutional Setup for Industrial Policy in Late Industrialization in the 21st Century."

20 Selwyn, "Beyond firm-centrism."

perspective. The power of the emerging labor class is thus not only understood in terms of its access to state power, but also in terms of labor's bargaining power vis-á-vis capital. The bargaining power of labor[21] is further conceptualized through workers' structural and associational power.[22] The structural power of labor stems from the workers' position in the production process and their ability to disturb it, which is why the structural power of labor highly depends on a variety of factors related to the structure of the local economy and GCCs. Structural power can be further differentiated in marketplace bargaining power, arising from tight labor markets, and workplace bargaining power, which is based on the workers' ability to disrupt the production process.[23] Since the structural power of labor can differ between firms given their different demands[24] (e.g., skill requirements), this chapter will take into account the different labor relations in various groups of leather manufacturing firms in Ethiopia. Further, associational power, which does not necessarily emerge from structural power, is determined by workers' collective organization and the different forms of power that result from it.[25]

## 3 The Leather Industry and the Global Leather Commodity Chain

The development of Ethiopia's leather industry, in particular since the 1990s, needs to be understood in the context of the leather GCC.[26] The leather GCC is a classic example of what has been described as a "buyer-driven" commodity chain. These types of chains are characterized by decentralized, globally dispersed production networks, coordinated by lead firms that control the key value-adding activities (e.g. design, branding), but often outsource all or most of the manufacturing processes to a global network of suppliers.[27] The leather industry has often played a central role in export diversification and the industrial development of peripheral countries, in particular in countries with large livestock sectors.

21 Ibid., p. 220f.
22 Wright, "Working-class power, capitalist-class interests, and class compromise."
23 Silver, *Forces of Labour*.
24 Selwyn, "Beyond firm-centrism," p. 220f.
25 Ibid.
26 Section 3 and section 4.2 draw on Grumiller, "A Strategic-Relational Approach to Analyzing Industrial Policy Regimes within Global Production Networks."
27 Gereffi, "The Organization of Buyer-Driven Global Commodity Chains"; Gereffi, "Global Production Systems and Third World Development"; Gereffi and Memedovic, *The Global Apparel Value Chain*.

The leather GCC can be roughly divided into five key segments: (i) the livestock sector and slaughterhouses, where hides and skins are collected as a byproduct of meat production; (ii) intermediaries, often playing an important role in collecting and trading raw hides and skins; (iii) tanneries, transforming raw hides and skins into finished leather through capital-intensive processing steps (i.e., tanning [producing i.e. wet blue leather], crusting [crust leather], and finishing [finished leather]). Many tanneries in the global (semi-)periphery do not have the capacity to perform all the processing steps and only produce lower-value and semi-finished, rather than finished, leather, with the latter being by far the most valuable processing step in tanning.[28] Finished leather is then used by (iv) leather manufacturers to labor-intensively produce leather products for a variety of end-use markets (e.g., footwear, apparel, bags, furniture, etc.). (v) Buyers (intermediaries, branders, retailers, etc.) play an important role in distribution through sales channels at the wholesale and retail levels, and different leather items are traded locally and internationally at different points in the leather GCC.

Upgrading for firms within the leather GCC includes process, product, functional, and end-market upgrading.[29] The functional upgrading trajectory for manufacturers in the leather GCC, which mirrors the degree of added value of different functions along the chain, includes cut-make-trim (CMT), original equipment manufacturing (OEM) or full-package supplier, original design manufacturing (ODM), and original brand manufacturing (OBM).[30] Memedovic and Mattila[31] argued that a major precondition for the development of an export-oriented leather manufacturing industry is a well-developed local or nearby material supply, since global buyers in the leather GCC prefer full-package services. The increasing relocation of global leather production from industry-dominating China to peripheral countries in the last decade has opened a window of opportunity for peripheral countries with locational advantages.[32]

---

28 Leather finishing can multiply the value added relative to previous processing steps, but there are large differences between market sectors (e.g. finishing for leather used in luxury cars or mass-market bags).

29 Humphrey and Schmitz, "How does insertion in global value chains affect upgrading in industrial clusters?"; Staritz, Gereffi, and Cattaneo, "Editorial."

30 Gereffi, "International trade and industrial upgrading in the apparel commodity chain"; Memedovic and Matilla, "The global leather value chain".

31 Memedovic and Matilla, "The global leather value chain," p. 512.

32 Grumiller and Raza, "The Ethiopian Leather and Leather Products Sector."

In Sub-Saharan Africa (SSA), many countries have a large livestock sector, but only a few countries have managed to integrate themselves into the leather GCC successfully beyond the supply of raw materials or low value leathers.[33] A major challenge for SSA countries is the development of a tanning industry, given the limited supply of quality raw hides and skins in the context of traditionally organized livestock sectors. Given the highly decentralized livestock production and the limited benefit for farmers and households to sell hides and skins – the production of skins and hides is of comparatively minor importance for the livelihood of farmers in comparison to the production of meat and dairy products, since skins and hides are only byproducts of meat production – the links between the livestock sectors and the leather sectors are often weak.

In 2018, Ethiopia has one of the world's largest livestock populations with around 58 million cattle (the largest in Africa and 6th in the world), 29 million sheep (3rd in Africa and 10th in the world) and 30 million goats (3rd in Africa and 8th in the world)[34] and suffers from similar structural constraints.[35] Until today, the Ethiopian livestock sector continues to be traditionally organized and largely involves small cattle farmers[36] and households without many large-scale ranches, which is why the links between the livestock and the leather sector continue to be relatively weak, severely constraining the growth of the leather industry.

The following section will highlight that in the last century, and in particular since the 1990s, the Ethiopian government was nonetheless able to support the development of a tanning industry and, consequently, a growing and increasingly export-oriented leather manufacturing industry emerged through the implementation of selective industrial policy. Despite insignificant levels until the 2010s, Ethiopia accounted for 85 percent of leather footwear and 19 percent of leather goods (excluding footwear) exports from SSA (excluding South Africa) by 2017.[37]

33 UN Comtrade database.

34 Data provided by the Ethiopian Leather Industry Development Institute (LIDI).

35 Abebe and Schäfer, "High Hopes and Limited Successes"; Abebe and Schäfer, "Review of Industrial Policies in Ethiopia"; Brautigam, Weis and Tang, "Latent advantage, complex challenges"; Lelena Global Consulting, "Value Chain Analysis of the Ethiopian Leather Sector"; Oqubay, *Made in Africa;* UNIDO, "Technical assistance project."

36 Today, around 12.5 million households, or 70 percent of the total population, depend fully or partly on cattle for their livelihoods (FAO 2018).

37 UN Comtrade data. Data refers to global imports.

## 4 The Emergence and Transformation of the Leather Industry in Ethiopia since the Early Twentieth Century

### 4.1 *Historical Contextualization*

During the early twentieth century, Ethiopia's leather sector was dominated by traditional leather soaking, tanning and handcrafting. Early industrialization processes were initiated with the establishment of two tanneries (1918 and 1927, respectively) by Armenian merchants, which was followed by local investments and the emergence of locally-owned tanneries since the 1950s.[38] Similarly, a formal leather manufacturing sector developed in the 1930s with the investment in two shoe factories belonging to the before mentioned Armenian families.[39] These firms promoted "modern" shoemaking skills and created spillovers that furthered the industry. However, production of manufactured leather products by formal firms remained at low levels until the 1960s due to a lack of local commercialization and exports.[40] In addition to the formal manufacturing sector, informal manufacturing also expanded and various "manufacturing clusters" with hundreds to thousands of workers, as well as (informal) micro and small firms, emerged and grew quickly (e.g. the Mercato footwear cluster in Addis Ababa). The raw hides and skins trade continued to be organized in a traditional way, limiting the supply of quality and raw hides and skins due to the traditional husbandry practices and the weak postmortem management of skins and hides (backyard slaughtering and sub-standard collection, storage, and transportation) until today.[41]

During the analyzed period of the Ethiopian Empire (since the early twentieth century until the Derg regime), few efforts have been made by the government to promote the formal leather and leather manufacturing industry, and raw hides and skins dominated exports.[42] The most important policy aimed at improving the supply of raw hides and skins, in terms of quality and quantity, to tanneries by setting up the Livestock and Meat Board (LMB) in 1964.[43] The

38 Mahmud, "Development potential and constraints of hides and skins marketing in Ethiopia".

39 Sonobe, Akoten and Otsuka, "An Exploration into the Successful Development of the Leather Shoe Industry in Ethiopia"; Lentakis, *Ethiopia*, pp. 153.

40 Sonobe, Akoten and Otsuka, "An Exploration into the Successful Development of the Leather Shoe Industry in Ethiopia"; van der Loop, "The Importance of the Leather Footwear Sector for Development in Ethiopia."

41 Abebe and Schäfer, "High Hopes and Limited Successes."

42 Cf. Ibid.

43 Mahmud, "Development potential and constraints of hides and skins marketing in Ethiopia."

LMB was in charge of providing technical assistance to modernize preservation practices by skin collectors and traders through training across the country. The government also introduced price regulations for different skin-qualities in order to improve the quality and incentivize the supply of high-quality hides and skins. Finally, the LMB also established market centers and monitored the establishment of slaughterhouses in various regions.[44]

The Derg, a Marxist-Leninist military dictatorship backed by the Soviet Union,[45] took power in 1974 and implemented an industrialization strategy that also had important implications for the leather industry. The Derg implemented industrial policy characterized by central planning, social ownership, self-reliance, and import-substitution.[46] The political change took place in the context of a war-economy that focused on military production and tried to manage the destruction and losses of civil war between the Derg and a heterogeneous coalition of forces led by the powerful Tigray People's Liberation Front (TPLF). Socialist movements from different regions and ethnic backgrounds within the coalition forces, including the TPLF, later united under the Ethiopian People's Revolutionary Democratic Front (EPRDF) umbrella.

The Derg nationalized firms in 1975 and the state-owned enterprises operated within a centrally planned quota system, prioritizing the leather, textiles and apparel, cement, food and beverages, and chemical industries. The state-owned National Leather and Shoe Corporation managed the eight tanneries and six shoe factories, which accounted for roughly 6,000 jobs by the end of the Derg regime.[47] During the Derg regime, the formal leather firms were particularly geared towards producing military boots – which is why the sector performed comparatively well in terms of output. The informal sector comprised of micro and small firms, on the other hand, was largely repressed.[48]

The Derg regime had also aimed to improve the link between the livestock and leather sector since the 1970s through regulating and licensing hides and skin traders and by promoting the livestock marketing infrastructure, most importantly through the construction and supervision of roughly five dozen slaughterhouses.[49] In 1986, a ban on raw hides and skins exports was introduced to ensure the local tanning and the production of semi-finished leather,

44 Ibid.
45 Clapham, "The Ethiopian developmental state," p. 1153.
46 Oqubay, "Industrial Policy and Late Industrialization in Ethiopia."
47 Abebe and Schäfer, "High Hopes and Limited Successes."
48 Gebreeyesus and Mohnen, "Innovation performance and Embeddedness in Networks."
49 Mahmud, "Development potential and constraints of hides and skins marketing in Ethiopia."

with limited success.[50] However, the ban not only incentivized hides and skins traders to sell to local tanneries, but also led to illegal smuggling activities.

### 4.2 *The Ethiopian Developmental State: Transforming the Leather Industry*

The end of the Derg regime in 1991 marked the beginning of Ethiopia's structural transformation and led to the emergence of what has been described in the literature, and not least by the government of the EPRDF itself, as a developmental state.[51] Ethiopia's new developmentalism was inspired by East Asian development models and can be characterized as an elite-driven legitimization project, led by the TPLF,[52] in the context of a multi-ethnic state. The development model includes a mix of import-substituting and export-oriented industrialization, making extensive use of selective industrial policy.[53] Overall, Ethiopia's developmental regime has been relatively effective in terms of promoting industrialization processes, exports, employment, and output growth given the high degree of state capacities geared towards the goals of the relative autonomous political elite, not shying away from conflicts with the emerging labor (section 5) and capitalist class.[54]

Since the emergence of Ethiopia's developmental state, the development of, and industrial policy targeting, Ethiopia's leather industry can be differentiated in three phases[55] that are characterized by shifting strategies of the political elite: The first phase (1991–1997/2000) was characterized by the implementation of the agricultural demand-led industrialization (ADLI) strategy since 1994 and a horizontal industrial policy, focusing on agricultural sectors with industrial linkages as engines of growth and promoting local investments. As a result, new investments by local entrepreneurs were incentivized and state-owned tanneries and leather manufacturing companies were privatized. This led to an increase of semi-finished leather exports (Figure 9.1) – in particular to tanneries in the EU (Italy). Informal and formal leather manufacturers, on the other hand, continued to produce almost exclusively for the local market. Even though the informal sector did not benefit from the government support

50 Abebe and Schäfer, "High Hopes and Limited Successes."

51 Clapham, "The Ethiopian developmental state."

52 The TPLF to some extent lost influence with the coming into power of Prime Minister Abiy Ahmed in early 2018. In late 2019, the EPRDF was renamed the Prosperity Party.

53 Oqubay, *Made in Africa*; Oqubay, "Industrial Policy and Late Industrialization in Ethiopia."

54 Cf. Pellerin, "The aspiring developmental state and business associations in Ethiopia"; Oqubay, *Made in Africa*.

55 Grumiller, "A Strategic-Relational Approach to Analyzing Industrial Policy Regimes within Global Production Networks."

that targeted formal and more export-oriented segment, the informal sector also started to reemerge and grow significantly.[56]

The second phase (1998/2001–2007) was characterized by a more selective approach to industrial policy with a focus on promoting the leather industry as a strategic sector in order to increase exports, foreign exchange income, and employment. The selective industrial policy included preferential access to finance and land, tax incentives for new firms and exports, and discretionary liberalization for foreign investments in the tanning segment. The newly established Leather and Leather Products Technology Institute (LLPTI) also provided sector-related training.[57]

Overall, the industrial policies during this phase were successful in terms of increasing local investments in the tanning and manufacturing segments as well as upgrading to exports of semi-finished leather (Figure 9.1), however, the local tanneries did not upgrade[58] to the finishing stage, limiting exports of higher value products as well as constraining the link between the tanneries and leather manufacturers.[59] The already established and newly emerging formal leather manufacturing firms, in addition, continued to focus on the protected local market and only a few firms succeeded in exporting significant volumes. Many of these firms suffered from cheap Chinese imports at the end of the 1990s and early 2000s, despite a 35 percent tariff on most leather product imports.[60]

As a result of the limited success, the government shifted its strategy towards promoting FDI-driven investments, upgrading, and exports during the third development phase (2008–2019) against the opposition of locally-owned tanneries. The introduction of an export tax on semi-finished leathers and a more active and successful approach towards attracting FDI – in particular from China – had profound impacts on the development of the sector. The implemented industrial policy mix, which also included a variety of additional supporting measures (e.g. strengthened institutional capacities, improved access to finance, foreign exchange and input supply for exporting firms, and more), incentivized upgrading towards, and exports of, finished leather, reducing the role of local tanneries at the same time. In 2018, Ethiopia had 30

56 Ibid.

57 Ibid.

58 In general, locally-owned tanneries aimed to export low-value leather in order to increase their foreign exchange earnings and finance their import businesses, thus shying away from investments (Ibid.).

59 Ibid.

60 Tegegne, "Impacts of Chinese imports and coping strategies of local producers."

tanneries, 10 of which were foreign-owned, with 7,516 employees and foreign firms dominating exports.[61] Exports of non-manufactured leather thus shifted from being dominated by local tanneries supplying tanneries in the EU for further processing to a mix of local- and foreign-owned tanneries supplying finished leather to mostly China and – to a lesser extent – local manufacturers.[62] Similar to locally-owned tanneries who preferred to export in order to access foreign-exchange, most foreign-owned firms also prefer to export to their mother companies and established sales channels abroad, limiting the access to export-quality finished leather for locally-owned and non-vertically integrated leather manufacturing firms, given their smaller and more infrequent orders. Locally operating foreign-owned manufacturers, on the other hand, source only from a handful of tanneries. The tanning segment thus continues to lack linkages to the local leather manufacturing sector, despite the success of upgrading towards finished leather in the last decade.[63]

The third development period, in addition, was also characterized by significant growth of the formal and exporting leather manufacturing sector. The major driver of manufactured leather exports (Figure 9.1), in particular footwear and gloves, were large Chinese and other FDI firms, and only few locally owned leather manufacturers were exporting successfully.[64]

The sector nonetheless continues to suffer from a wide range of challenges that hamper its economic development, including, most importantly, the weak linkages between the livestock and tanning segment as well as the tanning and manufacturing segment. Another major issue is the limited export success of locally-owned firms, which struggle to upgrade and fulfill global buyers' requirements despite continuous government support and in the context of so far limited spillover effects from FDI.

### 4.3 *Today's Structure and (Global) Market Integration of the Leather Manufacturing Sector*

The transformation of the leather sector in the last century until today led to the creation of a modern manufacturing sector that operates alongside[65]

61 Data provided by the Ethiopian Leather Industry Development Institute (LIDI).

62 Grumiller, "A Strategic-Relational Approach to Analyzing Industrial Policy Regimes within Global Production Networks."

63 Ibid.

64 Ibid.

65 In general, there are few functional links between the informal and formal sector. The main exception is the supply of low-quality leather of formal tanneries to informal local firms.

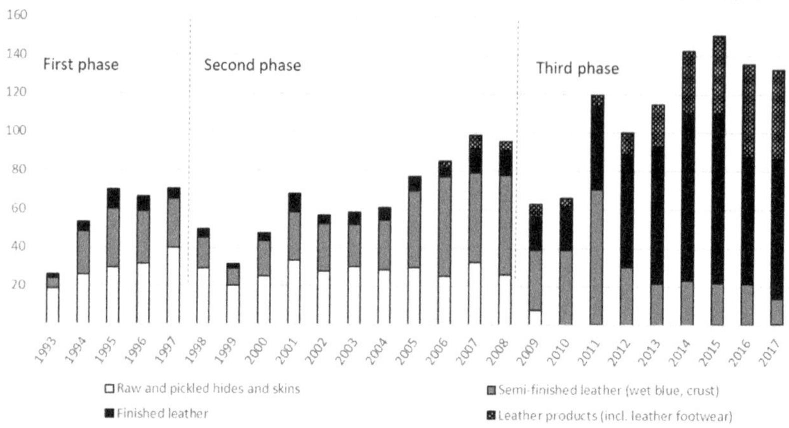


FIGURE 9.1 Ethiopia's leather export structure (1993–2017, USD millions)
SOURCE: ADAPTED VERSION OF GRUMILLER 2019, BASED ON UN COMTRADE (2019)
Note: Data reflects global imports.

informal activities. In particular since the 1990s, and following important structural shifts during the 2010s, a highly diverse manufacturing sector comprised of different types of firms in terms of ownership, products produced, size, and (global) market integration emerged, including: (i) foreign owned footwear and glove manufacturers exporting to key consumer countries (footwear to the US and China; gloves to the EU); (ii) locally-owned footwear manufacturers focusing on the local market, with limited export success; (iii) locally-owned leather goods manufacturers, focusing on the local market and/or exports to niche markets in key consumer countries; (iv) the informal sector, producing various leather products for the local market.

Foreign-owned manufacturers also developed to key actors in Ethiopia's leather industry, but they do not compete with locally-owned firms on the local market due to government restrictions. The six foreign-owned footwear firms that were established in the late 2000s and early 2010s mostly have Chinese/Taiwanese ownership and currently employ around 12 thousand people (one-third of the total employees[66] in the formal footwear sector) and dominate

66 There are unconfirmed rumors that the Huajin Group, the largest FDI company in the sector, might significantly increase investment to employ 50,000 persons or more in the near future.

exports.[67] Most of these firms tend to produce on a CMT/OEM basis for global buyers (they thus only manufacture the product and manage sourcing activities, without adding significant value), but they also produce their own designs and brands for the Chinese market. This group of firms tends to have the best access to local export-quality leather given their consistent large order volumes. Three foreign-owned glove manufacturers employing a little over one thousand employees, including the stock-listed and vertically integrated Pittards from the UK, are also present in Ethiopia.

The 16 locally-owned footwear firms with roughly 4,500 employees focus on the local market are given higher margins in the context of a protected market and almost all firms have their own designs and brands. Medium- and larger-sized companies are also able to offer a wide array of services to global buyers, offering CMT, OEM, and private labeling services depending on the buyers' demands. Some of these companies also successfully export their own brands to regional markets. Most of these firms, however, have not been successful in exporting to key consumer countries given that most firms do not fulfill global buyers' requirements in terms of price-quality ratios, high landing costs, timely delivery, and other requirements such as Corporate Social Responsibility (CSR) issues (e.g. occupational safety and health). As a result, Anbessa shoe, the largest locally owned footwear firm with shops all over Ethiopia, has recently built a new factory that fulfills the requirements of large buyers in key consumer countries and is potentially able to supply market segments demanding higher volumes. Competition on the local market, in addition, has increased in recent years due to the rising production capacities of local firms and imports.[68]

Locally-owned and formal small- and medium leather goods firms that focus on the production of bags, jackets, belts and wallets (excl. footwear and mostly gloves) also play an important role in Ethiopia's leather sector. Most of these 40+ firms, employing roughly 1,400 persons, are smaller in size compared to footwear firms[69] and have their own design and brand for the local market, but only a few of these companies have the capacity and capability to export a significant share of their production. However, the leather goods

67 Employment data provided by the Ethiopian Leather Industry Development Institute (LIDI) refers to mid-2018.

68 Ethiopian leather footwear imports increased from an average of 1.4 million USD between 2006 and 2010 to 9.6 million USD between 2012 and 2016, most of which is imported from China (56 percent in 2016), India (32 percent) and Turkey (14 percent), see: UN Comtrade database.

69 Footwear and leather goods firms are highly labor-intensive in nature, but footwear firms require more machinery, which is why they tend to be larger to achieve economies of scale.

sub-sector is also comprised of an innovative group of firms with a strong export orientation and focus on higher-end niche markets with larger margins in key consumer countries. Many of these firms are owned by well-educated female entrepreneurs (many of whom are also members of the Center for Accelerated Women's Economic Empowerment – CAWEE) with experience abroad and knowledge of Western designs and trends. These firms offer CMT/OEM services, but also often succeed in selling their own designs.

In addition to the expansion of the formal leather industry, micro- and small firms also continue to play an important role in the Ethiopian leather sector, in particular on the local market. Thousands of the micro- and small firms, many of which are informal or have an informal character despite official registration, are located in clusters that emerged spontaneously and without planning. These types of firms often have investment and working capital below 1,000 USD each.[70] The largest of these clusters is the Merkato footwear cluster in Addis Ababa, which is comprised of several thousand, mostly male, shoemakers from the Gurage ethnic group. The next section presents an analysis of the industrial and labor relations in Ethiopia's leather industry and highlights the large differences of bargaining power in the manufacturing segment depending on firms' strategies and market-orientation.

## 5 Labor Relations in Ethiopia's Leather Manufacturing Sector

The industrial policy regime implemented by the EPRDF, the ruling party, can be characterized by a centralized and hierarchical approach to industrial relations.[71] The export-oriented industrialization strategy and selective industrial policies in the context of Ethiopia's developmental state successfully supported industrialization processes in the context of intensifying contradictions with an emerging but relatively marginalized labor class. Demands of the labor class were often perceived to be contradicting, the export-oriented and – at least partially – FDI-led industrialization path furthered by the political elite. Even though various fractions of the EPRDF have strong links to Marxism, its ideological roots are more linked to regional liberation movements and the mobilization of peasants. The industrial proletariat thus only plays a minor role in the party and lacks access to state power.[72]

70 Tegegne, "Impacts of Chinese imports and coping strategies of local producers."
71 Hardy and Hauge, "Labour Challenges in Ethiopia's Textile and Leather Industries," p. 724.
72 Cf. Ibid.

The limited power of labor is closely related to its marginalized role in the party, constraining the associational power of labor. With the coming into power of the EPRDF, the state-controlled All-Ethiopia Trade Unions domination during the Derg regime was replaced by the Confederation of Ethiopian Trade Unions (CETU) in 1993, a national trade union organization.[73] Initially, CETU operated relatively independently, but conflicts in the context of the privatization processes and the structural adjustment program imposed by the World Bank led the EPRDF leaders to realign CETU with the party.[74] Nonetheless, CETU does not blindly support the government, but aims to mediate between the broader developmental objectives and policies of the EPRDF leadership and the interests of the workforce.[75] In this context, CETU is part of the tripartite committee that also includes the Ministry of Labor and Social Affairs and the Ethiopian Employer's Federation. The committee is the main body in which labor related issues are discussed with the government. With a labor union density of 15 percent (in 2010), CETU is comprised of nine sectoral associations, including the Industrial Federation of Textile, Leather and Garment Trade Unions (IFTLGTU) with almost 50 thousand members.[76]

The limited influence of labor in the party is most clearly visible in the lack of a minimum wage[77] – a long-standing demand of the Ethiopian labor movement. Given the absence of a minimum wage, there is no uniformity in the application of minimum wages.[78] Since the tax law exempts any monthly wage below 600 ETB from taxes, some employers consider this threshold – which is close to the international poverty line taking into account purchasing power parity – as a default minimum wage. At the current exchange rate of 32 ETB/USD (January 2020), this is equivalent to 19 USD per month in nominal terms. The information obtained from interviews suggest that wages paid typically exceed this threshold[79] in the leather sector, though in general, leather sector

73 Ibid.

74 Markakis, *Ethiopia*, p. 251f.

75 Cf. Hardy and Hauge, "Labour Challenges in Ethiopia's Textile and Leather Industries," p. 725.

76 Ibid.

77 With the reform of the labor law in 2019, the government set up a Wage Board that includes the tripartite and other stakeholders that discusses the implementation of a minimum wage, however, at the time of writing there are no signs that a minimum wage will be implemented in the near future.

78 Grumiller and Raza, "The Ethiopian Leather and Leather Products Sector."

79 Many leather firms are located in or near Addis Ababa, which is why wages in those leather firms also need to compensate for higher living costs.

wages are considered to be rather low, in particular when compared to service sector wages.[80]

The current Ethiopian labor law[81] contains articles with respect to the maximum working hours per week, overtime hours, and employment conditions. For instance, the law limits the maximum working hours to 8 hours per day and 48 hours per week, and caps overtime at 4 hours per day and 12 hours per week, respectively. Overtime work has to be paid extra, with remuneration rates equivalent to 1.5 to 2.5 times the regular hourly wage rate depending on the date, time and conditions of overtime hours worked. The ILO reports that an increasing share of both men and women work overtime, which indicates widespread poverty and the need for overtime work to secure a basic living standard.[82]

Currently, women account for between 70 to 80 percent of employees in leather manufacturing. Women are preferentially selected for some of the higher-detail work within the factories including finishing work, sewing, cutting and pattern-making. The Ethiopian labor code[83] has important provisions in connection with female employment. The law restricts any type of discrimination as regards employment and payment. It also contains provisions with respect to the special conditions of work for women particularly during pregnancy, allowing for a special leave of up to 120 days with payment during pregnancy, birth and after birth.

From a sectoral perspective, the associational power of labor is also limited in the leather industry given that the union is not active in all firms (in particular in smaller firms) or only has a passive role. Even in cases of active labor struggles that include work stoppages and strikes, the labor union was rarely responsible.[84] Instead, interviews with firm managers and employees suggest that labor unrest is often more connected with informal and spontaneous acts of solidarization or dissatisfaction, e.g. in case of perceived injustices due to unequal pay or dissatisfaction with the quality of food in the canteen. For this reason, labor struggles often seem to be short-lived and are not strategic in form, limiting the overall associational power of labor.[85]

80 Ibid.

81 The labor law was reformed in 2019 (Proclamation No.1156/2019), repealing the Labour Proclamation of 2003 and related amendments. The changes include some improvements for employees, but the effects on the leather industry are relatively minor.

82 ILO, "Decent work country profile".

83 Ethiopian Proclamation No.1156/2019.

84 Cf. Hardy and Hauge, "Labour Challenges in Ethiopia's Textile and Leather Industries," p. 725.

85 Cf. ibid.

Despite the lack of associational power,[86] the workforce in the leather industry has some degree of structural power that shapes labor relations in the sector, but there are important differences between various groups of firms. From the employer perspective in the formal sector, the main challenges in their management of labor relations are high turnover and related low productivity rates.[87] The high turnover rates can be explained by a variety of interlinked factors, including comparatively low wages in the sector, a favorable regional labor market (in particular in Addis Ababa where most leather manufacturers are located), dissatisfaction with factory work, distance from home, and workers that perceive their work in the leather sector as temporary and thus look for other opportunities (e.g. self-employment, jobs in other sectors such as construction, services, apparel, work in the Middle East, and more). The scale of the problem and its effect on the marketplace power of labor, however, differs between various groups of firms related to their strategies, (global) market integration, and skilled-labor demand.

Foreign-owned firms, in particular footwear and glove firms from China and Taiwan, have been affected the most by labor struggles and high turnover rates. These firms exported the Chinese factory model and associated authoritarian management style, which did not resonate well with Ethiopian employees who do not have factory experience[88] and often do not plan a career in the leather industry, given better job opportunities elsewhere. Some firms have reported around 70 percent of turnover rates per year, others of up to 10–20 percent per month, which is why a large share of workers in these firms are often semi-skilled and firms are more hesitant to offer more cost-intensive training (e.g. field trips to China).[89] As a result, output and quality tends to be relatively unstable, the complexity and value of products produced in foreign-owned Ethiopian factories tend to be lower, and changes between products produced tend to require longer periods.[90] The situation is, however, improving and the turnover rate for experienced workers has dropped significantly, likely due to implemented incentive schemes for skilled workers (e.g. piece rates, often raising their wages to over 1,500 ETB) and increasing adaptations to local customs. Experienced Ethiopian workers are also increasingly employed as trainers and lower-level managers. As a result, the number of Chinese managers and

86 The lack of associational power may likely be explained by the lack of structural power of labor in Ethiopia, but this analysis goes beyond the scope of this chapter.

87 Cf. Ibid.; Xiaoyang, "Export, Employment, or Productivity?"

88 Cf. Thompson, "Time, Work-Discipline, and Industrial Capitalism."

89 Xiaoyang, "Export, Employment, or Productivity?", p. 20ff.

90 Ibid.

trainers per Ethiopian worker has decreased in Chinese-owned leather manufacturing firms.[91] However, wages for new and unskilled workers continue to be low (generally around 700 to 1,000 ETB)[92] and turnover rates remain high.

Locally-owned firms generally have not struggled as much with strikes and labor unrest given that the owners and managers of these firms are more sensitive towards local workers' expectations and customs. High turnover-rates are nonetheless also a big challenge for locally-owned footwear firms, but their approach tends to differ compared to foreign-owned firms. Two approaches within the group of locally-owned footwear manufacturers can be differentiated: The first group focuses exclusively on the local market, which is characterized by higher margins and lower quality requirements, which is why these firms demand for skilled labor is comparatively low. As a result, some of these firms learned to manage high turnover rates in the context of their local market integration and lower-end quality production. The second group of firms has a hybrid strategy that aims to increase exports to low-mid market segments in key consumer and regional markets as a second source of income and in order to improve their access to foreign exchange (for imports of inputs and/or their import side-businesses). In order to tackle high turnover rates, these firms often pay higher wages at levels similar to or above foreign firms and have introduced a variety of benefits (e.g. free lunches, annual leave, medical services, etc.) with mixed success. The struggle for locally-owned firms to lower turnover rates is likely to be connected, in addition to the above mentioned challenges, with the competition of foreign firms that have a more consistent demand for skilled labor given more consistent export orders and – at least partially – pay higher wages for experienced workers.

The situation is different in the leather goods sub-sector (bags, jackets, wallets, belts, etc., excl. footwear and gloves) given that these firms are smaller in size and the owners often have stronger personal ties to their employees. The market-orientation (local vs. export) differentiates these firms in terms of quality, skilled labor required, and wage levels similar to locally-owned footwear firms, however, the leather goods firms that successfully integrated into niche markets – as discussed above – offer significantly better working conditions. Given the firms' higher quality and skill requirements (e.g. design), these firms often pay higher wages to experienced workers compared to most other

91 Cf. Ibid.

92 Wage data in this paper is indicative: There are big regional differences and differences between firms of the same group, i.e. wages in Addis Ababa tend to be higher compared to other regions.

leather firms (interviews suggest 2,000 to 3,500 ETB per month), often have stronger personal bonds with their key employees in the context of "family businesses", and thus do not struggle as much with high turnover rates or labor unrest.

The situation is not comparable with the informal sector, in which owners and workers of micro and small firms often work in more precarious conditions compared to the formalized sector.[93] The job opportunities in the informal sector are nonetheless often perceived as a safety net for employees and this positively affects their marketplace bargaining power.[94] Many leather firms located in leather clusters are organized in cooperatives as a strategy to counter major challenges such as a lack of safety net, poor rent conditions, and financial shortages. The Ethio-International Footwear Cluster Cooperative Society (EIFCCOS) is the largest and best-organized cooperative in the sector, linking 173 firms that employ roughly 1,500 workers.[95] EIFCCOS consists of seven sub-networks, has a common production facility for footwear with 70 firms, and many joint activities such as purchasing materials, manufacturing and marketing. The collaboration has also allowed its members to acquire larger orders and to receive support by donor agencies, in particular UNIDO, and the government.

## 6 Conclusion

This chapter has outlined the transformation process of Ethiopia's leather industry during the twentieth and early twenty-first century, highlighting the crucial role of industrial and labor policy. The transformation process since the 1990s needs to be understood in the context of the political elite-driven Ethiopian development regime furthering export-oriented industrialization through shifting strategies, with important implications for growth, upgrading processes, the role of FDI, and global market integration.[96] Today, the Ethiopian leather industry is comprised of heterogeneous groups of firms that can be differentiated in terms of ownership, size, market integration, products produced, and more. The most important group of firms in terms of exports are foreign-owned footwear and glove manufacturers, since only few

93 Cf. Tegegne, "Impacts of Chinese imports and coping strategies of local producers."
94 Cf. Hardy and Hauge, "Labour Challenges in Ethiopia's Textile and Leather Industries."
95 UNIDO, "Networking small enterprises in Ethiopia's leather sector."
96 Grumiller, "A Strategic-Relational Approach to Analyzing Industrial Policy Regimes within Global Production Networks."

locally-owned footwear and leather goods manufacturers successfully integrated into the leather GCC.

The Ethiopian development regime and export-oriented industrialization path builds on industrial relations that are characterized by a relative marginalization of labor. The Ethiopian government has a centralized and hierarchical approach to industrial relations, and the national trade union is closely linked to the party, in which it plays a minor role, limiting the associational power of labor. The labor code implemented by the government exemplifies this since it provides a regulatory framework that ensures some fundamental rights of employees within and beyond the leather industry (e.g., regulations regarding overtime, maternity leave, etc.), however, it also reflects the interest of the government to attract FDI to promote export-oriented industrialization by keeping wages low, explaining the lack of a minimum wage.

On the sectoral level, workers are relatively unorganized despite an active but harmless sector-specific labor union. Workers' struggles in the sector are thus more spontaneous in nature, enabling workers to fight for firm specific and often minor causes, but overall they lack strategic form. A key finding of this chapter is that the structural power of labor and the scale of labor unrest in the contemporary leather industry differs depending on the ownership, market integration and strategies of different groups of firms, which explains the large diversity of labor relations in the industry. Foreign-owned firms, in particular new Chinese firms that tried to export the Chinese factory model, have struggled the most with strikes and workers' dissatisfaction, but the management has adapted their strategies and the situation is improving.

From the employer perspective, high turnover rates are one of the biggest challenges in the manufacturing industry, affecting almost all firms. This problem is a key challenge for export-oriented firms integrated or wanting to integrate in GCCs since they need to produce higher-quality products consistently, increasing the marketplace power of higher-skilled and more experienced workers in these firms. Many locally-owned firms focusing on the local market, in contrast, have managed high turnover rates in the context of a less demanding local market, however, this situation may change in light of increasing local market competition. High turnover rates are thus not only limiting the GCC integration[97] of locally-owned firms, but are also a result of their strategies and market-orientation. The informal leather sector, on the other hand, continues

97 See Hardy and Hauge, "Labour Challenges in Ethiopia's Textile and Leather Industries," pp. 731–34.

to be characterized by precarious work and has its own dynamics, with cooperatives in clusters – often supported by donor agencies – being the main and most visible strategy to soften the challenges of the precariat.

## Bibliography


Abebe, Girum and Florian Schäfer. "High Hopes and Limited Successes: Experimenting with Industrial Polices in the Leather Industry in Ethiopia," *Ethiopian Development Research Institute, Working Paper, 11* (2014).

Abebe, Girum and Florian Schäfer. "Review of Industrial Policies in Ethiopia," in Akbar Noman and Joseph Stiglitz (eds), *Initiative for policy dialogue at Columbia. Industrial policy and economic transformation in Africa* (New York: Columbia University Press, 2015), pp. 123–161.

Bair, Jennifer. "Global Capitalism and Commodity Chains: Looking Back, Going Forward," *Competition & Change*, 9, 2 (2005), pp. 153–180.

Bair, Jennifer. "Analysing global economic organization: embedded networks and global chains compared," *Economy and Society*, 37, 3 (2008), 339–364.

Brautigam, Deborah, Weis, Toni and Tang Xiaoyang. "Latent advantage, complex challenges: Industrial policy and Chinese linkages in Ethiopia's leather sector," *China Economic Review*, 48 (2018), pp. 158–169.

Clapham, Christopher. "The Ethiopian developmental state," *Third World Quarterly*, 39, 6 (2018), pp. 1151–1165.

Evans, Peter. *Embedded autonomy: States and industrial transformation*. (Princeton NJ: Princeton University Press, 1995).

FAO. "Livestock and livelihoods spotlight. Ethiopia. Cattle Sector," in *Food and Agriculture Organization of the United Nations, Africa Sustainable Livestock 2050, Report* (2018), online available at: http://www.fao.org/3/i8676en/I8676EN.pdf.

Gebreeyesus, Mulu and Pierre Mohnen. "Innovation performance and Embeddedness in Networks: Evidence from the Ethiopian Footwear Cluster," *World Development* 41 (2013), pp. 302–316.

Gereffi, Gary. "The Organization of Buyer-Driven Global Commodity Chains: How U.S. Retailers Shape Overseas Production Networks," in Gary Gereffi and Miguel Korzeniewicz (eds), *Commodity Chains and Global Capitalism* (London: Praeger Publishers, 1994), pp. 95–122.

Gereffi, Gary. "Global Production Systems and Third World Development," in Barbara Stallings (ed.), *Global Change, Regional Response: The New International Context of Development* (Cambridge: Cambridge University Press, 1995), pp. 100–142.

Gereffi, Gary. "International trade and industrial upgrading in the apparel commodity chain," *Journal of International Economics*, 48, 1 (1999), 37–70.

Gereffi, Gary and Olga Memedovic. "The Global Apparel Value Chain: What Prospects for Upgrading by Developing Countries?" *United Nations Industrial Development,* Report (Vienna, 2003).

Grumiller, Jan. "A Strategic-Relational Approach to Analyzing Industrial Policy Regimes within Global Production Networks: the Ethiopian Leather and Leather Products Sector," *ÖFSE Working Paper, 60* (2019).

Grumiller, Jan and Werner Raza. "Towards an Institutional Setup for Industrial Policy in Late Industrialization in the 21st Century," *ÖFSE Working Paper, 61* (2019).

Grumiller, Jan and Werner Raza. "The Ethiopian Leather and Leather Products Sector: An Assessment of Export Potentials to Europe and Austria," *ÖFSE Report,* 11 (2019).

Hardy, Vincent and Jostein Hauge. "Labour Challenges in Ethiopia's Textile and Leather Industries: no voice, no loyalty, no exit?" *African Affairs,* 184/473 (2019), pp. 712–736.

Horner, Rory and Matthew Alford. "The roles of the state in global value chains: an update and emerging agenda," *Global Development Institute Working Paper Series,* 36 (2019).

Humphrey, John and Hubert Schmitz. "How does insertion in global value chains affect upgrading in industrial clusters?" *Regional Studies,* 36, 9 (2002), pp. 1017–1027.

ILO. "Decent work country profile: Ethiopia," *International Labour Office, ILO Country Office for Ethiopia and Somalia; Federal Democratic Republic of Ethiopia, Ministry of Labour and Social Affairs* (Addis Ababa, 2013).

Jessop, Bob. "The Strategic Selectivity of the State: Reflections on a Theme of Poulantzas," *Journal of the Hellenic Diaspora,* 25, 1–2 (1999), pp. 1–37.

Jessop, Bob. "Institutional Re(turns) and the Strategic – Relational Approach," *Environment and Planning A: Economy and Space,* 33, 7 (2001), pp. 1213–35.

Lelena Global Consulting. "Value Chain Analysis of the Ethiopian Leather Sector," *Unpublished Report* (Addis Ababa, 2016).

Lentakis, Michael. *Ethiopia: A View From Within* (London: Janus Publishing Company, 2005).

Mahmud, Ahmed. "Development potential and constraints of hides and skins marketing in Ethiopia," in R.C. Markel, Abebe, G. and A.L Goetsch (eds). *The opportunities and challenges of enhancing goat production in East Africa.* Proceeding of a conference held at Awassa, Debub University (2000), pp. 127–138.

Markakis, John. *Ethiopia: The last two frontiers* (James Currey, Woodbridge, 2011), pp. 251–252.

Memedovic, Olga and Heikki Mattila. "The global leather value chain: the industries, the main actors and prospects for upgrading in LDCs," *International Journal of Technological Learning, Innovation and Development,* 1, 4 (2008), pp. 482–519.

Neilson, Jeffrey, Pritchard, Bill and Henry Wai-chung Yeung. "Global value chains and global production networks in the changing international political economy: An introduction," *Review of International Political Economy,* 21, 1 (2014), pp. 1–8.

Oqubay, Arkebe. *Made in Africa: Industrial policy in Ethiopia* (Oxford: Oxford University Press, 2015).

Oqubay, Arkebe. "Industrial Policy and Late Industrialization in Ethiopia," African Development Bank Group, *Working Paper Series*, 303 (2018).

Pellerin, Camille Louise. "The aspiring developmental state and business associations in Ethiopia," Journal of Modern African Studies, 57, 4 (2019), pp. 589–612.

Pempel, T. J. "The developmental regime in a changing world economy," in Meredith Woo-Cumings (ed.), *The developmental state* (Ithaca, NY: Cornell University Press, 1999), pp. 137–181.

Selwyn, Ben "Beyond firm-centrism: re-integrating labour and capitalism into global commodity chain analysis," *Journal of Economic Geography*, 12, 1 (2012), pp. 205–226.

Silver, Beverly. *Forces of Labour: Workers' Movements and Globalisation since 1870*. (Cambridge: Cambridge University Press, 2003).

Smith, Adrian. "The state, institutional frameworks and the dynamics of capital in global production networks," *Progress in Human Geography*, 39, 3 (2015), pp. 290–315.

Sonobe, Tetsushi, Akoten, John and Keijiro Otsuka. "2An Exploration into the Successful Development of the Leather-Shoe Industry in Ethiopia," *Review of Development Economics*, 13, 4 (2009), pp. 719–36.

Staritz, Cornelia, Gereffi, G. and Olivier Cattaneo. "Editorial: Special Issue on Shifting End Markets and Upgrading Prospects in Global Value Chains," *International Journal of Technological Learning, Innovation and Development*, 4, 1/2/3 (2011), pp. 1–12.

Tegegne, Gebre-Egziabher. "Impacts of Chinese imports and coping strategies of local producers: the case of small-scale footwear enterprises in Ethiopia," *Journal of Modern African Studies*, 45, 4 (2007), pp. 647–79.

Thompson, Edward Palmer. "Time, work-discipline, and industrial capitalism," *Past and Present*, 38 (1967), 56–97.

UNIDO. "Technical assistance project for the upgrading of the Ethiopian leather and leather products industry," in *Independent Evaluation Report*. (Vienna, 2012), online available at: https://www.unido.org/sites/default/files/2013-02/Ethiopia_leather_evaluation_FINAL_report_130208_0.pdf.

UNIDO. "Networking small enterprises in Ethiopia's leather sector," in *UNIDO, Progress Report* (2016), online avaliable at: https://www.unido.org/sites/default/files/2016-04/CLUSTERS_ethiopia_leather_sectorpdf_0.pdf.

van der Loop, Theo. "The Importance of the Leather Footwear Sector for Development in Ethiopia," *Addis Ababa University, RLDS Policy Brief*, 1 (2003).

Xiaoyang, Tang. "Export, Employment, or Productivity? Chinese Investments in Ethiopia's Leather and Leather Product Sectors," *Johns Hopkins University, School of Advanced International Studies, China Africa Research Initiative*, Working Paper 32 (2019).

Wright, Erik Olin. "Working-class power, capitalist-class interests, and class compromise," *American Journal of Sociology*, 105 (2000), 957–1002.

Wylde, Christopher. *Latin America after neoliberalism: Developmental regimes in post-crisis states* (London: Palgrave Macmillan, 2012).

Wylde, Christopher. *Emerging Markets and the State: Developmentalism in the 21st Century* (London: Palgrave Macmillan, 2017).

# PART 4

## *Production Chains in (Post-)Socialist Eastern Europe*

CHAPTER 10

# Outward Processing Production and the Yugoslav Self-Managed Textile Industry in the 1980s

*Goran Musić*

The narrative of "industrial collapse", which has dominated discussions about manufacturing and labor in East, Central and Southeast Europe ever since the early 1990s, is shifting in recent years. Often described as the greatest fall of economic output during peacetime in modern history,[1] the traumatic experience of transformation from planned economies toward free market is open for reinterpretation in the new millennium as foreign direct investments into manufacturing picked up pace and many formerly state owned industries became integrated into global supply chains. Instead of being perceived as post-industrial wastelands, the industrial zones in former state-socialist countries are now seen more as dynamic spaces, where Western European and other producers are relocating parts of their operations, attracted by low labor costs. One of the key topics in many industries of the region today is upgrading strategies and labor shortages, not deindustrialization and unemployment.[2]

The reason why this chapter emphasizes moving away from the "rise and fall of socialist industrialization" paradigm is not to downplay the destruction of industrial infrastructure and the dissolution of Eastern European working classes during the 1990s, but rather to open the vista for a wider, global historical outlook on labor in this part of the world. A view that can better avoid the teleological assumptions of the dominant narrative frames, such as the inevitable decline of socialist modernization or gradual catching up with the economically most developed countries in the frame of European unification. The idea is to situate these processes in a broader chronological narrative of ever-changing international division of labor, or, as Adrian Smith and John Pickles suggest, to understand labor in former state-socialist countries as becoming:

1 See Rostowski, "Comparing two Great Depressions," pp. 225–41.
2 See Gerőcs, Tamás, Meszmann and Pinkasz in this volume.

 | DOI:10.1163/9789004448049_011

> ... differentially repositioned in relation to the (re)creation of international production networks and the reconfiguration of new geo-economic borders in Europe and beyond.[3]

This repositioning is usually associated with the "transitional period" of the 1990s, but it is certainly not a development without a precedence, with layers of East European working classes being exposed to similar pressures already under state socialism. New theoretical approaches to labor in the region often stress lineages of commodification as well as continuities in the region's interaction with Western capital. Besnik Pula challenges the transitology-inspired visions of 1989 as an absolute starting point for Eastern European capitalisms, pointing out how previous instances of entry into the international division of labor at various critical junctures during the Cold War greatly influenced the post-socialist developments of these economies.[4] Adrian Grama and Susan Zimmerman connect to the debates inside global labor history and Martha Lampland's anthropological work on rural labor in Hungary to argue for an extended historical perspective of various efforts to lower the cost of labor under the capitalist as well as socialist state formations.[5] Alina Sandra-Cucu looks at the incorporation of Romania's car industry into Western production chains during the late socialist period with the aim of:

> ... opening an analytical space in which block concepts like 'neoliberalism', 'state socialism', or 'postsocialism' can be historicized and problematized as encounters between different logics of accumulation, scaled political rationalities, managerial cultures, and workers' everyday struggles for planning and sustaining a future.[6]

An insight into the lived experience of the (post-)socialist working classes seems to confirm researchers' wariness toward a clear cut periodization and sudden ruptures. Basing himself on the oral history interviews with blue-collar workers in the Serbian capital Belgrade, Rory Archer shows how correspondents have a blurry memory of dividing lines between socialist and

---

3 Smith and Pickles, "Global value chains," p. 327.

4 Besnik Pula does not include Yugoslavia in his research even though its self-managed firms were the frontrunners of many technology transfers and coproduction schemes with the Westers enterprises described in his book, see: Pula, *Globalization Under and After Socialism*.

5 Grama and Zimmerman, "The art of link-making in global labour history"; Lampland, *The Object of Labor: Commodification in Socialist Hungary*; Lampland, Martha. *The Value of Labor*.

6 Cucu, "Go West."

post-socialist times, as crisis years of late Yugoslav socialism are often fused with the turbulent transformations of the 1990s.[7] Therefore, one of the results of a *longue durée* perspective is the toning down of the view of 1989 as the single, ultimate rupture point for Eastern European labor.

This chapter will contribute to the efforts of revising the prevailing research frames and point to the continuities of remaking socialist labor relations in accordance with the demands of the world capitalist market by looking at the phenomena of "production sharing" or "outward processing" in 1980s Yugoslavia. The concept of outward processing trade, where a contractor temporarily exports the necessary production components to a foreign manufacturer, only to import the finished product under a favorable trade agreement, is a well-known practice in the textile industry. It is thanks to the outward processing trade regime with European Union countries that employment in textile and clothing production stabilized on a smaller scale by the mid-1990s in large parts of East, Central and Southeast Europe, in some cases even becoming the cornerstone of total employment in manufacturing amidst the fall of other industries.[8]

The effects that the integration of formerly state-owned textile industries into global production chains and their transformation into low-cost export processing platforms had on working conditions, living standards and subjectivities of, mostly female, workers have been relatively well researched in recent years.[9] Most of these accounts recognize that the roots of outward processing are to be found in the late socialist period, yet none ventures to show how the practice actually evolved before the 1990s. By making a close inspection of a Yugoslav textile enterprise "Textind", this chapter sheds light on this early period of outward processing production, or "lon jobs" as they were colloquially called inside Yugoslavia.

7 Archer, " 'It was better when it was worst'."

8 Apart from Ukraine, Russia and Poland, the outward processing trade agreements played an important role in all former socialist countries of the region. The trade scheme became less significant after the EU accession of the Visegrád Four countries and the end of quota restrictions in the world textile trade in 2004, paving the way for a more direct integration into global production chains through foreign direct investments. Outward processing textile production continued to play an important role during early the 2000s, especially in Romanian and Bulgarian industries. See: Smith and Pickles, "Global value chains," p. 327.

9 See Bonfiglioli, "Gender, Labour and Precarity," Dima, "The evolution of textile and clothing industry," Vodopivec, "Textile Workers in Slovenia," Musiolek, "Tools for Enforcing Labour Rights," Luginbühl and Musiolek, "Stitched up," Plank, Staritz and Lukas, "Labour Rights in Global Production Networks."

Using the factory press as the main source, this chapter follows the consequences of the introduction of lon jobs on a larger scale in Textind in the mid-1980s. It looks at the changing attitudes of the enterprise management toward these types of contacts, their effect on the business results, as well as the impact they had on the shop floor, relation between different groups of workers and the articulation of workers' dissatisfaction. The fact that the Yugoslav state nourished an elaborate system of workers' self-management, adds an additional aspect to the analysis. The discussions taking place in the factory institutions offer an opportunity to see how the local workforce had perceived this increasing marketization of production and labor relations in the midst of the crisis of socialist modernization. They also give us clues to explain the worsening relations between the industrial workers and the ruling parties as well as the apparent weakness of labor in Eastern Europe on the eve of the political and economic transformations in the 1990s.[10]

## 1 Sharing Garment Production: EEC and Yugoslavia

In the high years of the post-World War Two economic boom, the Western European economies typically relied more on the import of cheap labor within their own borders than exporting technology and intermediary products for assembly in low-wage countries. During the economic slowdown of the 1970s however, the largest West European producers were forced to revise this strategy because of the rising unemployment at home and increasing competitiveness on the world market. Throughout the course of the 1980s, the European Economic Community (EEC) started to implement the so-called "outward processing relief arrangements", as a way of protecting domestic high value added production, while tapping into the lower labor costs of countries on its periphery.

Outward processing production implied "temporary export" of raw materials and intermediary products for further processing or assembly outside of the EEC and the subsequent return of the enhanced value products with partial or total relief from import duties. In other words, EEC companies were encouraged to search for subcontractors abroad and provide them with materials and blueprints for production. In return, the subcontractors

10 For methodological research of a Yugoslav self-managed enterprise, see: Archer and Musić, "Approaching the Socialist Factory." For the deteriorating relationship between the working classes and communist parties in the case of Hungary and GDR, see: Bartha, *Alienating Labor*.

were obliged to deliver the required quantities, meet the quality standards and respect the deadlines. The contractors' motivation for such arrangements was certainly the cost reductions made possible by transferring labor intensive operations to low wage countries, but also the utilization of the EEC trade duties relief and gaining access to foreign markets of developing economies on its periphery with high entry barriers, such as Eastern Europe and North Africa.[11]

Unlike the United States, which used production sharing schemes primarily for semi-conductors, office machines and automobile components, in the European case it was the textile and clothing industry that fully embraced this new trend by in the mid-1980s. Textiles and apparel made up one-half of the EEC's total global imports connected to outward processing trade in 1987. Faced with the rival producers from East Asia, the Western German textile producers were already pioneering this practice in the 1970s and evolved into the main users of the EEC's production sharing scheme in the following decade.[12] The West German companies were responsible for contracting 52 percent of EEC's total outward processing trade imports in 1987.[13]

On the other end, the majority of the subcontractors were located in Eastern Europe with Yugoslavia being the country of choice for most West German companies. Between 1984 and 1987, when Spain and Portugal intensified their EEC joining process, Eastern Europe had become the main target for outward processing. During this period, the value of production sharing imports from Eastern Europe to the EEC doubled to 2 billion US dollars. By 1987, due to its geographic proximity, trained workforce, relatively low wages[14] and well-established connections with the capitalist economies, Yugoslavia managed to capture 38 percent of this booming production exchange between the EEC and Eastern Europe.[15] After Eastern Europe, North Africa, especially Tunisia and Morocco, was the second most important assembly and producing region for EEC companies in the same period.[16]

11 United States International Trade Commission, *Production Sharing*, pp. 9–19.

12 Fröbel, Heinrichs and Kreye, *Die Neue Internationale Arbeitsteilung*, pp. 114–151.

13 Two thirds of West Germany's import volume consisted of apparel and textiles, mainly blouses, shorts, trousers and footwear, see: United States International Trade Commission, *Production Sharing*, pp. 9–6.

14 The basic manufacturing wage in late 1980s Yugoslavia was about seven times lower than corresponding wages in Western Germany, see: *Ibid.*, pp. 9–20.

15 The other main destinations for subcontracting in Eastern Europe were Hungary, Romania and Poland, together accounting for 47 percent of the total EEC production sharing imports from Eastern Europe, see: *Ibid.*, pp. 9–12.

16 *Ibid.*, pp. 9–17.

Traditionally the textile enterprises were among the Yugoslav producers most exposed to the world market. The textile industry had always been less protected by the state and received fewer investments in comparison to the strategically more important heavy industries. In this situation, the Yugoslav textile producers had been forced to be export oriented ever since the early 1960s, but they also became highly dependent on the import of raw materials, due to the underdevelopment of the local base for cotton, wool, silk and underinvestment in artificial fibers and chemical dyeing.

By the late 1980s, the Yugoslav textile industry employed 474,000 workers or some 17 percent of all workers in the industry. The sector was highly gendered with almost 80 percent of workers being women. It also distinguished itself by a high ratio of unqualified workforce, relatively low wage rates, night shift work and hard working conditions on the shop floor.[17] Still, the work security, ability to participate in the success of one's enterprise and the spread of social benefits guaranteed by Yugoslav socialism all contributed to the creation of a specific factory loyalty, identification with the system of workers' self-management and expectations of gradual progress among the Yugoslav female textile workers.[18]

The first attempt at opening the Yugoslav textile production toward Western European markets in the 1960s ended with a failure to sustain classical exports due to the inadequate quality of the fabric, poor design, and non-competitive prices. Stabilization ensued in the 1970s with a great expansion in the export of home brands finished textile goods. The boom was made possible by Yugoslavia's careful geopolitical balancing between East and West, as well as the economic engagement with the Global South through the Non-Aligned Movement. The insufficient domestic base for raw materials was compensated with imports of cotton from the Soviet Union, Egypt, and Sudan, but also Greece and the United States.[19] The surplus production of finished goods on the domestic market was resolved by export orientation toward the Comecon countries, primarily the Soviet Union, but also significant sales to developing markets in North Africa and the Middle East, such as Algeria, Libya, Egypt, and Iraq (Table 10.1).

17 Draganić, "Some Problems and Trend in the Development of Yugoslav Textile Industry," pp. 393–394.

18 Chiara Bonfiglioli develops the concept of "industrial structure of feeling" among the Yugoslav textile workers. See: Bonfigloli, *Women and Industry in the Balkans*.

19 Around 40 percent of raw cotton for the Yugoslav textile industry was imported from the Comecon, whereas developing countries contributed to additional 50 percent of cotton supplies.

TABLE 10.1 Regional structure of textile exports in percentages (export to all regions = 100)

| | Developed countries | | COMECON countries | | Developing countries | |
|---|---|---|---|---|---|---|
| | 1981 | 1988 | 1981 | 1988 | 1981 | 1988 |
| Total | 20 | 54 | 62 | 34 | 18 | 12 |
| Yarn and fabric | 25 | 61 | 54 | 21 | 21 | 18 |
| Finished products | 18 | 51 | 66 | 40 | 16 | 9 |

SOURCE: ČULAHOVIĆ, "THE YUGOSLAV GARMENT AND TEXTILE INDUSTRY," P. 90

The spread of outward processing production in the Yugoslav textile industry in the mid-1980s was tightly related to the changed geopolitical landscape and deep crisis of peripheral developmental models that took place a few years earlier. The early 1980s witnessed a cut back in the Soviet Union's import of Yugoslav apparel in the face of trade deficits and the partial opening of Moscow toward more price competitive Western European producers exporting at cheaper price due to high productivity. A drop was also recorded in Yugoslav exports to the Middle Eastern and African markets because of the falling oil prices and debt crisis in the developing world. In 1981, 66 percent of Yugoslavia's finished textile goods export went to Comecon countries, only to fall to 40 percent by 1988. Exports to developing countries, on the other hand, fell from 16 to 9 percent during the same period (Table 10.1).[20] In the midst of a prolonged economic slowdown of the Yugoslav economy, where wage freezes were introduced to battle the rising inflation, the domestic demand was not able to compensate for these drops in foreign sales.

The external shocks also affected suppliers. The irregular supplies of cotton and its oscillating quality placed great pressure on domestic spinning facilities. A factory newspaper article from 1983 reported that all cotton mills in the country were operating in three shifts under the brigade work regime. The basic textile industry was badly prepared for bottlenecks in cotton supply with entire work shifts adjourned due to irregular supplies and constant production stoppages. The economic reforms allowed spinning mills to raise prices and prioritize export or demand advance payments in hard currency from the local finished goods producers. The finished goods producers were thus left

20 Čulahović, "The Yugoslav Garment and Textile Industry," p. 20.

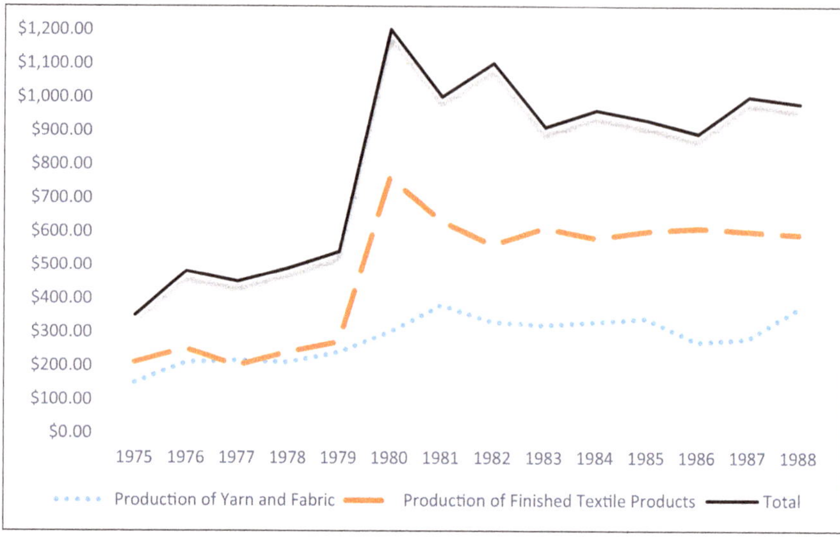


FIGURE 10.1 Yugoslav textile and garment export (in million US dollars)
SOURCE: ČULAHOVIĆ, "THE YUGOSLAV GARMENT AND TEXTILE INDUSTRY," P. 89

scrambling for the raw materials, facing blocked production on their own shop floors and penalties for undelivered shipments.[21]

It was in this context that the Yugoslav textile factories started repositioning from classical exports to sewing and finishing operations for larger West European companies. The main attraction of lon jobs was their apparent predictability. The contractor made sure the local finishing factory acquired raw materials and supplied all the necessary components. The local producers were able to secure export in advance and utilize the capacities previously made idle by the crisis. Moreover, an increase in exports to the Western markets became an official policy of the Yugoslav economic planners as the country struggled to accumulate hard currency and repay the mounting foreign debt.

After the success of the late 1970s, the export of finished textile goods and intermediary products fell sharply between 1980 and 1982, but managed to stabilize by relying on bilateral trade agreements and outward processing trade with EEC countries, such as Italy, France and the German Federal Republic in particular.[22] The share of developed industrial countries in the Yugoslav export of textile rose

21 Kirćanski, B., "Izvoz- ne po svaku cenu," *Textind*, May 28, 1987, p. 8.

22 Around 70 percent of lon exports were directed toward West Germany, followed by Italy, France and other Western European countries, but the case study shows that this type of production exchange was also developing with Comecon countries, such as Hungary and German Democratic Republic.

from 18 to 51 percent between 1981 and 1988. The lon jobs played a crucial role in this revival of textile production and export. The sewing and finishing operations for foreign companies amounted to one quarter of total foreign exchange receipts made by the Yugoslav textile industry in the second half of the 1980s, becoming an important source of hard currency inflow into the country. The net value of processing jobs nearly doubled between 1981 and 1988, with total exports reaching the value of 981 million US dollars in 1987 (Figure 10.1).[23]

Somewhat unexpectedly, the textile industry thus emerged as one of the more dynamic sectors in the largely depressed Yugoslav economy of the 1980s. Between 1983 and 1988, the demand of foreign partners for finishing services prompted the creation of some 90,000 new jobs. Solely in 1984, 34 new factories opened whereas longstanding enterprises began establishing new departments that specialized in lon jobs. Every eighth new jobs in the country that year was created in the textile industry.[24] Most of the newly opened facilities were funded by underdeveloped regions searching for a way to solve local unemployment and channel poorly skilled female workers into these labor-intensive factories.[25] The following section will focus on the case study of a large textile factory and show the challenges this producer faced when adjusting production to the new business trends.

## 2 The Illusive Gains of Lon

The relatively *laissez-faire* industrial policy of the Yugoslav state resulted in an atomized structure of producers where factories for finished textile goods were duplicated in almost every municipality or even within single municipalities.[26] Out of the total number of factories in the textile industry, 76.3 percent were finished goods producers, most of them without in house weaving and spinning facilities, thus competing for the scarce domestically produced yarn and fabric and strongly dependent on imports. The northern Serbian district of Central Banat in the Vojvodina province was one of the more economically

23 Čulahović, "The Yugoslav Garment and Textile Industry," p. 88.

24 Barjaktarević, M., "Sve dalje od tržišta," *Textind*, May 21, 1985, p. 2.

25 Čulahović, "The Yugoslav Garment and Textile Industry," p. 75.

26 In 1988 there were 817 factories in the country employing some 450, 000 employees. The average number of employees per enterprise was 551, with 728 in yarn and fabric production and 496 in the finished product producers. The average enterprise was larger than the standards in Western textile industries, but smaller and less concentrated than the giant conglomerates of the Soviet Bloc. See: Čulahović, "The Yugoslav Garment and Textile Industry," p. 77.

developed regions of the republic and Yugoslavia. Textile production was the second most important economic activity in Banat, right after food processing. It relied on the tradition of peasant household production and capitalist investments made in the rug industry under Austria-Hungary in the late Nineteenth Century.[27] A number of smaller, mid-sized and larger textile plants operated in Central Banat in the early 1980s, founded spontaneously out of the local peasant women cooperatives, surviving from the prewar period, established by municipal socialist authorities or set up as branches of successful self-managed producers.

In 1983, faced with the growing volatility in the textile industry, the local authorities decided to merge the four most important factories in the region. Aiming for the economies of scale, they formed a conglomerate named Textind. After the unification, the factories within Textind still kept great autonomy in determining their production profile and business strategies. Following the decentralizing ethos of workers' self-management, the four professional managements and workers' councils remained highly independent from each other, forming only a coordinating administrative unit at the top. The idea behind the fusion was primarily to unite the marketing efforts and stabilize production by appearing as a larger buyer on the supply side as well as utilizing the common sales network. Textind employed around 6,000 workers throughout the Central Banat district, most of them low-skilled women from the countryside.[28]

The most important founding companies of the new textile conglomerate were "Proleter" (carpet production), "Udarnik" (socks), and "Begej" (hats). However, the most prominent enterprise was certainly the undergarments producer "Sloga". The enterprise employed over 2,500 workers and sold more than half of its output on the foreign markets, in particular women's brassiere and baby apparel. Sloga had already established business connections with the German company "Triumph" by the mid-1960s, sewing bras for this multinational, sending workers to Germany for training and implementing western production technologies. Maintaining close collaboration with its Western partners throughout the 1970s, Sloga also found a lucrative export niche for its products in the Soviet Union, becoming one of the largest factories in Vojvodina and a model export-oriented Yugoslav enterprise during those years.[29]

While Sloga was able to compensate for the closing of the Soviet market in the early 1980s by intensifying its finishing services for Triumph and other

27 Erne, Martinov and Pavlović, *Tekstilna industrija regiona Srednji Banat*, p. 4.

28 *Ibid.*, p. 25.

29 *Ibid.*, p. 23.

Western producers, the smaller factories in the region were gravely affected by the lack of hard currency and supply bottlenecks of the early 1980s. The hope was that by forming a conglomerate, Sloga might pull other producers along in opening toward the EEC market and help the local textile industry overcome the crisis. Yet, as this section will show, the implementation of lon production was not a simple matter in all cases, and even when the contacts with Western European companies were established, the financial results did not always match the high expectations set by earlier successes of classical export to less demanding markets.

The share of lon jobs in Sloga's total exports jumped from 55 to almost 70 percent in the first year of the expanded enterprise, which confirmed the underclothes producer once again as the trendsetter in the Yugoslav textile industry. The socks producer Udarnik managed to sign outward processing deals with three foreign companies in 1982. Two of them came from West Germany, whereas the third was the East German socks producer "Esda".[30] The carpet manufacturer Proleter kept sinking into financial troubles, as there were few production sharing opportunities in its line of business. Proleter's products were not competitive on the Western markets and it kept exporting to the Middle East, even under the production cost, as these were important traditional markets where the company felt it had to maintain a presence. Obtaining raw materials without steady hard currency inflow became an ever-greater challenge and Proleter finished the 1983 business year with a net loss for the first time since its foundation in 1946.[31]

As the socks producer Udarnik was about to find out, a signed production sharing agreement did not guarantee avoiding financial troubles. The foreign contractors were the dominant side in the relationship, dictating prices and imposing tight deadlines. The clothing industry was becoming increasingly trend-oriented, demanding numerous turnover cycles during the business year and constantly changing production specifications. The outward processing scheme was one of the ways for the Western producers to relieve these pressures from their home factories. Over a nearly two-decade long experience in

30 The share of Comecon countries in the total textile outward processing agreements with Yugoslavia was negligible. Yet, in the case of Textind, orders from Hungary, Czechoslovakia and the GDR are often reported in the factory papers. It remains an open question whether these were autonomous production sharing agreements contracted between socialist companies or perhaps a further subcontracting of the existing deals these Eastern European countries made with the Western partners. The finishing services Texting had provided for Esda were compensated in production materials.

31 Kirćanski, B., "Gubici i kako ih prebroditi," *Textind*, May 27, 1983, p. 4.

direct business exchange with Triumph and other Western European companies, Sloga mastered the flexible production and work discipline demanded by lon jobs, but the smaller factories faced numerous problems trying to answer these same challenges in a short period of time.

One of the main issues was certainly the inability and unwillingness of the workforce to follow the intensification of the work processes. In the mid-1980s, Textind managers' chief appeal to the workers was an increase in work discipline, calling for higher piece rate quotas and stricter application of work shifts. As already mentioned, the majority of workers in these textile factories were women commuting to work from the local villages. The sick and maternity leaves in the textile sector were habitually higher than in the rest of the industry due to the poor working conditions and gendered workforce. The peasant workers were also in the habit of using sick leaves as a cover for work on the fields. The managers were well aware of this trend, counting ahead with workforce supply oscillations in the months of peak agricultural works.

In the summer of 1983, however the work absences increased beyond all expectations, with certain Textind workshops reporting up to 80 percent increases in sick leaves in comparison to the previous years. A part of the workforce, especially the older women, were physically unable to follow the increased tempo. Decades of unfavorable working conditions left many workers with chronic diseases and disabilities. Udarnik, for instance, had one of the highest percentages of employed work invalids in the province of Vojvodina, with 8.3 percent of its workforce diagnosed with permanent disabilities. In other workshops, where irregular supply of materials caused production stops and falling wages, workers drifted away to private agriculture in order to supplement their household budgets. The more severe work regimes, prolonging crisis and deteriorating living standards thus triggered mass leaves from the workplace.[32]

Additional problems were inadequate facilities and the constantly changing production orders. In Udarnik, the existing storage space proved too small to accommodate the growing production for export, causing mixing of different sock models and falsely sorted shipments.[33] Different orders for various foreign partners demanded continuous readjusting of the machines, causing pauses in production and grievances of the technicians and shop floor mechanics. It was not only the shop floor workers complaining about the lon jobs. Even though they were starting to be integrated into broader production chains, these were

32 Ćuk, A., "Kako poboljšati radne uslove," *Textind*, June 10, 1983, p. 3.

33 Stančić, J., "Jedini uslov kvalitet," *Textind*, January 31, 1986, p. 6.

still autonomous enterprises maintaining not only sewing, but also higher value added activities, such as engineering and economic departments, selling outlets, designing homemade fashion brands and running independent export networks. The finishing services were taking time and space away from the development of their own programs, degrading the efforts of local white-collar workers who nurtured pride in their own products, just as the manual workers producing them.

As 1983 ended, Udranik seemed to be on the path toward adopting a new model of growth despite the internal resistance. The exported quantities were rising with the help of finishing services. The management planned to sell 5 million pairs of socks via production sharing and an additional 3.6 million pairs through classical export in the following year. The share of Comecon and developing markets was decreasing and only 400,000 pairs were exported to non-convertible currency markets. The factory earned 2 million US $ of hard currency in 1983,[34] yet, the final balance sheet was disappointing. The rising price of raw materials was eating up the entire gain made through foreign trade. At the end of 1983, the net profit made from exports was only 23,000 US dollars. Next year the price of exported goods started to fall amidst the growing number of factories offering finishing services. The Textind paper complained that the company was "giving away socks for free" and that the "entire idea of export has been degraded".[35]

By 1987, the production sharing with the East German company Esta grew to 3 million pairs per year, yet in spring that year the contract was revoked. The pages of Textind's paper claimed Udarnik initiated the contract termination because of the low quality of Esta's materials.[36] However, it is very possible the factory was just saving face in front of its readers and the real reasons were Udarnik's late shipments, dissatisfying product quality and the penalties it was forced to pay as a result. The dynamic of the total export value of Textind's plants over this period shows the plants were losing the initial momentum of lon job contracting. The exports jumped from 14.8 to 17 million US dollars during the first year of merger in 1983, but fell back to 15.4 million US dollars the next year. The downtrend continued, reaching 12.7 million US dollars earned from exports in 1986 and 1987. The internal distribution of foreign trade contracts in 1987 reveals the smaller factories failed to catch up with Sloga. The underwear producer accumulated 56 percent, Udarnik and Begej around 14 percent and Proleter only 8 percent of Textind's total export.

34 Barjaktarević, M., "Sve dalje od tržišta," *Textind*, May 21, 1985, p. 2.

35 *Ibid.*

36 Stančić, J., "Uslugom do deviza," *Textind*, April 19, 1987, p. 8.

In the next section, this chapter will look more closely into the evolving attitudes toward lon jobs among the management and the shop floor workers. It shows how workers and management reacted differently to the increasing pressures of production for export and the emergence of internal conflict. The following section will also situate the enterprise grievances into a broader understanding of the economic crisis of Yugoslav socialism and the effects the new business model had on the system of workers' self-management.

## 3 The "Necessary Evil"

An article published by the factory press in early 1984 vividly described changes brought by lon jobs to Udarnik's shop floor. Textind's journalists noticed how the production hall seemed moribund in the early months of 1983 as the enterprise was unable to procure production materials and workers were often sent home from work, receiving 70 percent of their wages. A couple of months later the situation was altered to a point where all work shifts were in full operation while workers were "buried under the piles of socks".[37]

In order to meet the contracted obligations, the factory management hired new trainees and formed two production units numbering around 250, mostly younger workers, specialized in finishing sewing operations of socks. Still, the machines they used were timeworn while the production process was plagued by sloppy organization and holdups, making it hard to finish orders on time. The management campaigns for technological and work discipline forced the production supervisors to exert more authority and press for an orderly appearance on the shop floor, despite the chaotic work process. This was specially the case when delegations from potential foreign partners were visiting the factory and workers had to make an added effort to represent the factory in the best light.

Facing constant threats of late shipments and penalties, the sloppy production process and inadequate technology had to be overcome through overtime work. Mandatory work weekends or extended shifts in the days before important deadlines were a regular occurrence in the Yugoslav textile industry even during the stable 1970s. However, the former extraordinary measures were becoming a norm by the mid-1980s due to the frantic tempo of lon production. The Yugoslav industrial enterprises usually scheduled collective holidays in the summer, during which the workers could enjoy heavily subsidized stays in the

37 Stančić, J., "Obnavlja se mašinski park," *Textind*, February 10, 1984, p. 7.

enterprise-owned resorts.[38] As of 1984, however, Textind's paper started to report about the allegedly voluntary abstention from holidays among workers from the key work groups and mechanics in order to meet the production targets.[39] In September 1985, the management decided to turn each Saturday into a workday until the end of the year. In December, Sundays were introduced as workdays as well, whereas the final days before the New Year were marked by twenty-four-hour work shifts.[40]

The proliferation of outward processing underlined the implicit divisions between not only different textile factories, but also within single enterprises. Workers' self-management cherished decentralization and efficiency on the market, encouraging each part of the enterprise to maximize its work results autonomously, distinguish itself, and reap the rewards of better work.[41] Workers employed on lon jobs were quick to realize their importance and request better payment and recognition.

Udarnik's specialized divisions for finishing services were of the opinion that other parts of the factory were unfairly appropriating part of the income made by productivity gains in lon production. Calling on their self-management rights, lon workers demanded complete control over the distribution of profits made through outward processing. Various administrative units and less productive parts of the enterprise were allegedly passively relying on the success of export production, thus losing motivation to improve their own work efforts. The request was to prioritize the payment of export specialized units and reward all other workers based on how well they contribute to servicing this most important activity.[42]

Ironically, the introduction of Western-oriented and modern business methods was followed by a short revival of stakhanovite labor culture, which was still marginally present after the introduction of workers' self-management but still to a much lesser extent than in other East European socialist economies. On Udarnik's 1985 factory day celebration, the outward processing departments were promoted as "shock work" units. The individual norm breakers were recognized as "heroes of work" and given silver coins engraved with the portrait of Josip Broz Tito. Unable to answer the demands

38 For trade union and enterprise-organized tourism in Yugoslavia, see Duda, "Workers into Tourists."

39 Miklušev, M., "Prvo Remont pa odmor," *Textind*, July 18, 1985, p. 5.

40 Stančić, J., "Još jedan radni dan," *Textind*, September 27, 1985, p. 3.

41 For income distribution policies and market incentives within workers' self-management, see: Archer and Musić, "When Workers' Self-Management met Neoliberalism."

42 Stančić, J., "Koga stimuliše 'lon' posao," *Textind*, March 9, 1984, p. 9.

for wage increases the management relied on symbolic recognition and attempts to revive old traditions connected to the ideological language and the revolutionary zeal.

Yet, the importance of political work in the factory was waning overall. A report from Sloga's factory communist party cell conference in the summer of 1985 mentioned the delegates showed little interest in discussions with many of the women from direct production bringing their work into the meeting hall, using the time to fix elastic bands on robes in their seats.[43] Of course, political passivity of shop floor workers was not a new phenomenon in Yugoslav factories with highly skilled manual and white-collar male workers traditionally showing more incentive to take part in self-management activities.[44] However, in a situation where business results and payment became less dependent on the political mediation, and where strict productivity measuring made every second spent on the shop floor count, probably more than ever before the party and self-management meetings were becoming a luxury reserved for the professional management.

An additional reason for disinterest was certainly the inability of workers to have their grievances heard among the enterprise elites. As already mentioned, the spread of production sharing was initially greeted with skepticism not only on the shop floor, but also among many political functionaries and experts inside the textile factories. In 1984, talking about lon jobs, Lazar Erne, an economist and member of Textind's managerial board, stated the following in the factory press:

> It is good that the textile industry joined international division of labor on time … but it is bad that the foreign partner can endanger the material existence of all those workers employed under production sharing schemes at any time for political or any other reason. It remains an open question for how long and in what form we should maintain our connections with foreign companies. It is not easy to resolve this dilemma when confronted with falling exports and the shrinking domestic market.

With top management sending out this type of critical messages, the unionists spoke in even sharper words. The same article quoted Vojica Danilov from the municipal trade union organization saying the following:

---

43 Z.D., "Izostala diskusija," *Textind*, June 14, 1985, p. 4.

44 For political participation of blue-collar workers in Yugoslav political institutions, see: Seroka and Smiljković, *Political Organizations in Socialist Yugoslavia*, p. 66.

> If we take into account that our workers in lon production earn approximately 250 German marks, while in Germany an ordinary manual worker earns 1,000 marks, then we do not need any other figures. It is clear that these jobs represent a new form of economic domination of highly developed nations, if not an outright exploitation of our human and technological resources.[45]

The term commonly used inside the factories for outward processing production in these initial years was "necessary evil". It implied the adoption of finishing services for larger Western producers was a downgrade in comparison to the previous models of export-oriented growth, a hurtful and exploitative practice, which the Yugoslav textile industry should not follow as a long-term orientation. In a situation where all alternative markets were shutting down, demand and raw materials became more expensive, there was no other solution to keep the production materials flowing in and the facilities running. Thus, production sharing was openly presented as an involuntary, tactical move, made until the changed circumstances on the global market allowed for a return to more independent growth model.

By the second half of the decade however, this type of critical language was all but gone. The growing restlessness on the shop floor combined with the rising dependency of the Yugoslav textile industry on outward processing contracts changed the political undertones of the management and the overall perspectives for future economic development. An article from the summer of 1986, indicatively titled "Everything for the sake of export", had the following to say:

> In order to succeed we must take into account the global benchmarks of productivity and quality ... it is of the outmost importance that we join the international division of labor as an opportunity for development. We can only benefit from this process.[46]

The article then went on to explain how, by collaborating with foreign companies, the local factories can learn about new materials, new packaging techniques, etc. The importance of work discipline and precision in sewing operations was stressed even more severely than in the initial phases of outward processing orientation. Now however, instead of lon production being placed

45 Z.D., "Samo da je više sirovina," *Textind*, March 23, 1984, p. 2.
46 Stančić, J., "Sve za izvoz," *Textind*, July 13, 1986, p. 4.

in the context of sacrifice for building socialism, the dominant discourse invoked visions of foreign partners as strict, but beneficial teachers helping to spread diligence and enabling the Yugoslav workers to come closer to Western production standards.

The fact that most of the contractors were German companies facilitated the projection of stereotypes about German industriousness to these business relationships. Another text from 1986 recognized that "Germans demand a lot", but argued that they have every right to do so, as they invest materials, organize transport, and it was supposedly only normal that they expected a quality service in return.[47] Thus, the claims of unequal relations of power were pushed aside in the late 1980s. Production sharing was about a mutually beneficial partnership in which the Yugoslav producers were supposed to rise to the challenge and match the quality levels already attained by the foreign companies.

With room for the expression of grievances becoming ever smaller inside the factory, the shop floor workers turned toward self-organization and direct action. In April 1987, 70 workers of Udarnik's outward processing production line went on strike. Strikes were not officially recognized in the Yugoslav labor code and workers usually resorted to this measure in extreme situations.[48] The direct causes for the strike action were late wages and management's demand that workers pay back one part of their previous monthly wage to the company because an important export job failed to materialize and the factory was supposed to pay unexpected penalties abroad. The workers' dissatisfaction burst out during the open negotiations with the management where workers launched a series of accusations. Apart from wage payment, the striking workers demanded to be better informed about the business negotiations with the foreign companies. Assuming foul play, they asked for a list of trips abroad, exact calculations of business dinners and representation expenses, posing the question, who benefits from these business deals.[49] The outward processing contracts were obviously recognized as a problematic practice, yet, apart from the customary suspicion of the management, the exact mechanisms and

47 Stančić, J., "Jedini uslov kvalitet," *Textind*, January 31, 1986, p. 6.

48 Industrial action was seen as a paradoxical occurrence in a self-management economy and it was not recognized by the labor code. Strikes did occur regularly in Yugoslav socialism, at least since the late 1950s, but they were usually small, isolated and of short duration. Amid the prolonged economic crisis, strikes started to become more common in the second half of the 1980s. Still, striking workers could not count on the support of official workers' institutions and undertaking this type of action carried risk of political and legal prosecution. For more on strikes in socialist Yugoslavia see: Jovanov, *Radnički štrajkovi*.

49 Stančić, J., "Obustavom do zaokreta," *Textind*, April 27, 1987, p. 4.

actors responsible for the fact that workers were constantly getting the short end of the stick remained opaque.

One month later, Milica Blagojević, a worker from Udarnik's outward processing production line explained she felt like the more she was working the less she was being rewarded. However, Blagojević did not search for the root of the problem in the nature of the lon jobs, but the egalitarian redistribution of income in the self-management system and its failure to stimulate the most productive workers. In her own words:

> Despite our very best effort, we are not productive enough in the factory and the country as a whole. I have read somewhere Albania is the only European country behind us in productivity. We can and must perform better … it turns out that work and results of work do not determine the success of a factory or single workers. In some cases, those who work less earn much more money and those who work well end up being short. In order to get out of the crisis we must give more attention to ones who make the most effort, we must put an end to *uravnilovka* [income levelling].[50]

As we can see, the grievances over production sharing agreements on the shop floor were not automatically framed in the binary of "exploitative foreigner" and "exploited domestic worker". Without a doubt, many workers were suspicious of the foreign companies and some probably blamed them directly for the crisis, yet, unlike during the first half of the decade, this sentiment was rarely voiced openly. When the strikers examined lon jobs during the negotiations the mistrust was not with the contractors, but chiefly with the local management, allegedly contracting the lon deals for their own enrichment and perks. The last citation shows how another way of conceptualizing the problematic business relationship was to internalize the dominant notions of industriousness and self-blame. The competitive rules of the international textile market were recognized as unavoidable and eventually adopted. The fall of the domestic textile industry in this case was seen as a direct result of Yugoslav socialism's inability to discard the less profitable parts of its economy, raise productivity and catch up with Western production standards.

In a situation where finishing contracts with foreign companies came to be seen as the only hope for the preservation of local textile manufacturing, it was hard to identify this very activity as the cause for the falling living standards.

50 Stančić, J., "Kako da budemo produktivniji," *Textind*, May 28, 1987, 4.

It seems that those groups of younger workers hired and trained for finishing sewing operations were especially prone to adopt this logic, despite, (or exactly due to) the fact that they were exposed the most to market pressure. They could envision themselves profiting from outward processing, if it were not for the bulky, inflexible enterprise structures inherited from the 1970s. Some may have still perceived the lon jobs as the "necessary evil", but there were a growing number of managers and workers who saw them as a necessary outside stimulus for modernizing the Yugoslav textile industry in accordance with global trends.

## 4 Conclusion

This chapter has shown how global production networks influenced labor relations and conditions of work for an entire section of workers in the Yugoslav textile industry years before the fall of the state socialist regimes in Eastern Europe. The production sharing agreements are a common reference point in the research of the post-socialist textile industries. Still, the spread of global production chains in the region took place in specific social, economic and political conditions created by the prolonged crisis of planned economies. Extending the study frame backwards to the late socialist period and seeing how transnational capital interacted with labor in the socialist institutional setting is therefore a worthwhile research agenda. Yugoslavia was the most prominent destination place for production sharing deals between the EEC and Eastern Europe during the 1980s, yet a similar dynamic was well in place in Hungary, Romania, and many other socialist countries.

The reason why Yugoslav textile companies became the prime subcontractors for EEC's outward processing schemes at the time was their experience in dealing with Western companies since the break with the Soviet Union in the late 1940s. As we have seen in the case of Sloga, close business relations with Western European producers were well in place already by the mid-1960s. The Yugoslav manufacturers were very active in acquiring licenses for modern production technologies, starting in the early 1950s, and various forms of cooperation, subcontracting and even joint venture investment inside Yugoslavia ensued in the 1960s and 1970s. Still, the proliferation of outward processing textile agreements marked a qualitative and quantitative shift in these relations. First, the orientation toward production for Western markets became much more widespread in the 1980s. Second, instead of using Western technologies to produce domestic brands finished goods and export them to markets under favorable terms of trade, the production sharing agreements made the self-managed factories enter a much stricter and more controlling relationship with foreign partners.

The outward processing agreements allowed the foreign companies unprecedented influence over the daily business of self-managing factories in which the workers' councils were supposed to regulate management regimes. The internal equipment and the workforce were adjusted to service outside production orders, thereby pushing out the traditional company production programs. The local companies were becoming ever more dependent on lon jobs as they stopped relying on classical export. The foreign partner dictated the export prices and imposed quick turnover rates, thus placing the local enterprises and their work organization under great production strains. Moreover, the finishing factories had little chance for long term planning as the contractors kept the right to break the contract at any point.

In order to be a successful subcontractor, a company had to maintain relations with a great number of potential partners, keep maximum production flexibility and introduce strict work discipline. But, these were usually not specialized subcontractors, but hybrid companies trying to maintain independent in-house product development and classical export, while entering production sharing in order to earn hard currency and obtain production materials. This duality proved unsustainable, as lon jobs were taking away time and space from other production tasks, exposing the inherited divisions inside the factories and drawing new lines of conflict.

The longstanding tensions between the shop floor workers and the management had exacerbated under production sharing, with workers accusing the directors of profiting personally from business relations with West European companies. Another cleavage was the newly created animosity between the factory units specialized in production sharing and other parts of the enterprise dedicated to domestic market and traditional export. In the past, workers' self-management enabled representation, making sure that all sections of the workforce would ultimately gain material benefits from enterprise successes. Moreover, the management knew that the organization of work had to be adjusted in accordance with workers' work capabilities and collective sense of moral economy. The hectic production tempo of outward processing production left little room for internal mediation and joint discussion, thus facilitating industrial conflict. For decades socialist Yugoslavia seemed to strive on integrating collectively owned industry and participatory decision making into capitalist world economy. The spread of outward processing in textile production helped expose the limits of this developmental concept.

## Bibliography

Archer, Rory and Goran Music. "Approaching the Socialist Factory and its Workforce: Considerations from Fieldwork, in (former) Yugoslavia," *Labor History*, 57, 5 (2016).

Archer, Rory and Goran Music. "When Workers' Self-Management met Neoliberalism: Positive Perceptions of Market Reforms among Blue-Collar Workers in late Yugoslav Socialism," in Marsha Siefert (ed.) *Labor in State Socialist Europe after 1945: Contributions to a History of Work* (Budapest, CEU Press, 2020).

Archer, Rory. " 'It was better when it was worst': blue-collar narratives of the recent past in Belgrade," *Social History*, 43, 1 (2018), pp. 30–55.

Bartha, Eszter. *Alienating Labour. Workers on the Road from Socialism to Capitalism in East Germany and Hungary* (New York: Berghahn Books, 2013).

Bonfiglioli, Chiara. "Gender, Labour and Precarity in the South East European Periphery: the Case of Textile Workers in Štip," *Contemporary Southeastern Europe*, 1, 2 (2014), pp. 7–23.

Bonfiglioli, Chiara. *Women and Industry in the Balkans: The Rise and Fall of the Yugoslav Textile Sector* (London: I.B.Tauris, 2019).

Cucu, Alina-Sandra. "Go West: industrial production between socialist flexibility and the capitalist dynamics of the 1970s," online available at: <http://research.gold.ac.uk/28310/>; last accessed June 16, 2020.

Čulahović, Besim. "The Yugoslav Garment and Textile Industry," *Yugoslav Survey: A Record of Facts and Information*, XXXI, 2 (1990), pp. 71–94.

Dima, Adriana. "The evolution of textile and clothing industry – Romania: From Lohn to Loss," *Revista Economica*, 67, 4 (2015), pp. 176–187.

Draganić, Ilija. "Some Problems and Trend in the Development of Yugoslav Textile Industry," *Ekonomika preduzeća*, 7, 8 (1991), pp. 391–405.

Duda, Igor. "Workers into Tourists: Entitlements, Desires, and the Realities of Social Tourism under Yugoslav Socialism," in Hannes Grandits and Karin Taylor (eds), *Yugoslavia's Sunny Side: A History of Tourism in Socialism (1950s–1980s)*, pp. 33–68.

Erne, Lazar, Milorad Martinov and Radoslav Pavlović, *Tekstilna industrija regiona Srednji Banat u vremenu od kraja 19. veka do početka 20. veka* (Art Concept: Zrenjanin, 2009).

Fröbel, Folker, Jürgen Heinrichs and Otto Kreye. *Die Neue Internationale Arbeitsteilung: Strukturelle Arbeitslosigkeit in den Industrieländern und die Industrialisierung der Entwicklungsländer* (Hamburg: Rowohlt, 1977).

Grama, Adrian and Susan Zimmerman. "The art of link-making in global labour history: subaltern, feminist and Eastern European contributions," *European Review of History: Revue européenne d'histoire*, 25, 1 (2017), pp. 1–20.

Jovanov, Neca. *Radnički štrajkovi u Radnički štrajkovi u SFRJ od 1958. do 1969. godine.* (Belgrade: Zapis, 1979).

Lampland, Martha. *The Object of Labor: Commodification in Socialist Hungary* (Chicago: University of Chicago Press, 1995).

Lampland, Martha. *The Value of Labor: The Science of Commodification in Hungary, 1920–1956* (Chicago: University of Chicago Press, 2016).

Luginbühl, Christa and Bettina Musiolek. "Stitched up: Poverty wages for garment workers in Eastern Europe and Turkey," Clean Clothes Campaign Report (2014).

Musiolek, Bettina. "Tools for Enforcing Labour Rights and Ensuring Corporate Social Responsibility in the Garment Sector: The South-East European Context," *SEER-South-East Europe Review for Labour and Social Affairs*, 3, 3 (2000), 123–35.

Plank, Leonhard, Cornelia Staritz and Karin Lukas. "Labour Rights in Global Production Networks: An Analysis of the Apparel and Electronics Sector in Romania," Kammer für Arbeiter und Angestellte für Wien (2009).

Pula, Besnik, *Globalization Under and After Socialism: The Evolution of Transnational Capital in Central and Eastern Europe* (Stanford: Stanford University Press, 2018).

Rostowski, Jacek. "Comparing two Great Depressions: 1929–33 to 1989–93," in Salvatore Zecchini (ed.), *Lessons from the Economic Transition: Central and Eastern Europe in the 1990s* (Dordrecht: Kluwer Academic Publishers, 1997), pp. 225–241.

Seroka, Jim and Radoš Smiljković, Political Organizations in Socialist Yugoslavia (Durham: Duke University Press, 1986).

Smith, Adrian and John Pickles. "Global value chains and business models in the central and eastern European clothing industry," in Béla Galgóczi, Jan Drahokoupil and Magdalena Bernaciak (eds), *Foreign investment in eastern and southern Europe after 2008. Still a lever of growth?* (Brussels: European Trade Union Institute, 2015), 319–53.

United States International Trade Commission, *Production Sharing: U.S. Imports Under harmonized Tariff Schedule Subheadings 9802.00.60 and 9802.00.80, 1985–1988* (Washington, DC: USITC, 1989).

Vodopivec, Nina. "Textile Workers in Slovenia: From Nimble Fingers to Tired Bodies," *Anthropology of East Europe Review*, 28, 1 (2010), pp. 165–183.

CHAPTER 11

# Uneven Development in the European Automotive Industry

## *Labor Fragmentation and Value-Added Production in the Hungarian Semi-periphery*

*Tamás Gerőcs, Tibor T. Meszmann and András Pinkasz*

## 1 Introduction

Since the global economic crisis of 2008, automotive production has been increasingly relocated from Western Europe to Eastern Europe, leading to a growing demand for semi-skilled labor.[1] This process was especially visible in the relocation of automotive MNC plants from Germany to some regions of Hungary. Moreover, it is not only capital that has become increasingly mobile in the recent years, but labor too. One of the major push factors behind labor migration in Eastern Europe has been the opening of EU labor markets and the wage gap between Western and Eastern European labor markets. As Altreiter et al.[2] underlined, this dual mobility – i.e. capital and labor – causes disembeddedness in employment relations. These challenges have made new tasks for manufacturing companies to both organize production and extract surplus value, and also for trade unions to represent the sometimes conflicting interests of workers. Our general question is whether we can still observe a reproduction of the dependencies characteristic to the semi-periphery, and if so, what concepts may help us in analyzing the mechanisms of this reproduction in labor relations.

We examine whether a sub-national region in the semi-periphery can reach the 'high road work model.' Besides observing changes in value-added in production, we also integrate organized labor into our inquiry, where strong labor interest representation is a key component. Our research design and analysis prioritized the latter criteria: we selected local subsidiaries of transnational companies with private governance strategies that provide ground

1 Pavlínek, "Foreign Direct Investment and the Development"; Krzywdzinski, "Automation, Skill Requirements."

2 Altreiter et al., "Capital and Labour on the Move."

 | DOI:10.1163/9789004448049_012

for unionization and worker representation, therefore creating the prospect of a high road model. Thus, we could explore whether negotiations between unions and companies have taken new directions, and whether labor interest representation indicates an upgrade.

We analyze the question not only from the point of view of industrial sociologists, but also address it from a more global and encompassing perspective by applying the concept of uneven development. Based on the concept of uneven development, we see that the high road and low road work models – seemingly separable – are complementary parts of the same global system. Moreover, we argue that in order to understand why labor representation develops in a particular way in a particular location, we need to bring in the perspective of value chain governance. The latter includes concrete production in which labor is organized, and therefore it is the context in which the particular form of representation also occurs. The global automotive value chain breaks down into a hierarchical system where firms attempt to improve competencies and also to the particular context of industrial relations in which workers struggle for the representation of their interests. These struggles are intertwined and sometimes in opposition, but nevertheless are embedded in the wider structure of value chain.

In this chapter we first show that, irrespective of massive relocation to the Hungarian sub-region, value-added production stagnated. Moreover, contrary to what industrial sociologists describe as a limited upgrading to the high road work model in Eastern Europe, we see no evidence for real improvement in terms of labor interest representation.[3] We investigate what this so-called 'limited high road model' really means for workers in practice, and what the possibilities and obstacles are when enhancing labor representation vis-á-vis capital.

Our aim in this chapter is to understand the impact of the automotive value chains' global expansion strategy on the Hungarian labor market. To add additional depth, we have supplemented our country-level assessment with an additional case study focused on four supplier companies from a county of the Central Transdanubian region. We use macro-statistics to assess changes in production and interviews with workers and union representatives to assess the development of labor representation. Although we do not address the way certain managerial decisions are made, we do introduce the concept of rent-seeking, which combines both the hierarchical structure of production and the sphere of labor relations.

3 Jürgens and Krzywdzinski, "Work Models."

The chapter is structured in the following way: in the next section we elaborate on the concept of uneven development, while taking into account industrial sociologists' findings in different economic locations. The social-institutional case to which we apply our theory is the Hungarian automotive industry in the period since the global economic crisis. In the third we point out regional production hierarchies; in section four, using concepts of industrial sociologists, especially the high road and low road work models, we study the development of labor relations within the value chains of particular automotive enterprises since the global economic crisis. Our aim here is to determine why organized labor was not able to bring an upgrading mechanism into motion. As is also discussed in more detail in the concluding section, our research found that fragmentation is a key force behind production and labor models with which trade unions were unable to cope. Although there are signs that unions have strengthened since 2016, due to the recent extremely tight labor market, the prospects for labor representation and for corresponding upgrading are rather gloomy.

## 2 Theoretical Framework: Industrial Sociology Combined with Uneven Development and Value Chain Analysis

To analyze the organization of production and labor relations in the Hungarian automotive industry, we use the categorization of two work models of industrial sociologists.[4] The first is the high road work model – 'constructive competitiveness' – which, because companies are interested in taking a long-term, investment-oriented attitude towards employee training and significant job security, involves high levels of employee expertise and long-term skill and competence development. The second is the low road work model – 'destructive competitiveness' – that implies low labor costs, employment of semi-skilled labor, highly limited skill formation, low job security, and weak interest representation of workers. In these models, it is the strength of labor interest representation that is key to guaranteeing the emergence of a constructive or destructive model. While studying the relocation of German automotive subsidiary plants to Eastern Europe, Krzywdzinski and Jürgens found that the high road work model characteristic to labor relations in Germany was only being transferred to a limited extent to Eastern Europe.[5]

4 Singenberger and Pyke, "Industrial Districts"; Krzywdzinski, "Work Models," p. 4.
5 Jürgens and Krzywdzinski, "Work Models."

Going a step further, we want to understand recent developments but also to consider the structural factors that are shaping the prospects of a high road work model. For this purpose we rely on the theory of uneven development and the Global Value Chain (GVC) framework. Combined with the GVC framework, uneven development is a critical concept that highlights the spatial-geographical component in order to analyze the highly uneven distribution of value-added within a production chain at given localities during the process of global capital accumulation.[6] For example, global lead firms, as well as sectors, use various instruments, including global value chains, to reinforce and reproduce center-periphery relations[7] (Milberg 2007). Moreover, uneven development denotes a power relation that appears in a hierarchical structure, but also an interconnectedness of the seemingly separate work models within the international division of labor. The GVC framework helps us in a dynamic analysis of development(s). It is not only the structure that is of interest but also those exploitative mechanisms through which the above mentioned hierarchies are constantly reproduced. The core issue in the analysis of these mechanisms is the creation and appropriation of (surplus) value. Moreover, the analysis of the multi-scalar system has to consider questions of accessibility to the state of the art technologies, world market opportunities and financial dependence.[8]

From this global perspective, however, the asymmetries in the labor relations highlighted by industrial sociologists are usually missing, or at least underexplored within the GVC framework.[9] Despite its limitations, the GCC framework has allowed analysts to include discussion on labor conditions, particularly within the categories of rent-seeking, power and the (dis)embeddedness of workers, in/from the hierarchical structure of global production.[10] The GCC framework includes the broader social-institutional context in which labor relations are embedded, or from which these relations become disembedded.[11] Thus, this approach incorporates the vocabulary of industrial sociology

6 For a thorough review of the concept and the harmonization of GVC/GCC approach and its economic geographical critique, Global Production Network (GPN), see: Hess, "Investigating the archipelago economy" and Bair, "Global Capitalism and Commodity Chains."

7 Milberg, "Shifting Sources and Uses of Profits."

8 On finance see: Gereffi and Evans, "Transnational Corporations"; on Eastern European development see: Gerőcs and Pinkasz, "Debt-Ridden Development."

9 For a major exception see: Newsome, *et al.*, (eds) *Putting Labour in Its Place. Labour Process Analysis and Global Value Chains.*

10 Werner and Bair, "Loosing our Chains."

11 Hess, "'Spatial' Relationship?"

to deal with issues such as the role of unions, employment relations etc. in a regional context.

In this chapter, we hypothesize that these hierarchies reproduce over time, especially during global and sector level crises. High road and low road work models are interconnected and can be identified with particular positions in the same value chain. Although most industrial policy experts expect the high road work model to adapt,[12] in our understanding, none of the models are transferable independently from the structure of production at the particular location in the value chain. Companies of a given industry – which are at the same time participants in multinational enterprises' value chains – position themselves at various locales in the production process, a movement that might be also understood as rent-seeking.[13] Rent-seeking comprises of a diverse pool of features, including monopolies or technological advantage, brand ownership, policy protection or any other activity which is related not only to production in a narrow sense, but to the form of integration into global value chains.

We analyze the uneven development of automotives in Hungary in a production cluster in order to test the reproduction of the dependency relation. We do this in two steps. First, we empirically analyze value-added production, as is suggested by GVC scholars;[14] second, to assess labor representation we analyze labor relations in the automotive supply chain at different levels (from Tier 1 to Tier 3) in one of the most highly industrialized regions (Central Transdanubia) in Hungary. We argue that these components, value-added production and labor relations, are inseparable and good indicators for understanding both dependencies, and at a different level, these two components indicate the rent-seeking strategies of companies that participate in the chain.

The economic and social aspects of work have changed in accordance with new modes of integration of international division of labor.[15] Since the 1980s, new forms of uneven development have emerged as a consequence of the overproduction crisis in manufacturing.[16] This has forced automotive companies – among others – to seek new solutions to fierce competition. One strategic response to the crisis was technological, i.e. the standardization of the

12 Krzywdzinski, "Work Models"; Boyer and Freyssenet, *The Productive Models*.
13 Kaplinsky, "Globalization, Industrialization"; Henderson *et al.*, "Global Production Networks," pp. 448–450.
14 Sturgeon *et al.*, "Direct Measurement of Global Value Chains."
15 Fröbel *et al.*, *Krisen in der kapitalistischen Weltökonomie*.
16 Gereffi and Korzeniewicz, *Commodity Chains and Global Capitalism*; Gereffi, "Global Value Chains."

traditional 'Fordist' mass production, which culminated in the fragmentation of production and the subsequent global reintegration of production processes through international trade.[17] Sources of rent and the distribution of the volume of realized value-added in the value chain changed radically. It was after the regime change of 1989 that countries in Eastern Europe were reintegrated into the new structures of international division of labor. Fragmentation of production on a global scale affected production profiles in the region. Hungary, among other countries, witnessed rapid relocation as a consequence of the fragmentation of production and the global expansion of value chains. The country has provided opportunities for lower value-added segments of the production process, which had been exposed to overproduction and relocation from the West.[18] Specialization in low-value-added activities has had significant consequences for the economy in general and for the emerging work models in Hungary in particular. In the next section we look into this specialization from the perspective of value-added production in the 1995–2016 period. The fourth section addresses specialization from the perspective of labor relations and its consequences for labor representation.

## 3 Fragmentation of Production: Value-Added

In this section we investigate the production of value-added that is determined by world economic hierarchies in order to link particular labor relations to the evolution of the global automotive value chain. In a model distinction, the production process can be divided into high value-added and low value-added activities. High value-added activities that can be characterized by the high road work model require a highly skilled labor force for which there is competition in the market. Skilled labor is therefore almost always in relative shortage and access to this labor pool is limited. Companies need to attract skilled labor. In order to retain skilled labor they must sustain generous investments in their employment relations such as those suggested by the high road work model. High labor investments are responsible for embedded labor relations. One characteristic is a low level of labor turnover. An integral part of embedded labor relations is a high rate of unionization. A high union density rate translates both into bargaining strength vis-á-vis the company attempting to attract labor, but also into long-term investments and settlements that are guaranteed

17 Feenstra, "Integration of Trade."
18 Cf. Gerőcs and Pinkasz, "Debt-Ridden Development."

by permanent contracts. Furthermore, there is a geographical concentration of high value-added activities in the center of production. These activities are the least transferable precisely because of limited access to the skilled workforce, which is usually available in industrial clusters where they are able to perform high value-added manufacturing activities.[19]

Contrary to high value-added activities performed by skilled labor at the core of production, asymmetrical specialization in lower value-added activities concentrate in other geographies, typically those on the periphery, such as Hungary. In peripheral positions, production profits are sustained by cheaper and more flexible labor, therefore rents are more exploitative in these geographic regions. Cheap labor is more abundant, though much less skilled.[20]

The volume of value-added is a market price based numerical measure; therefore we can make our calculation for individual companies and for an industrial average as well. We refer to 'value-added' based on the definition of economic statistics, i.e. the difference between Output (net sales without goods and services for resales) and Intermediate Consumption (expenses for raw materials, intermediaries and services).[21] The Gross Value-Added in the equation (after being corrected by the tax base) is split between compensation of employees and capital income. We must underline that value-added is a constituent of a given, usually non-market price-system, in which companies are already pursuing rent-seeking strategies, e.g. through intra-company transfer pricing. Subsequently, prices and the value-added itself exhibit forms of various rent-seeking behavior.

Gross Value-Added (GVA) is measured in the share of output. In the case of the Hungarian automotive industry we have found relatively low levels of value-added production. The industrial average has been between 18–20 percent (see Figure 11.1), which is below the average of 25–30 percent in manufacturing. It is interesting to note that prior to the world economic crises we found a decreasing tendency of value-added production of 25–28 percent in the automotive industry in Germany, but since the crisis there has been a recovery. We suspect the reason is the relocation of production. Namely, lower value-added activities have been transferred to Eastern Europe, whereas Germany

19 High value-added activities typically include research, product development and branding. Szanyi *et al.*, "Cluster Development."

20 We do not need to presume that skills are always optimally priced and used. As a legacy of the structural crises during the Eastern European transition, highly skilled workers became underemployed, or employed for tasks that required a lower level of qualification than what they had. In short, labor can be both cheap and skilled as several examples show in the region.

21 We use the categorization of the UN System of National Accounts.

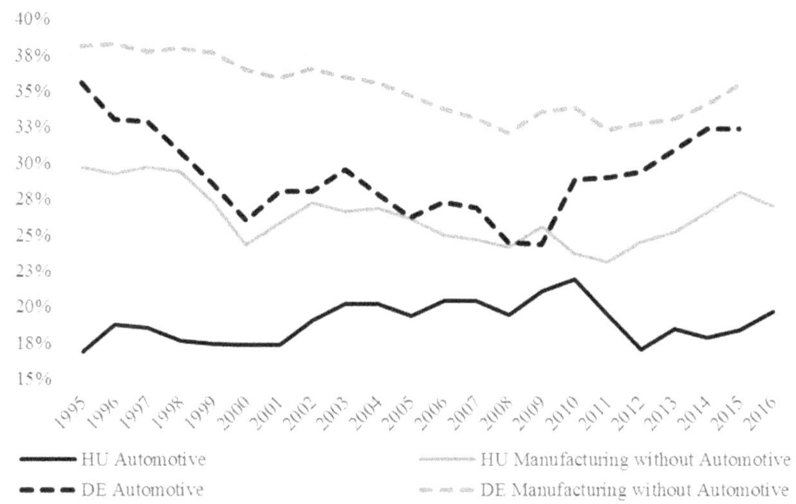


FIGURE 11.1 Gross Value-Added (GVA) in the share of output
SOURCE: EUROSTAT

specialized in higher value-added activities. During the crises years, especially between 2009 and 2012, we saw a temporary upward trend in Hungary too, but this does not contradict the long-term tendency. In fact, the tendency of decreasing value-added has reappeared since 2012. It is not certain what caused the temporary uptick. We suspect that the average level of output must have fallen more than what companies could adjust to by reducing the wage sum of the workforce.

Neither the average GVA/Output in the county of our research, nor the company level data of the four companies studied, deviate from the national average (see Table 11.1).

We see relocation as the driving force behind the fragmentation of production. Automotive companies in German headquarters have been able to specialize in high value-added activities as part of the management's global rent-seeking strategy. They relocated low value-added activities to Eastern European countries and as a consequence, Hungary emerged as a destination for low value-added activities in the automotive industry, pushing average value-added production below even the industrial average of manufacturing in the country. Comparatively low average wages have had serious consequences for labor relations. As Drahokoupil and Piasna[22] argue, despite differences in

22 Drahokoupil and Piasna, "Dependent Market Economies."

TABLE 11.1 Automotive industry in Hungary

| Year | Case study | | Central Transdanubia | | National economy | |
|---|---|---|---|---|---|---|
| | GVA / output | Weigh (GVA) | GVA / output | Weigh (GVA) | GVA / output | Weigh (GVA) |
| 2013 | 17,5% | 3,8% | 16,6% | 5,7% | 18,4% | 100,0% |
| 2014 | 19,6% | 3,9% | 16,5% | 5,3% | 17,8% | 100,0% |
| 2015 | 19,4% | 3,6% | 16,7% | 5,3% | 18,3% | 100,0% |
| 2016 | 21,3% | 3,9% | 18,7% | 6,4% | 19,6% | 100,0% |
| 2017 | 14,9% | 2,5% | 15,2% | 5,0% | 19,3% | 100,0% |

SOURCE: EUROSTAT, PROFIT AND LOSS STATEMENTS, OWN CALCULATION

productivity levels, i.e. skill and technological performances, wages are still undervalued in Eastern Europe compared to their western counterparts, which is not only the outcome of different value-added activities but the consequence of historical and political struggles.[23]

## 4 Fragmentation of Labor: Labor Relations

Lipietz[24] observed that a new hierarchy of labor regimes emerged in reaction to the exhaustion of the Fordist production model in the West. Our empirical findings in Hungary verify his observations. We discovered that fragmentation of labor and the subsequent disembeddedness of labor relations are dominant in the lower value-added segments of production. There has been a flexibilization in the labor regulation[25] that has further strengthened the fragmentation of the workforce. Our research on labor relations in Hungarian automotives showed that fragmentation of both production and labor relations is the

23 "In this context, both employees and firms can enjoy rents from their market power. Such rents are then split between employers and employees in the bargaining process over wages. High-profitability firms can thus be expected to pay higher wages. The low rate of unionization and higher levels of unemployment are likely to undermine the market power of employees, and this has often been seen as an explanation for the low wage share that can be observed in many CEE [Central and Eastern European] countries" (Drahokoupil and Piasna, "Dependent Market Economies").

24 Lipietz, "The Post-Fordist World," p. 2.

25 Laki *et al.*, "Az új Munka Törvénykönyvének."

crucial component-drive that structurally destroys prospects of constructive labor representation.

We can see workers' or 'workforce' fragmentation evolving in the Hungarian labor market. Beyond the low level of unionization described by the low road work model, fragmentation is manifest in cyclical developments affecting the labor market participation of various social groups.[26] Since 2016, when a new cycle began in Hungary, we have been witnessing a systemic realignment in the flexible labor regime along the geographical expansion of the automotive global value chain. This new cycle affects not only negotiations between labor and capital, but also impacts on intra-labor relations. One consequence of these processes has been an overall upward pressure on wages in manufacturing. Negotiating for higher wages caused conflicts among workers as former wage category systems required modifications, causing new grounds for competition and cooperation among the various segments of the fragmented workforce. As Altreiter et al.[27] have demonstrated, "workforce fragmentation leads to rivalry among workers and makes solidarity difficult". One cause of labor dissatisfaction was articulated in intra-labor relations, instead of capital-labor negotiations, which clearly undermined the power of the union.

The drive behind wage increases stems not only from the workers' increased bargaining power but also from the strategic needs of capital. There are companies facing increased pressure and competition for labor, which drives an increase in wages. The threat of industrial disobedience, strike action, or any other form of labor militancy has been relatively absent in the Hungarian automotive industry. As a result, companies have been capable of managing their employment relations with control over wage hikes despite the sudden shift in the economic cycle.

Both companies and unions had to accommodate their strategies in accordance with the acceleration of relocation and the subsequent labor shortage. The greatest pressure was on the workers, therefore, from a systemic point of view, the unions' strategic response was telling. In what follows, we elaborate on the development of this strategic response in order to better understand its potential and the limitations it encountered.

Observing general developments in Hungarian manufacturing, with a special focus on four automotive supplier companies, we found that workforce fragmentation put labor representation in a weak state, in turn also ruining prospects of upgrading. The main obstacle for accurate labor representation,

26 Beblavý *et al.*, "Linking Labour Regimes."

27 Altreiter *et al.*, "Capital and Labour on the Move," pp. 81–82.

i.e. for a general articulation of the interests of all workers regardless of their position in the production, was the high degree of workforce fragmentation embedded in flexible and unstable industrial relations.

According to our study, labor fragmentation emerges in the automotive industry along three dividing lines: insiders versus outsiders; blue-collar versus white-collar; and old versus new employees. The first division has traditionally been the result of the default strategy of plant level trade unions in Hungarian manufacturing, which has been following and protecting the interests of core workers, in other words, insiders.[28] This was especially true during the acute crisis year of 2009, when unions barely questioned the dismissal of agency and fixed term temporary workers, or of other outsiders, and concentrated on the protection of core employees. Some of the largest companies, in agreement with local unions, ensured the protection and job security of their core skilled workers.[29] Typically, trade unions were not able to find ways of challenging insourcing while maintaining the core competencies of the skilled workforce.[30] That is, solidarities also did not spread beyond the workplace. When the hiring process restarted and grew exponentially from 2012/2013, employers were increasingly hired on atypical contracts: either on fixed term contracts or indirectly through temporary agencies. The main strategy of trade unions was to try to restrict the use of atypical employment forms, and gently convince individual employers that workers on permanent contracts are more committed and loyal. Workers on atypical contracts were usually more difficult to organize. Incorporation of outsiders – especially temporary agency workers – was not at all common in the automotive sector, but more prevalent in some large plants in the electronics sector.[31]

The second division and a potential labor-labor conflict occurs at plants that also have significant R&D functions in product development. These are special divisions between 'replaceable' semi-skilled blue-collar workers on the ground floor of the production line and engineers and office workers on the first floors or in separate buildings, where the former are often unionized and the latter are typically not. Most commonly, unions are unable to recruit white-collar workers or convince them to take part in work council elections. Among white-collar workers, individual bargaining is the norm. Nonetheless, when white-collar workers are unionized, it seems more likely that they would have a separate union, resulting in a situation that could lead to potential conflict.

28 Crouch, "Labour Market Governance."
29 Neumann and Boda, "A válság hatása"; Neumann, "Az új Mt. a munkahelyen."
30 Cf. Crouch, "Labour Market Governance."
31 Meszmann, "The Rise of Dual Labour Market."

The most recent visible case of this kind of conflict in Hungary appeared during Mercedes wage negotiations in Kecskemét, preceding a strike, when a union of white-collar workers – organized in another union – reached an agreement with management and in the process sidelined the most numerous representative union of blue-collar workers.[32]

The third labor-labor division and potential conflict continues to emerge, arising from a situation of intense competition and anarchic struggle for new workers/entrants. From 2017, 80 percent of manufacturers complained that they had to reduce production capacities due to a lack of workers.[33] Whereas companies attempts to hire new entrants with comparatively high wages on the production line, at times even higher than those of its own core trained workers – simultaneously lowering qualification requirements – feeds resentment towards both new entrants and management. A major resentment among core workers is that new employees are hired with the same hourly wage as more experienced employees who have proven to be loyal. Another issue is that many recently hired temporary workers are from foreign countries and are offered free housing.[34]

At the core of all labor representation problems in Hungary lies an underlying paradigm of business unionism.[35] Neither plant level nor sectorial level unions can find ways to voice an autonomous vision or strategy regarding more encompassing industrial development. Unions are concentrated on plant level bargaining. In the present situation of tight labor market, management offer concessions to plant level trade unions in order to handle the difficult period. Industrial conflicts, particularly capital-labor conflicts, first appeared in late 2016, with many large automotive companies facing strikes and strike threats. However, cleavages, division, and hidden conflicts in the workplace have reduced the chances and scope of a constructive and prolonged battle.

32 See Autopro.hu's news: „Az MTSZSZ bérmegállapodást kötött a kecskeméti Mercedes gyárral," available at <https://autopro.hu/gyartok/Az-MTSZSZ-bermegallapodast-kotott-a-kecskemeti-Mercedes-gyarral/20722/>; last accessed 30 January, 2018.

33 See Napi.hu's news: "Tömegek mondanak fel a magyar munkahelyeken," available at: <https://www.napi.hu/magyar_gazdasag/tomegek_mondanak_fel_a_magyar_munkahelyeken_elvadult_a_helyzet.649110.html>; last accessed 30 January, 2018. See also G7's news: "A régióban panaszkodnak, Magyarországon sírva üvöltenek a cégek a létszámhiány miatt," available at: <https://g7.24.hu/allam/20171030/a-regioban-panaszkodnak-magyarorszagon-sirva-uvoltenek-a-cegek-a-letszamhiany-miatt/>; last accessed 30 January, 2018.

34 Meszmann, "Temporary Agency Work."

35 Frege and Tóth, "Institutions Matter."

The three dividing lines that cause fragmentation among workers occur with various intensity depending on positive and negative economic and regulatory cycles. This was most visible in 2009, when the protective-insider line strengthened as the main agenda for the union was to obtain job security for its members and the core workforce. However, since 2016, with labor force shortages and flexible legislation in place, we have seen that these privileges have deteriorated dramatically. Fragmentation also overlaps to a certain extent with social groups and spatial categories of workers (e.g. migrant, commuting vs. local workers). The result has been that such fragmentation has hampered prospects of inclusion or integration and thus also the bargaining position of workers.

Apart from the industrial trends in Hungary mentioned above, we have also compared the labor relation characteristics of four companies in different positions, specialized in the German automotive value chains. Our aim with this research was to understand how this specialization circumscribes labor relations and how unions adjust to? We conducted interviews with union representatives from a large Tier 1 company, as well as union representatives from three small to medium-sized companies: two Tier 2 companies and one Tier 3 company among automotive supplier companies from the Central Transdanubian region.

The Tier 1 (1,000+ employees) and the two medium-sized Tier 2 (250+ employees) companies are multinational. Semi-automated production with limited value-added is characteristic of these companies; short duration of training (two months), expansion in the volume of production, especially in the case of the Tier 1 company. All companies began production prior to the EU accession, and up until the global economic crisis all had experienced stable production. Meanwhile, employers enjoyed high social prestige and were respected as being law abiding and for providing generous wage levels. Gradual or wave-like expansion in production was characteristic of all companies, whereas improvement in technological endowments was limited. The Tier 1 company and the larger of the Tier 2 companies doubled their production. However, the relocation of some operations was retrospectively considered a drawback to the relative status of the plant within the multinational company. Namely, the relocated production lines generated very little income. The Tier 1 company also had 500 white-collar workers in a separate R&D facility.

In contrast, the Tier 3 company is a previously state owned, privatized company, with Hungarian ownership that has gradually reduced its employment without affecting production. Its position in the automotive supply chain deteriorated in the late 1990s. It lost its Tier 2 status and moved to Tier 3, resulting in greater reorientation towards other industrial sectors. The company has been suffering from a lack of capital, exemplified also by poor (dusty, noisy) working conditions. The company therefore could not afford to offer higher wages and has lower prestige. For decades it has mostly employed women on the production lines, paying them the minimum wage.

We detected the effects of fragmentation concerning the social division of labor and the forms of labor representation at play in all four companies analyzed. We found that companies have benefited from the fragmentation of labor from the start. Moreover, fragmentation has further increased with environmental shocks, regulatory changes as well as changes in plant-level labor relations. Also, unions only emerged as vocal actors relatively late in the history of the plants, and they were thus unable to influence work models from the beginning. Unions started to represent interests in crisis periods, and they only represented a segment of insiders.

Changes in company strategies toward production and labor relations also demonstrate features of uneven development. There was a fragmentation in the employment structure of 'our' case studies, mirroring social division of work and various spatial and social inequalities within the hierarchical structure of global value chains. In recent years, in the Tier 1 company, among production workers, there have been comparatively more female workers (the assessment had a 60 to 40 ratio), which is a change from previous years. White-collar workers, especially engineers, are predominantly male. Even more pronounced was the share of women in the larger Tier 2 company (80 percent), which, although employing a total of 750 women, only about 75 percent of those were full time. Young mothers receiving child-care benefit were more often working part time jobs and they were typically employed on separate production lines. The smaller Tier 2 company remained relatively stable on the 2006 level, employing about 300 workers, of which about 250 worked in production. Since physical strength was a prerequisite of the job, the production workers were unanimously male, the core of whom were long-term employees in their 40s. Whereas originally the company had only employed locals and commuters, temporary agency workers and new direct employees came from a less visible social strata, and often lacked education and work-qualification requirements. The Tier 3 company had 120 employees at the time of the interview, the majority of which were women, production workers, and specifically assembly line workers (85–90). Most of them were close to retirement age, and a small number had returned to work as retirees via temporary agencies (students were also working during summer breaks) after decades of working in the plant. The major change here, as in the smaller Tier 2 company, is that although earlier temporary and agency workers had been hired on a large scale (also via chain contracting and with at least 20 percent temporary agency workers), this practice has ended in the last year, and all employees are now on permanent standard employment contracts. In all analyzed companies, with the partial exception of the Tier 1 company, trade union members, trustees, and representatives formed a closed group of long-term employees with no connection to outsiders or temporary agency workers. In the smaller Tier 2 company and in the Tier 3 company, it appeared that the union was an association of a closed circle of long time colleagues, with limited interest in representative functions. In the 2009–2014 period, temporary workers in the Tier 1 company were isolated and without job security whereas white-collar workers were entirely segregated, and impossible for the union to access. Since 2016, core workers in the Tier 1 and larger Tier 2 companies have considered the competitive entry wage bid for newcomers to be an insult. While some realigned as a new core, many others left the labor market.

Labor fragmentation was intensified by flexibilization and instability of labor relations. In the Tier 1 company, the first major change towards flexibilization occurred around the EU accession in 2004–2005. Under the pretext of increasing competitiveness, a multiple-shift workforce scheduling model was developed: thus securing a larger work base with minimal workforce. It also included the introduction of working Saturdays without supplementary compensation, as well as radically reducing overtime and the corresponding recompense. The global economic crisis of 2008/09 and its immediate aftermath brought about further changes in flexibility. The company only made minimum reductions to its core workforce for a few months in 2009. In addition, a reduced working time of 32 hours per week was introduced. Soon thereafter, production recovered, but with major cuts in compensation. Most notably, technicians and skilled workers found that their tariff category had undergone a negative change, and they experienced status degradation. An extended reference period, or "working time frame", was also introduced to calculate average working time so that in the first few years there would be no supplements for overtime work. In practical terms, this meant that worker income decreased or could only be sustained by adapting to flexible work. Although production soon started to peak, wage negotiations were still modest.

After the adoption of the new Labor Code, the newly concluded collective agreement of 2013 maximized the threshold of overtime work to 300 hours annually.[36] Such flexibilization also brought about significant shop floor collisions: employees found it increasingly difficult to reconcile family and work,

36 The overarching reform of the 2012 labor code made it possible for companies to extend working time frames and force overtime work when demand is high but put workers into un- or underpaid idle when demand is low. Further restrictions were enacted by 2018 amendments, called the Slave Law by the Hungarian public: companies can now demand up to 400 hours of overtime work, and to delay payments up to 3 years.

while production workers had daily conflicts with immediate superiors due to improper address and poor treatment of employee requests. Blue-collar workers who experienced the regulatory changes of the 2009–2013 period felt that the company added insult to long-standing injuries. After 2013, as many loyal workers felt betrayed and left the workplace, labor turnover gradually increased, first with the British and then followed by other Western EU level migration.

As flexibilization intensified fragmentation, the question is to what extent did labor unions or organized labor in the analyzed companies attempt to overcome forces of fragmentation, and prevent potential labor-labor cleavages. Typically, active labor representation started late in 'employee-friendly' workplaces. It is intriguing that in two cases, instead of general conflicts, labor-labor conflicts prompted the established formal or more active representation of the interests of organized workers. Only recently, with the trade union playing a more active role, did management finally address some of the grievances. The forms of labor representation varied in the four companies. There were existing works councils in all the companies,[37] but in all foreign companies, work councils were established before a meaningful, representative trade union organization. In two cases, the Tier 1 and the larger Tier 2 companies, unions had either only recently been established or have only started to play a more meaningful role in the last few years – after internal conflicts had occurred. But in the case of the smaller Tier 2 company, internal conflict led to the formation of a union in 2006, despite a works council already being in place. Whereas the union remained, the works council did not operate in 2017 due to lack of interest. Characteristic to all three union representatives was a positive acknowledgment of the Western work model, specifically in the praise of the foreign, mostly German managers. Changes in management (a criticism against younger, Hungarian managers and HR personnel was typically voiced), and also external shocks seemed to push towards self-organization and unionization.

37 Since 1992, the workplace in Hungary (more precisely, a company or a separate division, part of the company operating independently that employs more than 50) could have a dual worker representation system. Besides the plant level trade unions, the work councils have a more pronounced role in consultation and requesting information affecting jobs and incomes. Co-determination powers of work councils are restricted only to the distribution of the company social funds. The recent changes in Labor Code weakened the power of local trade unions, and only partially compensated the work councils. Since 2012, the local union representative is no longer responsible for monitoring compliance with the provisions of employment regulations – this right has passed to the works council. For more details see: <https://www.worker-participation.eu/National-Industrial-Relations/Countries/Hungary/Workplace-Representation>.

Neither of the two Tier 2 companies have a collective agreement. In the Tier 3 company, the trade union was an inherited union from the previous era. Since this company was the smallest, and in terms of employment numbers, the most constant, all these factors appeared to have contributed to good union-management relations, and regular consultations. Nevertheless, as noted by the union official, collective bargaining was reduced to a minimum over the years. Both Tier 2 companies had a narrow understanding of their unionist role, concentrating on wage negotiation, working time, and contracting standards. All three Tier 2 and the Tier 3 companies had modest unionization rates, although still above national averages, ranging from 10–15 percent in the Tier 2 to 20 percent in the small Tier 3 company. In all interviewed companies there was information provided and regular consultation with unionists.

The Tier 1 company had atypical trajectory in terms of interest representation. For almost 20 years, until 2015, the main channel for interest representation was the works council. Until then the union, although present, did not reach the strategically important 10 percent threshold to be eligible to conclude collective agreements. In collective bargaining, it was again the works council that represented labor interests. In the assessment of the current union head, the industrial relations and work culture of the plant exemplifying a 'good German model' stopped any need for real representation of interest. Only with the emerging crisis situation and changed 'market position' of the firm was there an impetus on the part of worker activists to revitalize the trade union organization. Over a period of two years following 2015, the unionization rate reached 30 percent, and about 37.5 percent among production workers. It was therefore only the Tier 1 company which could press strategically and constructively towards collective regulation and wage agreements – but only from/beginning in 2015.

Industrial conflicts, especially along the line of capital-labor have only surfaced since late 2016, with strikes and strike threats in many large automotive companies. However, trade unions in our companies did not find decisive ways to cope with divisions among worker groups stemming from fragmentation. Moreover, unusually in both instances the general shocks resulted in labor-labor conflicts, where the influence of trade unions increased, mostly reaffirming these divisions. Labor-labor conflicts were also visible in Tier 1 and especially the larger Tier 2 companies, which were recruiting new entrants on a mass scale, and where labor turnover was extremely high, also via temporary agencies. In the larger Tier 2 company, there was a 'wild' work stoppage due to core workers resenting the high entrance wages for new employees. Core workers were also displeased that temporary migrant workers from both inside and outside of Hungary were provided free accommodation, which, they considered to be unequal treatment. It was in the immediate aftermath of the work stoppage that the union was formed. However, it could not prevent the resolute decision of the management to attempt to recruit new entrants by any means possible. The conflict was resolved in an unusual manner: wage increases for a unionist core insider group, symbolic benefits for loyal workers on seniority basis, and acceptance of equal wages for new entrants.

Thus, in the absence of an integrating labor organization and encompassing interest representation, fragmentation was considered the norm. Unions emerged late and typically only represented a core group of experienced long-term employees. In two cases, self-organization peaked at unfavorable times, which, by default, followed insider logic. Trade unions were not able to exert organizational influence as a counterweight to fragmentation, let alone to articulate interests more inclusively or efficiently.

In response to an earlier question posed by Jürgens and Krzywdzinski,[38] we can highlight that Hungarian automotive companies are too precarious to preserve or establish a high road model, and therefore, with very few exceptions, seem to be predominantly locked in a specialization of low-skill and low-wage manufacturing. Companies might be rational in using a hybrid, technological-exploitative rent.

From a historical perspective, the so-called 'global economic crisis' of 2008/09 had two significant consequences. At first, it weakened even further the regulatory power of trade unions, and more generally that of associational power of employees, and then opened space for relocations and job openings in Hungary. The second major shock, however, occurred on the opposite side of the spectrum with the opening of the EU labor markets – a situation where workers expressed their voice with their feet.[39] Yet, even in these beneficial times for self-organization, unions do not seem to have encompassing strategies to emerge from a sidelined minor position.

Unstable labor relations, characteristic to uneven development, systematically undermine labor organization and representation. We found that at the time of relocation, management style was originally friendly towards employee rights, but not necessarily towards labor self-organization. What we learnt from our interviews is that cooperative industrial relations – even if earnestly thought out as firm strategies – fell on fragile environments exposed to macro shocks, and were shallowly adopted organizationally as a nurturing ground from the side of plant level trade unions.

38 Jürgens and Krzywdzinski, "Work Models."

39 Meardi, "Social Failures of EU Enlargement."

## 5 Conclusion

Labor representation is key to the adaptability of a high road work model in the automotive industry, but its introduction depends on the organization of global production. Despite the intense specialization of Central and Eastern European countries in the German automotive industry, the potential to upgrade to the high road work model has been largely limited. In this chapter we investigated the mechanism of uneven development. This approach allowed us to analyze labor relations combined and embedded within the evolution of global automotive value chains. We linked the high road and low road work models into global value chains in which different rent-seeking strategies could reproduce hierarchies in both the production of value-added and particular labor relations. At a different point these empirical measures – value-added production and the particular labor relations – might serve as proxies to rent-seeking strategies which automotive companies have pursued in Hungary.

The results of our research indicate a specific environment, with fragmented labor and production that seems to be beneficial for exploitative rent-seeking strategies for organizing production. In the case of Hungary and its region, labor fragmentation and disembedded and unstable labor relations are the main causes for weak or limited capacity of labor representation. In fact, trade unionism was typically concentrated, limited to a narrow group of workers, which was thus unable to exercise inclusive interest representation. Moreover, it often generated inter-labor division lines. We therefore explain the weakness of labor representation not as the consequence of the limited upgrading from low road to high road work model, but as a result of simultaneous fragmentation of production and labor caused by global forces of uneven development.[40]

## Acknowledgments

This research was co-financed by the project "From developmental states to new protectionism: changing repertoire of state interventions to promote development in an unfolding new world order" (OTKA FK_124573), supported by the NRDIO (NKFIH) in Hungary.

40 In this chapter, we did not investigate how the global market environment circumscribes companies' rent-seeking behavior. A different research rational to investigate company strategic decisions and managerial capacity could certainly enrich our findings.

## Bibliography

Altreiter, Carina, Theresa Fibich, and Jörg Flecker. "Capital and Labour on the Move: the Dynamics of Double Transnational Mobility," in Jan Drahokoupil (ed.), *The Outsourcing Challenge: Organizing Workers Across Fragmented Production Networks* (Brussels: European Trade Union Institute, 2015), pp. 67–87.

Bair, Jennifer. "Global Capitalism and Commodity Chains: Looking Back, Going Forward," *Competition & Change*, 9 (2005), pp. 153–180.

Beblavý, Miroslav, Lucia Kureková, Jan Drahokoupil, Martin Myant, and Stefan Domonkos. *Linking Labour Regimes and Technological Innovation in Central and Eastern Europe: The Case of Automotive and Software Industries* (Neujobs, 2012).

Boyer, Robert and Michel Freyssenet. *The Productive Models: The Conditions of Profitability* (London: Palgrave, 2002).

Crouch, Colin. "Labour Market Governance and the Creation of Outsiders," *British Journal of Industrial Relations*, 53 (2015), pp. 27–48.

Drahokoupil, Jan and Agnieszka Piasna. "Dependent Market Economies and Wage Competition in Central and Eastern Europe," in Tamás Gerőcs and Tibor Szanyi (eds), *Market Liberalism and Economic Patriotism in the Capitalist World-System*. Pp 43–66. https://link.springer.com/chapter/10.1007/978-3-030-05186-0_4 (London: Palgrave, 2019).

Feenstra, Robert C. "Integration of Trade and Disintegration of Production in the Global Economy," *Journal of Economic Perspectives*, 12 (1998), pp. 31–50.

Fröbel, Folker, Jürgen Heinrichs, and Otto Kreye. *Krisen in der kapitalistischen Weltökonomie* (Reinbek: Rowohlt Verlag, 1981).

Frege, Carola and András Tóth. "Institutions Matter: The Case of Union Solidarity in Hungary and East Germany," *British Journal of Industrial Relations*, 37 (1999), 117–140.

Gereffi, Gary. "Global Value Chains in a Post-Washington Consensus World," *Review of International Political Economy*, 21 (2014), pp. 9–37.

Gereffi, Gary and Peter Evans. "Transnational Corporations, Dependent Development, and State Policy in the Semiperiphery: A Comparison of Brazil and Mexico," *Latin American Research Review*, 16 (1981), pp. 31–64.

Gereffi, Gary, John Humphrey, and Timothy Sturgeon. "The Governance of Global Value Chains," *Review of International Political Economy*, 12 (2005), pp. 78–104.

Gereffi, Gary and Miguel Korzeniewicz (eds.). *Commodity Chains and Global Capitalism* (Westport, CT: Praeger, 1994).

Gerőcs, Tamás and András Pinkasz. "Debt-Ridden Development on Europe's Eastern Periphery," in Manuela Boatcă, Andrea Komlosy and Hans-Heinrich Nolte (eds), *Global Inequalities in World-Systems Perspective: Theoretical Debates and Methodological Innovations* (New York, NY: Routledge Publishing, 2018), pp. 131–153.

Henderson, Jeffrey, Peter Dicken, Martin Hess, Neil Coe, and Henry Wai-Chung Yeung. "Global Production Networks and the Analysis of Economic Development," *Review of International Political Economy*, 9 (2002), pp. 436–464.

Hess, Martin. "'Spatial' Relationship? Towards a Reconceptualization of Embeddedness," *Progress in Human Geography*, 28 (2004), pp. 165–186.

Hess, Martin. "Investigating the Archipelago Economy: Chains, Networks and the Study of Uneven Development," *Journal für Entwicklungspolitik*, 25 (2010), pp. 20–37.

Jürgens, Ulrich and Martin Krzywdzinski. "Work Models in the Central Eastern European Car Industry: Towards the High Road?," *Industrial Relations Journal*, 40 (2009), pp. 493–512.

Kaplinsky, Raphael. "Globalization, Industrialization and Sustainable Growth: The Pursuit of Nth Rent," *IDS Discussion Paper*, 365 (Sussex: Institute of Development Studies, 1998).

Krzywdzinski, Martin. "Work Models Under Strain of Offshoring East-West Competition in the European Car Industry," paper for the 16th GERPISA International Colloquium, Turin, 19 June 2008.

Krzywdzinski, Martin. "Automation, Skill Requirements and Labour-Use Strategies: High-Wage and Low-Wage Approaches to High-Tech Manufacturing in the Automotive Industry," *New Technology, Work and Employment*, 32 (2017), pp. 247–267.

Laki, Mihály, Beáta Nacsa and László Neumann. "Az új Munka Törvénykönyvének hatása a munkavállalkók és a munkáltatók közötti kapcsolatokra," *MTA KRTK Közgazdaság-tudományi Intézet Műhelytanulmányok*, MT-DP-2013/2 (2013), pp. 1–66.

Lipietz, Alain. "The Post-Fordist World: Labour Relations, International Hierarchy and Global Ecology," *Review of International Political Economy*, 4 (1997), pp. 1–41.

Meardi, Guglielmo. *Social Failures of EU Enlargement: A Case of Workers Voting with their Feet* (New York, NY: Routledge, 2012).

Meszmann, T. Tibor. "The Rise of the Dual Labour Market: Fighting Precarious Employment in the New Member States Through Industrial Relations (Precarir) Country Report: Hungary," *CELSI Research Report*, 12 (2016).

Meszmann, T. Tibor. *Temporary Agency Work as a Form and Channel of Labour Migration.* (Budapest: Friedrich-Ebert-Stiftung, 2018), online available at: <https://library.fes.de/pdf-files/bueros/budapest/14597.pdf >; last accessed June 15, 2020.

Milberg, William. "Shifting Sources and Uses of Profits: Sustaining U.S. Financialization with Global Value Chains." *Schwartz Center for Economic Policy Analysis and Department of Economics, The New School for Social Research, Working Paper Series*, 2007–9 (2007).

Neumann, László and Dorottya Boda. "A válság hatása a vállalatok gazdálkodására," in Károly Fazekas and György Molnár (ed.), *Munkaerőpiaci Tükör 2010: Közelkép: A válság munkapiaci hatásai* (Budapest: MTA KTI and OFK, 2010), pp. 85–105.

Neumann László. "Az új Mt. a munkahelyen – két év után," manuscript. (Budapest, 2014).

Pavlínek, Petr. "Foreign Direct Investment and the Development of the Automotive Industry in Central and Eastern Europe," in Béla Galgóczy, Jan Drahokoupil and Magdalena Bernaciak (eds), *Foreign Investment in Eastern and Southern Europe After 2008: Still a Lever of Growth?* (Brussels: European Trade Union Institute, 2015), pp. 209–255.

Singenberger, Werner and Frank Pyke. "Industrial Districts and Local Economic Regeneration: Research and Policy Issues," in Frank Pyke and Werner Singenberger (eds), *Industrial Districts and Local Economic Regeneration* (Geneva: International Labour Organization, 1992), pp. 3–29.

Sturgeon, Timothy J., Peter Bøegh Nielsen, Greg Linden, Gary Gereffi and Clair Brown. "Direct Measurement of Global Value Chains: Collecting Product- and Firm-Level Statistics on Value Added and Business Function Outsourcing and Offshoring," in Aaditya Mattoo, Zhi Wang and Shang-Jin Wei (eds), *Trade in Value Added: Developing New Measures of Cross-Border Trade* (Washington, DC: World Bank, 2013), pp. 289–319.

Szanyi, Miklós, Ichiro Iwasaki, Péter Csizmadia, Miklós Illésy, and Csaba Makó. "Cluster Development in Hungary: Searching for a 'Critical Mass' of Business via Cluster Mapping" in Bruno Dallago and Chiara Guglielmetti (eds), *Local Economies and Global Competitiveness* (London: Palgrave Macmillan, 2010), pp. 113–133.

Werner, Marion and Jennifer Bair. "Loosing our Chains: Rethinking Commodities through Disarticulations," *Environment and Planning A*, 43 (2011), pp. 998–1015.

# PART 5

## *Trade Union Networks, NGO Campaigns, Workers' Agency*

CHAPTER 12

# Transnational Solidarity Networks between Workers and Global Production Networks

*Jörg Nowak*

The debate about transnational solidarity between workers has seen an upsurge since the late 1990s and into the twenty-first century as a response to the increasing internationalization of production and services.[1] In the course of this debate, continually pointing out the necessity of a transnational cooperation between workers and unions, the different locations of workers in richer and poorer countries have been examined. For example, it has been underlined that unions in imperialist countries tend to support free trade policies, while unions in the South tend to oppose them.[2] Workers in imperialist countries profit from the superexploitation of workers in non-imperialist countries since many products produced in low-wage countries, especially food, can be bought for comparably low prices in imperialist countries[3] – at times at lower prices than in non-imperialist countries, even when differences in purchasing power are taken into account.[4] At the same time, these low prices of some consumer goods allow employers in imperialist countries to save on wages of

---

1 Johns, "Bridging the Gap"; Pasture and Verberckmoes, *Working-class Internationalism*; Wills, "Taking on the CosmoCorps?"; Harrod, and O'Brien, *Global Unions?*; Herod, "Geographies of labor internationalism"; Ghigliani, "International trade unionism"; Anner, *Solidarity Transformed*; Ryland, "Exploring the grassroots' perspective"; Bieler and Lindberg, *Global Restructuring, Labour and the Challenges for Transnational Solidarity*; Bieler et al., *Labour and Transnational Action;* McCallum, *Global Unions, Local Power*.

2 Bieler, "The EU, Global Europe, and processes of uneven and combined development," p. 181.

3 Smith, *Imperialism in the 21st century*.

4 The debate around a labor aristocracy that sets itself apart from the majority of the working class started with Friedrich Engels and was applied to the division between workers in imperialist and non-imperialist countries by Vladimir Ilyich Lenin, in Imperialism. The question if workers in imperialist countries participate in the exploitation of workers in non-imperialist countries remains controversial. One issue is that different concepts of exploitation have been used in this debate. One line emphasies superexploitation as the payment of wages (or wage substitutes such as housing and food) that do not guarantee the physical reproduction of workers. e.g., Ruy Mauro Marini, *Subdesarollo* could show how foodstuff production in Brazil under conditions of slavery facilitated the industrialization of England in the nineteenth century through cheap imports of canned beef. Another line looks at the rate of exploitation: Michael Roberts, "Imperialism and super exploitation" could show convincingly

 | DOI:10.1163/9789004448049_013

workers in those countries. But as Bieler et al. 2011 underline,[5] workers and trade unions in imperialist countries can also decide to take another course of action, for instance to coordinate their activities in solidarity with workers and their organizations in non-imperialist countries. Political ideologies have a key influence in this respect.

Many of the studies on transnational solidarity focus on the efforts of big trade union bodies or global union federations. The evidence here is mixed. Andrew Cumbers and Paul Routledge provide a rather bleak example of the global union federation the International Chemical, Energy, Mining and General Workers Federation (ICEM).[6] Other authors found successful but limited action of the ICEM in a case of a subsidiary of a German pharmaceutical company in Turkey.[7] The International Union of Food, Agricultural, Hotel, Restaurant, Catering, Tobacco and Allied Workers' Associations (IUF) runs a pretty engaged and successful campaign and alliance that brings together workers from Coca-Cola factories and of Coca-Cola bottlers which are outsourced, but due to internal strife between different trade union organizations, the IUF stayed away from an international support campaign for the Colombian union, SINALTRAINAL, that organized Coca-Cola workers, of which some had been murdered by death squads.[8] Frequently, initiatives on a more rank-and-file basis, that are not run by the union headquarters, do not receive adequate attention, even though they sometimes have almost equal, or even better, political and economic success than top-down campaigns. I will engage with two of these campaigns in this text: First, the ExChains network, a linkage of workers from H&M and Zara fashion retail shops in Germany and of garment workers who produce for these companies in Bangladesh, Sri Lanka and India. The second example is *Réseau Rail sans Frontière* (Rails without Borders), a network of railway unions from various West European and North African countries. The findings about these cases stem from around twelve interviews that I conducted in December 2014 in the framework of a research project that was funded by the Rosa Luxemburg Foundation.[9] Before I analyze these cases, I will draw on the debate on transnational union action and on global production networks.

---

that the rate of exploitation of workers in imperialist countries is higher than the one in non-imperialist countries.

5 Bieler and Lindberg, *Global Restructuring*, p. 14.

6 Cumbers and Routledge, "The Agency of Unions."

7 Fougner and Kurtoglu, "Transnational Labour Solidarity."

8 Nowak, *Grenzüberschreitende Solidarität*, pp. 12–15.

9 See Nowak, *Grenzüberschreitende Solidarität*, for the results of this research project.

A debate on the relevance of international labor action restarted in the 1960s and 1970s when the first postwar wave of relocation to low wage countries gathered pace, especially in the automotive industry.[10] Since the late 1960s, trade unions established global committees in several multinational enterprises in which they coordinated their activities.[11] These committees were first founded in 1966 in General Motors, Ford, Chrysler, Volkswagen and Mercedes-Benz, and then, during the next ten years, in more than twenty multinationals in the chemical, electronics, petrochemical, food and automobile industries. At the same time, representatives of German metal union IG Metall banned any direct contacts between unions of plants from different countries explicitly in 1974 at the Second General Meeting of the European Metalworkers Federation.[12]

Hildebrandt et al.[13] stress the thesis that trade unions in imperialist countries focus on national strategies in times of growth, while they tend to engage in international activities in periods of economic stagnation and decline. It is in this situation that the living standard of the working class in these countries is under threat, and jobs in imperialist countries come under pressure to be relocated to low wage countries. Hildebrandt et al. therefore claim that the substance of international trade union action can be understood as a form of national protectionism. As an example they point out that the United Autoworkers trade union from the United States was keen to seek connections with West European metal workers unions in the 1950s, when jobs were relocated to Western Europe where wages were lower at the time. However, German IG Metall blocked this initiative. Tellingly, the IG Metall union agreed to a similar initiative when German car producers began making massive foreign direct investments in low wage countries during the 1960s. Rebecca Johns analysed a similar schema for some US unions in the 1990s that became interested in narrowing the gap between wages in the US and in Guatemala when they saw the jobs of their members in the US under threat by competition from workers in Central America.[14] Given the vast wage differences between workers in OECD and non-OECD countries,[15] there will necessarily be a tension

10 This process has been analysed by Beverly Silver in her book *Forces of Labour.*

11 The following account is based on Olle, "Internationale Gewerkschaftspolitik am Beispiel der IG Metall" and Hildebrandt et al., "National unterschiedliche Produktionsbedingungen."

12 Olle, *Internationale Gewerkschaftspolitik*, pp. 169 ff.

13 Hildebrandt et al., "National unterschiedliche Produktionsbedingungen."

14 Johns, "Bridging the Gap."

15 Cope, *Divided World*, calculates a difference of 1:10 for male industrial workers after inflation between OECD and non-OECD countries. Note here that Mexico is part of the OECD, pp. 316 ff.

in transnational co-operations of workers, and even more so if those workers create the same product and are in direct competition.

Since the 1990s, global commodity chains have been seen as potentially weak links vulnerable to labor action due to just-in-time production being more sensitive than earlier supply models. Andrew Herod provides some examples in his research, such as the General Motors strike of 1998, in which 9,200 workers kept 193,500 other workers in 144 factories from working due to disruption to supply networks.[16] 'Organizing along the value chain' became a slogan in part of the academic and trade union literature during the 2000s, at times making bold claims to include all workers involved in a chain, even beyond the core product – which would include integrating iron-ore miners in the case of automobile production, and also rubber tappers.[17]

Since 60 percent of global manufacturing consists in the production of intermediate goods, the question arises if the concept of global production networks (GPN)[18] is perhaps more adequate to grasp the nature of global production. The concept of GPN is more diffuse than the firm-centered, earlier concepts of global commodity chains and global value chains,[19] but it is better able to integrate the different types of production-related services that are integral to facilitate surplus production. In this case, attention is also given to government and private services that provide infrastructure and oversee labor relations inside the factories, such as security services, the provision of land, traffic and energy, as well as the implementation of trade and legal regimes by national and international institutions.[20] The concept of GPN also allows us to go beyond the focus on consumers and the end product by including intermediate goods or transport services that form an integral part of production in most cases.

In light of these theoretical considerations, I will move on to my two case studies in the next section. The research question that informs these case studies are the organizational forms that workers, activists and trade union officials found to act beyond national borders. One of the central challenges for a transnational organization of workers is the mastering of the two contradictory tendencies of an overt centralization of leadership bodies and the decentralization and fragmentation that often comes with grassroots-led networks and campaigns. Another challenge arises in in overcoming tendencies

16 Herod, "Organizing globally, organizing locally."
17 Hübner, *Globale Wertschöpfungsketten organisieren.*
18 See Andrea Komlosy in this volume.
19 Gereffi, and Korzeniewicz, *Commodity Chains and Global Capitalism.*
20 Kelly, "Production networks."

to focus on specific sectors at the expense of broader perspectives at the level of the social formation.

## 1 ExChains Network

The ExChains Network is a network of representatives of work councils of the fashion retail sector in Germany, mainly from H&M and Zara, and of garment workers from Sri Lanka, Bangladesh and India that produce, among others, for H&M and/or Zara.[21] On the German side, the ExChains Network is composed of works council members from Kaufhof, Karstadt, Metro, Ikea, H&M and Zara, and was in the process of expanding to Esprit fashion shops during the time of my research in late 2014.

The formation of the network began when activists who worked in H&M and Zara made contact with and maintained links to the international network Transnationals Information Exchange (TIE). The active works council members delivered education seminars together, in which the activities of the network were planned and strategies developed. These were focused on issues of health, safety and organizing strategies. Retail workers from H&M and Zara visited works council meetings and employee meetings across the two companies. Especially in the case of H&M and Zara, the works council members see the contact with workers at supplier companies and the conflicts around their conditions of work as a part of their everyday works council activities.

The ExChains Network is built on the experiences of TIE, which created networks of workers in chocolate production in Latin America in the 1980s. Since the late 1990s TIE supported a process of union organizing led by employees of H&M in Germany during which more than one hundred works councils were installed. The notable characteristic of this organizing process was the fact that there were no professional organizers and no trade union officials leading the process. It was led by the workers, jointly with TIE, and the works councils then joined the German service union Ver.di, but without Ver.di being involved in the organizing drive. The central actors were the works council members, who visited shops without works councils and established contacts. During this process, a study mapped the enterprise organization and the human relations politics of H&M, which included the conditions of work at supplier

21 The information on the ExChains Network is based on two interviews with German members of the network, conducted in December 2014, a more detailed account can be found in Nowak, *Grenzüberschreitende Solidarität.*

companies. The initiative within H&M to connect with garment workers was based on this information.

The workers in Germany were outraged by the stories they heard about the supplier companies and sought to make connections with the workers in south Asia. Regular visits were established, and the German workers took their first trip to Sri Lanka in 2004. The groups of workers going from Germany to South Asia were always larger than those of South Asian workers coming to Germany, where there were only two or three able to travel. The reason for this was rooted in the structure of available funding on the German side, which allowed for travel to Asia rather than the other way around, while funding in South Asia is much harder to organize. This situation represents and reinforces the ongoing colonial divide. Nonetheless, participants on both side of this divide stress the common class perspective against management.

The extension of the network beyond the works councils of H&M and Zara is a part of the actual planning processes, but the different patterns of relations to suppliers in companies such as the two most important German department store chains, Karstadt and Kaufhof, pose a serious challenge. While H&M and Zara maintain comparably long-term relations with a considerable number of suppliers, other retail corporations have rather mediated supplier relations that are distributed across various trading companies and therefore come with more complex supplier networks. Thus, for the suppliers of Karstadt – which has much more product diversity across the board and is not restricted to fashion – the product demand of Karstadt represents a much smaller amount of their total production, and therefore is less significant for single suppliers as is the case for some of the suppliers of Zara and H&M, which might provide twenty or fifty percent of their total production to a single buyer company.

The cooperation takes place between members of work councils at H&M and Zara in Germany and active trade unionists in India, Sri Lanka and Bangladesh. In this way, the contacts to workers in supplier companies for these brands are mediated by the trade unions that represent them. For example, in the Indian states of Tamil Nadu and Karnataka in the southeast of India, workers in supply companies are members of the left independent New Trade Union Initiative (NTUI). Another cooperation runs in Sri Lanka with the National Garment Workers Federation. Many companies from the three South Asian countries are suppliers of all three retail companies – H&M, Zara and Esprit – at the same time. The contact between German workers and garment workers in South Asia is supported by a regional coordinator of the TIE, who is located at the Center for Workers Management in New Delhi, which maintains close relations to the NTUI. The Center receives financial support from the German Rosa Luxemburg-Foundation, aligned with the German socialist party *Die*

*Linke*. This regional coordination is an essential part of the contact between the workers across continents, partly due to the use of different languages.

The regional coordination is also a central device for the formation of common demands and the development of common strategies of organization of both German and South Asian workers in the face of the "buyers" (H&M, Zara, Esprit). Since 2015, the health mappings have been an important instrument for both areas of action. These start with the question, "What is it in the work process that makes us sick?" The responses to this question are a starting point to identify problems and conflicts in the workplace, to devise strategies and to formulate demands. This way, the workers see what has to be done in order to avoid work processes that lead to sickness. The aim of this organizing process is that workers do not only respond to measures of management, but that they develop their own strategy of change. The health mappings are done both by workers in the North and South, and despite large differences in the general context, health issues are very important to both retail and garment workers. The aim is to build or strengthen a local bargaining power and bargaining process that enables the participants in the ExChains network to act at the same time on a local, regional (across South Asia) and international level.

The fact that unions in the network only organize specific suppliers based on a local strategy comes with the danger that corporations may change their suppliers – for example, to the Philippines, where H&M already has a presence, and where unionists are routinely threatened and killed by death squads. Apart from India and Bangladesh, Esprit has supplier relations in China, while H&M have outsourced some specific work processes to home-based work in Bulgaria (a move which was revealed by a union of those home-based workers). A defining principle of the network is that demands and strategies are decided upon and enforced in the factories and trade unions in the South, not in the North. This implies that the risk of union organizing and negotiations is being evaluated on a local basis.

The meetings between workers from different continents aim to create a common debate and a common class consciousness. This means that the paternalistic expectations addressed to the unions in the North are avoided, including information about experiences and situations of workers in Germany. Early in the process, workers from South Asia tended to overestimate the ability to act and the resources of unions and workers in Germany, e.g. the fact that unions in Germany have more financial resources than South Asian ones led to the assumption that German unions would also be able to exert economic or political power regarding the decisions of employers as to how the supply chain should be organized. One issue of debate during the common meetings was the question of whether workers in both continents should demand a special add-on to the price that the retail corporations pay for the commodities in order to raise wages in the garment factories. This strategy was seen as a way to use the transnational power of workers on different continents for the benefit of the South Asian workers in textile production. This idea was dropped since it could potentially split the workforce – for example, given the case that only H&M and not Esprit would pay the add-on.

Two other demands were taken up, and then addressed by the works council members in Germany: transparency regarding the prices that retail chains pay to the suppliers and transparency regarding the entire supply chain. This demand stems from the suspicion that the retail chains pay much lower prices than they claim. The national works council of Zara is currently preparing a court case in this respect – but without much hope of winning. The main aim of this initiative is to put pressure on the management and to politicize the conflict. Since production in India is not directly paid for by Zara itself but via the larger trust Inditex (that owns Zara), there are additional opportunities to hide the prices paid. The supplier for H&M Germany is H&M Sweden, which creates a similar problem when enforcing transparency. The working conditions in supplier companies are a regular topic for workplace and works council meetings at H&M and Zara, in the newsletter and the journal of the works council, and also during the monthly talks between the works councils and management.

The ExChains Network relies on contacts within the service union Ver.di, especially in the twelfth department (retail). But union officials lack the capacity to actively support this work. It is partly connected to the rather decentralized structure of the service union that this networking project, with support of the union, became possible. The division of Ver.di into thirteen departments creates problems related to parallel structures in and conflicts between the departments as to which workers should be organized within which department. But this division also enables more political autonomy for union officials, in distinction to the top-down structures in the metal workers union IG Metall. The ExChains network also reinforces the close relations between the works council members of H&M and Zara in Germany.

One of the recent common actions of the ExChains Network dealt with the dismissal of three union members in a factory close to Bangalore. A video related to this was shown in workplace and works council meetings of H&M and Zara in Germany. The engagement with colleagues in other countries regularly leads to confrontations between workers in Germany and their management. The work in the ExChains Network contributed to the politicization of labor relations in Germany and created new avenues for debate among German workers in general. In the case of the three dismissed garment workers there were parallel negotiations with the local union in Bangalore and works council members of H&M in Germany. The three workers were finally reinstated. A second success came when workers in Bangladesh were paid compensation after a factory closed down. In this case there was also pressure put on management in Germany.

One of the problems for the ExChains Network is that – as always – the organization of workers at both ends of the supply chain is only partial. All three retail companies have a presence beyond Germany, and the company headquarters are in Sweden (H&M) and Spain (Zara). Esprit maintains two headquarters, in Hong Kong and Germany. Among the supply companies, workers from twelve factories have joined the network. H&M reported in 2011 to have 750 suppliers, of which 150 are long-term suppliers that cover 58 percent of the production.

Within Germany the affiliation to the same sectorial union Ver.di is a crucial issue, while in South Asia different trade unions join the network, and the political contacts to the NTUI are important. Thus, the model of organization for this network is based on chains of supply and sale for the products sold by those retail corporations. The commonality of the workers in Germany and South Asia consists in raising joint demands against the management of the same retail corporations. But the garment workers are additionally confronted with the management of the garment factories, and in many cases also with intermediary traders that sell to retail corporations.

One of the features of the network is that the garment workers are in competition with one another. The retail workers in Germany are in competition as well – but the retail workers do not really compete with the garment workers since they are placed in different parts of the supply chain. Since the garment workers in Asia are not delegating their decision power to a larger federation, there is no avenue to control them via a global union federation or a Northern trade union. The contacts are rather between workplace or between national works councils and workplace delegates. Moreover, the TIE as a coordinator means that a third institutional level is involved. But this rank-and-file model has certain limits since it only covers a part of the supply chain – H&M comprises of a larger number of stores in other countries and its supply chain extends way beyond the factories in the three South Asian countries included in the ExChains Network. Within the German retail sector, H&M is now one of the strongholds during strikes. In South Asia, which does not have many sectoral unions in the garment sector, the participating unions 'jump scales' from the local to the transnational level of organization. The health mappings and the common networking aim to link demands for better conditions of work with a broader politicization of union activities.

## 2 Network Rails without Borders

Strikes in the transport sector have had a significant impact across many European countries in recent years, among airline companies, airports, train drivers and truck drivers. During the past eighty years, strikes in transport and logistics outnumbered strikes in manufacturing, and this continues to be the case. Several authors argue that a large swath of transport can be counted as a part of production and surplus creation.[22] Many of the strikes in Europe were attacked by state security forces, e.g.: railway strikers in France in June 2014 by police; air controllers in Spain were forced back to work by military in 2012; and in summer 2017 airport personnel was forced back to work by police in Catalonia, ordered by the Catalan government.

Across all transport sectors in Europe privatization, casualization and outsourcing are major issues. In 1992 there was the first European transport strike against the implementation of rule 91/440/EWG of the Council of European Communities that initiated the privatization of railways in Europe. Since the European Trade Union Council did not coordinate this movement further, different railway unions grouped in the succeeding years under the name Réseau Rail sans Frontière.[23] Another impetus for the foundation of the network was the strike movement in France in 1995. One of the founders of the network, Sud Rail, emerged from this movement. Railway workers were on strike for a longer period than other workers in the 1995 movement since they aimed to extend gains for some workers to all occupational groups.

The formal foundation of the network took place in 2000. In the beginning, it consisted of railway unions within europe National Union of Rail, Maritime and Transport Workers (RMT) (UK), Langile Abertzaleen Batzordeak (LAB) (Euskadi), Confederación General del Trabajo (CGT) (Spain), Sveriges Arbetares Centralorganisation (SAC) (Sweden), Netzwerk Bahn von unten in Transnet (Germany), Sud Rail (France), Organizzazione Sindacati Autonomi, Confederazione Unitaria di Base (CUB) and Sindacato Unitario Lavoratori Trasporti (Italy). The most influential of those unions are Sud Rail und RMT. Sud Rail is only the third biggest among unions in the French rail sector, but it has a strong basis with some of the train stations in Paris, representing 8,000 members overall. It differs from other French railway unions in that it organizes employees at railway stations and workshops independent of their company

22 Smith, *Imperialism*; Tonak and Shaikh, *Measuring the Wealth*.

23 The information on Réseau Rail sans Frontière is based on one interview with a member of the French part of the network conducted in December 2014, a more detailed account can be found in Nowak, *Grenzüberschreitende Solidarität*.

affiliation. This includes private cleaning companies as well as train drivers in the state railway company. RMT has 80,000 members and organizes, among others, the workers of the London Underground. Like Sud Rail it can be classed as a radical political trade union. Italian CUB has about 500,000 members across all industrial sectors. The Netzwerk Bahn von unten in Transnet (later: in EVG)[24] comprises of some members of works councils, but is not able to make much headway in the union EVG. The basque leftist union LAB has 45,000 members in various sectors, and the Spanish anarchist union CGT has 8,000, also across various sectors. The Swedish anarchist union SAC has 5,000 members overall, and later on unions from Belgium and Switzerland came to join the network.

Among the first actions organized by the network was a European strike against the opening up of freight transport to private companies on March 18, 2003. The EU Commission planned to push through a related regulation, urging national governments to open their rail infrastructure to private companies. Trade unions were concerned that privatization and competition would come with wage cuts and an erosion of established minimum working conditions. The mobilization for the strike extended well beyond the network, since a huge number of trains did not run in Portugal, the Netherlands, Luxemburg, Belgium and Greece. In Germany, Austria and the United Kingdom the action was restricted to leafletting due to the ban on political strikes in these countries. The strike caused at least a delay to the privatization plans, which are still only proceeding in small steps in the EU. At least a rapid privatization could not be enforced on the workers.

The network called for further strike action for the meeting of EU transport ministers at March 2, 2006. In May 2010 a protest was organized in Lille, France, which included 1,000 members of 20 unions from the UK, Ireland, France, Spain, Portugal, Belgium, Germany, Switzerland, Italy, Cyprus, the Basque Country and Greece. The protest took place in front of the headquarters of the European Railway Agency (ERA) and was directed against a softening of security standards, mainly in the tunnel between France and the UK.

The languages used in the network are mainly French and Spanish; the biannual bulletin covers five languages: French, Spanish, Catalan, Italian and English. An extension of the network to other countries faces difficulties since in many countries railway workers are part of larger federations that do not want

24 Transnet fused in 2010 with the union *Gewerkschaft Deutscher Bundesbahnbeamten und Anwärter* to *Eisenbahner- und Verkehrsgewerkschaft* (EVG).

to compromise themselves with smaller political unions which are present in the network.

In a second phase of action, the network was extended to Africa. This goes back to an initiative of French railway workers with Senegalese roots. In 2014, the network comprised of unions from Morocco (ODR, Organisation Démocratique du Rail), Senegal (Syndicat Autonome des Travailleurs du Rail, Syndicat Unique des Travailleurs du Rail, Regroupement des Cheminots Deéflatés, Syndicat du Petit Train de Banlieue), Mali (Syndicat de Travailleurs du Rail, Cheminot Retraités), Burkina Faso (Syndicat Libre de Cheminots du Burkina), Benin (Syndicat des Travailleurs du Bénin et du Niger) and Tunisia (rail union of UGTT). These unions are in most cases the majority unions in the sector. But also citizens' committees that accompany developments in the railway networks, and represent the users of the railways, are part of the network, for example, Attac Morocco and the Collectif Citoyen pour la Restitution et le Développement Intégré du Rail Malien from Mali. In Africa, privatization of the railways is a big issue, too. In 2003, the state railways in Mali and Senegal were sold to the French-Canadian consortium Transrail S.A. This led to massive protests, since it came with a closure of two thirds of the railway stations.

The network intervened in several campaigns in Africa with success, for example in the case of the planned relocation of the central station in Dakar, the capital city of Senegal. International investors, mainly from Libya, favored relocation to a suburban part of Dakar and aimed to rebuild the old station building as a shopping center. This would have meant a more stressful and time-consuming commute for poorer parts of the population. In Senegal the intervention of the network was perceived as the action of a European organization and therefore caused much attention. The first response was that the government co-opted one of the union leaders of the network and made him chief manager of the railway company. In April 2013, the station was given back to railway transport after a renovation.

The second campaign that included the network revolved around the dismissal of the general secretary of the railway union ODR in Morocco, and the relocation of several union members to remote parts of the country. The ODR is the only trade union in Morocco with a special section for immigrants, and many rail employees stem from Mauritania and Mali. The pressure from the network led to the reinstatement of the general secretary in 2012, but in a lower position, and the relocated workers received new offers.

The railway workers from different countries are not in mutual competition. It is rather that a well-maintained railway network in one country will enhance the use value of a network in another one. But if railway workers strike simultaneously, it maximizes their negotiation power. Longer railway strikes lead to decreased income for railway companies since customers will use alternative means of transport. However, a more encompassing network of railway workers beyond the network Rails without Borders inside of Europe is impeded by the political divisions between social democratic and radical left unions in Europe that were only partially lifted during European mobilizations.

The political aims of the network go beyond working conditions, focused on resistance against privatization and the closure of stations and rail tracks. In this case, the specificity of the product links workplace struggles with broader political perspectives. The workers refer to the product of rail transportation in a positive notion that links up with general ideas about mobility and society. This aspect is more relevant in Africa than in Europe since larger parts of the population depend on the railways as a means of transportation. The positive reference to the product increases conflict with management: Austerity comes not only with the closure of transport routes, but also with a decrease in security for workers and passengers. In other words, while the neoliberal organization of production does not come with an immediate impact on product quality, as in the case of fashion retail in the first example, the reorganization of rail transport affects both the conditions of work and the health of workers and the quality of passenger rail transport itself. The perspective of public transport as a common good comes as an immediate contradiction to the strategies of flexibilization, privatization and competition that are increasingly imposed on rail transport. On a theoretical level, the concept of global production networks, which can be adapted to the sector of fashion retail, does not yield many insights into the sector of rail transport. Although there is substantial cross-border investment in the European rail sector, markets in rail transport are primarily national. The regulation of rail transport in Europe is a hybrid of transnational EU and national regulations, but the product markets in passenger transport are dominated by national patterns of demand. In contrast, freight transport occurs both on a national and international level to a significant extent. Despite the relevance of international freight transport, railway concessions are distributed on a national level, so that an approach that looks at global networks of production encounters significant limits. This then had an impact on the forms of organization that railway workers chose: they did not start with international contacts along the supply chain in one company and then link up with workers from other companies in the same sector, as in fashion retail. Railway workers first organized at the national level either in one railway company, or in several, and then established international contacts. The common characteristic for a common identity of workers is sectorial, as it is in fashion retail and production, but the identification with the product of passenger transport, which is more effective and ecologically less damaging than road or air transport, adds another layer of identification of workers with product quality.

## 3 Conclusions

The solidarity networks portrayed here cut across the (post-)colonial divide between imperialist and non-imperialist countries and put effort in not replicating hierarchical relations between those world regions, although they are embedded into quite different contexts. Due to the political background of the workers involved, there is no hidden or covert trade union-management coalition in the North against Southern workers as has been analyzed on other occasions.[25] Although these networks might wield less power than larger union federations, they do not hesitate to use it for the sake of their members. In the best case, these networks can also be models for future networks.

With the example of the railway workers, it is the identification with both the product and the sector that provides for unity across and within countries, but this is hampered in Europe by political divisions between trade unions. The outsourcing of cleaning, catering and repair staff makes the common organization of all railway related workers more difficult, and, networks with other transport workers in air or road traffic, to dockers or seafarers are usually not very developed. Coordination across the different sections of transport workers could have a significant potential for disruption.

The problems of fragmentation have much more salience in the fashion industry. The technology of garment production allows for more rapid relocation due to the nature of production machines and skills needed, and more recent developments witness the relocation of garment production from Turkey and Southeast Asia to Ethiopia where wages are below those in Cambodia, Vietnam and Bangladesh. H&M has begun to source increasingly from Ethiopia, but also relocation from China to India is an increasing trend. The large number of suppliers, but also of retail shops creates significant hurdles for the organization of workers across the supply chain. The number of suppliers is even multiplied if we go from fashion to retail sectors like larger supermarkets or department stores with an even bigger number of suppliers. Department store chains like Karstadt have several thousand suppliers, which shows that, 'unionization along the supply chain' is a great slogan, but not a viable strategy in all sectors.

25 See the free trade agenda of European unions analyzed in Bieler, "The EU, Global Europe."

The territorial organization of workers will continue to play a role and can have significant effects, as the successful two day strike of more than 120,000 garment workers against cuts in social security benefits in Bangalore (India) proved in April 2016.[26] One of the problems that workers' movements are facing is that the rhizomatic model of organization of capitalist production is challenging for all types of workers' organization: Supply chains in many sectors are organized in a decentralized fashion in order to avoid bottlenecks in case of industrial unrest or other problems that might have a negative impact on the supply chain. It is this decentralized and nonlinear organization of supply chains that the concept of global production networks tries to capture – in distinction to the concepts commodity chains or value chains that insinuate a linear organization. The colonial divide requires worker organization across this divide, and at the same time national, regional or local territorial organization of workers has to be complemented with a transcontinental one. While an over-centralization of worker organization can result in bizarre strategies that ignore local contexts and might lead to dysfunctional outcomes, the current under-centralization, with a few power centers integrated into compromises with capital, does not seem to be the solution either. If organizations of workers limit themselves by imitating this decentralized pattern without a coordinating center that national and multinational companies use to control the supply chains, they can only have an impact on single parts of the production network but not engage into a coordinated action. Thus, workers organizations are confronted with the challenge of navigating between a decentralized fragmentation of their actions and an over-centralization: Their strategies have to respond to specific logics in local, regional and national contexts, and thus develop sensitivity for specific labor markets and production arrangements, and at the same time they need some amount of centralization to coordinate action across these specific places.

## Bibliography

Anner, Mark. *Solidarity Transformed. Labor Responses to Globalization and Crisis in Latin America* (New York: Cornell University Press, 2011).

Bieler, Andreas. "The EU, Global Europe, and processes of uneven and combined development: the problem of transnational labour solidarity," *Review of International Studies* 39, 1 (2013), pp. 161–183.

26 People's Union of Civil Liberties – Karnataka, *Bangalore Garment Workers'*.

Bieler, Andreas and Ingemar Lindberg (eds). *Global Restructuring, Labour and the Challenges for Transnational Solidarity* (London: Routledge, 2011).

Bieler, Andreas, Roland Erne, Darragh Golden, Idar Helle, Knut Kjeldstadli, Tiago Matos, and Sabina Stan (eds). *Labour and Transnational Action in Times of Crisis* (London: Rowman and Littlefield, 2015).

Cope, Zak. *Divided World, Divided Class. Global Political Economy and the Stratification of Labour Under Capitalism* (Montreal: Kersplebedeb, 2015).

Cumbers, Andrew, Paul Routledge. "The Agency of Unions: The entangled geographies of transnational labour solidarity," in Ann Cecilie Bergene, Sylvi B. Endresen, Hege Merete Knudsen (eds), *Missing Links in Labour Geography* (Farnham: Ashgate, 2010).

Engels, Friedrich. "Preface to German Edition 1892", in Karl Marx, *Capital*, Volume 1 (Moscow: Progress Publishers, 1970).

Fougner, Tore and Ayca Kurtoglu. "Transnational Labour Solidarity and Social Movement Unionism: Insights from and beyond a Women Workers' Strike in Turkey," *British Journal of Industrial Relations*, 49, s2 (2011), pp. 353–375.

Gereffi, Gary and Korzeniewicz, Miguel (eds). *Commodity Chains and Global Capitalism* (Westport: Praeger, 1994).

Ghigliani, Pablo. "International trade unionism in a globalizing world: a case study of new labour internationalism," *Economic and Industrial Democracy*, 26, 3 (2005), pp. 359–382.

Harrod, Jeffrey and Robert O'Brien (eds). *Global Unions?* (New York: Routledge, 2002).

Herod, Andrew. "Geographies of labor internationalism," *Social Science History*, 27, 4 (2002), pp. 501–523.

Herod, Andrew. "Organizing globally, organizing locally. Unions spatial strategy in a global economy," In Jeffrey Harrod, Robert O'Brien (eds), *Global Unions?* (New York: Routledge, 2002).

Hildebrandt, Eckart, Werner Olle and Wolfgang Schoeller. "National unterschiedliche Produktionsbedingungen als Schranke einer gewerkschaftlichen Internationalisierung. Zur Kritik des syndikalistischen Internationalismus," *Prokla*, 24, 6 (1976), pp. 27–57.

Hübner, Carsten. *Globale Wertschöpfungsketten organisieren. Eine Herausforderung für die Gewerkschaften* (Berlin: Friedrich Ebert-Stiftung, 2015).

Johns, Rebecca A. "Bridging the Gap between Class and Space: U.S. Worker Solidarity with Guatemala," *Economic Geography*, 74, 3 (1998), pp. 252–272.

Kelly, Philip F. "Production networks, place and development: Thinking through Global Production Networks in Cavite, Philippines," *Geoforum* 44 (2013), 82–92.

Lenin, Vladimir Ilyich. *Imperialism: The Highest Stage of Capitalism* (London: Penguin, 2010).

Maurini, Ruy Mauro. *Subdesarrollo y revolución* (México D.F.: Siglo XXI, 1969).

McCallum, Jamie. *Global Unions, Local Power. The New Spirit of Transnational Labor Organizing* (Ithaca: Cornell University Press, 2016).

Nowak, Jörg. *Grenzüberschreitende Solidarität unter ArbeiterInnen. Eine Bestandsaufnahme anhand von vier Fallstudien* (Berlin: Rosa Luxemburg-Stiftung, 2016).

Olle, Werner Olle. "Internationale Gewerkschaftspolitik am Beispiel der IG Metall," *Kritik der politischen Ökonomie*, 3–4 (1975), pp. 145–172.

Pasture, Patrick and Johan Verberckmoes. *Working-class Internationalism and the Appeal of National Identity: Historical Debates and Current Perspectives on Western Europe* (Oxford: Berg, 1998).

*People's Union of Civil Liberties – Karnataka (PUCL-K) and Women Against Sexual Violence and State Repression-Karnataka (WSS). Bangalore Garment Workers' Protest Demonstration: A Preliminary Fact-finding Report,* June 9, 2016, online available at: http://sanhati.com/blog/17090/; last accessed, June 10, 2020.

Roberts, Michael. "Imperialism and super exploitation," March 7, 2016, online available at: https://thenextrecession.wordpress.com/2016/03/07/imperialism-and-super-exploitation/; last accessed October 2, 2018.

Ryland, Rebecca. "Exploring the grassroots' perspective on labour internationalisms," in Ann Cecilie Bergene, Sylvi B. Endresen, Hege Merete Knudsen (eds), *Missing Links in Labour Geography* (Ashgate, 2010).

Shaikh, Anwar and Ahmet Tonak. *Measuring the Wealth of Nations: The Political Economy of National Accounts* (Cambridge: Cambridge University Press, 1994).

Silver, Beverly. *Forces of Labor. Workers' Movements and Globalization since 1870* (Cambridge: Cambridge University Press, 2003).

Smith, John. *Imperialism in the 21st century* (New York: Monthly Review Press, 2016).

Wills, Jane. "Taking on the CosmoCorps? Experiments in transnational labor organisation," *Economic Geography*, 74, 2 (1998), pp. 111–130.

CHAPTER 13

# Corporate Social Responsibility in the Global Cocoa Chocolate Chain

## *Insights from Sustainability Certification in Ghana's Cocoa Communities*

*Franziska Ollendorf*

## 1 Introduction

Over the last three decades the notion of Corporate Social Responsibility (CSR) has become an important element in the public debates on normative sources, scope and practical implementation of corporations' societal role in the countries in which they operate. International civil society and transnational corporations alike use this concept for the articulation of their interests.[1] Researchers have discussed CSR as a battlefield of interests,[2] showing how the transnational business lobby managed to influence the broad conception of CSR in terms of a public-private cooperation for the benefit of the society as a whole.[3] Meanwhile, CSR has also become an integral part of national and international policy making. All the major multilateral institutions favor the concept of voluntary social responsibility of transnational corporations (TNCs), which is often seen as the best way to tackle value chain grievances.

This contribution sheds light on how CSR is implemented at the local level of the Global Cocoa Chocolate Chain in Ghana and elaborates on its social and institutional effects. It approaches the field of CSR research from a neo-Gramscian inspired perspective that understands CSR as a contested field of struggle over influence and value distribution in global value chains.[4] Contrary to an understanding of CSR as a mere tool for TNCs to manage their public relations, CSR activities are described here as a proactive governance strategy of TNCs. The main assumptions are as follows: 1) CSR strategies aim to increase TNCs' freedom to operate and incorporate profound critique of their hegemonic practices. 2) CSR allows TNCs to enhance their sphere of influence by transforming the institutional environment of the value chain. Thereby, TNCs

1 Utting, "Corporate Responsibility and the Movement of Business," pp. 375–88.
2 Levy and Kaplan, "CSR and Theories of Global Governance," pp. 432–51.
3 Ungericht, "Die Regulation transnationaler Wertschöpfungsketten,", pp. 58–75.
4 Bair and Palpacuer, "CSR beyond the corporation," pp. 1–19.

 | DOI:10.1163/9789004448049_014

achieve improved control over production and resource flows in their chains. While the former assumption has been broadly discussed in the literature under the key term "greenwashing", CSR as a proactive private governance tool that is used to shape local production processes has received little attention so far.

There are many different ways in which CSR can be put in practice. However, codes of conducts, sustainability standards and ethical certification schemes have become major instruments for TNCs to implement their voluntary self-commitment to better sourcing practices.[5] Hence, during the last decade, the number of voluntary sustainability standards has grown exceptionally in global commodity chains. In 2014, the leading commodities produced in compliance with various sustainability standards were palm oil, sugar, cocoa and cotton.[6]

Based on the empirical insights gained during fieldwork on one sustainability certification project in Ghana's cocoa sector in 2015 and 2017, this contribution describes the implementation process of one proactive CSR strategy and its social and institutional effects at the local level. Moreover, the proposed critical assessment of CSR's transformative potential in the Global Cocoa Chocolate Chain seeks to demonstrate the limitations of the prevailing understanding of global value chain governance as the internal management of value chains, meaning the inter-firm relations. CSR nowadays is an important tool for TNCs to shape conditions in their value chains and to communicate these efforts to consumers and regulators. Thus, it is the very nature of CSR to be addressed to both internal and external actors of the chain. Considering CSR as a private governance tool in global value chains therefore requires an understanding of chain governance that goes beyond the common restriction to internal management efforts. Therefore, based on the intermediary findings presented here, I argue for a combination of global value chain governance theory with a concept of structural power exercised by the leading firms in a chain. This allows for an improved consideration of the diversity of TNCs' efforts to control their supply chains and the environments in which they operate.

For the discussion of the transformative potential of proactive CSR in the Global Cocoa Chocolate Chain, this chapter will examine the implementation process of a particular UTZ certification project in Ghana. UTZ Certified is a Dutch NGO that specializes in sustainable agriculture standards and provides

5 Blowfield and Dolan, "Stewards of Virtue?," pp. 1–23.

6 Potts *et al.*, *The State of Sustainability Initiatives Review 2014*, p. 8.

certification services to both producers and buyers.[7] Many TNCs from the various tropical agriculture value chains, in the frame of their CSR strategies, use UTZ certification to prove the sustainability of their supply chains. The analysis is guided by the following research question: how does the implementation of proactive CSR interventions transform the institutional setting and social conditions in Ghana's cocoa sector? In other words, which new forms of sector coordination, norm diffusion and local interventions are established by certification programs? What kind of development is fostered by such private sector-led sustainability initiatives? A particular emphasis is given to cocoa producers' perceptions regarding societal shifts in their communities induced by proactive CSR projects.

## 2 Research Approach

In 2015 and 2017, a case study of one major sustainability certification project in Ghana's cocoa sector (hereafter the project) was conducted. The project is one of the biggest cocoa sustainability certification programs in Ghana. It is implemented in the most prolific area of cocoa production in the country, the Western Region. In 2015, forty-two semi-structured expert interviews with representatives from various public cocoa-related institutions, NGOs, and national as well as transnational companies from the cocoa and chocolate industry were carried out. Furthermore, forty-eight semi-structured interviews with cocoa producers participating and non-participating in this CSR intervention were conducted in five target communities of the project. The selection process of the communities and survey participants combines purposeful and random sampling elements. The project administration is divided into the three zones A, B, and C with each having a certain number of operational districts. As a first step, one zone was selected randomly. The selected zone consists of six operational districts with each having up to fifty target communities. The purpose was to include different types of communities with different characteristics to the sample. Therefore, the communities from the six operational districts were classified into three types:

(1) very remote and difficult to access,
(2) remote but good access to road,
(3) near town, close to main road.

---

7 In January 2018, UTZ Certified has merged with the US based NGO Rainforest Alliance, which is also active in sustainable agriculture certification. The two certification bodies state to seek to improve their efficiency and to "join forces for a better future", see: www.utz.org.

In the next step, a random selection of five communities out of the classified pool was made: two communities have been chosen from type (1), another two from type (2), and one community from type (3). In each community, an initial focus group discussion with project participants and non-participants was held. Attendees were invited to register for the survey pool out of which survey participants were purposely selected. In each community two female and three male cocoa farmers participating in the project, holders of key positions (chiefs, lead farmers and purchasing clerks), two share-croppers and two non-participating farmers were included the sample.

Besides, participatory observations during the training of farmers in UTZ standards, lead farmers' workshops and public-private sector meetings were also undertaken. In 2017, the author went back to the same communities to conduct ten follow up interviews with those cocoa farmers interviewed in 2015 who were still available. Additionally, seventeen experts from the public and private cocoa industry were interviewed.

The study applies elements from the global value chain approach (GVC) to the discussion of proactive CSR's potential to transform the Global Cocoa Chocolate Chain. Particularly its axis "governance" is of importance for the argumentation developed here. Early GVC research made an important distinction between producer and buyer-driven chain governance, originally introduced by Gereffi.[8] The governance axis was further developed in the mid-2000s by Gereffi and colleagues who refined this somehow simplified breakdown. They came up with five scaled types of governance structures that a lead firm may apply in its supply chain: market, modular, relational, captive and hierarchical governance.[9] Still, the producer-buyer divide of chain governance remained one of the most common features. The Global Cocoa Chocolate Chain has been analyzed by researchers mainly in terms of buyer-drivenness. But there is a particular dynamic that Fold[10] refers to as a bi-polarity in the chain. Accordingly, lead firms are the brand chocolate manufacturers but the cocoa processors also play a pivotal role due to their intermediary position in the Global Cocoa Chocolate Chain. In a recent report,[11] Gereffi and colleagues also highlighted the role of these powerful first-tier suppliers, which they see as actually functioning as the managers of the Global Cocoa Chocolate Chain. Maintaining direct relationships with both the local suppliers from which they purchase the raw beans and the transnational buyers, to which they sell the

8 Gereffi, "Global Production Systems and Third World Development," p. 113.

9 Gereffi *et al.*, "The governance of global value chains", pp. 78–104.

10 Fold, "Lead Firms and Competition in 'Bi-polar' Commodity Chains", pp. 228–47.

11 Abdulsamad, *et al.*, *Pro-Poor Development and Power Asymmetries in Global Value Chains.*

processed produce, provides them with an advantaged position as intermediaries in the chain.

Recently, the value chain researchers Bair and Palpacuer[12] have argued for an understanding of value chain governance that goes beyond such assessments of inter-firm relations and organizational patterns in a chain. They suggest combining the prevailing understanding of GVC governance in terms of industrial or chain internal governance with a concept of global governance. Fuchs[13] has carved out different channels of business' structural power in global governance. Accordingly, next to business' agenda-setting power through the allocation of capital or in the frame of public-private partnerships, sector specific codes of conducts have become an important tool for private influence and power in global governance. Whereas codes of conduct were initially developed by business actors themselves, they are now often generated in cooperation with civil society actors, and this is particularly the case for sustainability standards.[14] Combining the concepts of GVC governance and structural power in global governance they provide an understanding of lead-firms' governance from a neo-Gramscian inspired perspective of "contested governance". Following Levy's adaptation of Gramscian theory to global value chains,[15] the latter are objects of social construction and meaning creation. They are integrated economic, political, and discursive systems that should be understood as the locus of contestation and collaboration between a multitude of actors. Therein, many more struggles than simply market competition and value-adding will occur. In this light, the present contribution follows Bair and Palpacuer's suggestion and applies it to the study of sustainability certification in Ghana's cocoa sector. Approaching CSR from a "contested governance" perspective allows analysis of the transnational cocoa and chocolate industry's efforts to transform existing production norms and practices in the Global Cocoa Chocolate Chain as well as its local institutional setting.

## 3 The Global Cocoa Chocolate Chain: Emergence, Sustainability Challenges and Certification as a Response

The consumption of processed cocoa products goes back to the pre-Columbian societies, the Olmecs, Mayans and Aztecs, who already used cocoa for a hot

12 Bair and Palpacuer, "CSR beyond the corporation," pp. 1–19.
13 Fuchs, *Understanding Business Power in Global Governance.*
14 Fuchs, *Understanding Business Power in Global Governance,* p. 133.
15 Levy, "Political Contestation in Global Production Networks," pp. 943–63.

and spicy drink during religious celebrations. Nevertheless, cocoa originates from the Amazonian lands and only arrived in Mesoamerica due to merchant relations. After the arrival of the colonial rulers, similar as with tea from China and coffee from the Arab World, cocoa was brought from Mesoamerica to Europe as early as the sixteenth century. It remained an exclusive and exotic drink consumed only by the aristocracy and clerics for the next two centuries. During the nineteenth century, it finally spread over to other parts of the population in many European countries. Increasing demand triggered a rise in cocoa prices, which led the colonial rulers and traders to push cocoa production.[16] First, cocoa cultivation was expanded to other parts of Latin America to such regions as present Ecuador, Venezuela and Brazil where huge plantations were established and slaves displaced from West Africa to work there. The Portuguese brought cocoa to the island of São Tomé and Principe in the Gulf of Guinea, from where it was taken to Fernando Po. Tetteh Quarshie, a blacksmith from the Gold Coast (now Ghana), brought the first cocoa seeds to the West African country when returning home from Fernando Po in 1876. Cocoa easily flourished in the tropical belt of West Africa and, by the 1890s, its distribution to African farmers was actively supported by the British colonial administrations and some missionaries.[17]

By the late nineteenth century, European chocolate manufacturers had invested in product innovations and began to produce new types of chocolate products such as chocolate bars or pieces. Cocoa for the consumption of the masses was now imported from West Africa, mainly from the Gold Coast, which by the 1940s already supplied 40 percent of the raw material needed to meet the increasing demand for chocolate.[18] Whereas in Latin America cocoa was initially grown on huge plantations, cocoa in West Africa was produced by small-scale farmers from the beginning.[19] During the first part of the twentieth century, cocoa became one of the major income sources of the producing colonies and a central occupation for thousands of rural dwellers. However, cocoa world market prices were volatile and often very low. The living conditions of most cocoa farmers remained very poor.

After the colonial period, which in Ghana ended in 1957 and in Côte d'Ivoire in 1960, both countries managed to keep their leading positions in the global cocoa market. In the cocoa production season 2015/16, 73 percent of the whole world cocoa production came from Africa, where the two countries together

16 Durry and Schiffer, *Kakao: Speise der Götter*, pp. 11–12.
17 Ludlow, "Ghana, cocoa, colonialism and globalisation," pp. 5–7.
18 Muojama, "The First World War and the Cocoa Industry in Ghana," p. 5.
19 Durry und Schiffer, *Kakao: Speise der Götter*, p. 39.

accounted for 60 percent, 17 percent came from Latin America and 10 percent from Asia.[20] Apart from cocoa production at farm level, there are four main activities in the Global Cocoa Chocolate Chain: cocoa marketing, chocolate processing, manufacturing, and retailing to consumers.[21]

*Cocoa production* is only possible in the warm and humid equatorial belt. Up to 90 percent of the world's cocoa is produced by millions of small-scale farmers who grow their cocoa on small plots of land typically 2 to 4 hectares in size.[22] Local activities surrounding cocoa production comprise of the supply of inputs such as financials, chemicals, seedlings, agricultural training and extension services, cocoa cultivation, and postharvest handling. When cocoa beans are fermented, dried and packed in bags by the cocoa farmers themselves, the system of *internal marketing* depends on the producing country's policy. However, the main steps include transportation and storage, quality control and traceability, which are carried out either by public agents or companies. The *external marketing,* that is the selling of the cocoa beans to the international buyers, in most of the producing countries is in the hand of a public entity. Traditionally, after the beans had been sold to the export market, they were shipped directly to the importing countries for grinding and further *processing*. Only a marginal share remained in the origin countries for local processing and consumption. Recently, however, the transnational processing companies have established factories in the producing countries, which has enabled local processing capacities to rapidly increase. Local processing in Ghana grew by 17 percent and in Côte d'Ivoire by 5 percent per annum, making Côte d'Ivoire the world's second largest processing country after the Netherlands.[23] Nevertheless, in 2013, 86 percent of the Ivorian grinding capacities were owned by five TNCs and not much of the value added remained in the country.[24] The *manufacturing* of the end product, chocolate, is mainly done in the consumer countries.

There is a high level of concentration in the processing and manufacturing segments of the Global Cocoa Chocolate Chain. Over the past few years, many mergers – both within the same production segments, as well as in between

20 International Cocoa Organisation, *Production of cocoa beans.*

21 Gayi and Tsowou, *Cocoa Industry: Integrating small farmers into the global value chain,* pp. 10–13.

22 Gayi and Tsowou, *Cocoa Industry: Integrating small farmers into the global value chain,* p. 10.

23 ACET, "The Cocoa AgriProcessing Opportunity in Africa," p. 14.

24 Araujo Bonjean and Brun, Concentration and Price Transmission in the Cocoa-Chocolate Chain, p. 344.

them – have occurred. Currently, the joint market share of the top five chocolate manufacturing companies (Mars Incorporated, Mondelez International, Nestlé, Ferrero and Hershey) account for more than half (55 percent of the global chocolate market).[25] Even more remarkably, the two biggest cocoa processing companies, Barry Callebaut and Cargill, alone produce 70–80 percent of the world's couverture.[26] High asymmetries of value distribution along the chain are characteristic of the Global Cocoa Chocolate Chain. In 2014, the millions of cocoa farmers worldwide together made only 6.6 percent of the price of the end product, whereas the few processors and grinders together make 7.6 percent, the manufacturers 35.2 percent and the retailers 44.2 percent.[27] The poverty among cocoa farmers has become a topic for Western consumers due to the child labor scandals in the early 2000s. TNCs of the cocoa and chocolate industry increasingly had to respond to this new consumer awareness, which they mainly did within the frame of their CSR strategies. However, the industry faces more challenges in order to assure a sustainable flow of their most important input – cocoa beans – and more sophisticated responses can be observed since the introduction of CSR.

While the global demand for cocoa is rapidly increasing, mainly due to new demands in Asia and other Newly Industrialized Economies, the industry faces a number of severe challenges to meet this increasing demand and assure cocoa sustainability. TNCs have started to act to combat/prevent a future cocoa bean shortage. They mainly consider farmers' techniques to be inadequate and state a need for the modernization of agricultural practices to enable the desired productivity increase. Additionally, both cocoa farmers and trees are aging while the youth are not necessarily interested in continuing their family's cocoa business. The companies are aware that, due to small income and hard physical work, the attractiveness of cocoa farming decreases as soon as alternative income options are in reach.[28] Other major sector challenges possibly jeopardizing the future sustainable flow of the raw material and worrying the industry are local marketing challenges, pests and diseases, and, importantly, climate change.

In addition to these problems at the production level, the industry has to handle the growth of consumer awareness about child labor problems and severe poverty within the supply chain. Hence, consumers' demand for more

25 Statista, *Statista dossier on the chocolate industry*, p. 20.
26 Fountain and Hütz-Adams, *Cocoa Barometer 2015*, p. 6.
27 Fountain and Hütz-Adams, *Cocoa Barometer 2015*, p. 1.
28 Anyidoho, "Young people's aspirations in agriculture: a case study of Ghana's cocoa sector."

equitable cocoa products has rapidly increased over the past decade. Fair trade and sustainable production goods no longer occupy a niche position and are increasingly part of the mass consumption market. By 2012, 22 percent of the whole cocoa production was already standard-compliant and 10 percent[29] of the whole global export market was sold certified by one of the four main sustainability labels existing in the cocoa/chocolate market: Organic (0.2 percent) Fairtrade (4.5 percent), Rainforest Alliance (7.6 percent) or UTZ Certified (9.8 percent) of total cocoa production.[30]

In the course of the 2000s, both pressures – consumer awareness of ethical grievances and the need for an improved sustainability of supply – led to the rapid move of TNCs towards the implementation of more proactive CSR strategies in the Global Cocoa Chocolate Chain. Since the beginning of the 2010s, all major chocolate brands and main cocoa processors have implemented sophisticated CSR strategies. From the chocolate brand side, for example, there is Mars Incorporated's 'Sustainable Cocoa Initiative', Mondelez' 'Cocoa Life' or Nestlé's 'Cocoa Plan'. Equally, the processors have their own programs in place: For instance, Cargill runs its 'Cocoa Promise' and Barry Callebaut the 'Cocoa Horizons'. Most of the companies translate these CSR efforts into one of the four private sustainability certification labels of the Global Cocoa Chocolate Chain mentioned above.

## 4 Evolution and Institutional Setting of Ghana's Cocoa Sector

Since the beginning of cocoa cultivation in Ghana during the colonial period, cocoa is one of Ghana's main export commodities.[31] Today, after Côte d'Ivoire, Ghana is the second largest cocoa exporter in the world. About 720,000[32] small-scale farmers cultivate cocoa on an average of 5 hectares[33] and earn a mean daily income of 0.84 USD.[34] Furthermore, about 30 percent of the whole population of Ghana depend, in different ways, on activities linked to the cocoa sector.[35]

29 Potts *et al.*, *The State of Sustainability Initiatives Review 2014*, p. 134.
30 Cosbey, *Policy case study – Food labelling*, p. 12.
31 Kolavalli and Vigneri, "Cocoa in Ghana," pp. 201–17.
32 Institute of Development studies and the University of Ghana, "Mapping sustainable production in Ghanaian cocoa – Report to Cadbury" (2008), cited by Hütz-Adams, p. 27.
33 Hainmueller *et al.*,"Sustainable Development for Cocoa Farmers in Ghana."
34 Fountain and Hütz-Adams, *Cocoa Barometer 2015*.
35 Hütz-Adams, *Vom bitteren Kakao zur süßen Schokolade: Der lange Weg von der Hand in den Mund*, p. 9.

After Tetteh Quarshie brought cocoa seeds to his village in the Eastern Region of the former Gold Coast in 1876, cocoa spread over the whole tropical belt of the country. Farmers from the Southern and Eastern Provinces migrated west- and northwards into the tropical forest zones where plenty of sparsely populated virgin forest-land was still available for cocoa production.[36] Merchants brought it to the powerful Ashanti kingdom and many chiefs began to participate in the cocoa business. Quickly, the Ashanti region became a dominant production area. By 1911, the Gold Coast was already the world's biggest cocoa producer. The improvement of the local transport system in the 1920s also later expedited the rapid expansion of the industry. More and more European and American firms moved to British West Africa where cocoa export was their major business activity.[37]

Since its emergence, the cocoa sector has been a contested terrain, strongly influenced by the respective political economy prevailing in the country. Therefore, its development has taken place in several stages.[38] During the colonial period, within a free market system, the European companies had direct control over the internal and external marketing of the cocoa beans. By then, the colonial public sector encouraged cocoa farmers' cooperatives since they were seen as a driver of quality cocoa production.[39] Yet, following two major cocoa farmers strikes from 1930 to 1931 and in 1937, where higher prices for the produce were demanded, the colonial administration established two institutions that were supposed to improve control over the sector, namely the West African Produce Control Board and the Cocoa Marketing Board. In this system, the foreign companies continued to be the only buying agents.[40,41]

After the gain of independence from Britain led by Dr. Kwame Nkrumah in 1957, cocoa continued to be an important revenue source for the state. Dr. Nkrumah's post-colonial government took back control over the chain and the direct influence of expatriate industry was interrupted. The Cocoa Marketing Board (COCOBOD) was kept in place but reconfigured internally. Importantly, the Cocoa Marketing Company (CMC) was created as a subsidiary that came to be in charge of all commercial activities linked to cocoa. During the following years, the public integration of the chain was advanced and further divisions

36 Knudsen and Agergaard, "Ghana 's cocoa frontier in transition," p. 329; Ross, "The plantation paradigm," pp. 49–71.

37 Muojama, "The First World War and the Cocoa Industry in Ghana," p. 5.

38 Ton, *et al.*,"Chain governance, sector policies and economic sustainability in cocoa," p. 7.

39 Laven, *The risks of inclusion*, pp. 78–79.

40 Ton, *et al.*,"Chain governance, sector policies and economic sustainability in cocoa," p. 7.

41 Laven, *The risks of inclusion*, p. 79.

of the COCOBOD were implemented.[42,43] Thus, most importantly, the decolonialized cocoa chain in Ghana was characterized by a strong public position to manage and control the sector and the sharp decrease of direct foreign influence through the private sector. During the first years of independence, farmers benefitted from improved support through public outreach activities and extension services, which, however, were very resource intensive and later came to be strongly criticized by the international donor community. Unfortunately, the flourishing period was short-lived and by the 1970s, military coups brought political turmoil to the country that also hit the cocoa sector and production subsequently reduced significantly. In the early 1980s, the country stabilized and Flight Lieutenant Jerry John Rawlings, who came to power through another military coup, entered negotiations on economic reforms with the World Bank and the IMF. As part of the negotiated Economic Recovery Programme, the Cocoa Rehabilitation Programme was launched which aimed at cutting down costs and establishing a slim and efficient marketing board.[44] Hence, the number of COCOBOD's staff was drastically reduced and extension services for cocoa farmers transferred to the Ministry of Food and Agriculture, which, also had to cover the whole range of crops and therefore could not provide appropriate support to cocoa farmers.

Nevertheless, contrary to other African cocoa producing countries, Ghana only partially introduced sector liberalization reforms and managed to keep its influence in the cocoa sector.[45] Until today, COCOBOD, under the supervision of the Ministry of Finance, remains in charge of managing most aspects of the national cocoa value chain.[46] Currently, it has five subsidiaries that are in charge of ensuring the accurate functioning of the sector. Together they cover a large panel of sector responsibilities: research on as well as regulation of chemical inputs and plant material (Cocoa Research Institute Ghana), seed production (Seed Production Unit), quality control (Quality Control Company), pest and disease control and the provision of extension services to cocoa farmers (Cocoa Health and Extension Division), as well as storage and external marketing (Cocoa Marketing Company).[47]

42 *Ibid.*, pp. 78. Ton, *et al.*,"Chain governance, sector policies and economic sustainability in cocoa," p. 7.

43 Laven, *The risks of inclusion,* pp.78–79; Vellema *et al.*, "Policy Reform and Supply Chain Governance," pp. 235–37.

44 Fold, "Lead Firms and Competition in 'Bi-polar' Commodity Chains," pp. 228–247.

45 Kolavalli, *et al.*, "Cocoa in Ghana," p. 209.

46 See <https://cocobod.gh/structureand_operations.php>; last accessed on February 2, 2018.

47 See <https://cocobod.gh/oursubsidiaries.php>; last accessed on February 2, 2018.

Keeping these important responsibilities at the central level, it was the internal marketing system that was liberalized. In 1992/93 full responsibility for buying cocoa beans from the farmers was devolved to the private sector.[48] However, every buying company has to register with the board and demonstrate sufficient financial and operational capacities. Once approved, these Licensed Buying Companies (LBCs) work through a local purchasing clerk at community level. The LBCs buy the cocoa beans from the farmers for a price that is annually fixed by COCOBOD. In 2014, there were 41 LBCs active out of which only four shared 64 percent of the local market.[49] In 2014 these four most active LBCs were: the public Produce Buying Company which was a former subsidiary of COCOBOD and has long history in local purchasing; the Lebanese LBC Akuafo Adamfo, Amajaro Ghana Limited with its parent company based in London; and Kuapa Kokoo, a Ghanaian farmer-based LBC,which receives support from international NGOs.

After purchasing the beans, the LBCs are obliged to sell them to COCOBOD. COCOBOD runs quality controls of the beans through its subsidiary Quality Control Company and manages the storage of the beans in warehouses. It has a traceability system in place and knows the origin of the beans. However, once the beans arrive at the warehouses, beans from different locations are stored together and mixed. COCOBOD's Cocoa Marketing Company arranges forward sales contracts on the traded quantity of cocoa beans with the international buyers. Raw beans are mainly sold to transnational cocoa processing companies, only very few chocolate manufacturers still buy raw beans to process them in-house. International trading houses are now almost non-existent in the Global Cocoa Chocolate Chain.

Two key aspects are of main importance for this study: First, under the conditions of this conventional marketing system, the international buyers do not know the concrete origin of their beans since they only arrange a contract with the Cocoa Marketing Company on the quantity of beans they will buy. Furthermore, in Ghana, they do not operate at the community level since it is the Licensed Buying Companies (LBCs) that purchase the beans from the farmers. In this scenario, TNCs in the Global Cocoa Chocolate Chain, that is the cocoa processors and the chocolate manufacturers, in Ghana generally do not have any direct link to the farmers or the LBCs. Before the spread of sustainability certification projects, only the LBCs entered the communities to purchase cocoa. Second, COCOBOD's Cocoa Health and Extension Division

48 Kolavalli, *et al.*, "Cocoa in Ghana," p. 209.

49 COCOBOD, "45th Annual Report and financial statements for the year ended 30th Sept. 2014."

(CHED) is the main public agency in charge of providing extension services to the farmers and conducting other outreach activities such as the control of cocoa pests and diseases or the rehabilitation of old and unproductive cocoa farms. CHED's extension services include the training of farmers with agronomic practices and basic economics aiming at increasing their productivity. However, after the Cocoa Rehabilitation Programme of the 1990s and the following drastic reduction of resources for cocoa extension services, the public cocoa extension system became very weak during the 2000s and a huge extension gap appeared leaving farmers to deal with their challenges alone. In 2010, COCOBOD began to reinvest into extension and much improvement was seen. Nevertheless, until today, CHED's agents have had to struggle to reach the most remote and marginalized communities and to deliver adequate services to them.

Meanwhile, in the course of the 2000s, the private sector entered the extension vacuum at the local level. Mainly in the frame of their CSR strategies, transnational cocoa processors and chocolate manufacturers began to engage in the training of farmers with the so-called "Good Agricultural Practices". Most of them are operating in parallel to CHED's extension structure and have not joined the public-private partnership structure under which COCOBOD first sought to manage private extension activities and align them with its own activities.

In the following chapter, one major cocoa sustainability certification project will be presented as a case of proactive CSR strategies in the form of private cocoa extension activities at the community level. This provides the basis for the following discussion on structural transformations in Ghana's cocoa sector stemming from TNCs' CSR activities.

## 5 Case Study on One Major Cocoa Sustainability Certification Project in Ghana

For the study of proactive CSR's effects in the Global Cocoa Chocolate Chain, one of the biggest UTZ sustainability certification projects in Ghana's cocoa sector is analyzed. The project is run by one of the world's most important cocoa processors, as an integral part of its CSR strategy. The transnational processing company aims to foster cocoa sustainability through the promotion of productivity and quality increase, facilitated by training on the UTZ sustainability certification requirements. Thus, the core of the certification project is the training of cocoa farmers with UTZ sustainability standards. Those farmers adopting the requirements receive a premium for their produce. Thereby, their livelihoods are supposed to improve and poverty to diminish.[50]

Since its launch in 2011, by mid-2015, more than 15,000 cocoa farmers have already been UTZ certified in the frame of the project. For its implementation, a tripartite cooperation among private actors had been established. In Ghana's system of local marketing, the transnational cocoa processor is not familiar with the local conditions and therefore needs to cooperate with an actor with a broad network on the ground. The processor therefore cooperates with one of the largest LBCs in Ghana. Also partnering in the project is the Dutch-based NGO Solidaridad, which acts as a facilitator in this strategic partnership. Solidaridad plays an important role by providing logistics, knowledge and infrastructure to the two partnering project companies. Importantly, there is UTZ, the standard-setting body, and another Dutch NGO. However, regarding the project implementation, UTZ limits its role to the training of the companies' project staff on UTZ standards and requirements. UTZ designs the sustainability standards that the farmers have to adopt. Although the standards are developed on a multi-stakeholder partnership basis, having public, private and civil society involved, an interview statement of a representative of the transnational cocoa processing company indicates that the company plays an important role in the standard development process. The adoption of the standards by the project participants is evaluated by external certification bodies, licensed by UTZ. The managers of each certification project have to select one certification body for external audit. In Ghana's cocoa sector, in 2016, there are ten certification bodies active for UTZ.

The UTZ sustainability standards applied by the project contain a Core Code of Conduct that covers all commodities certified by UTZ and a cocoa specific part. The Core Code of Conduct spells out the need for implementing standards on sustainable farm management and farming practices, social and living conditions, and environmental protection.[51] The Cocoa Module contains particular control points on farm maintenance and postharvest processing[52] that have to be fulfilled by the farmers. The training of cocoa farmers with UTZ sustainability standards is achieved through the establishment of a sophisticated Internal Management System (IMS). The IMS is a central UTZ

---

50 <http://www.solidaridadnetwork.org/news/west-africa-ghana-cocoa-farmers-receive-first-utz-incentive-bonuses>; last accessed on February 2, 2018.

51 <https://utzcertified.org/attachments/article/2172/CoC-Summary.pdf>; last accessed on February 2, 2018.

52 <https://www.scsglobalservices.com/files/en_utz_code_of_conduct_cocoa_module_2014.pdf>; last accessed on February 2, 2018.

requirement. It is a hierarchical project administration system (in contrast to a participatory, bottom-up system) and in the case of the project is built upon the already existing structure of the LBC's decentralized purchasing system, which reaches down to the community level. Down from the top level, there are IMS officers at each administrative level, that is to say the zonal, district and local levels in charge of program management who report frequently to the top-level management. At the local level, together with the IMS officer (who is often a young Ghanaian agronomy graduate), the LBC's purchasing clerk (often a successful cocoa farmer) invites farmers to participate in the certification project. Those who decide to join have to organize themselves into a farmers group, which will have the name of the project LBC. Nevertheless, and importantly, not all farmers within a community can join since the number of participants is restricted due to the limited international demand for UTZ certified beans. Thus, the community is divided into project participating and non-participating farmers. The participating farmers will sign a contract that defines duties and responsibilities of all parties. The farmers commit themselves to adopt the standards of and sell their produce only to the project LBC. The two project companies are responsible for the provision of training and some equipment. However, most of the farmers are illiterates and only understand the content of the contract from the LBC clerk's explanation.

The delivery of the training is organized based on a train the trainers approach. Each of the LBC's farmers' groups need to have a lead farmer positioned, who in theory is elected by the group but, in reality, might also be appointed by the LBC clerk or the technical IMS officer. The lead farmer is supposed to attend a workshop where he[53] receives advanced training on the UTZ Code of Conduct. In turn, this should enable him to conduct the training with the group. Both attendance at the workshop and the conduct of biweekly training sessions are not paid but a time-consuming responsibility. For all project participating farmers, the presence at the biweekly training is mandatory and has to be documented in their personal project passbooks. They also have to document the application of farming practices, such as the usage of chemicals, pruning or fermentation, their sales, as well as their social and environmental conditions. After a few months, with the group having considerably advanced with these practices, the IMS officer calls first for an internal and afterwards, if the degree of adoption seems to be high enough, for an external audit. Consultants from the contracted Certification Body will then check the

53 In a lead farmer workshop where the author assisted, no single female lead farmer participated.

level of adoption of the UTZ standards. A number of farms will be selected randomly and the control points are evaluated on-site. The whole project's farmers group is assessed jointly and receives a group certificate, administered by the project companies. Those farmers unable or unwilling to fulfill the requirements repeatedly will be excluded from the group. However, after a positive audit, group members are allowed to sell their 64kg bag of cocoa beans with a premium of 8 GHC (equal to 2 Euros in 2016 and to 8 percent of the price for conventional beans). The bags with certified beans are encoded and the UTZ traceability system being part of the IMS allows the separation of them from conventional beans along the whole upwards marketing chain in Ghana. Most of the bags will go from the project LBC's depots directly to the processing company's factory in Tema, with the public Quality Control Company of COCOBOD conducting a quality inspection there. Contrary to the public marketing system of conventional beans, where the transnational processor cannot identify the origin of the beans, the new traceability system and the direct link to the LBC allow the company to know exactly from which community the beans originate.

The introduction of the sustainability certification project opens a new sphere of action and influence on production for the transnational processor. Before, there was no direct link to the community level. But how does this new role of the transnational private sector in community extension services as part of its CSR strategy change local conditions? How does this shape the position of other stakeholders and which new dynamics evolve at the community level? The next section will present the social and institutional effects of transnational CSR interventions at the local level of Ghana's cocoa sector.

## 6 Social and Institutional Effects of the Studied Certification Project

The analysis of one sustainability certification project and particularly of its core element, the IMS system, reveals the immediate effects at the community level and structural transformations regarding the institutional environment of the cocoa sector in Ghana.

Most importantly, the survey among cocoa farmers indicates that participating farmers perceive an improved access to agricultural extension services and training as one of the most valuable changes linked to the project. Indeed, the approach to train the trainers and enable a local person – the lead farmer – to facilitate training is much more effective than COCOBOD's extension system which depends on a limited number of extension agents.

Many of the interviewed project participants reported their adoption of new farming practices, especially pruning, mistletoe removal, weeding and some farm sanitation practices such as the removal of diseased cocoa pods or tree branches. These are physically demanding practices and especially women and elderly workers stated difficulties with their execution. Another requirement of the UTZ standard is soil and pest management. Therefore, farmers receive training on the appropriate application of approved fertilizers and pesticides. Still, many interviewees highlight the struggle to get these products either because of local market shortages or their lack of financial means to purchase them. Hence, many farmers particularly complained about the difficulty to comply with the requirement of agrochemical application since they don't have access to them. Whereas these farming practices are similar to the ones taught by COCOBOD staff, the need to keep a record of farming performance and attendance at training sessions in project passbooks is completely new to the farmers and especially challenging for those who are illiterate or have only a very basic level of education. When asked for their experiences with social and environmental aspects of the training, many farmers could not easily comprehend what was being referred to. The most often mentioned social standard was the prohibition of child labor. This indicates a much higher prioritization of the production standards against the social and environmental standards during the trainings. Yet, one aspect of the program that falls into the social category is the formation of the farmers' groups. Indeed, participants mainly perceive this as a positive development that would ease the delivery of training and the sharing of other information. Nevertheless, statements about the inconvenience of the mandatory biweekly meetings indicate the missing emancipatory nature of company-driven farmers' organization. Problematically, the restriction of group membership results in the exclusion of many cocoa farmers from the ongoing development process. In fact, the project divides the cocoa communities into certified and non-certified cocoa farmers and thereby reinforces existing or creates new local inequalities. Project targeted farmers learn how to improve their farming practices, often achieving a production increase and are able to sell their beans with a premium. At the same time, the rest of the community lags behind, does not receive training and other benefits from the program and sells their cocoa beans for less money even though their quality might be the same. In several instances, the group members were invited to join mainly based on personal relations of the LBC's local purchasing clerk. Thus, practices of nepotism risk to be fostered. Furthermore, in some cases, disputes about participation in the project's farmers' group have been reported. Some interviewed farmers even expected to be members but the purchasing clerk reported otherwise. Many farmers were waiting to join the group and widely different information about the membership circulated. In sum, the participation was very attractive for many non-participants in the communities and it became clear that the limited membership was a very conflicting issue. Cases have been reported where the project structure even collided with traditional local authorities, which were not included the project. Some people explained how an already existing farmers' group came to its end because most of its members left the group and joined the project's farmers' group. Considering these dynamics, it became apparent that the changes triggered through the project actually shape more deep-rooted aspects of social life in the communities than mere cocoa production issues.

Besides these immediate dynamics at the community level, more structural effects of the project can be observed. They become particularly important considering the multitude of ongoing certification projects in Ghana's cocoa sector that are operating in a similar way. Changes in the institutional structures linked to CSR occur along the whole Global Cocoa Chocolate Chain. At the local level in Ghana, which was the main interest of this study, the transnational cocoa and chocolate industry's CSR strategies create at least two new spheres of private influence: the community extension and the internal marketing systems, both central parts of the project's Internal Management System. The IMS establishes a number of new local institutions that materialize, for instance, in local offices, new positions, and staff members carrying out tasks and responsibilities in the field of community development. Hence, the project directly shapes the local institutional constellation, particularly the sphere of responsibility of COCOBOD's Cocoa Health and Extension Division, which was formerly the only agent in charge of extension services. Duplication of efforts is one of the major concerns of COCOBOD's staff and was often stated in the interviews. But at the same time, there is hope that the private sector's engagement will diminish the existing lack of resources and help to push productivity upwards. Therefore, COCOBOD staff are generally rather positive towards the new private commitment. However, the increase of local influence of TNCs seems to be accompanied with a decrease of COCOBOD's regulatory capacity. The local dominance of the public agency is likely to drop rapidly.

Next to the extension system, the marketing system is also affected by private sustainability certification. Yet, the scope of transformation may only become clear during the following years. Participating farmers enter a quasi-contract farming since the members of the project are obliged to sell their produce to the project LBC. The participation in a certification project becomes increasingly attractive for farmers since the premium and training are strong incentives. Thus, for the program studied, the participating LBC enjoys a large influx of farmers willing to sell their produce to them. The transnational processing company running the project in the frame of its CSR strategy, however, manages to enhance the vertical integration of its supply chain. The establishment of the project structure allows the company to reach down to the local level of cocoa production and to shape farmers' production practices. The certification project can be understood as a way to effectively diffuse agricultural production norms and to ensure their adoption. Partnering with the successful LBC and the NGO Solidaridad, the company takes decisions affecting local development perspectives. Finally, the two main pillars of the project, the community extension and the traceability systems, extend the transnational processing company's influence on the small-holder cocoa farming and improve its control over the origin of the beans.

## 7 Conclusion: CSR, Control over Production, and Local Development Perspectives

As has been shown, CSR has a high potential to improve the value chain governance of transnational corporations. The presented case reveals that both aspects of value chain governance, that is internal chain governance and structural power, are needed to understand the overall functioning of transnational corporations' governance efforts in global value chains. On the one hand, the concept of structural power helps to understand the transnational cocoa processor's efforts to establish local structures to improve its control over dispersed smallholder cocoa production. Through UTZ sustainability training, new forms of community extension are established and new production norms successfully introduced to farmers. In addition, their compliance is monitored through detailed record keeping that is mandatory for participants. With the introduction of a quasi-contract farming system, the flow of standard compliant beans to the processor is also assured. Both aspects shape the institutional environment of Ghana's cocoa sector and result in lasting transformation. This, however, is another indicator for an improved power position of the transnational cocoa processor in the struggle for control over resource allocation and value distribution in the Global Cocoa Chocolate Chain. On the other hand, the concept of global value chain internal governance helps to explain why the transnational cocoa processor needs a close relationship with the partnering Licensed Buying Company, which is an important actor in Ghana's internal marketing segment. Both firms share the common objective of controlling farmers cocoa production and the strategic partnership allows both of them to introduce the needed structures.

Looking at the outcomes for the target group, that is Ghanaian cocoa farmers, the results of these dynamics seem to be ambivalent. Even though an immediate increase in quality and quantity of cocoa beans might occur for the certified farmers and translate in a slight income increase, the net benefit and long-term sustainability are still less evident. A higher workload and more difficult farming practices as well as a surge in input application are often stated challenges and might outweigh the immediate benefits. However, the new extension system for cocoa farmers is highly welcomed by project participants. Problematically, the ongoing developments and benefits only target a part of those living in Ghana's cocoa communities. The cocoa farmers not participating in the project and not becoming certified producers are excluded from the ongoing developments. In fact, target communities become divided into participants and non-participants or so to say certified and non-certified people. There are indications that this division also affects other social domains than cocoa farming.

The presented dynamics highlight the need to continue a critical examination of deeper-seated social effects of business-driven sustainability projects as part of their CSR strategies. Even if the transnational cocoa and chocolate industry aims to increase certified cocoa purchase to 100 percent, it appears that an improvement in a company-led farmers' livelihood tends to neglect important aspects of social development and, due to its very top-down nature, doesn't foster an intrinsic local empowerment. In the presented case, sustainability certification is shown to be an appropriate tool to improve aspects of production sustainability. Hence, it can be considered as a successful "contested governance" intervention by the project leader, one of the world's biggest cocoa processors. Nevertheless, transnational CSR in the form of sustainability certification should not be confused as a tool for more fairness in the cocoa chain or for an inclusive local development. Yet both would be urgently needed if the objective is to end the poverty cycle in which most of the Ghanaian cocoa farmers are trapped.

## Bibliography

Abdulsamad, Ajmal, *et al. Pro-Poor Development and Power Asymmetries in Global Value Chains*. Center on Globalization, Governance & Competitiveness (Durham: Duke University, 2015).

Anyidoho, Nana Akua *et al. Young people's aspirations in agriculture: a case study of Ghana's cocoa sector* (2012), online available at: <https://youtheconomicopportunities.org/sites/default/files/uploads/resource/Ghana%27s%20Cocoa%20Sector%20Case%20Study.pdf>; last accessed February 2, 2018.

Araujo Bonjean, *et al.*, "Concentration and Price Transmission in the Cocoa-Chocolate Chain," in Mara Squicciarini and Johan Swinnen (eds) *The economics of chocolate* (Oxford: Oxford University Press, 2016), pp. 339–362.

Bair, Jennifer and Palpacuer, Florence. "CSR beyond the corporation: contested governance in global value chains," *Global Networks*, 15, supplemental issue (2015), pp.1–19.

Blowfield, Michael and Dolan, Catherine. "Stewards of Virtue? The Ethical Dilemma of CSR in African Agriculture," *Development and Change*, 39 (2008), pp. 1–23.

COCOBOD (2014): *45th Annual Report and financial statements for the year ended 30. Sept. 2014*, online available at: <https://cocobod.gh/index.php>; last accessed February 2, 2018.

Cosbey, Aaron. *Policy case study – Food labelling Climate for Sustainable Growth.* CEPS Carbon Market Forum Centre for European Policy Studies Brussels, (2015), online available at: <https://papers.ssrn.com/sol3/papers.cfm?abstract_id=2696716>; last accessed February 2, 2018.

Fold, Niels and Neilson, Jeff. "Sustaining Supplies in Smallholder-Dominated Value Chains: Corporate Governance of the Global Cocoa Sector," in Mara Squicciarini and Johan Swinnen (eds), *The Economics of Chocolate* (Oxford: Oxford University Press 2016), pp. 195–212.

Fold, Niels. "Lead Firms and Competition in 'Bi-polar' Commodity Chains: Grinders and Branders in the Global Cocoa-chocolate Industry," *Journal of Agricultural Change*, 2 (2002), pp. 228–247.

Fountain, A.C and Hütz-Adams, F. *Cocoa Barometer 2015*, online available at:<www.cocoabarometer.org>; last accessed February 2, 2018.

Gayi, Samuel and Tsowou, Komi. *Cocoa Industry: Integrating small farmers into the global value chain.* UNCTAD Special Unit on Commodities. New York, Geneva (2016), online available at: <http://unctad.org/en/PublicationsLibrary/suc2015d4_en.pdf>; last accessed February 2, 2018.

Gereffi, Gary. "Global Production Systems and Third World Development," in Barbara Stallings (ed.), *Global change, regional response. The new international context of development* (Cambridge, New York: Cambridge University Press, 1995) pp. 100–42.

Gereffi, Gary *et al.* "The governance of global value chains," *Review of International Political Economy*, 12 (2005), pp. 78–104.

Godson Muojama, Olisa. "The First World War and the Cocoa Industry in Ghana: A Study of the Hazards of Economic Dependency," *Global Journal of Human-Social Science: Arts & Humanities – Psychology*, 16 (2016), pp. 33–41.

Hütz-Adams, Friedel. *Vom bitteren Kakao zur süßen Schokolade. Der lange Weg von der Hand in den Mund* (SÜDWIND e.V. –Institut für Ökonomie und Ökumene, 2011), online available at: www.suedwind-institut.de; last accessed February 2, 2018.

Knudsen Helt, Michael and Agergaard, Jytte. "Ghana 's cocoa frontier in transition: The role of migration and livelihood diversification," *Geografiska Annaler*, Swedish Society for Anthropology and Geography (2016), pp. 325–342.

Kolavalli, Shashi and Vigneri, Marcella. "Cocoa in Ghana: Shaping the Success of an Economy," in World Bank (ed.): *Yes, Africa can: success stories from a dynamic continent* (Washington, DC, 2011): pp. 20–217.

Laven, Anne. *The risks of inclusion: Shifts in governance processes and upgrading opportunities for cocoa farmers in Ghana* (Amsterdam: KIT publishers, 2010).

Levy, David. "Political Contestation in Global Production Networks," *The Academy of Management Review*, 33 (2008), pp. 943–963.

Levy, David and Kaplan, Rami. "CSR and Theories of Global Governance: Strategic Contestation in Global Issue Arenas," in Andrew Crane *et al.* (eds), *The Oxford Handbook of Corporate Social Responsibility* (Oxford: Oxford University Press, 2008), pp. 432–451.

Ludlow, Helen. "Ghana, cocoa, colonialism and globalisation: Introducing historiography," *Yesterday&Today*, 8, (2012), pp. 1–21.

Potts, Jason *et al. The State of Sustainability Initiatives Review 2014. Standards and the Green Economy*. International Institute for Sustainable Development and the International Institute for Environment and Development (2015), online available at: <http://www.iisd.org/library/state-sustainability-initiatives-review-2014-standards-and-green-economy>; last accessed February 2, 2018.

Ross, Corey. "The plantation paradigm: colonial agronomy, African farmers, and the global cocoa boom, 1870s–1940s," *Journal of Global History*, 9 (2014), pp. 49–71.

Ton, Giel *et al. Chain governance, sector policies and economic sustainability in cocoa: a comparative analysis of Ghana, Côte d'Ivoire, and Ecuador* (Wageningen: Amsterdam Institute for Social Science Research, 2008).

Ungericht, Bernhard. "Die Regulation transnationaler Wertschöpfungsketten als interessenpolitisch umkämpftes Terrain," in Karin Fischer, Christian Reiner and Cornelia Staritz (eds), *Globale Güterketten: Weltweite Arbeitsteilung und ungleiche Entwicklung* (Wien: Promedia, 2010), pp. 58–75.

Utting, Peter. "Corporate Responsibility and the Movement of Business," *Development in Practice*, 15, (2005), pp. 375–88.

CHAPTER 14

# On the (Re)Production of Informal Work in Argentina's Auto Industry

*Stefan Schmalz and Johanna Sittel*

## 1 Introduction

Argentina's car industry is usually considered a sector with decent wages and comparatively good working conditions. However, this assessment is not true for the overall sector. In particular, production in local car suppliers is often based on informal labor and workers and their families have developed a number of informal survival strategies in order to cope with flexibility requirements and low wages. These forms of informal labor are a part of globalized car production, as the large transnational companies, such as VW, Renault and Fiat, and their global production networks dominate the Argentinean car industry today.

The automotive industry is known as a frontrunner of globalization, at least since the 1980s, when European and US car markets experienced sluggish growth and emerging markets became more important.[1] The restructuring of the production model of the auto sector in the last few decades ran in parallel with an increasing flexibilization of production and employment. This process impacted both precarious formal, regular employment and in particular in the Global South, informal, non-registered labor, which is not regulated by labor laws. The informal sector offers an abundant pool of cheap labor: According to recent estimates, about 60 percent of all workers in the non-agricultural economy worldwide are informal workers.[2] These informal jobs can take different forms, such as informally employed workers at the plant level or self-employed waste-collectors who are responsible for the plant's waste disposal. Argentina is a semi-peripheral country, where highly developed economic sectors coexist amongst less developed sectors and the informal economy comprises about one third of the overall workforce.

1 Sturgeon *et al.*, "Globalisation of the automotive industry: main features and trends," pp. 7–24; Morales, *Flexible production: restructuring of the international automobile industry.*

2 OECD, *Is Informal Normal? Towards More and Better Jobs in Developing Countries.*

 | DOI:10.1163/9789004448049_015

This chapter examines the way in which informal work is integrated into presumably formal production networks. In our case study we argue that the risks and costs of flexibilized car production are outsourced to the lower tier supply industry and the households of the workers, which leads to a number of informal practices. In other words, we argue that informality is reproduced by intentional company strategies of cost reduction and flexibilization. This outsourcing of jobs into the informal sector forces workers and their families to seek a wide range of individual survival strategies, often on the black market.

The paper is divided into three parts. In the first part, we present our theoretical framework on informality. We then proceed to the empirical part of the paper by analyzing the context of the Argentinean automobile industry. This section is based on the qualitative research conducted in Córdoba and Buenos Aires.[3] It outlines different forms of informal work found in the lower tier companies in Argentina's automotive production networks and how they are reproduced in households and the daily life of workers. By doing this we simultaneously describe both, company strategies of flexibilization and workers' survival strategies used to cope with these requirements. Finally, we conclude that in the case of Argentina, formal production inside the global production chains is highly dependent on informal work, which is often disguised by outsourcing processes to small enterprises, the informal sector and the households. Thus, informality tends to be (re)produced as an entrepreneurial strategy of cost reduction and flexibility, but also as an individual survival strategy of the workers and their families.

## 2 Theoretical Foundations: The Dialectics of Informal and Formal Labor

Informality comprises a wide range of activities, among them, irregular informal work in factories, self-employed craftspersons, domestic workers, street

3 The findings are based on qualitative research results of the PROALAR Joint Project: "FlexTrans: Flexibility in Transnational Value Chains – Precariousness, Work and Territory in Germany and Argentina" (Jena and Córdoba/Buenos Aires; 2012–2013) and the PhD project of Johanna Sittel. This is an empirical study based on qualitative interviews with experts, employers' representatives and trade union officials, workers and some household members mainly in Córdoba and some in Buenos Aires. In addition, we did participatory observations of production and housing conditions. In the DAAD-funded FlexTrans project, 37 interviews were conducted. Also, 55 more interviews have been conducted as part of Johanna Sittel's dissertation project on the "The Double production of informal work in the Argentinean automotive sector" (09/2015–12/2015 and 04/2016).

vendors, etc. There are different readings of the phenomena of informal work.[4] The term *informality* goes back to the studies commissioned by ILO about the informal sector in Africa.[5] From this modernization theory perspective, informality usually tends to be perceived as a result of underdevelopment in the so-called *Third World*, which should be overcome by the modern sector.[6] The dependency theory and structuralist approaches are in turn critical about these assessments.[7] They offer a broader definition of informal work, arguing it is not only a phenomenon of less developed societies, but rather comprises all income-generating activities, which are not regulated by the state.[8] Moreover, from a dependency theory perspective, informal labor is a functional necessity of capitalist accumulation in order to cut down on labor costs and compete in the world market.[9]

More recently, institutionalist and ethnographic approaches have tried to grasp informality. While Perry et al. perceive informality as individual exit options from ill-functioning laws and rules,[10] Belvedere et al. highlight the importance of households for informal activities.[11] They distinguish between two forms of informality, subsistence informality (*informalidad de subsistencia*) based on mere informal subsistence production – which does not create additional income, but aims at livelihood and reproduction – and informality of accumulation (*informalidad de acumulación*), which aims at gaining an additional income in order to sustain or increase ones material living standard. The feminist Bielefeld school also refers to the relationship between subsistence work and formal capital accumulation by pointing out the inseparable connection between *housewifization* and the capitalist economy.[12] Scholars such

4 For details, see: Komlosy *et al.*, *Ungeregelt und unterbezahlt. Der informelle Sektor in der Weltwirtschaft*; Sittel *et al.*, "Reflexionen zum Informalitätskonzept am Beispiel der argentinischen Automobilindustrie."

5 Hart, "Informal Income Opportunities and Urban Employment in Ghana"; ILO, *Employment, Incomes and Equality: A strategy for Increasing Productive Employment in Kenya.*

6 ILO, *Employment, Incomes and Equality: A strategy for Increasing Productive Employment in Kenya.*

7 Santos, *The shared space. The two circuits of the urban economy in underdeveloped countries*; Portes *et al.*, *The Informal Economy. Studies in Advanced and Less Developed Countries.*

8 Portes and Sassen-Koob, "Making it Underground: Comparative Material on the Informal Sector in Western Market Economies"; Portes *et al.*, *The Informal Economy. Studies in Advanced and Less Developed Countries.*

9 Portes *et al.*, *The Informal Economy. Studies in Advanced and Less Developed Countries.*

10 Perry *et al.*, *Informality: Exit and Exclusion.*

11 Belvedere *et al.*, "Trayectorias Laborales en tiempos de crisis."

12 Mies, *Patriarchy and Accumulation on a World Scale*, p. 16. The notion *housewifization* describes how capitalist development is based on the exploitation of women as

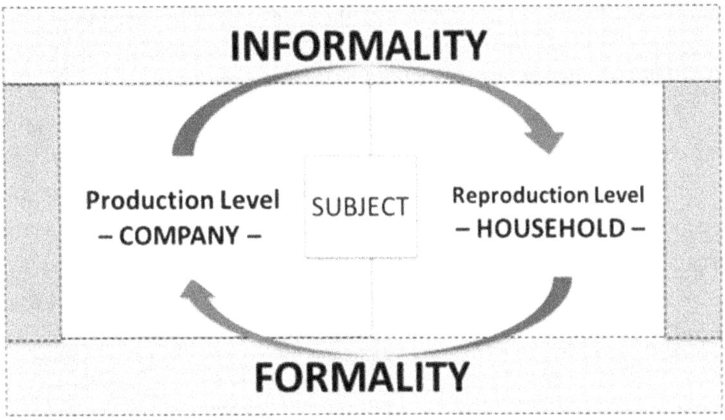


FIGURE 14.1 Dynamic concept of informality

as Maria Mies and Claudia von Werlhof show how reproductive work (domestic work, etc.), subsistence, but also productive production, are shifted to the responsibility of households and that it falls mostly on the shoulders of female workers.[13] Although these authors do not focus on the term of informality, they point out its relation to different forms of domestic work.

Even though dualistic understandings of informal work continue to be prominent, today dialectic approaches analyzing the relationship between informal and formal production and labor are gaining importance.[14] This chapter draws on such a dynamic, dialectical concept of informality. Formality and informality are hereby not perceived as self-contained, but as standing in a dialectical relationship that manifests itself in both industrial value creation and at the household level. Consequently, informal labor tends to be closely connected to both formal and reproductive activities (see Figure 14.1).[15]

Our working definition of informality for the following analysis thereby refers to non-registered work activities beyond institutional regulation, which aim at the creation of income and can comprise different forms of labor in

housewives. In the context of global capitalism, housework and other forms of unpaid work as typical female work are devalued.

13 *Ibid.*; Werlhof, "The Proletarian is dead: Long live the Housewife?".

14 Neffa, "Modelos productivos y sus impactos sobre la relación salarial. Reflexiones a partir del caso argentino"; Komlosy, *Work. The Last 1000 Years;* Webster *et al.*, *Making visible the invisible: confronting South Africa's Decent Work Deficit, Research Report prepared for the Department of Labour.*

15 Sittel *et al.*, *Reflexionen zum Informalitätskonzept am Beispiel der argentinischen Automobilindustrie*, p. 63.

companies and households. Informal labor may thereby refer to wage labor (regular or casual), self-employed and unpaid contributing family workers in family businesses.[16] Generally, trade unions do not represent these groups. In many cases, informal workers have to organize themselves and struggle for particular rights. The dialectical concept of informality highlights the grey zones between formal and informal labor in particular. We therefore point out the practices of informal over-time work at a formal workplace or informal extra payments as a form of semi-informality. In addition, informal work often overlaps with unpaid subsistence and domestic work, which we do not subsume under informality but regard as separate categories.

## 3 Argentina: Between Crisis and Progress

In the case of Argentina, three characteristics seem to be crucial to understanding how informality unfolds. Firstly, Argentina is a semi-peripheral, structurally heterogeneous country. Secondly, economic development in Argentina used to be characterized by economic cycles that repeatedly lead to crisis. And thirdly, the country has gone through recurrent periods of institutionalization and de-institutionalization of labor standards.

(1) The global capitalist economy is characterized by structural dependencies and a hierarchical international division of labor.[17] Argentina is a *semi-peripheral country* and, thus, occupies an intermediate role between countries of the core, which tend to produce capital goods and highly specialized services, and the periphery, which mainly produces raw materials and agricultural goods. These different zones of the world-system are closely connected by global commodity chains.[18] Argentina's labor market reflects *structural heterogeneity* as a result of the country's semi-peripheral position.[19] Its economy is characterized by different forms of production, which range from small *backyard-production facilities* to modern export-oriented companies. Historically, structural heterogeneity has persisted despite attempts of formalization

16 Chen *et al.*, "Informality, Gender and Poverty: A Global Picture," p. 2137.

17 Wallerstein, *World-Systems Analysis. An Introduction.*

18 Hopkins and Wallerstein, "Commodity Chains in the World-Economy Prior to 1800"; Fischer et al., *Globale Güterketten. Weltweite Arbeitsteilung und ungleiche Entwicklung.*

19 The notion of *structural heterogeneity* was developed by dependency theory authors and describes social polarisation and inequalities as a main feature of peripheral, so-called underdeveloped countries, Córdova and Michelena, *Aspectos teóricos del subdesarrollo.* See also: Frank, *1929–2005. Crisis in the world economy.*

of the labor market and in the face of segmented labor markets with diverging wage levels and working conditions and a large informal sector.[20]

(2) Along with structural heterogeneity, the Argentinian economy is characterized by pronounced cyclical oscillations of economic growth, which is the second characteristic of Argentinean development we underline. Historically, Argentina has been through instable junctures,[21] which had a dramatic impact on the labor market. For instance, the 1982 debt crisis was succeeded by a period of hyperinflation in 1989 – the worst crisis since the end of the period of import-substituting industrialization –, then followed by the impact of the Mexican "Tequila crisis" in 1994. These crises led to a temporary increase in unemployment, underemployment and informality (see Figure 14.2). Throughout the 1990s, the situation remained unstable. Neither the dollar-peso currency peg, the so-called *convertibilidad* (1991–2002), nor the Carlos Menem government's neoliberal reform policy of the 1990s helped to re-stabilize Argentina's economy on a long-term basis. Instead, the era led to one of the most serious economic, social and political crises in the country in 2001/2002.

During the Kirchner governments (2003–2015 – Nestor Kirchner: 2003–2007; Cristina Kirchner Fernández: 2007–2015) Argentina experienced a period of relatively political, social and economic stability. The so-called period of *postconvertibilidad* was characterized by comparatively high GDP growth rates and a regeneration of the industrial sector in the Metropolitan area of Córdoba.[22] This development also had an impact on the labor market with formal employment rising and un/under-employment being reduced to under 10 percent. However, between 2014 and 2016 the Argentina's economy went through a slump once again with labor market indicators deteriorating.

(3) Third, Argentina's development ran along periods of institutionalization and de-institutionalization of labor standards that were characterized by cycles of formalization and informalization respectively.[23] The "moving boundaries of informality"[24] changed frequently. During the era of Peronism (1946–1955) Argentina developed a comparatively comprehensive system of industrial relations.[25] In particular, industrial workers gained significant

20 Schmalz *et al.*, "Unsicherheit als Alltagserfahrung: Abgestufte Beschäftigungshierarchien im Wertschöpfungssystem Automobil in Argentinien"; Groisman, "Gran Buenos Aires: Polarización de ingresos, clase media e informalidad laboral, 1974–2010."

21 Boris, "Argentinien und der 'K-Faktor'."

22 Buffalo, *Reestructuración productiva y configuración territorial.*

23 Weinmann, "Los ciclos de la política del trabajo formal e informal en América Latina."

24 Castells and Portes, "World Underneath: The Origins, Dynamics and Effects of the Informal Economy," p. 32.

25 Álvarez *et al.*, *Estado actual del sistema de relaciones laborales en la Argentina.*

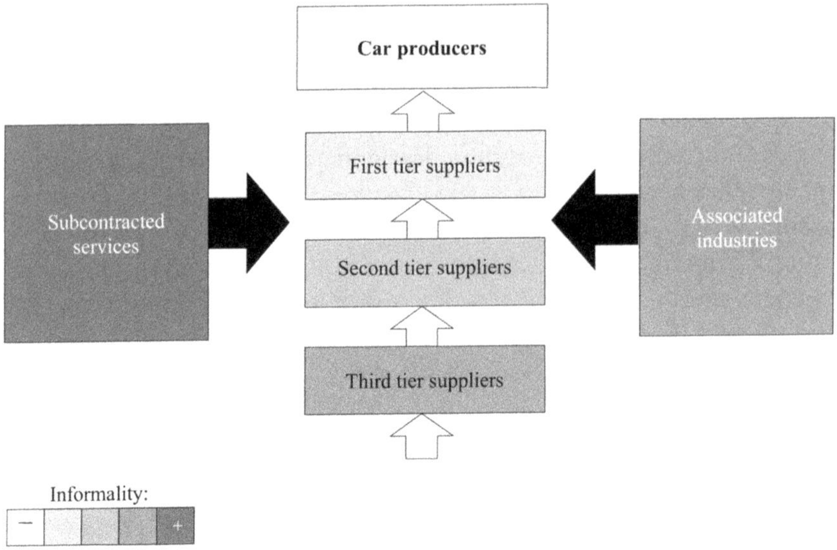


FIGURE 14.2 Development of formal and informal employment in Argentina 1974–2014: employment rate (in percent of population) and unregistered employees (share of employed persons in percent)
Note: the data between 1980–1989 refer to the greater Buenos Aires area, the only methodologically corresponding data available for this period; from 2003 the measurement method was changed.
SOURCE: EPH-INDEC

institutional rights. However, these rules were partially dismantled during the military dictatorship between 1976–1983 and particularly by Menem's neoliberal reform policies in the 1990s.[26] The government deregulated the labor market and made cuts to welfare. For instance, the government repealed the minimum wage and privatized the pension system. These measures led to an increase in informality by more than one fifth (see Figure 14.2).

After the 2001/2002 financial crisis, the Kirchner government implemented policies to reinstitutionalize labor standards.[27] About 182 labor laws were reviewed, changed or adopted. The Menem government's law of flexibilization of labor relations ("Ley Banelco") was cancelled (2004) and in 2013, there was an attempt to regulate (mainly informal) domestic work. In addition, a new legal procedure in order to legalize informal activities in general was initiated in May 2014. Moreover, the government reintroduced the minimum wage

26 Harvey, *A brief history of Neoliberalism.*

27 Boyer and Neffa, *Salida de crisis y estrategias alernativas de desarrollo. La experiencia Argentina.*

and public pensions. The economic boom of the 2000s and the reform policy beginning in 2003 led to an improvement of labor market indicators. Until 2010 about four million new jobs were created.[28] Moreover, the Kirchner government increased the number of labor regulation inspectors from 40 (2013) to 568 (2015) which helped to reduce informality. The share of informal jobs, which had increased tremendously again after the 2001/02 crisis, was reduced to under 35 percent. Overall, the political representation of informal workers during the Kirchner governments was strengthened. In 2011, for example, the first association of informal workers, the so-called popular movement, CTEP (*Confederación de Trabajadores de la Economía Popular*), was founded.

After the latest disruptions to the financial markets in 2013, the implementation of measures to reduce informality had slowed down and real wages stagnated. The minimum wage amounting to 9,500 pesos (412 Euros) remained at a rather low level. The inflation rate went up to more than 25 percent yearly. The reregulation of the labor market did not change most informal practices with the majority of newly created jobs lacking stability and quality. Since the assumption of office of the Mauricio Macri government, in December 2015, labor market indicators have further deteriorated. Under Macri, inflation has reached its highest annual rate since 1989/90 at 46 percent. Real wages dropped to an all-time low in 2016 and more than half a million workers lost their jobs in his first year in office. Moreover, the share of informal work is rising again. Similarly, control mechanisms introduced by the Kirchner government, such as labor inspections, are gradually being phased out as part of so-called de-bureaucratization measures. For example, at the beginning of 2018 the *Administración Federal de Ingresos Públicos* (AFIP) decided to close three departments, which controlled informal work. Although the planned reform of the labor market by the Macri government envisages the creation of new jobs, it mainly includes measures to flexibilize and informalize work, such as the reintroduction of an internship system or the facilitation of dismissals and cuts in social security. The planned cuts and reforms have already led to three general strikes and several mass mobilizations.

The automobile sector reflects the overall changes in the labor market quite well. In Córdoba, Argentina, transnational companies such as Fiat, VW, IVECO and Renault dominate car production. After the creation of the free trade area Mercosur (founding members: Argentina, Brazil, Paraguay, Uruguay) the Argentinean supply industry began to hold a strategically important position for transnational companies in the *Cono Sur*, the Southern Cone of South America,

28 CIFRA, *Informe de Coyuntura, No. 7*, p. 25.

in particular for the dynamic Brazilian market and its highly developed auto industry. The auto industry in Córdoba has a heavy presence of component suppliers. Both cars and car components are mainly exported to Brazil (about 60 percent of all exports). Apart from the dependency on export markets, Argentina's car industry also has to import raw materials and components. In Argentina's semi-peripheral industrial structure there are few high-tech car suppliers that are able to cope with modularized just-in-time production to successfully compete in the world market, as the technologically advanced car producers in the core countries today rely on highly flexibilized and competitive production networks.[29]

Argentina's automotive industry is increasingly under pressure by market liberalization and deindustrialization. Whereas the auto sector played a key role in import-substituting industrialization (1930–1976), there was a significant fall of industrial production after the 1982 debt crisis, which continues to have a lasting impact. This was further coupled by the 2001/02 crisis in which the car sector shrank to a historic low. Between 1995 and 2011 employment in the supplier industry decreased by 28 percent and in the final assembly plants by 25 percent respectively. During the period of reindustrialization, after 2003, the auto sector recovered. In comparison to 1997 the number of employees has increased by about 37.5 percent. The industry in Córdoba also experienced a regeneration.

By 2010, there were about 20,000 workers employed in Cordoba's automotive sector, about a third of the overall industrial employment. However, in the last few years the sector has suffered another crisis period. The production collapsed in 2014 with 3,100 workers in the assembly plants forced to go on unpaid leave[30] and 400 of them dismissed.[31] In 2016, once again suspensions and reduced working hours affected around 2,900 workers at the manufacturers and 3,000 at the suppliers respectively.[32] Since 2017, the automotive sector seems to be recovering as investments and sales went up sharply and (in Córdoba) about 1,500 new jobs in the car factories were created.

Labor in the Argentinean automotive industry is said to be regulated by strong trade unions and to be mainly formalized. However, there are divergent assessments. The plant-corporatist automotive union SMATA (*Sindicato de Mecánicos y Afines del Transporte Automotor*) estimates the share of informal labor in the overall sector to be about 40 percent, a number that was also

29 Humphrey *et al.*, *Global Strategies and Local Realities*.
30 Redacción LAVOZ, "Hoy las suspensiones en Córdoba llegarán a los 3.100 trabajadores."
31 Kempa, "Automotrices desvincularon a casi 400 trabajadores."
32 Kempa, "Smata y UOM acuerdan una grilla de suspensiones para frenar despidos."

confirmed by an oppositional trade union delegate.[33] However, this number is not stable. It is highly dependent on the changing labor laws. Labor laws and policies, such as the re-regulation of the labor markets during the Kirchner government, hampered the strategies of informalization in order to increase competitiveness. This is of importance, as labor costs went up by 30 percent between 2001 and 2012 and companies were forced to reduce costs. However, with the Macri government a new period of deregulation and informalization of the labor market seems to have started.

Taken together, although Argentina has comparatively high standards of legal protection, informal work and underemployment are still structural features of the labor market. These structural conditions are present even in highly regulated sectors such as the automobile industry, in particular in the lower tier supply industry. The 2014–2016 crisis and the policies of the Macri government once again highlighted the insecurity of employment in this sector, which led to an increase of informality.

## 4 (Re)Production of Informal Work in Argentina's Automobile Sector

The automobile industry is a rather privileged sector in Argentina's economy and it is usually ignored when analyzing informality, as official estimations do not involve informal work in SMATA-organized manufacturing plants. There are other economic sectors such as domestic work (85 percent), construction (65 percent) or the textile industry (37 percent) with higher shares of informal labor.[34] However, in the lower tiers of the automotive supply industry one finds widespread informal work as well. In Argentina, risks and costs of automobile production are outsourced to the lower tiers of the value chain, in particular to workers and their households. The informal practices are reproduced by the strategies of employers to reduce costs and increase flexibility in order to compete in global markets and meet the high requirements set by the car manufacturers, but also by individual survival strategies of workers and their families.

### 4.1 *Informality on the Plant Level*

Informal labor in the car and car supplier industry is often only visible upon close inspection. For employers and employer representatives, informality is

33 Interview with union official SMATA, Córdoba, 20 September 2012; Interview with a delegate of transnational car company, Córdoba, 27 September 2013.

34 Bertranou and Casanova, *Informalidad laboral en Argentina: segmentos críticos y políticas para la formalización.*

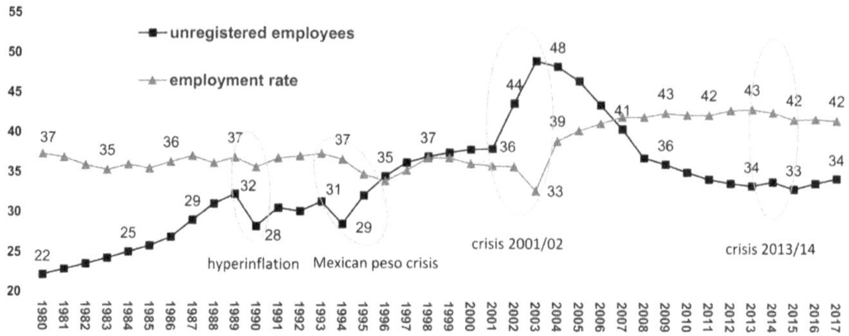


FIGURE 14.3 Informality along the automobile value chain in Argentina (own depiction)

still a taboo issue, as there used to be strict controls of informal practices under the Kirchner government. In the important car producers, informality is not an important issue. The comparatively strong presence of trade unions at the plant level leads to a de facto non-existence of informality in most final assembly plants. Accordingly, car producers are a guarantee for comparatively stable formal employment under relatively privileged working conditions: "Working at VW is like playing football with Barcelona",[35] a worker in Córdoba told us. However, the further the plant is positioned from the final product within the production chain, the more precarious the labor.[36] The (semi-)informal practices are quite common in outsourced production stages and ancillary services (see Figure 14.3).

The main reasons for subcontracting are cost reduction and specialization.[37] In the automotive sector the easiest way to achieve this cost reduction is by outsourcing external service providers for security, sanitation, maintenance, catering, logistics or even individual production stages crucial for the overall production process. For instance, the externalization of logistics and accounting results in lower costs. The risk of informality is higher at these outsourced facilities and along the supply chain. In particular, in the second, third or even fourth tier component producers informal work is quite common. The same is true for final product-related services (e.g. automobile workshops) and

35 Interview with a worker from transnational car company, Córdoba, 22 September 2012.

36 Schmalz *et al.*, "Unsicherheit als Alltagserfahrung: Abgestufte Beschäftigungshierarchien im Wertschöpfungssystem Automobil in Argentinien."

37 On outsourcing in a global perspective see: Smith, *Imperialism in the 21st Century*, pp. 39–100. On subcontracting in Latin America, see: Robinson, *Latin America and global capitalism*. On subcontracting in car industry see Humphrey *et al.*, *Global Strategies and Local Realities*.

the associated industries that are indirectly related to car production (e.g. machines, spare parts, packaging, waste disposal).

Most (sub)suppliers in the car industry are national small and medium enterprises (SMEs) with low trade union density at the shop floor level. In these small (sub)suppliers and associated industries semi-informal practices are widespread. The semi-informal wage-payments and irregular overtime work are common forms of informality. They are quite widespread among both small and larger supply companies: "There are always some companies that employ people full-time paying half of them under the counter."[38] For instance, in the case of spare parts producers, semi-informal jobs are quite common.[39] Parts of the wage are paid informally in order to reduce costs: "Overtime was always paid under the counter",[40] explained a worker in a tire factory. In the metal industry, one finds similar practices. For example, in the company *Iron*[41] in Córdoba all 15 employees have a permanent contract. However, there are also a number of (semi)informal practices at the plant level. When demand for their output spikes, most workers work from 7 am to 6 pm, instead of 7 am to 4 pm, and receive informal extra-payments. "Overtime is typical for our firm", summarizes the chief executive personally.[42]

Workers in turn report that all overtime work has been paid under the counter.[43] Workers were financially dependent on overtime work, as the payment for regular working days were insufficient to support a family, even though it is set by a collective agreement. For instance, Marco earns about 12,000 pesos (around 1,100 Euros, December 2015) monthly, with about 30 percent of the monthly salary being paid informally for overtime work. In addition, there are other (semi)informal practices. Some employers accumulate high debt with workers' social insurance by not paying the contributions. Even worse, there is a high level of *monotributo*[44] work, which is comparable to service contracts for small entrepreneurs or pseudo self-employment. In the co-oporative *Iron sheet*

38 Interview with UOM-delegate of different car parts manufacturers, Córdoba, 25 June 2012.

39 Interview with a worker from car parts factory, Córdoba, 1 June 2012.

40 Interview with a worker from tire factory, Córdoba, 19 November 2015.

41 Names of companies and persons have been changed or made anonymous for data protection reasons.

42 Interview with a chief of small car parts factory, Córdoba, 11 December 2015.

43 Interview with a worker from small car parts factory, Córdoba, 11 December 2015.

44 The *monotributo* regime was introduced in 1998 as part of the flexible labor market reforms for temporary low-income commercial activities. In contrast to self-employment (working on "cuenta propia"), it is possible to contribute to the pension fund, but the payments are limited to minimum contributions, which usually do not reflect the hours worked.

all 25 workers are such pseudo self-employed small entrepreneurs (*monotributo*), effectively working on the basis of service contracts. The same is true for external employees of a steel producer in Rosario who founded a co-operative after dismissal from the main factory. Today this company does the same work and is directly involved in the production of their former employer. Such *café con leche* practices, located in the grey zone between formality and informality, have increased in the last few years.[45]

Even though the suppliers and service providers that are involved in car production networks usually have to register their employees,[46] these companies find loopholes in official regulations that enable informality. Most small service providers in sanitation, logistics, maintenance and catering draw extensively on informal labor. In addition, trade union representation is much lower than in the core automotive sector. For instance, in the case of one company in our sample, waste disposal is done informally. "Waste disposal has been outsourced. Well, there is this guy who asks for cardboard, nylon and other stuff, he takes it to sell. The company gives it to him because it is garbage."[47] This practice is not completely altruistic, as the company is able to dispose their waste without any costs. Moreover, most externalized services in the factories of car producers contain frequent (semi-)informal labor. Many drivers are self-employed workers,[48] while small machinery maintenance factories do not pay wages or social insurance on time or do not comply to labor laws.

Most *tercerizados – outsourced workers* – are temporary agency workers or employees of subcompanies that do not have well-paid formalized jobs. Informality is also quite widespread at small car workshops. The large contracted workshops fall under the same legal regulations as car manufacturers, but the small workshops – about 35,000 in Argentina, producing very simple to highly specialized components for the car body, transmissions or the engine – do not comply with legal standards and employ informal workers. There are quite a few experiences of informality in these workshops: "I worked there for 5 years, officially [formally]. But they tricked me. They did not pay the social security contributions, neither pension nor health insurance. Since our boss knew both the president of the employers' association and the union well, nobody noticed it."[49]

45 Neffa *et al.*, *La crisis de la relación salarial: naturaleza y significado de la informalidad, los trabajos/empleos precarios y los no registrados*, p. 58. *Café con leche* is the Spanish term for coffee with milk.

46 Interview with human resource manager of car parts factory, Córdoba, 29 May 2012.

47 Interview with a delegate of car parts factory, Córdoba, 11 June 2012.

48 Interview with a sociologist, Buenos Aires, 18 September 2015.

49 Interview with a car mechanic in a small workshop, 17 October 2015.

There are a number of reasons for these (semi-)informal practices. They include cost reduction, flexibilization, but also disciplining the workers by fragmenting the workforce in order to increase competitiveness. For instance, informal overtime work is a useful tool for employers to temporally cope with sudden spikes in demand. Moreover, parts of the production process are outsourced to subcontracted firms that extensively draw on informal labor in order to externalize the risks and costs of market volatility. Similar effects can be achieved by externalizing services as most employees of service providers work under comparatively bad working conditions.

### 4.2 *Household Level*

The close relationship between informal and formal labor is not only apparent in industrial production, but also in the households. The wage earner should not be perceived as a single, isolated person, as he/she is usually embedded in a household.[50] The household tends to be a crucial unit for global production, while several forms of income do persist within households at the same time.[51] The income of industrial workers is often insufficient to support the family. The household of a worker in Argentina typically comprises of a nuclear family even though family arrangements are getting more heterogeneous. Although the number of female principal earners increased between 2001 (27,7 percent) and 2010 (34,2 percent) by 7 percent, the Argentinean worker family usually comprises of a male principal earner, his wife and at least two children. Two thirds of interviewees are in similar conditions with the rest of them being single or divorced.

The precarious jobs, whose numbers oscillate together with the economic conjunctures, recurrent crises and unstable income and underpayment have an impact at the household level: "Ever since I have been working and I can remember ... we are not able to make plans such as 'in five years I will have a car, a house'. Even my father was not able to do so ... We just live day by day, there has never been stability."[52] This is why workers and other household members develop ways to cope with these instabilities, with informality being an important strategy. Many households reduce their expenditures for consumption goods by buying them in the informal sector. They also rely on

50 Smith *et al.*, *Households and the World Economy*; Wallerstein, *World-Systems Analysis. An Introduction*; Komlosy, *Work. The Last 1000 Years*.

51 *Ibid*; see also: Huws, "The Reproduction of Difference: Gender and the Global Division of Labour"; Werlhof, "The Proletarian is dead: Long live the Housewife?"; Dunaway, *Gendered Commodity Chains: Seeing Women's Work and Households in Global Production*.

52 Interview with a worker from transnational car company, Córdoba, 22 September 2012.

additional sources of informal income of non-registered work or they pick up informal jobs for a brief period of time. Wages are too low to have a decent living and it is nearly impossible to receive larger bank credits. "To ascend, you have to do without: do not go out, not enjoy a beer, no new jeans, do not go to the cinema. […] I have been working for 10 years and for what? For a computer from 2003 […] and an old TV set".[53] Almost every worker seems to have an additional income to get along: "There are many people, that have a second job … as car mechanics, repairers, painters … Of course these jobs are undeclared and realized at home or in a tiny workshop."[54]

Consequently, informality in Argentina is often an additional source of income to a fixed job, even though official labor market statistics record only a few second sources of income. This also applies to the automotive industry.[55] In our sample, about half of all interviewees declared a stable second income or a so-called *changa*. Changas are mainly referring to casual work such as irregular activities in handicraft, trade or services, which are sometimes related to the qualification of workers and involve – mostly unpaid – family work:

> There are many who sell food, they sell it once in a while. The hardest part is for those who have children, because not all the family can go to work because going to work means paying someone to look after the children. That's why many women sell food or earn something in a variety of ways. On the weekend, the workers work on their own account: in construction, electrical installations/repairs, as plumbers, selling things or repairing mobile phones. In the factories you can see every kind of business trying to make a little more money. But you cannot have a second formal job. That's impossible because you're in the factory for at least nine hours a day.[56]

There are diverging forms and intensity of these *changas*. "After work, I work as a taxi driver", explained a 32-year-old mechanic.[57] Others do gardening work or provide car maintenance services to close friends and neighbors. Some are doing the *changas* temporarily, others as a source of additional income. For

53 Interview with a worker from car parts factory, Córdoba, 1 June 2012.

54 Interview with a self-employed taxi driver (former worker in automobile supplier), Córdoba, 21 September 2012.

55 Sevilla, *Une comparaison de la fabrication de la violence liée à l'emploi. Licenciements massifs et intérim chez les ouvriers de l'automobile en Argentine et en France.*

56 Interview with a worker and student, Córdoba, 27 November 2015.

57 Interview with a car mechanic in small workshop, 17 October 2015.

instance, a retired former worker of a car supply company sells cookies in front of the factory gate in order to have some additional income to his low pension, and a former worker with a fixed contract at an automobile plant who had to stop work due to health issues, has organized a driving service for former colleagues.[58] However, usually *changas* are mainly used to finance daily life. "My changa helps me with the children, in particular to buy clothes for them", stated a 47-year-old worker at a tire factory. For most workers, *changas* seem to be a necessary survival strategy.[59] Those interviewees who did not indicate having a *changa,* who work more than 10 hours due to informal over-time work, receive seniority payment due to their high age/experience or are still quite young and live at their parents' house and thus do not yet have their own family to support.

Although already showing signs of erosion, the male-bread-winner model is still quite common in Argentina's working class. Labor participation of women increased between 1990 and 2006 by 10 percent.[60] The rising demand for female labor is also due to the deregulation and precarization of the labor market. In most cases, the need for a second income is unavoidable, in particular when there is no stable *changa* in the household. Women are particularly vulnerable to informality as the gendered workplaces hiring women usually have high shares of informal positions.[61] The workers' wives often work as domestic workers or in the public sector on a part time basis. Despite Kirchner's reforms, they work informally. Apart from paid or unpaid informal work contributing to a household's income, workers try to keep living costs low by avoiding unnecessary costs for formal services and by relying on subsistence production and their own workforce in the household: "Being able to repair by myself helps to live better and it helps you at home, because if the kids have broken shoes and one cannot buy new ones, I will fix them. I will fix everything".[62]

Taken together, informality in households seems to be an important part of workers' survival strategies. Besides overtime work in factories, *changas* are also important for making a decent living. They help "to live better"[63] and act

---

58 Interview with an informal vender in front of car factory, Córdoba, 10 December, 2015.

59 Interview with a worker from tire factory, Córdoba, 19 November 2015.

60 Águila, "Tendencias contrapuestas en la participación de las mujeres en el mercado laboral argentino: Un análisis desagregado del empleo femenino para el período 2003–2013," p. 2.

61 On the relationship between gender inequality and the global division of labor see Huws, "The Reproduction of Difference: Gender and the Global Division of Labour"; on the role of female labor in value chains see Dunaway, *Gendered Commodity Chains: Seeing Women's Work and Households in Global Production.*

62 Interview with a worker in tire factory, Córdoba, 10 November 2015.

63 *Ibid.*

as a *shock absorber* during times of crisis when unemployment, lower income or unforeseen expenditures hit workers' households.[64] "It's hard to live in these times (...) because the [formal] economy does not support you", explained a 46-year-old worker in a tire factory.[65] Consequently, workers are highly flexible and creative in order to cope with conjunctural changes and to develop *survival strategies*[66] beyond formal wage labor.[67] "It is worthwhile to expand your skills and your horizon (...) and solidify what you can do. Because in the periods between one and the next job, it will support you, even as you will just use your skills for a kind of *changa*."[68] Or, as another worker formulated "I think that just a few metal workers do not have the ability to find work [...] when they are dismissed from the factory [...] you learn to do other things".[69] Therefore, one sees multiple work biographies at the households and various employment and consumption strategies.

Informality in the household serves as a flexibility buffer during economic downturns, thereby subsidizing companies indirectly.[70] The underpayment and insecurity in the companies is also based on informal practices within families as economic risks are outsourced to the households. Moreover, multiple patterns of income and consumption in the households are a precondition for the reproduction of the automotive workforce. Even the better-paid interviewed workers' households rely (partially) on additional informal income for larger expenditures such as a possible annual holiday.

## 5 Conclusion

The following rule of thumb is helpful to understand informality in Argentina's automotive industry: the lower the plant is positioned along the production chain, the higher the risk of informal practices. This rule is valid for both local

64 Cardoso and Faletto, *Development and Dependence in Latin America.*
65 Interview with a worker in tire factory, Córdoba, 19 November 2015.
66 Neffa, *La crisis de la relación salarial: naturaleza y significado de la informalidad, los trabajos/empleos precarios y los no registrados,* pp. 81–85; Komlosy, *Methoden und Theorien der Globalgeschichte,* p. 135.
67 Schmalz *et al.* "Unsicherheit als Alltagserfahrung," pp. 88–93.
68 Interview with a young temporary worker, Córdoba, 30 November 2015.
69 Interview with a self-employed taxi driver (former worker automobile supplier), Córdoba, 21 September 2012.
70 This corresponds with Andrea Komlosy's concept on "transfer value" and underlines the huge share of informal work. For details of transfer value, see: Komlosy, *Work. The Last 1000 Years,* p. 88.

suppliers and service providers and also applies to the households of workers. There are a number of informal practices to be found at plant level, such as irregular overtime work, short-term contract work and the non-payment of social welfare provisions. Informality is therefore an employer strategy of supplier companies to save costs and make the labor supply flexible in order to cope with the high pressure from car producers. In addition to these plant-based informal practices, there are also different informal sources of income at the household level such as so-called *changas* and the semi-informal income (of women) both of which are part of survival strategies of workers and their families.

The high share of informal labor in the highly globalized Argentinean automobile production chain shows how a complex entanglement of both formal and informal labor is the dominant mode for the exploitation of workforces in the semi-periphery. The informal wage payments also contribute to the fragmentation of the working class. Additionally, low wages in the industry tend to be subsidized by survival strategies and informal practices in the workers' households. For instance, informal labor in households leads to a double burden for women who are usually also responsible for unpaid care work. Therefore, one cannot fully grasp the functioning of informal labor and its entanglements with formal production without including paid and unpaid household contributions in the analysis.

The informal labor is also influenced by state policies. The austerity policies of the Macri government are currently leading to increasing poverty and social unrest. Several measures, such as the pension cuts worth about 4.8 billion Euros, are having an impact on about 17 million Argentineans (in late 2017) and have led to large protest in Buenos Aires. Some of these measures, such as the cuts for labor control authorities, are likely to increase the role of informal labor in Argentina's industry. Together with the increasing pressure on the supplier industry in automotive production networks, informality will continue to persist in both Argentina's factories and households.

## Bibliography

Águila, Nicolas. "Tendencias contrapuestas en la participación de las mujeres en el mercado laboral argentino: Un análisis desagregado del empleo femenino para el período 2003–2013," *Congreso Nacional de Estudios de Trabajo 5.-7. August, Thematic Group No. 6: Género, mercado de trabajo y cuidado* (Buenos Aires: aset, 2015).

Álvarez, Eduardo O. et al. *Estado actual del sistema de relaciones laborales en la Argentina* (Buenos Aires: Rubinzal-Culzoni Editores, 2008).

Belvedere, Carlos *et al.* "Trayectorias Laborales en tiempos de crisis," in Jorge Carpio, Jorge Emilio Klein, and Irene Novacovsky (eds), *Informalidad y exclusión social* (Buenos Aires: FCE-Siempro-OIT, 2000).

*Bertranou, Fabio and Luis Casanova. Informalidad laboral en Argentina: segmentos críticosy políticas para la formalización* (Buenos Aires: ILO, 2013).

Boris, Dieter. "Argentinien und der 'K-Faktor'," *Blätter für deutsche und internationale Politik* 56 (2011), pp. 23–26.

Boyer, Robert and Julio C. Neffa (eds). *Salida de crisis y estrategias alernativas de desarrollo. La experiencia Argentina* (Buenos Aires: CEIL-PIETTE, 2007).

Buffalo, Luciana. *Reestructuración productiva y configuración territorial. Pequeña industria metalmecánica en la Ciudad de Córdoba 2002–2012. Tesis para optar por el grado de Doctor en Geografía* (Universidad Nacional de La Plata: Inédita, 2013).

Cardoso, Fernando H. and Enzo Faletto. *Development and Dependence in Latin America* (Berkeley: University of California Press, 1979).

Castells, Manuel and Alejandro Portes. "World Underneath: The Origins, Dynamics and Effects of the Informal Economy," in Alejandro Portes, Manuel Castells, and Lauren A. Benton (eds), *The Informal Economy. Studies in Advanced and Less Developed Countries* (Baltimore and London: The John Hopkins University Press, 1989), pp. 11–40.

Chen, Martha, Joann Vanek, and Kames Heintz. "Informality, Gender and Poverty: A Global Picture", *Economic and Political Weekly*, 41, 21 (2006), pp. 2131–2139.

CIFRA. *Informe de Coyuntura No. 7. El nuevo patrón de crecimiento. Argentina 2002–2010* (CIFRA, 2011).

Córdova, Armando and Héctor S. Michelena. *Aspectos teóricos del subdesarrollo* (Caracas: Insituto de Investigaciones, 1967).

Dunaway, Wilma (ed.). *Gendered Commodity Chains: Seeing Women's Work and Households in Global Production* (Stanford: Stanford University Press, 2013).

Fischer, Karin, Christian Reiner, and Cornelia Staritz (eds). *Globale Güterketten. Weltweite Arbeitsteilung und ungleiche Entwicklung* (Wien: Promedia, 2010).

Frank, André Gunder. *1929–2005. Crisis in the world economy* (New York: Holmes & Meier Publishers, 1980).

Hart, Keith. "Informal Income Opportunities and Urban Employment in Ghana," *The Journal of Modern African Studies*, 11, 1 (1973), pp. 61–89.

Harvey, David. *A brief history of Neoliberalism* (Oxford: Oxford University Press, 2005).

Hopkins, Terence and Immanuel Wallerstein. "Commodity Chains in the World-Economy Prior to 1800", *Review*, 10 (1986), pp. 157–170.

Humphrey, John, Yveline Lecler, and Mario S. Salerno (eds). *Global Strategies and Local Realities. The Auto Industry in Emerging Markets* (Palgrave Macmillan: Springer Palgrave Macmillan, 2000).

Huws, Ursula. "The Reproduction of Difference: Gender and the Global Division of Labour," *Work Organisation, Labour and Globalisation*, 6 (2012), pp. 1–10.

ILO (ed.). *Employment, Incomes and Equality: A strategy for Increasing Productive Employment in Kenya* (Geneva: International Labour Organisation, 1972).

Kempa, Luis Roberto. "Automotrices desvincularon a casi 400 trabajadores," *La Voz del Interior* (25 January 2015).

Kempa, Luis Roberto. "Smata y UOM acuerdan una grilla de suspensiones para frenar despidos," *La Voz del Interior* (3 September 2016).

Komlosy, Andrea. *Work. The Last 1000 Years* (New York: Verso Books, 2018).

Komlosy, Andrea. *Methoden und Theorien der Globalgeschichte* (Stuttgart: UTB, 2011).

Komlosy, Andrea *et al. Ungeregelt und unterbezahlt. Der informelle Sektor in der Weltwirtschaft* (Frankfurt am Main: Brandes & Aspel/Südwind, 1997).

Mies, Maria. *Patriarchy and Accumulation on a World Scale* (London: Zed Books, 1986).

Morales, Rebecca. *Flexible production: restructuring of the international automobile industry* (Cambridge: Polity Press, 1994).

Neffa, Julio C. "Modelos productivos y sus impactos sobre la relación salarial. Reflexiones a partir del caso argentine," in Julio C. Neffa and Enrique de la Garza Toledo, *Trabajo y modelos productivos en América Latina. Argentina, Brasil, México, Colombia y Venezuela luego de las crisis del modo de desarrollo neoliberal* (Buenos Aires: CLACSO, 2010), pp. 261–376.

Neffa, Julio C. *et al. La crisis de la relación salarial: naturaleza y significado de la informalidad, los trabajos/empleos precarios y los no registrados* (Buenos Aires: CEIL-PIETTE CONICET, 2010).

OECD. *Is Informal Normal? Towards More and Better Jobs in Developing Countries*, (Paris: OECD, 2009).

Perry, Guillermo E. *et al. Informality: Exit and Exclusion* (Washington, DC: Worldbank, 2007).

Portes, Alejandro, Manuel Castells, and Lauren A. Benton (eds). *The Informal Economy. Studies in Advanced and Less Developed Countries* (Baltimore and London: The John Hopkins University Press, 1989).

Portes, Alejandro and Saskia Sassen-Koob. "Making it Underground: Comparative Material on the Informal Sector in Western Market Economies," *American Journal of Sociology*, 93 (1987), pp. 30–61.

Redacción LAVOZ. "Hoy las suspensiones en Córdoba llegarán a los 3.100 trabajadores," *La Voz del Interior*, June 6, 2014.

Robinson, William I. *Latin America and global capitalism: A critical globalization perspective* (Baltimore: John Hopkins University Press, 2008).

Santos, Milton. *The shared space. The two circuits of the urban economy in underdeveloped countries* (London, New York: Methuen, 1979).

Schmalz, Stefan *et al.* "Unsicherheit als Alltagserfahrung: Abgestufte Beschäftigungshierarchien im Wertschöpfungssystem Automobil in Argentinien," in Hajo Holst (ed.), *Fragmentierte Belegschaften – Globale Perspektiven auf Leiharbeit, Werkverträge und freie Mitarbeiter* (Frankfurt am Main: Campus, 2017), pp. 69–98.

Sevilla, Ariel. *Une comparaison de la fabrication de la violence liée à l'emploi. Licen- ciements massifs et intérim chez les ouvriers de l'automobile en Argentine et en France* (Paris: Congress "l'Association Française de Sociologie," 14–17 April 2009).

Sittel, Johanna et al. Reflexionen zum Informalitätskonzept am Beispiel der argentinischen Automobilindustrie, *Journal für Entwicklungspolitik*, 31 (2015), pp. 59–82.

Smith, John. *Imperialism in the 21st Century: Globalization, Super-Exploitation and Capitalism's Final Crisis* (New York, London: Verso, 2016).

Smith, Joan, Immanuel M. Wallerstein, and Hans-Dieter Evers (eds). *Households and the World Economy* (Beverly Hills: Sage, 1984).

Sturgeon, Timothy J. et al. "Globalisation of the automotive industry: main features and trends," *International Journal of Technological Learning, Innovation and Development*, 2 (2008), pp. 7–24.

Tomadoni, Claudia. *Los autos nunca compran autos: Territorio, reestructuración y crisis en la industria automotriz* (Madrid: Ediciones Encuentro, 2009).

Wallerstein, Immanuel M. *World-Systems Analysis. An Introduction* (Durham/London, 2004).

Webster, Edward et al. *Making visible the invisible: confronting South Africa's Decent Work Deficit, Research Report prepared for the Department of Labour* (Johannesburg: The Sociology of Work Unit, University of Witwatersrand, 2008).

Weinmann, Nico. "Los ciclos de la política del trabajo formal e informal en América Latina," in Hans-Jürgen Burchardt and Fernando Groisman (eds), *Desprotegidos y desiguales. ¿Hacia una nueva fisonomía social?* (Buenos Aires: Prometeo, 2015).

Werlhof, Claudia von. "The Proletarian is dead: Long live the Housewife?," in Joan Smith, Immanuel M. Wallerstein, and Hans-Dieter Evers (eds), *Households and the World Economy* (Beverly Hills: Sage, 1984), pp. 131–147.

# PART 6

## *Conclusion*

CHAPTER 15

# Global Labor and Labor Studies – Breaking the Chains

*Karin Fischer*

Labor is the black box of global value chains (GVC s). GVC research suffers from profound labor blindness.[1] It is primarily concerned with firm strategies and the possibilities for economic upgrading. These statements were true for quite a long time. GVC research treated labor like a commodity input into production or a cost factor with regard to decisions made on sourcing and location.[2] This has changed. Scholars in the field have opened up to labor issues and comprise a lively research area that productively absorbs inputs from different disciplines and theories. This edited volume is further evidence of that. It combines, as the editors wrote in their introduction, historical with contemporary social science perspectives, all engaging with commodity chains from the perspective of labor relations and work experiences in various locations, and the possibility of workers' agency within the complex spatial arrangements of global production.

The afterword takes up developments, issues and controversies surrounding labor in global commodity chains. It revisits "nodes" of the chains and networks analyzed in the book, including, among other sites, Slovakian mining districts, tea, soy, and sugar plantations in India, Brazil and Hawaii, Hungarian and Argentinian car factories and leather production companies in Ethiopia. Embedded in a brief history of commodity chain research, I will delineate theoretical approaches (part one), sources of inspiration (part two) and the question of labor agency (part three), both by referring to seminal literature in the field and the contributions in this book. The afterword ends with some thoughts on the theoretical and epistemological foundations for integrating global labor and commodity chain research.

1 The author thanks Johanna Grubner and the editors for valuable comments and suggestions.

2 Thompson, Parker and Cox, "Labour and Asymmetric Power," p. 53; Selwyn, "Global Value Chains," p. 1774. See also Selwyn, "Poverty Chains and Global Capitalism."

 | DOI:10.1163/9789004448049_016

## 1 Commodity Chain Research: Approaching Labor

"First generation" GVC research, which proliferated in the late 1990s, was above all concerned with inter-firm relations, the resulting modes of governance, and the possibilities for economic or industrial upgrading. Made up of different academic disciplines but closely associated with development studies, "upgrading" was seen as a viable strategy to development: companies and producers in developing countries should strive to shift to higher value activities, thus strengthening their bargaining capacity vis-à-vis the lead firm and, in the end, increasing their share of the total surplus.

Critique pushed the research community forward – and sometimes it called upon the researchers in the field to look back to the roots of commodity chain studies, namely to the world-systems approach.[3] Instead of exploring the upgrading possibilities for firms or industries, "world-systems theorists are most fundamentally interested in how commodity chains structure and reproduce a stratified and hierarchical world-system,"[4] or, as Komlosy and Musić write in the introduction to this book, how commodity chains "reproduce imbalances and polarizations between high- and low-end positions along the chain."

For original world-systems theorists, although they never thoroughly investigated labor and labor agency along chains, labor was of course a constituent element. Wallerstein and Hopkins defined a commodity chain as "a network of labor and production."[5] For Christopher Chase-Dunn the "tree-like sequence of production processes and exchanges" included "raw materials, labor, the sustenance of labor, intermediate processing, final processing, transport, and final consumption."[6] Instead of seeing economic upgrading as the main strategy for development, world-systems theorists advocated to increase the value of labor at every single "node of the chain," whether by bargaining or militancy.

Critical commodity chain studies were always closer to this kind of theorizing, i.e. seeing global commodity chains as an expression of uneven and combined development. This approach is present in this book. As Gerőcs, Meszmann and Pinkasz put it, combined with the GVC framework, uneven development highlights the spatial-geographical dimension of global production. It enables an analysis of the highly uneven distribution of value-added within a commodity chain at given localities that reproduce and reinforce center-periphery relations. Uneven development denotes a power relation

3 Bair, "Global Capitalism."
4 Bair, "Global Capitalism," p. 156.
5 Hopkins and Wallerstein, "Commodity Chains," p. 159.
6 Chase-Dunn, *Global Formation,* p. 346.

that appears in a hierarchical structure, but also the interconnectedness of seemingly separate labor regimes.

Immanuel Wallerstein conceived capitalism as an expanding system, incorporating regions and peoples of the periphery into a hierarchical international division of labor, though in a subordinated way. Contemporary contributions in the field of commodity chain studies, however, draw attention to the cyclical nature of expansion and contraction of global production or – put another way – to globalization and de-globalization tendencies. It is not only the integration or inclusion but also disintegration or exclusion of places and people that constitutes uneven development and commodity chains. In a nutshell, global production reflects "moments of inclusion *and* exclusion."[7]

The historical contributions collected in this book strengthen this perspective. By applying the concept of the "commodity frontier", Ernst Langthaler traces the expansion and contraction of boundaries of global agri-food chains in different world-historical contexts. In the "frontiers" metaphor, it is the shift between the widening of external frontiers (through land grabbing and the extension of capitalist power to new, uncommodified spheres of social life) and the deepening of internal frontiers, i.e. the more intensive use of already commodified spaces and labor (through mechanization or high-tech innovations, for example). Andrea Komlosy shows the cyclical phenomenon in the textiles and garment chain with alternating periods of rise and decline as well as non-synchronicity between the sectors and regions involved in production. In terms of labor relations, Komlosy uncovers the cyclical shifts of in-house centralization and putting-out decentralization. In a similar vein, Stefan Schmalz and Johanna Sittel detected cycles of formalization and informalization in their study on the automotive supply chain in Argentina. The social protection and a formalization of labor regimes took place in contraction phases – although unequally distributed among different classes of laborers, economic sectors and regions. Shifts between expansion and contraction, widening and deepening were always contested. This also comes to light due to a trans-regional and labor-oriented perspective.

Returning to the short history of GVC research, after a first phase dominated by policy orientated studies aiming to identify local upgrading opportunities, scholarly attention then turned towards the obstacles of upgrading. A large number of studies started to dismantle the "optimistic upgrading narrative."[8] If upgrading was successful, for example in terms of technology intensity, secure

7 Bair and Werner, "Commodity Chains," p. 989, italics in the original, pp. 992–993.

8 Thompson, Parker and Cox, "Labour and Asymmetric Power Relations," p. 54.

orders, and profitability, firms did not necessarily spread their gains evenly. More concretely, rewards were not passed on to workers in the form of higher wages, greater job security and/or improved working conditions. What applies to global industries is also true for commodity food chains. Integration into agribusiness supply chains did not inevitably enable smallholders and contract farmers to adopt modern technology and raise their incomes. More often than not they became increasingly dependent upon inputs, proprietary seeds, and the regulation of production by agribusiness. Finally, family farmers lost control over processing and marketing.[9]

Following from this insight, researchers defined social upgrading as a distinct process. Extensive literature emerged studying if, how, and in what form workers or contract farmers could increase their benefits and improve their working conditions during economic upgrading processes.[10] Work can be improved in many ways, for example, in terms of qualification, social security, working hours, income, gender equality, or freedom of association. These dimensions can change independently from each other. This was again the central insight from a trans-regional and labor-oriented commodity chain perspective.[11] If firms take on further and/or higher value activities within global value chains, a core of workers might profit. In other areas of the production, or at other locations, there might emerge a new demand for flexible – and therefore unsecured and underpaid – workers. Industrial upgrading can go hand in hand with the squeezing-out of female workers and, thus, enhance gender inequality. Such findings are also valid for agrarian value chains. More "entrepreneurial" farmers might profit from integration into agrarian value chains. Although dependent on international markets and durable ties with the lead firm, they might be able to raise their profits – at the expense of (part-time, casual or informal) rural wage laborers they hire on poor and ever worsening employment conditions. It is now clear that social upgrading and downgrading processes cannot be accurately captured without taking power relations between the actors involved into account.[12]

Many chapters in this book highlight the interconnectedness of "high road" work models, as Gerőcs, Meszmann and Pinkasz put it, associated with skill

9 Anner, "Social Downgrading"; Fischer, "Dependenz trifft Güterketten"; Fischer, Reiner and Staritz, "Einleitung"; Amanor, "Global Value Chains"; Gibbon and Ponte, *Trading Down.*

10 Barrientos, Gereffi and Rossi, "Economic and Social Upgrading".

11 Selwyn, "Social Upgrading"; Bair and Werner, "Commodity Chains"; Rossi, Luinstra and Pickles, *Towards Better Work.*

12 Selwyn, "Global Value Chains," p. 1781; Marslev, Staritz, Raj-Reichert and Plank, "Soziales Upgrading und ArbeiterInnenmacht."

development, significant job security etc., and "low road" work models that rely on low labor costs, temporary employment, etc. Both models can be identified at particular positions (lower or higher tier suppliers) and particular locations in the same value chain. It becomes clear that high road and low road work models – seemingly separable – are indeed complementary parts of the same global system of accumulation. Some workers' gains are structurally linked to other workers' losses. Christin Bernhold's chapter on an agro-industrial chain emanating from Argentina makes this point clear when she asks in the title "who's upgrading?" In the chapter, Bernhold shows that the lead firm's sourcing practices are based on existing class differentiations. Economic upgrading strategies even deepen these divisions: capitalist "middle" farmers lease land to the lead firm while others with access to some land and capital become subcontractors. In this way, both segments profit from the – although subordinated – integration in the global agro-chain. Hired smallholders and rural laborers are at the end of the chain. Some of them are precariously and temporarily integrated into the circuits of agribusiness, while others are expelled and have to find other sources for subsistence.[13] Similarly, but in terms of time and space far-off, Klemens Kaps exemplifies in his study on the transnational grain chain in Habsburg Galicia that upgrading in crop production and related industries had nothing to do with a strategy for long-term development. They were little more than contingency measures implemented by landowners to compensate for the lost grain trade by mobilizing and redirecting resources. Economic upgrading brought productivity gains – but not better working conditions or higher wages for the peasants and rural workers. By tracing the changing social arrangements of trans-regional production, these chapters demonstrate the usefulness of a chain perspective for understanding the combination of different types of labor and labor regimes.

Returning to the introspection of the research field, it is fair to say that the GVC camp needed some time to approach the labor issue. The framework of global production networks (GPNs), however, was more open to labor issues from the very beginning. GPN researchers, predominantly economic geographers, do attempt to include a range of the relevant – non-corporate – actors and relationships involved in global production, such as national states, regions, supra-national institutions, business associations and trade unions.[14] Even though the chain metaphor should not be equated with an essentially linear structure or solely vertical processes, the network perspective illuminates

13 See also Fischer and Langthaler, "Soy Expansion and Countermovements."

14 Coe, Dicken and Hess, "Global Production Networks."

the wider social conditions in which production, reproduction, and consumption is embedded. The focus is therefore on broader economic, social and political arrangements and on how these structures affect agents at the various sites of global production networks. Although the GPN framework acknowledged the importance of integrating labor in the picture, studies rather tended to treat labor as the passive victim of restructuring, thus reproducing the factor of production approach.[15]

Labor geographers within the field then made a plea to place exploitation and labor agency at the center of GPN dynamics.[16] Mentioning labor geographers brings me to a delineation of the research communities at the intersection of global production and labor, which enrich the subject from different disciplinary and theoretical angles.

## 2 Labor-Oriented Commodity Chain Research: Sources of Inspiration

When considering global production and labor, a source of inspiration is clearly global labor history. This is very much felt in this book as many authors have their academic roots in this field. Introduced in the late 1990s, global labor history has significantly broadened the conceptual understanding of work, workers and the working class.[17] It counters the disproportionate emphasis in Northern dominated academic discourses on free and waged labor and gainful employment. It "alerts us to the variety of possible permutations in labor relations."[18] Most people and households in the world are semi-proletarized and merge, as Wilma Dunaway put it, "erratic wages with resources acquired from nonwaged efforts."[19] Global labor history transcends the Eurocentrism present in much academic labor research.

Many forms of labor exist beside formal wage labor, both in history and nowadays, that co-exist in global chains or networks. They range from forced labor with different degrees of coercion of workers in different regions, to different forms of informal labor in companies and households. Unfree labor must be considered, as Komlosy and Musić point out in the introduction, as "a constitutive component of capitalism." Specific forms of unfree labor such as serfdom, slavery, or servitude "have been integrated into commodity chains

15 Taylor, Newsome, Bair and Rainnie, "Putting Labour in its Place," p. 2.
16 Cumbers, Nativel and Routledge, "Labour Agency."
17 van der Linden, "The Promise and Challenges."
18 van der Linden, *Workers of the World*, p. 26.
19 Dunaway, "Through the Portal," p. 60.

in different periods of history until today, contributing to the same product together with free labor."

Klemens Kaps's contribution on the "peripheral labor regime" in Galicia and the chapters on plantation export agriculture in Hawaii (Uwe Spiekermann) and India (Santosh Hasnu) remind us that the shift from unfree labor to wage labor was neither a sudden nor a homogeneous phenomenon. Instead, the authors discover flexible labor arrangements according to the needs of employers and the industrial metropole. In agriculture and the related industries they find labor regimes with different degrees of (and lack of) freedom. This is also true for copper mining, processing, and marketing in the Habsburg Monarchy, as Miroslav Lacko has shown. The whole copper chain proved very heterogeneous in terms of labor relations – despite substantial state regulation. An extended historical perspective shows that clear-cut periodizations and ruptures are seldom. In this respect, Goran Musić points to the continuity of production chains across "system boundaries." He demonstrates that outward processing industries in Yugoslavia existed well before the "transition." The spread of global textile chains dates back to various forms of subcontracting and joint ventures in the 1960s and subordinated the region to the position of a low-cost export processing platform for Western buyers.

Vulnerable labor arrangements in global chains or networks include migrant labor. Seasonal or otherwise time-bound migrant work is intrinsic, particularly in globalized agri-food chains, labor-intensive global industries, and care work in Northern countries. Migrant work is most often explored in the historical contributions of this book. Bad living and transport conditions, the lack of sanitary provisions, and low wages, leaving many coolie workers undernourished, led to high mortality rates on the colonial plantations and *en route*, as Santosh Hasnu shows in his study on the interconnectedness of global commodity production, migrant labor and transport infrastructure in India. Uwe Spiekermann, although more concerned with the side of capital, namely with a leading sugar planter in Hawaii, describes entrepreneurial recruitment practices, thereby illuminating a hierarchically organized labor regime in which imported "white," "black" and "yellow" coolie workers were differentially exploited based upon their racialized location. Ernst Langthaler's chapter on the diverse histories of soy chains, however, reveals different drivers and expectations behind migration: while in China, mass migration from South to North was related to the expectation of social upward mobility, large-scale displacements forced peasants in Brazil into precarious wage work at the low end of agri-food chains.

Households and families, and within families predominantly women, provide unpaid or underpaid labor to household enterprises, family businesses or other kinds of commodity production. The survival of workers very often remains partly dependent on unpaid subsistence labor. Outsourcing work for commodity chains into the family household allowed appropriating unpaid subsistence work and low-paid nonwaged labor, transferring values to those who were in command of the chain, as Komlosy explains in her chapter. It is, according to Wilma Dunaway, the household and gender which ensures the maximal exploitation of underpaid and unpaid labor within every single node as well as between the nodes in the commodity chain.[20] Stefan Schmalz and Johanna Sittel describe in their case study a wide range of informal practices in Argentinian car workers' households. "Changas" – as informal activities from selling food to fixing things for others are called in Argentina – are at the same time a cost-saving strategy of supplier firms, a shock absorber during times of crisis, and a survival strategy of the extended household.

Family households serve as "reproductive and income pooling units," often on a trans-regional basis, as Komlosy writes. Making the social reproduction of labor visible is what gender/feminist theorists contribute to the GVC/GPN research agenda. Feminist scholars inform our understanding of how global chains or networks are embedded in and exploit gender relations. They point to the place-specific, but transnationally interconnected dynamics of gender, race, and class. In feminist and world-systems inspired theorizing, global commodity chains rely on the i) intermingling of several forms of waged and nonwaged, free and unfree labor; ii) extraction of visible and hidden surpluses from households; iii) gendered and racial exploitation of workers; and iv) the economic devaluation of household-based work, especially that of women.[21] This definition addresses the power relations and inequality in global chains or networks defined as a *social relation* of *exploitation.* From the outset studies on female workers in global production have made us aware of gender hierarchies and discrimination in global chains or networks: the majority of the workforce in export production zones in the global South are young, semi-proletarized women. They are attributed worldwide with the same gender stereotypes ("nimble fingers") and more affected by precarious and informal working conditions, violence and lay-offs during economic crisis then men.[22]

"Subcontracting," which GVC/GPN literature brought to the foreground, directly points to the multi-faceted hidden and informal labor armies. Informal

20 Dunaway, "The Double Register," p. 10. See also Dunaway, "Through the Portal," pp. 60–63; Komlosy, *Work.*

21 Dunaway, "Introduction," p. 2.

22 Elson and Pearson, "Nimble Fingers." For an overview on the gender dimension in the commodity chain literature see Sproll, "Ungleichheit in globalen Wertschöpfungsketten."

labor in global chains or networks can be wage labor (regular or casual). "Hidden" wage labor includes self-employed workers and sharecropping peasant families, among others. Stefan Schmalz and Johanna Sittel use the term "subsistence informality," based on mere informal subsistence production, which aims at livelihood and reproduction, and "informality of accumulation," which aims at gaining an additional income in order to sustain or increase ones material living standard. Schmalz and Sittel illustrate how informal work is intentionally and systematically integrated into the presumably formal production network of the automotive industry – within companies and along the chain. This is precisely where the essence of global commodity chains is to be found: it is the uneven and unequal combination of different modes of labor exploitation that makes cross-border production profitable. This is what Andrea Komlosy highlights in her chapter on textiles and garments. She shows how the West European industrial system has been combined with industrious handicraft and home industries across far-flung regions. The GVC/GPN framework enables us to recognize that the structuring of global value chains is closely associated with an aim to have a flexible workforce.[23]

For the variegated groups of workers addressed in this book, Marcel van der Linden coined the term "subaltern workers." The term clarifies that labor power is commodified in many different ways. Formal and informal, regular and irregular is by no means a binary opposition but rather a process with many gradations and dimensions. The distinction between these different forms is fluid. They can be understood only by their relationship to each other and in a transnational perspective.[24]

Besides global labor history and gender/feminist theorizing, a third source of inspiration is provided by labor geography. It was labor geography in particular that criticized GVC approaches as capital- and state-centric and introduced global production networks as "networks of embodied labor."[25] The central tenet of labor geography "is the claim that the geography of capitalism makes a difference to workers and that workers make a difference to the geography of capitalism."[26] A central motive is to show that workers are not powerless and condemned to follow the dictates of global capital. Instead, they actively create and shape geographies, even when exposed to high vulnerability and

23 Selwyn, "Social Upgrading"; Bair and Werner, "Global Production."

24 van der Linden, *Workers of the World*, p. 32.

25 Cumbers, Nativel and Routledge, "Labour Agency," pp. 371–372. See also Thompson, Parker and Cox, "Labour and Asymmetric Power Relations," pp. 52–53; Herod, "Labour Geography," p. 24.

26 Herod, "Labour Geography," p. 16.

insecurity. Significant here is labor and its "geographical condition": actions of labor play out in complex social geographies and, at the same time, can be seen as spatial phenomena themselves. Therefore labor geography is interested in workers' economic and political practices.[27]

Last but not least, sociologists of work and employment with a Marxist background entered the field of global value chains by introducing labor process theory (LPT).[28] LPT is above all concerned with forces of control, consent and resistance at the point of production, i.e. within firms, in the factory, at the workplace.[29] The prism of labor control brings labor exploitation and disciplining to the foreground and provides a deeper understanding of the constitutive role of labor and the position of workers within global chains or networks. Researchers in the LPT field that seek to transcend the narrow focus on workplace relations and local agencies (situated in the global North) find it fruitful to turn to the concepts of GVC/GPN. While sociologists of work highlight asymmetries in labor relations, the multi-scalar GVC/GPN framework brings in the broader social-institutional context and the spatial interconnectedness of the seemingly separate work models within the hierarchical structure of global production. In this way, the labor process in particular places is integrated as a constitutive network element. Local labor control practices at the places of production such as, for example, labor-saving mechanization, informality, subcontracting, or gender segmentation can be analyzed with broader dynamics of labor control. It becomes clear how the lead firm channels labor control pressures "through the chain." Musić's case study on workers' experiences in the outward processing industries in 1980s Yugoslavia is an excellent example of this: Western buyers ordered maximum production flexibility and local management introduced strict work discipline while "at home" high value added production and relatively better jobs were protected. Strategies of managerial control do not end at the factory gate. Social disciplining can even be traced "down" to households, as feminist studies at the intersection of LPT and GVC/GPN framework show.[30]

Labor process theory highlights the relational nature of labor control and resistance. The labor process is a site of class relations as well as a site of class struggle. Labor geography considers how workers develop solidarity across

27 Coe and Jordhus-Lier, "Re-Embedding the Agency of Labour"; Herod, "Labour Geography". For a summary see Rainnie, Herod and McGrath-Champ, "Review and Positions," pp. 160–163.

28 Newsome, Taylor, Bair and Rainnie, *Putting Labour in its Place.*

29 Thomson and Smith, "Labour Power," p. 915.

30 Baglioni, "Labour Control."

space and how the changing spatialities of production encourage them to develop new organizing strategies. This said, we arrive at the debate about transnational labor agency to which labor-oriented GVC/GPN research contributes. The discussions circle around the question of how workers and their allies can mobilize and leverage power against employers at different "nodes" in a global production network or play it out on multiple scales simultaneously.

## 3 Labor as a Transnational Actor

Relocation and outsourcing are not only driven by cost and profitability. It is also a corporate strategy to escape unionized workers and to disrupt workers' capacity to organize and defend their interests. The combined processes of offshoring and outsourcing have "strongly undermined traditional strategies of labor to protect itself against exploitation, turning the global supply chain into a barrier both for organizing and collective bargaining."[31] While lead firms can pit workers in different localities and different geographical jurisdictions against one another, labor is to a much greater extent locked into a particular place.[32] At the same time, control can never be absolute. In her study on transnational relocation strategies of industrial capital, Beverly Silver comes to the conclusion that the interrelationship between capital relocation and labor movements is far more complex than a race-to-the-bottom in labor standards. She put it in the famous sentence: "where capital goes, conflict goes."[33] This too is an area where labor and GVC/GPN scholars find common ground. They portray workers not (only) as victims, but as having agency and the ability to actively shape the structures of global chains or networks.

"Jumping scale and bridging space," a concept developed by labor geography and used by Jörg Nowak in his chapter, is not only the lead firm's "weapon" to divide and weaken labor – also workers and their allies attempt "to meet capital at its own scale."[34] They scale up their activities geographically to shift the power-balance in the workplace. They bridge space to expand the terrain of struggle outside the factory, the export processing zone, the region and the country, and seek to mobilize support on various scales.[35] Jumping scale and

31 Merk, "Jumping Scale," pp. 605–606.
32 Merk, "Jumping Scale," p. 603.
33 Silver, *Forces of Labor*, p. 41.
34 Brookes and McCallum, "The New Global Labour Studies," p. 201.
35 Merk, "Jumping Scale," p. 606.

bridging space promises to be an effective strategy as global production networks are particularly vulnerable to disruption.

Transnational labor activism offers a broad spectrum for research. As it is always dangerous to distill a diverse field into a small number of topics for the purposes of outlining its structure, I am limiting myself in identifying two broad camps. The first stream of researchers places global union efforts and bargaining campaigns at the head of collective labor agency. Accordingly, the focus is on the global structures of the trade union movement and the "governance struggles"[36] that are directed at modifying employment regulations at a transnational level. Most prominent governance tools are global framework agreements and labor related corporate codes of conduct.[37] The second stream focuses on broader advocacy networks that support particular struggles linked to global production networks. Alliances not only cut across the boundaries of national/transnational, but also across production/consumption and labor/community.[38] Campaigns often articulate a broader political, social and environmental agenda, including anti-privatization, migrant workers' rights or the de-commodification of nature. In contrast to the first stream, researchers focus more closely on grassroots mobilizations around labor and want to bring "non-unionized (or not solely unionized) worker agency into focus."[39] This form of labor-oriented activism is often separate from formal trade union organizing and comparable with a new social movement unionist perspective. Accordingly, activists and academics take a critical view of (Northern dominated) global unions that remain closely allied with political parties and are unwilling or afraid to take on global capital.

The cases of labor agency portrayed in this book clearly fall into the first stream. This said, Jörg Nowak's case study on two union initiatives seems to form a bridge between the two streams.[40] Generally, transnational union alliances tend to be dominated by their most powerful and financially strong affiliates, i.e. European- or U.S.-based unions, and their views and practices.[41] In his contribution, Nowak depicts two union networks "from below." The ExChains

36 McCallum, "Governance Struggles."

37 See, for example, Brookes, "Labour as a Transnational Actor"; Brookes and McCallum, "The New Global Labour Studies." On global framework agreements see Helfen and Fichter, "Building Transnational Union Networks."

38 Munck, *Globalization and Labour*, pp. 154–173.

39 Zajak, Egels-Zandén and Piper, "Networks of Labour Activism," p. 901; Nowak, "Mass Strikes in India and Brazil."

40 See also Nowak, "Mass Strikes in India and Brazil."

41 Lindberg, "Varieties of Solidarity"; Helfen and Fichter, "Building Transnational Union Networks," p. 560.

network connects garment workers in South and South East Asia with works councils of big buyers in Germany. Goals, strategies, and action are developed on an equal footing. The Rails without Borders network is made up of small and independent unions in European and African countries. Both initiatives cut across the North-South divide and established horizontal, nonhierarchical relationships between its members. It is no coincidence, Nowak argues, that these labor alliances do not revolve around big Northern based global union federations. Nowak's research shows, at the same time, that union networks are in fact rather diverse.[42]

In any event, the organization of cross-border agency presents a great challenge for the actors involved. Nowak's case studies make that very clear. While an over-centralization and top-down approach can result in strategies that ignore local contexts and might lead to dysfunctional outcomes, a decentralized structure does not seem to be the solution either, as Nowak points out. If workers and their allied organizations do not establish a coordinating center – be it a global union federation or an experienced global grassroots network as in the case of ExChains –, they can only have an impact on single nodes of the production network, at best. Thus, as he concludes, workers organizations have to respond to specific logics in local and national contexts; at the same time, they need a certain degree of centralization to coordinate action across specific places.

Within the first stream, a separate but important research area is labor-oriented corporate social responsibility (CSR) by lead firms, particularly their corporate codes of conduct to regulate labor standards in supplier factories in the global South. Research deals predominantly with the structural limits of private regulation in the form of CSR mechanisms. CSR is often characterized as a top-down instrument and a routine management function between suppliers and lead firms, without involving workers and their organizations. Some even classify private governance regulations of this type as "abject failures".[43] Franziska Ollendorf also takes this line. She describes CSR, in her chapter on a certification project in Ghana's cocoa sector, as an instrument of structural power and a hegemonic practice of transnational buyers. More than a mere marketing tool for corporate "green-washing," CSR turns out to be a pro-active private governance tool, not only to control and shape the conditions in a GVC but to control the broader environment in the main consumer markets and the local settings in which the lead firm operates. Ollendorf`s study also

42 Helfen and Fichter, "Building Transnational Union Networks."

43 McCallum, "Governance Struggles," p. 149. See also Lund-Thomsen and Lindgreen, "Corporate Social Responsibility"; Wells, "Local Worker Struggles"; Merk, "Jumping Scale."

transcends a narrow perspective on work and workers, thereby connecting the two streams of research. By taking local conditions and livelihoods into account, she demonstrates that the CSR program under study created new insiders and outsiders at the local level.

Following the two delineated research communities, a dividing line seems to exist between those who give priority to the labor issue and labor agency (stream one) and those who see livelihood struggles and rainbow coalitions as transformative forces (stream two). For researchers of the first stream, workers and their organizations are strategic actors. They argue that workers have a unique capacity to physically disrupt production and to invoke employment relations institutions on various scales. Only workers, unions, and other members of the labor movement have structural and institutional power. Thus, transnational labor alliances can afford a set of strategic tools that are unavailable to other types of actors.[44]

As part of this stream, the focus on various sources of workers' power draws attention to the room for maneuver and strategic choices of workers in concrete contexts. In this book, Gerőcs, Meszmann and Pinkasz, as well as Jan Grumiller, adopt the power resources approach to analyze spaces of workers actions (and their limits).[45] In his investigation of the Ethiopian leather industry, Jan Grumiller explains that the structural power of workers differs according to the firm type and the firm's position in the globally dispersed leather chain. Even if workers dispose of structural power, their capacity to transform it into associational and bargaining power is severely limited because of labor's marginalization within the export-oriented Ethiopian developmental regime. Gerőcs, Meszmann, and Pinkasz conclude from their case study on the automotive industry in semi-peripheral Hungary, that only the perspective of value chain governance helps to explain why labor representation, i.e. associational power, develops in a particular way in a particular location. Thus, up-scaling the – originally place-based – power structure approach is indeed a viable undertaking and is once again proving the "added value" of a GVC/GPN perspective: whether, and, if so, in what manner workers organize themselves depends

---

44 Brookes, "Labour as a Transnational Actor"; Selwyn, "Global Value Chains." See Burawoy, "From Polanyi to Pollyanna," for the second stream, arguing that commodification (and not exploitation) is the key experience in our world today and that nature- linked struggles for land *and* labor will take the lead.

45 The basic concepts of the approach were originally created by Erik Olin Wright and then adopted by Beverly Silver. For further elaborations of the concept see Schmalz, Ludwig and Webster, "The Power Resources Approach," and the contributions in the respective issue of the Global Labour Journal. See also Selwyn, "Poverty Chains"; Selwyn, "Global Value Chains."

on their position within the local labor regime *and* their position within the global chain or network, i.e. whether they are employed by a lead firm, a strategically important supplier or a low end supplier, for example. Power resources of workers are expanded or constrained, on the one side, by the local labor control regime and capital-labor relations and, on the other side, on a transnational scale by GVC/GPN relations and chain governance. In other words, structural and associational power are related to the workers' position and relationship along the vertical axis of transnational power relations in GVC s, and the horizontal axis of local political economy contexts.[46]

Although the bigger picture provided by Beverly Silver shows that labor activism is continuously transforming the spatial and social landscape of production (and capitalism more broadly), there are different kinds of boundary drawing at work. Boundary drawing goes on by capital in terms of outsourcing, offshoring and segmenting labor markets, but there is one, as she said, that comes from the workers themselves: workers maintain boundaries against others in order to defend particular privileges.[47] In other words, conflicts often do not develop along the line of capital, but take on the form of labor-labor conflicts. This problematique is also present in this book. Plant level trade unions often only protect the interests of core skilled workers at the dispense of temporary workers, as Gerőcs, Meszmann, and Pinkasz revealed in the case of Hungarian supplier companies in the German automotive value chain. They detected labor-labor dividing lines on a plant level between blue-collar and white-collar, as well as between old and new employees. Also in good times, when trade unions disposed of relatively high structural and bargaining power, encouraging workers to strike or threaten strike action, internal divisions and hidden conflicts in the workplace reduced the chances and scope of a prolonged battle. In the end, this weakened the bargaining position of the entire work force.

The Yugoslav outward processing textile industry exemplifies two further challenges for workers organizing as Goran Musić shows. Firstly, workers in the export specialized units who were confronted with a tight labor control regime and produced higher output demanded greater rewards. Thereby new divisions within the workforce of a single factory between those producing for the domestic market and those integrated in the circuits of cross-border production networks were created. Secondly, the workers in the outward processing

46 Marslev, Staritz, Raj-Reichert and Plank, "Soziales Upgrading und ArbeiterInnenmacht."

47 Wildcat, "Forces of Labor. Interview with Beverly J. Silver," (June 2005), available at: <https://www.wildcat-www.de/dossiers/forcesoflabor/bs_interview.htm>; last accessed July 15, 2020.

production were confronted with mandatory work weekends, extended shifts and a strict technological and work discipline. The discontent with the disciplining labor regime, however, was not targeted at the foreign buyers. Neither jumping scale nor bridging space took place. Discontent was directed solely against the local management, with workers accusing them of profiting personally from the contracts with the foreign firms. The competitive rules of the international textile market and global production, however, were recognized as unavoidable.

Connecting the local to the global is a difficult task, in theory, and even more so in practice. The GVC/GPN framework can help us to understand the material possibilities and limitations of solidarity between workers in different positions in the chains.[48] Strategic research sheds light on value expropriation and distribution, the structure and power relations of the global chain or network, and on inter-firm-relationships. In this sense, research findings can help the transnational labor movement and social justice networks to find the leverage points to interfere with a company's key relationships around the world.

## 4 Concluding Remarks: Theoretical-Epistemological Considerations

Critical commodity chain and network studies are primarily interested in globalized production and how powerful actors, in particular lead firms, are enabled to increase their profits. Labor studies, however, focus on working conditions and labor relations in specific contexts and tend to emphasize wage-worker exploitation and resistance. While the former often neglect the labor relations and workers' power, the latter usually leave out the hierarchical connection of labor regimes at different locations and the maintenance of income differentials between the "high" and the "low ends" of a commodity chain, situated in different parts of the world. Engaging in a dialogue is therefore a highly productive endeavor, and something that this book has attempted to do.

The authors of this book have analyzed the working conditions and labor relations embedded in diverse social relationships ranging from the household, through the dialectics of control and resistance in the labor regimes at the firm level, to transnational labor agency and alliances. What makes the case studies unique is the chain or network perspective. The authors remain focused on transnational interrelationships and ask how these different types of labor and

48 van der Linden, "The Promise and Challenges," p. 68.

labor regimes are connected by transregional commodity chains or networks. Situating seemingly separate local labor regimes within global commodity chains or networks exposes the hierarchical structure among the combined locations and within the capitalist world-system more broadly.

The authors adopt the concepts of the GVC/GPN framework, some of them more, some less. Given the extensive research agenda of the paradigm, shortcomings are unavoidable, leaving much space for further investigations and interchange. While coming from different home disciplines, from social and economic history through industrial sociology to development economics, none of the authors hide behind disciplinary boundaries or theoretical convictions.

Do we need a new paradigm or label to characterize the research field connecting GVC/GPN research and labor studies? I don't think so. The "new global labor studies" that emerged as an interdisciplinary research community with the dawn of the "new international division of labor" at the beginning of the 1980s already provide some theoretical and epistemological fundamentals. They are an excellent guidance for what the research collected in this book stands for.[49] Firstly, GVC/GPN and labor scholars are aware that individual lives, local and national phenomena are in various ways shaped by global dynamics. They are fully cognizant of uneven development and the complexity of the politics of scale in today's world. Secondly, the notion of uneven development includes attention to hierarchies and power relations, again on different scales. Thirdly, labor takes on many forms. GVC/GPN and labor scholars recognize the synchronicity of labor and look at their combination in local, regional and global commodity chains or networks. They adopt a broadened understanding of work, which includes that the household is as crucial as the factory and that production is not possible without reproduction. From here it follows, fourthly, that labor-oriented GVC/GPN studies never ignore that the working class has two sexes. To this we add the dimension of race/ethnicity in the making and remaking of the global working class. The racial grammar of the labor market has to be seen as one of its structuring principles. Fifthly, history matters. Only through a historically informed analysis do continuities and change in labor regimes become apparent.

This ambitious program can of course not be fulfilled by individual researchers or single case studies. It is a multi-stranded endeavor undertaken by an interdisciplinary research community that is united, not only in its intellectual ambitions, but also in its social concerns. In the face of repeated multiple

49 Munck, *The New International Labour Studies;* Goodchild, "Interview – Ronaldo Munck"; Munck, "Afterword."

crises and climate change, not to mention the recent COVID-19 pandemic, a labor-oriented GVC/GPN perspective is key to articulate the "old" emancipatory agenda of social justice (against exploitation) and "new" themes such as sustainability (against the commodification of nature and the destruction of livelihoods). Global labor and commodity chain studies stands by its normative commitment.

## Bibliography


Amanor, Kojo S. "Global Value Chains and Agribusiness in Africa: Upgrading or Capturing Smallholder Production?," *Agrarian South – Journal of Political Economy*, 8, 1–2 (April 2019), pp. 30–63.

Anner, Mark. "Social Downgrading and Worker Resistance in Apparel Global Value Chains," in Kirsty Newsome, Phil Taylor, Jennifer Bair and Al Rainnie (eds), *Putting Labour in Its Place: Labour Process Analysis and Global Value Chains* (London and New York: Palgrave Macmillan, 2015).

Baglioni, Elena. "Labour Control and the Labour Question in Global Production Networks: Exploitation and Disciplining in Senegalese Export Horticulture," *Journal of Economic Geography*, 18, 1 (January 2017), pp. 111–137.

Bair, Jennifer. "Global Capitalism and Commodity Chains: Looking Back, Going Forward," *Competition and Change*, 9, 2 (June 2005), pp. 153–180.

Bair, Jennifer and Marion Werner. "Commodity Chains and the Uneven Geographies of Global Capitalism: A Disarticulations Perspective," *Environment and Planning A: Economy and Space*, 43, 5 (May 2011), pp. 988–997.

Bair, Jennifer and Marion Werner. "Global Production and Uneven Development: When Bringing Labour In isn't Enough," in Kirsty Newsome, Phil Taylor, Jennifer Bair and Al Rainnie (eds), *Putting Labour in Its Place: Labour Process Analysis and Global Value Chains* (London and New York: Palgrave Macmillan, 2015).

Barrientos, Stephanie, Gary Gereffi and Arianna Rossi. "Economic and Social Upgrading in Global Production Networks: A New Paradigm for a Changing World," *International Labour Review*, 150, 3–4 (December 2011), pp. 319–340.

Brookes, Marissa. "Labour as a Transnational Actor: Alliances, Activism and the Protection of Labour Rights in the Philippines and Pakistan," *Development and Change*, 48, 5 (September 2017), pp. 922–941.

Brookes, Marissa and Jamie K. McCallum. "The New Global Labour Studies: A Critical Review," *Global Labour Journal*, 8, 3 (September 2017), pp. 201–218.

Burawoy, Michael. "From Polanyi to Pollyanna: The False Optimism of Global Labor Studies," *Global Labour Journal*, 1, 2 (May 2010), pp. 301–313.

Chase-Dunn, Christopher. *Global Formation: Structures of the World-Economy* (Oxford and Cambridge, MA: Basil Blackwell, 1989).

Coe, Neil M., Peter Dicken and Martin Hess. "Global Production Networks: Realizing the Potential," *Journal of Economic Geography*, 8, 3 (May 2008), pp. 271–295.

Coe, Neil M. and David C. Jordhus-Lier. "Re-Embedding the Agency of Labour," in Ann Cecilie Bergene, Sylvi B. Endresen and Hege Merete Knutsen (eds), *Missing Links in Labour Geography* (Farnham: Ashgate Publishing, 2010).

Cumbers, Andy, Corinne Nativel and Paul Routledge, "Labour Agency and Union Positionalities in Global Production Networks," *Journal of Economic Geography*, 8, 3 (May 2008), 369–387.

Dunaway, Wilma A. "Introduction," in Wilma A. Dunaway (ed.), *Gendered Commodity Chains: Seeing Women's Work and Households in Global Production* (Stanford: Stanford University Press, 2014).

Dunaway, Wilma A. "The Double Register of History: Situating the Forgotten Woman and Her Household in Capitalist Commodity Chains," *Journal of World-Systems Research*, 7, 1 (Spring 2001), pp. 2–29.

Dunaway, Wilma A. "Through the Portal of the Household: Conceptualizing Women's Subsidies to Commodity Chains," in Wilma A. Dunaway (ed.), *Gendered Commodity Chains: Seeing Women's Work and Households in Global Production* (Stanford: Stanford University Press, 2014).

Elson, Diane and Ruth Pearson. "'Nimble Fingers Make Cheap Workers': An Analysis of Women's Employment in Third World Export Manufacturing," *Feminist Review*, 7 (Spring 1981), pp. 87–107.

Fischer, Karin. "Dependenz trifft Güterketten: Zur Überausbeutung von Arbeit im Globalen Süden," *PROKLA. Zeitschrift für Kritische Sozialwissenschaft*, 50, 1, 198 (March 2020), pp. 33–51.

Fischer, Karin, Christian Reiner and Cornelia Staritz. "Einleitung: Globale Güterketten, weltweite Arbeitsteilung und ungleiche Entwicklung," in Karin Fischer, Christian Reiner and Cornelia Staritz (eds), *Globale Güterketten: Weltweite Arbeitsteilung und ungleiche Entwicklung* (Wien: Promedia, 2010).

Fischer, Karin and Ernst Langthaler. "Soy Expansion and Countermovements in the Global South: A Polanyian Perspective," in Roland Atzmüller, Brigitte Aulenbacher, Ulrich Brand, Fabienne Décieux, Karin Fischer and Birgit Sauer (eds), *Capitalism in Transformation: Movements and Countermovements in the 21st Century* (Cheltenham: Edward Elgar Publishing, 2019).

Gibbon, Peter and Stefano Ponte. *Trading Down: Afrika, Value Chains and the Global Economy* (Philadelphia, PA: Temple University Press, 2005).

Goodchild, Laurence. "Interview – Ronaldo Munck," *E-International Relations* (May 25, 2015), online available at: <https://www.e-ir.info/2015/05/25/interview-ronaldo-munck/>; last accessed July 27, 2020.

Helfen, Markus and Michael Fichter. "Building Transnational Union Networks across Global Production Networks: Conceptualising a New Arena of Labour-Management Relations," *British Journal of Industrial Relations*, 51, 3 (September 2013), pp. 553–576.

Herod, Andrew. "Labour Geography: Where Have We Been? Where Should We Go?", in Ann Cecilie Bergene, Sylvi B. Endresen and Hege Merete Knutsen (eds), *Missing Links in Labour Geography* (Farnham: Ashgate Publishing, 2010).

Hopkins, Terrence K. and Immanuel Wallerstein. "Commodity Chains in the World Economy Prior to 1800," *Review (Fernand Braudel Center)*, 10, 1 (Summer 1986), pp. 157–170.

Komlosy, Andrea. *Work: The Last 1,000 Years* (London: Verso, 2018).

Lindberg, Ingemar. "Varieties of Solidarity: An Analysis of Cases of Worker Action across Borders," in Andreas Bieler and Ingemar Lindberg (eds), *Global Restructuring, Labour and the Challenges for Transnational Solidarity* (New York: Routledge, 2011).

Lund-Thomsen, Peter and Adam Lindgreen. "Corporate Social Responsibility in Global Value Chains: Where Are We Now and Where Are We Going?," *Journal of Business Ethics*, 123, 1 (2014), pp. 11–22.

Marslev, Kristoffer, Cornelia Staritz, Gale Raj-Reichert and Leonhard Plank. "Soziales Upgrading und ArbeiterInnenmacht in Globalen Wertschöpfungsketten," *WSI-Mitteilungen* (forthcoming).

McCallum, Jamie K. "Governance Struggles and Worker Power," in Andreas Bieler et al. (eds), *Labour and Transnational Action in Times of Crisis* (London and New York: Rowman & Littlefield, 2015).

Merk, Jeroen. "Jumping Scale and Bridging Space in the Era of Corporate Social Responsibility: Cross-Border Labour Struggles in the Global Garment Industry," *Third World Quarterly*, 30, 3 (2009), pp. 599–615.

Munck, Ronaldo. "Afterword: beyond the 'new' international labour studies," *Third World Quarterly*, 30, 3 (2009), pp. 617–625.

Munck, Ronaldo. *Globalization and Labour: The New 'Great Transformation'* (London: Zed Books, 2002).

Munck, Ronaldo. *The New International Labour Studies* (London: Zed Books, 1988).

Newsome, Kirsty, Phil Taylor, Jennifer Bair and Al Rainnie (eds), *Putting Labour in Its Place: Labour Process Analysis and Global Value Chains* (London and New York: Palgrave Macmillan, 2015).

Nowak, Jörg. "Mass Strikes in India and Brazil as the Terrain for a New Social Movement Unionism," *Development and Change*, 48, 5 (September 2017), pp. 965–986.

Rainnie, Al, Andrew Herod and Susan McGrath-Champ. "Review and Positions: Global Production Networks and Labour," *Competition & Change*, 15, 2 (July 2011), pp. 155–169.

Rossi, Arianna, Amy Luinstra and John Pickles (eds). *Towards Better Work: Understanding Labour In Apparel Global Value Chains* (Basingstoke: Palgrave Macmillan, 2014).

Schmalz, Stefan, Carmen Ludwig and Edward Webster. "The Power Resources Approach: Developments and Challenges," *Global Labour Journal*, 9, 2 (May 2018), pp. 113–134.

Selwyn, Benjamin. "Global Value Chains and Human Development: A Class-Relational Framework," *Third World Quarterly*, 37, 10 (2016), pp. 1768–1786.

Selwyn, Benjamin. "Poverty Chains and Global Capitalism," *Competition & Change*, 23, 1 (February 2019), pp. 71–97.

Selwyn, Benjamin. "Social Upgrading and Labour in Global Production Networks: A Critique and an Alternative Conception," *Competition & Change*, 17, 1 (February 2013), pp. 75–90.

Silver, Beverly J. *Forces of Labor: Workers' Movements and Globalization since 1870* (Cambridge: Cambridge University Press, 2003).

Sproll, Martina. "Ungleichheit in globalen Wertschöpfungsketten: Eine intersektionale Perspektive auf soziale Reproduktion," *Österreichische Zeitschrift für Soziologie*, 45, 4 (forthcoming Winter 2020), Special Issue Gender, Race and Global Capitalism at Work – gesellschaftliche Umbrüche, Kontinuitäten und Kämpfe.

Taylor, Phil, Kirsty Newsome, Jennifer Bair and Al Rainnie. "Putting Labour in its Place: Labour Process Analysis and Global Value Chains." in Kirsty Newsome, Phil Taylor, Jennifer Bair and Al Rainnie (eds), *Putting Labour in Its Place: Labour Process Analysis and Global Value Chains* (London and New York: Palgrave Macmillan, 2015).

Thompson, Paul, Rachel Parker and Stephen Cox. "Labour and Asymmetric Power Relations in Global Value Chains: The Digital Entertainment Industries and Beyond," in Kirsty Newsome, Phil Taylor, Jennifer Bair and Al Rainnie (eds), *Putting Labour in Its Place: Labour Process Analysis and Global Value Chains* (London and New York: Palgrave Macmillan, 2015).

Thompson, Paul and Chris Smith. "Labour Power and Labour Process: Contesting the Marginality of the Sociology of Work," *Sociology*, 43, 5 (October 2009), pp. 913–930.

van der Linden, Marcel. "The Promise and Challenges of Global Labor History," *International Labor and Working-Class History*, 82 (Fall 2012), pp. 57–76.

van der Linden, Marcel. *Workers of the World: Essays Toward a Global Labor History* (Leiden and Boston: Brill, 2008).

Wells, Don. "Local Worker Struggles in the Global South: Reconsidering Northern Impacts on International Labour Standards," *Third World Quarterly*, 30, 3 (2009), pp. 567–579.

Wildcat. "Forces of Labor. Interview with Beverly J. Silver," (Berlin, June 2005), online available at: <https://www.wildcat-www.de/dossiers/forcesoflabor/bs_interview.htm>; last accessed July 15, 2020.

Zajak, Sabrina, Niklas Egels-Zandén and Nicola Piper. "Networks of Labour Activism: Collective Action across Asia and Beyond: An Introduction to the Debate," *Development and Change*, 48, 5 (September 2017), pp. 899–921.

# Index of Places, Persons, Companies and Institutions

Tables, figures, and boxes are indicated by an italic *t*, *f*, and *b* following the page numbers.

www.ingramcontent.com/pod-product-compliance
Lightning Source LLC
LaVergne TN
LVHW021724021026
849161LV00004BA/674
* 9 7 8 9 0 0 4 4 4 8 0 3 2 *